ONE FAITH

Biblical and Patristic Contributions Toward Understanding Unity in Faith

WILLIAM HENN, OFM Cap.

D1595924

PAULIST PRESS
New York/Mahwah, N.J.

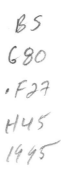

Excerpts from:
Unity and Diversity in the New Testament by James Dunn (Trinity Press International, Valley Forge, PA 1990) and *The Faith of the Old Testament: A History* by Werner H. Schmidt (Westminster John Knox Press, Louisville, KY, 1983) are reprinted with permission.

Library of Congress Cataloging-in-Publication Data

Henn, William.
   One faith : biblical and patristic contributions toward understanding unity in faith / William Henn.
      p.   cm.
   Includes bibliographical references and index.
   ISBN 0-8091-3577-9 (alk. paper)
   1. Faith–Biblical teaching. 2. Faith–History of doctrines. 3. Church–Unity–Biblical teaching. 4. Church–Unity–History of doctrines. 5. Creeds–Biblical teaching. 6. Creeds–History and criticism. I. Title.
BS680.F27H45   1995   95-9146
234′.2—dc20   CIP

Published by Paulist Press
997 Macarthur Boulevard
Mahwah, NJ 07430

Printed and bound in the United States of America

CONTENTS

PART TWO:
FAITH AND ITS UNITY ACCORDING TO THE
PATRISTIC LITERATURE 87

PART THREE:
IMPLICATIONS OF THE INVESTIGATION 193

INTRODUCTION

Charles the Fifth, who reigned as Holy Roman Emperor during the years when new divisions severed the Christian communities of Western Europe in the aftermath of the Reformation, retired to the monastery at Yuste for the last years of his life. There he was able to indulge his fascination for clocks, which led to a comment that might be particularly germane to the topic of this book. William Prescott relates the following anecdote:

> Charles took, moreover, great interest in the mechanism of timepieces. He had a good number of clocks and watches ticking together in his apartments; and a story has obtained credit that the difficulty he found in making any two of them keep the same time drew from him an exclamation on the folly of attempting to bring a number of men to think alike in matters of religion....[1]

A political leader, even one who, like Charles V, had been at times significantly engaged in efforts to preserve the unity of Christianity, might consider as "folly" any attempt to bring people "to think alike in matters of religion." But for the believer, such folly is a good example of the inscrutable wisdom of God, which cannot be understood by the rulers of this age (see 1 Cor 2,6-9). God's wisdom shines forth in Jesus' prayer "that they all be one...so that the world may believe" (Jn 17,20-21). It is revealed in the proclamation that "There is one Lord, one faith, one baptism" (Eph 4,5). Unity in faith is the scope and purpose of so much of the labor of those gifted with various charisms in the Church: they are sent to build up the body of Christ "until we all attain to the unity of the faith and of the knowledge of the Son of God...to the measure of the stature of the fulness of Christ" (Eph 4,13).

From its very inception, the contemporary ecumenical movement has harbored the conviction that unity in faith is one of the most essential pre-requisites for the re-establishment of full unity among currently divided Christian communities. The representatives from the various communities who founded the World Council of Churches in Amsterdam in 1948 boldly professed that, despite their many divisions, they nevertheless remained united in faith in Jesus Christ, a unity which provided the foundation and impetus for that new instrument for promoting Christian unity which the World Council constituted. Earlier, the delegates of the first world conference on Faith and Order (Lausanne, 1927) had likewise noted: "we feel united in the common Christian faith, proclaimed in Sacred Scripture and witnessed to and preserved in the ecumenical creed, commonly called 'Niccan,' and in the Apostles' Creed." Still earlier, the ecumenical patriarch of Constantinople (1920), the Lambeth Conference of the Anglican churches (1920) and the bishop of Rome (1894 and 1896) had all pointed out the absolutely essential character of unity in faith for the re-establishment of full communion between divided Christian communities.

Yet, notwithstanding such affirmations concerning the importance of unity in faith, the strikingly varied response to what has been, until now, the most widely distributed and discussed product of ecumenical dialogue—the Lima document of the Faith and Order Commission on "Baptism, Eucharist and Ministry" (1982)—shows that unity in faith is not only an elusive goal which is yet to be achieved, but that much work remains to be done simply to bring into sharper focus just what it means to be one in faith. That is the aim of the present book. It grew from the author's dual conviction that more explicit reflection is needed on the precise topic of unity in faith and that such widely acknowledged sources as the scriptures and the patristic literature might offer a rich basis for further reflection upon this theme. Naturally, one could hardly inquire into these sources with regard to unity in faith without first coming to some understanding of the way in which these privileged texts understand "faith" as such. And so, a simple two-step procedure came to characterize the methodology which has shaped the research and the results to be found in the following pages. What is faith, according to the Old Testament? In what way may one speak of the unity of Old Testament faith? How does Clement of Alexandria or Basil the Great or Augustine of Hippo describe faith? What can these great leaders of the early Church provide to help us better understand faith unity today?

As these questions already suggest, the research which went into the writing of this book opened up vistas which are quite beyond the sole topic of unity in faith. Themes such as the justifiability of speaking of an Old Testament creed, the variety of New Testament theologies of faith, the possibility of accounting for unity within diversity in the New Testament, the harmony of the community in shared faith according to Clement of Rome and Ignatius of Antioch, faith's credibility in the thought of great apologists such as Justin and Theodoret, the apostolicity of the one faith in Irenaeus and Tertullian, the immense growth in faith which lies open to the childlike believer in Clement of Alexandria, Origen and Gregory of Nyssa, the relation between shared faith and creed in Cyril of Jerusalem and Basil the Great, the responsibility of Christian leaders to foster unity in faith according to Gregory of Nazianzus, the beautiful biblical images for faith in Origen, Hilary, Ambrose and John Chrysostom, the orthodoxy of faith in Athanasius and Cyril of Alexandria and the profound philosophical reflection on the epistemological status of faith by Augustine which was at the same time intimately related to his very dramatic personal conversion—all of these have opened up to the author a rich sequence of studies and reflections which go quite beyond the precise topic of unity in faith, a wealth which hopefully will come through for the enrichment of the reader as well. Moreover, unity in faith shows itself in the course of this research to be not simply an ecumenical question. It is a matter of the very life of the Church as a community of believers. Even if all divisions were already healed, or even if they had never occurred in the first place, the task of promoting the one mind and one confession of faith in Jesus Christ would remain. The proclamation by Peter and the apostles at Pentecost, under the awesome influence of the Holy Spirit, produced communion in faith. From that day, such has always remained one of the most essential features of the life of the Church. And it will always be so, even after our current divisions are long overcome.

Unity in faith is the miracle which God works when the human beings who comprise the Church respond with humble intelligence and obedient will to the gentle inspiration of God's revelation and grace in such a way that communion comes to be. This communion with God and with other human persons is the aim of all of God's saving action. Its realization is not only possible; it is a certainty, guaranteed as part of the victory of Christ over the power of sin and error. It remains only for us to remove those obstacles to its more perfect realization at the present moment. The aim of this book is to gaze patiently and lovingly into the heritage which we have received in the scriptures and the writings from the patristic era so as to grasp more fully the nature of this unity and to sketch out in a more explicit way the guidance that these treasured sources can offer to us in that special quest of our time to join together in communion of faith.

PART ONE:
FAITH AND ITS UNITY IN SCRIPTURE

Unity in faith is of central importance not only as a focal point in the contemporary quest of the ecumenical movement to draw divided Christian communities into full communion but also as a foundational element in the nature of the Church itself, a Church which is a communion of believers united in a common faith. Its vital importance justifies an attempt to come up with a well informed and sufficiently nuanced description of precisely what it means to be united in faith. Pride of place in developing such a description must be given to whatever may be gleaned from the Word of God as contained in the Scriptures. The aim of Part One of this book is to examine what the Bible has to say about faith, particularly from the angle of asking how the biblical doctrine of faith might offer perspectives for better understanding unity in faith.

It must be noted from the outset that an exhaustive inventory of biblical texts which concern faith and, a fortiori, of the many articles, monographs and books on faith according to the Scriptures is not possible within the confines of these opening chapters.[1] Nor is it necessary. For our purposes one need not enter into all of the nuances, let us say, of faith according to one specific source such as the book of Isaiah or the gospel of Mark.[2] Rather it will suffice to take a more panoramic view, allowing the major features of faith in the two Testaments to emerge and raising the question as to whether and how this material might offer useful perspectives for understanding unity in faith.

Part One will approach the respective Old and New Testaments with a basically similar pattern of questions. First, it will inquire into the terminology for faith, its frequency of occurrence and the experience or conception of faith which this terminology conveys. A preoccupation will be to remain attentive to the various nuances and wealth of meaning which the various biblical authors and commentators may bring to light.

5

A second line of inquiry concerns the profession or professions of faith which may be discerned in each of the two Testaments. Here the focus of attention will be the question of whether or not one may properly speak of a "creed" as present explicitly or implicitly in the Old and New Testaments and, if so, what doctrinal content may be said to be included respectively in such creeds. A final line of inquiry concerns the precise question of unity in faith. To what extent, especially in light of the pluri-formity of expression which runs throughout both Testaments, may one speak of a unified faith within either the Old Testament or the New?

The first chapter will consider all three of these sets of questions as they concern the Old Testament. Turning to the New Testament, the extent of the relevant material and secondary literature necessitates that these three lines of inquiry be treated in three distinct chapters (Chapters Two through Four).

Chapter One
THE OLD TESTAMENT
ON FAITH AND ITS UNITY

Toward the beginning of their study of the biblical doctrine of faith, Jürgen Hermisson and Edward Lohse write: "If one asks the Old Testament about the word 'faith' it is initially not very talkative."[1] Nevertheless a significant number of studies have appeared over the years attempting to give voice to what the Old Testament might have to say about faith. Based upon an overview of a number of these studies, what follows will approach the Old Testament doctrine of faith under the following headings: 1. Old Testament Terminology for and Experience of Faith; 2. An Old Testament Creed? and 3. Unity of Faith in the Old Testament.

1. OLD TESTAMENT TERMINOLOGY FOR
AND EXPERIENCE OF FAITH

A. A Variety of Terms and Experiences

Many scholars approach the topic of faith by analyzing the terminology used to describe it.[2] Weiser notes that, should one consider faith as a human being's relation and attitude toward God, a number of different Hebrew words are used to convey this relationship, only one of which, 'âman, was translated by the Septuagint with the Greek words pisteúein, pistis.[3] In secular usage, the hiphil of 'âman means saying "Amen" to some object, recognizing the relation of object to reality (it is so) as well as the relation of the believing subject to witnesses (they are telling the believer what is so). This meaning of faith as referring to some objective state of affairs which a subject acknowledges often appears in the negative. Thus when Jacob's sons report to him that Joseph is alive and holding power in Egypt, he cannot believe them (Gen 45,26); Moses fears that when he returns to tell the Israelites that

he has been sent by God they will not believe him (Ex 4,1.8–9); the
Queen of Sheba tells Solomon that, before she visited him and saw the
extent of the grandeur of his court, she could not believe the reports of
it (1 Kings 10,7 = 2 Chr 9,6). Weiser underscores the importance of *relationship* in the use of this verb.[4] He further notes that this meaning is
used analogously to express the relation of human beings to God.
Believing in God, saying "Amen" to God, entails:

> ...recognizing and acknowledging the relation into which
> God enters with man, i.e., setting oneself in this relation, so
> that here, too, the mutual relation between God and man is
> of the very essence of faith and is so in such a way that, even
> where faith is a human activity for which man may be held
> responsible (the requirement of faith), man is never the one
> who initially establishes this relation.[5]

Examples of how the verb *'âman* can express the total relationship between God and human beings include Ex 14,31: "And they
beheld the great power that the Lord had shown against the Egyptians,
they feared the Lord and believed in him and in his servant Moses";
and Nm 14,11: "And the Lord said to Moses, 'How long will this people spurn me? How long will they refuse to believe in me, despite all
the signs I have performed among them?'"; and again Ps 78,22, where
the Lord's anger rises against Israel, "because they believed not God
nor trusted in his help." In this context of the all-encompassing relation between God and human beings, *'âman* refers to "all the elements
whereby God is God and seeks to establish a relation to man, namely,
His might, His miraculous power, His electing will, His love, the steadfastness and faithfulness of His conduct, the actualising of His word
and plan, His demand, His righteousness...."[6] Correspondingly, *'âman*
"brings into the relation with God the totality of the expressions of
human life."[7] This totality includes the nuance of knowledge, as in Is
43,10: "You are my witnesses, says the Lord, my servants whom I have
chosen to know and believe in me and understand that it is I. Before
me no god was formed, and after me there shall be none." However it
can also include elements of feeling, will and behavior, as in Hos
4,1–2: "There is no fidelity (truth = *emeth*, which shares the same stem
mn as *'âman*), no mercy, no knowledge of God in the land. False swear-
ing, lying, murder, stealing and adultery! In their lawlessness, bloodshed follows bloodshed."

The context for what is meant by faith in the Old Testament is that
of the covenant with Yahweh, a relation "which embraces the whole man

in the totality of his external conduct and inner life."[8] This meaning of faith reaches its apex in the prophet Isaiah, whose well-known saying "Unless your faith is firm you shall not be firm!" (7,9) seems to connote a certain correspondence between faith and existence:

> The positive meaning of the saying, then, is that the particular mode of life and the permanence of the people of God are to be found in faith itself. This goes hand in hand with the rejection of all fear of human might (7:1ff.) or trust in it (30:15f.), since human might is transitory. It also carries with it an incorporation of fear of God alone into the relation of faith (8:13). From this one may see that faith is for Isaiah the only possible mode of existence; it radically excludes any autonomy of man or any commitment to other gods. In Isaiah, Yahweh alone, His plan and will, and the corresponding attitude of man, are the only things which count in respect of all occurrence or understanding.[9]

The other Hebrew word most commonly commented upon in scholarly presentations of Old Testament faith is *batah*.[10] Weiser notes a rather sharp difference between this word and *'aman*, in that "Even where the word relates to persons...one may see that the self-relation of the subjective feeling of security is to be distinguished from the concepts of relationship denoted by *'aman*."[11] *Batah* means "to feel secure on the basis of..." and is often spoken of negatively by the prophets who condemn finding such security in chariots (Hos 10,13; Is 31,1), cities (Am 6,1), deceitful words (Jer 7,4.8), riches (Jer 49,4), beauty (Ez 16,15), oppression (Is 30,12), wickedness (Is 47,10) or even idols (Is 42,17; Jer 46,25).[12] But *batah* also is used positively in the sense of placing one's trust in God. Thus Jer 39,18 reads: "Your life shall be spared as booty, because you trusted in me, says the Lord." The psalms use the word about a hundred times, where it is often rendered by the verbs "believe," "trust" and "hope."[13] Thus Ps 4,6 states: "Offer just sacrifices, and trust in the Lord"; Ps 25,2: "In you I trust; let me not be put to shame"; Ps 55,24: "But I trust in you, O Lord." Weiser sees Isaiah once again as marking a climax in the way in which the Old Testament employs the word *batah*, particularly in Is 30,15: "For thus said the Lord God, the holy One of Israel: By waiting and by calm you shall be saved, in quiet and in trust your strength lies."[14] Here Isaiah transfers to God that trust which, when it is placed in human devices, is roundly condemned:

Because you reject this word, and put your trust in what is
crooked and devious, and depend on it, this guilt of yours
shall be like a descending rift bulging out in a high wall
whose crash comes suddenly, in an instant (Is 30,12–13; see
also Is 31,1 and 32,9–10).

This contrast between trusting in the Lord and trusting in human
powers highlights another dimension of the relation between human
beings and God.[15]

To believe, to trust, to hope, to seek refuge in—these are all words
which the Old Testament employs to express that relation between God
and human beings which can properly be called faith.[16] Juan Alfaro sums
it up in this way:

> ...faith in the OT expresses that integral attitude of man with
> respect to Yahweh, the God of the Covenant, who reveals
> himself as liberator of the chosen people. The partial aspects
> which are vitally included and unified in this whole are: A)
> knowledge-recognition of Yahweh, of his saving and govern-
> ing power revealed in the history of Israel; B) trust in his
> promises (in reverential fear); C) obedience to Yahweh's
> commandments. The fiducial aspect is generally (not always)
> more visible and to some extent more prevalent in OT faith;
> but the vital and integral reality of this faith includes the *total*
> affirmation (engaging all human faculties) of acknowledging
> and worshipping Yahweh alone, Israel's savior. By faith, man
> trusts in the divine word and promises, *in God himself*, and
> enters into vital communion with him. But that faith is also
> about some more or less implicitly affirmed content, express-
> ing the salvific intervention of Yahweh for his chosen people;
> bound to this is also human submission to the will of God. *To
> believe* in the OT is to say *Amen* to the words, promises and
> commandments of Yahweh.[17]

B. A Common Thread: Faith and History

At the opening of his discussion of faith in the Old Testament,
André de Bovis quotes a sentence from the famous phenomenologist of
religion, G. van der Leeuw: "In this insignificant people, living in a forgotten corner of the world, was accomplished an immense achievement,
the birth of faith."[18] Insofar as it connotes a beginning that leads to further growth, the word "birth" here is a happy choice, for a common

thread among commentators is the affirmation that Old Testament faith developed over the course of Israel's history.[19]

When did the faith which finds expression in the Old Testament begin? Hermisson and Lohse state that we don't really know the answer to that question.[20] The Old Testament confronts the reader first of all with stories of faith, which were passed on from generation to generation by means of a complex process of narrating the faith of the fathers.[21] In this context one might begin with the story of Abraham, whose father served other gods (Jgs 24,2).[22] Yahweh calls Abraham and promises him a land and numerous progeny (Gn 12,1–3) and Abraham "went as the Lord directed him" (Gn 12,4). The promise is repeated in Gn 15,1–5 and Abraham "put his faith in the Lord, who credited it to him as an act of righteousness" (Gn 15,6).[23] Even when this faith in God is severely tried in the test of Gn 22, where Abraham is asked to sacrifice his son Isaac, the apparent means by which the promise of a vast progeny would be fulfilled, Abraham remained steadfast and "was found to be loyal" (Sir 44,20).

Blackman notes that the theme of promise, which appears as a recurrent refrain in the various narratives about the patriarchs (Gen 17,1–8.19–21 [Abraham]; 26,3–5.24–29 [Isaac]; 28,13-15 [Jacob]; 35,11–12 [Jacob]; 48,4 [Jacob]; cf Ex 32,13; Dt 34,4), is related to the foundation of the covenant between Israel and Yahweh. "God guarantees it [the promise], and this is his 'truth', or faithfulness. On man's side, faith is simply believing that God is of such a character, even when the evidence seems to point the other way (see Gn 17:17–18)."[24] Later, Joshua 21,45 will express God's fidelity with the words: "Not a single promise that the Lord made to the house of Israel was broken; every one was fulfilled."

Mindful of his covenant with Abraham, Isaac and Jacob, the Lord hears the groaning of his suffering people in Egypt (Ex 2,24), calls Moses, reveals himself to him and promises to be with him in bringing Israel out of slavery (Ex 3,4–15). Seeing the great signs that the Lord works in bringing them out of Egypt, "they believed in God and in his servant Moses" (Ex 14,31; see Ex 19,9). Duplacy notes:

> The covenant consecrates this engagement of God in the history of Israel. In return Israel was asked to obey the Word of God (Ex 19,3–9). Now, "to hear Yahweh" is first of all "to believe in Him" (Dt 9,23; Ps 106,24f); the covenant, then, asks for faith (cf Ps 78,37). The life and death of Israel will depend henceforth on its free fidelity (Dt 30,15–20; 28; Heb

> 11,33) in maintaining the Amen of faith (cf Dt 27,9–26)
> which has made of it the people of God.[25]

The book of Deuteronomy nicely captures the mutuality of the covenant between God and Israel (see Dt 26,16–19). Yahweh chooses the people (Dt 7,6–7) and can be relied upon to be faithful down to the thousandth generation (Dt 7,9). Israel must show faithfulness by carefully observing the commandments, the statutes and the decrees which the Lord enjoins upon her (Dt 7,11). Blackman compiled a list of some of the key words in Deuteronomy which convey more precisely what response is expected of Israel in being faithful to the covenant:

> ...man is to heed (lit., "hear") the statutes (4:1; 7:12); to cleave or hold fast to Yahweh (4:4; 10:20); to seek and turn to him (4:29–30); to turn, in the sense of "repent," after apostasy (30:2–10); to obey his voice (4:30); to love him "with all your heart," etc. (6:5); to fear him (6:2, 13; 10:20); to remember him (7:18–19; 8:2–3, 18–20; 9:7).[26]

Following Bauer's affirmation that faith is, in the first place, the response of the people to the covenant, it is clear then that faith is an all engrossing commitment, an attitude which seeks to encounter Yahweh "in all things and in all events, which alone in the last resort can make sense of everything and which shows a way out of present tribulation for a man whose life is based on the bible and who stands in the presence of God and says 'yes' to his summons."[27] In the midst of the vanity, impermanence and suffering of human life, faith means finding solidity in God, convinced that it is God who stands at the center of all history, guiding and directing everything.[28] Faith is an act in the strong sense of the term which, unlike a natural inclination, requires a conscious effort and has practical consequences for the way in which one lives.[29]

De Bovis places this fundamental life-stance toward God in a strictly historical setting.[30] *Faith is confident trust in the promises of the Lord, turned toward a yet unseen future* in which God will faithfully bestow his blessings on his people: "I believe that I shall see the bounty of the Lord in the land of the living" (Ps 27,13; see also Ps 35,9–10; 37,34; 62,2; 107; 121,2; 130,7). In this way faith is almost imperceptibly transformed into hope: "In you I trust; let me not be put to shame, let not my enemies exult over me. No one who waits for you shall be put to shame; those shall be put to shame who heedlessly break faith" (Ps 25,2–3; see also Ps 28,7; 32,10; 33,21–22; 37,5; 55,24; 62,6–8; 71,5; 115,9–11; 127,1). Such trusting confidence finds its support in *recollection of God's great deeds of the past*. Tempted to doubt (Ps 77,10), the psalmist prays: "I remember the deeds of the Lord; yes, I remember your wonders of old. And I meditate on your works; your exploits I ponder" (Ps 77,12–13). This past is the history of the Lord's dealings with Israel over the many generations (Ps 77; 78; 105; 106; 114) and reveals Yahweh as a God of love: "Merciful and gracious is the Lord, slow to anger and abounding in kindness" (Ps 103,8; see also Ps 66,20; 103,6–10; 118,1; 136; 145). Recalling the fidelity of God in the past gives rise to joyful hymns of thanksgiving: "Shout joyfully to God, all you on earth, sing praise to the glory of his name; proclaim his glorious praise. Say to God, 'How tremendous are your deeds!'" (Ps 66,1–3; see also Ps 28,7; 30; 40; 65; 68; 105; 111; 116; 136). Finally, the stance of faith entails *an attentiveness to seek the will of the Lord in the present moment*, to live in the presence of God: "Your ways, O Lord, make known to me; teach me your paths. Guide me in your truth and teach me, for you are God my savior, and for you I wait all the day" (Ps 25,4–5; see also Ps 27,11; 86,11). Such an attitude of looking to follow the Lord's ways in the present circumstances of life includes the nuance of obedience: "Then said I, 'Behold I come; in the written scroll it is prescribed for me. To do your will, O my God, is my delight, and your law is within my heart!'" (Ps 40,8–9; see Ps 119,1–8).[31] As is clear from the texts listed here, the psalms offer a unique source for the language and expression of faith in the Old Testament.[32]

The theme of faith and history might suitably be brought to a conclusion with a brief discussion of the prophet Isaiah, who, according to Schnackenburg, is rightly called "the prophet of faith."[33] In Chapter 7, the prophet calls Ahaz from fear to confident trust in Yahweh, warning him against placing his hopes in human safeguards, such as the construction of fortifications and alliances with other nations, and culminating with the often discussed saying: "Unless your faith is firm, you shall not be firm" (7,9). Isaiah's proclamation and the reaction of the king set a pattern that can be traced throughout the book.[34] Isaiah calls for faith even when the Lord seems to be hiding his face (8,17; cf 33,2), thus drawing close to the eschatological attitude of faith and hope (25,4.9; 28,16; 30,15.18).[35] Eichrodt notes that everywhere Isaiah performed his ministry in the face of approaching disaster and understood God and the human relation to God in light of such a crisis situation.

> The antinomy which is beyond the comprehension of human thought, namely that the implacably just, holy and pure gives life and pardon in and through the execution of his judg-

ment—indeed, that there is no other way to him than along
the way of death—this antinomy is an element which can
never be removed from the revelation of God to Isaiah....In
every passage where Isaiah summons men to faith he is aware
of both himself and his hearers as confronted by the reality
of the wrathful and yet gracious God, the God who by his
concrete promise breaks through the total darkness of the
historical situation sufficiently for men to lay hold on him,
and by an act of profound inward assent to say a free Yes to
his offer.[36]

Faith is thus a comprehensive term for the total relationship
between human beings and God, in which one places one's whole trust in
God's sovereignty and governance of human life. In Deutero-Isaiah this
will find expression in a magnificent presentation of how God will be the
strength and salvation of his people (40,31; 57,13), will be the source of
their justice and salvation (51,5). "No ear has ever heard, no eye ever seen,
any God but you doing such deeds for those who wait for him" (64,2).

2. AN OLD TESTAMENT CREED?

From what has been said above, it would appear that faith in
the Old Testament accentuated the existential element of belief in, trust
in and commitment to God. While such a predominantly existential
thrust certainly can and did include convictions which are cognitive in
nature and which might be called, perhaps somewhat anachronistically,
doctrinal truths or beliefs, the question as to whether a listing of the
essential doctrines in terms of a creed can be distilled from the general
presentation of Old Testament faith has produced no little discussion.[37]
The name most often associated with originating this discussion is
Gerhard von Rad. In 1938 he proposed the theory that the Hexateuch, a
designation for the first six books of the Bible, was shaped on the basis
of Israel's fundamental faith, which is summarized in several ancient,
cultic creeds.[38] The most important of these in von Rad's presentation
was Dt 26,5b-9:

My father was a wandering Aramean who went down to
Egypt with a small household and lived there as an alien. But
there he became a nation great, strong and numerous. When
the Egyptians maltreated and oppressed us, imposing hard
labor upon us, we cried to the Lord, the God of our fathers,

and he heard our cry and saw our affliction, our toil and our oppression. He brought us out of Egypt with his strong hand and outstretched arm, with terrifying power, with signs and wonders; and bringing us into this country, he gave us this land flowing with milk and honey.

This historical credo contains four principal elements: the patriarchs, the oppression in Egypt, the Exodus, and the march to and entry of the promised land, elements which are confirmed in the other two credos to which von Rad gives prominence: Dt 6,20–24 and Josh 24,2b–13. For von Rad, the whole of the Hexateuch is to some degree contained in and governed by these short historical credos.[39]

One striking difficulty seemed apparent in von Rad's theory: there is no mention of the covenant at Sinai in these short credos, a tradition whose importance in the opening books of the Old Testament could hardly be overestimated. Von Rad explained this by positing that Sinai material was from a later, independent tradition, only subsequently integrated with the traditions represented in the historical credo by the Yahwist redactor. This position, with some modification, was reaffirmed by M. Noth and found its way into a number of more popular presentations of the development of the Old Testament.[40]

The theory of an ancient historical credo underlying the formation of the opening books of the Old Testament ran into a number of criticisms. First of all, it was argued that the language of the texts is very close to that of the Deuteronomist, who is to be dated much later, with the result that the credos were not as ancient as von Rad and Noth had assumed and consequently could hardly be considered as having a formative influence on the Hexateuch (or the Pentateuch).[41] Furthermore, it was questioned whether these texts should really be called credos. C. Brekelmans argued that Dt 6,20–24 should be considered a catechetical instruction, while Josh 24,2b–13 is more properly classified as an historical prologue to a covenant formulary, a comment which, with modification, applies also to Dt 26,5a–9 when verses 10–11 are added to it.[42] Finally, A. Weiser suggested that the Sinai material is not present in the three credos located by von Rad, not because it is a later tradition, but rather because the Sinai traditions and the traditions reflected in the credos concern different aspects of Israel's experience of God.[43] Sinai represents an encounter in which the people come to accept the will of God as reflected in the Law. The credos, on the other hand, speak of Yahweh's great acts of salvation in Israel's history. The two are to some extent heterogeneous and thus do not naturally go together.

While these concerns about the dating, the literary form and the relation to the Sinai covenant are of significance for any theory about the influence of these brief summaries upon the development of the early books of the Bible, the ultimate judgment upon such theories need not detain us here. Regardless of the outcome of the debate about the success of particular aspects of the theories of von Rad and Noth, the debate itself acknowledges that these texts do represent attempts to encapsulate some of the essential elements of Old Testament belief. Nor are these the only such summaries. Ex 15; 1 Sam 12,8f; Neh 9,6–37 and a number of Psalms (78; 105; 106; 135; 136) can be seen as free adaptations of the basic material contained in the historical credos.[44] Psalm 136, for example, follows the ancient pattern in vv. 10–12 but introduces a significant alteration by incorporating the divine action of creation in vv. 4–9.[45] Psalm 78 elaborates many of the details contained in the more streamlined presentations of the shorter summaries, placing the whole within the context of "the dark background of divine judgment" and a warning "against apostasy and obduracy."[46] Ps 78,68–70 and Ex 15,17 introduce the themes of David and Sion into the more traditional credal material, while Ps 105,8–10 injects the covenant theme and Psalm 106 casts the whole in a context of petitionary prayer.[47] J. Schreiner concludes his account of the adaptations in the creed-like passages with comments about Nehemiah:

> The penitential prayer of Nehemiah 9 marks a kind of final stage in the development of the Israelite credo. The tradition of salvation history which has evolved through the psalms mentioned above is incorporated in this confession of sin. The confession of God the creator, the covenant of Sinai, the Law and God's judgment, the saving gifts of prophecy and kingship—all are introduced from the narrative in the Pentateuch into the ancient schema, considerably enlarged. The whole becomes a cry of repentance and petition, but at the same time it is praise of God (v. 5). The confession of faith always had to be the praise of God. Israel knew no other way.[48]

Thus it is clear that, while one can locate any number of creed-like formulations of some of the basic elements of Israel's belief, the Old Testament gives evidence of a certain liberty in the content of these formulations and in the particular underlying theme within which this content is placed.[49]

Other shorter texts can also be pointed to as expressing Israel's faith. "Yahweh brought us out of Egypt" (Ex 20,2; Num 23,22; 24,8; Dt 5,6), for example, seems to be one of the oldest confessional formulas of the Old Testament. Schreiner notes: "This proclamation, praising the redeeming intervention of the Lord, became Israel's primal confession. No other event and no later manifestation of divine glory and divine will could displace this article of faith."[50] To this should be added other brief acknowledgments of Yahweh's Lordship, such as "The Lord is greater than all gods" (Ex 18,11); "I say to the Lord, 'My Lord are you'" (Ps 16,2); "You, O Lord, are the Most High over all the earth" (Ps 97,9); and "The Lord is king forever and ever" (Ps 10,16).[51] Deserving special notice are short acclamations of faith recited by the community as a whole. An example of such appears at the end of the contest between Elijah and the prophets of Baal on Mount Carmel: "Seeing this, all the people fell prostrate and said, 'The Lord is God! The Lord is God!'" (1 Kgs 18,39; see also Ps 100,3). Other examples include: "The Lord is king" or "The Lord reigns" (Ps 93,1; 96,10; 97,1; 99,1); and "The Lord is great" (Ps 35,27; 40,16; 70,4; Mal 1,5), "the latter always accompanied by an explicit invitation to the community to join in making it."[52]

Several authors further point out the importance of the *Shema* as an expression of the faith of Israel.[53] In this regard Hyatt comments:

> It is perhaps significant that Judaism came to consider its confession of faith as being embodied in the *Shema*, Deut. 6:4–9 (to which were often added Deut. 11:13–21; Num. 15:37–41), rather than in any of the so-called historical Credos. The *Shema* emphasizes (1) the oneness and sovereignty of Yahweh, (2) the obligation to serve and obey him through love, and (3) the obligation to remember his commandments and teach them to the children.[54]

What can be drawn from all of these reflections about the possible creed of the Old Testament? Durham proposes the following as a definition of the word creed: "A credo is a summary statement of belief encompassing the irreducible minimum sustaining a common faith."[55] Such a general description may be intended to take into account the fact that some authors are cautious about claiming that Israel had a creed.[56] Nevertheless, it is clear that the Old Testament recognized Yahweh as God and focused upon God's activity in history. The cult provided the

privileged milieu for the repeated recollection of the sovereignty of God
and of his mighty deeds. Durham's conclusion displays enough balance
to account for the various points of view:

> That there was "credo" in ancient Israel now seems assured.
> Too detailed an assertion of its exact contents and too close
> an association of the credo with one cultic occasion or one
> particular locale must be avoided. Credo as a literary type
> must be allowed both considerable flexibility and broad com-
> prehensiveness. The given form of the credo at any point in
> Israelite history must be regarded as determined more by the
> needs of the occasion and the persons involved than by a
> fixed outline. The credo might be as short as a single word or
> phrase ("Yahweh" or "Yahweh is King") or as long as the
> summaries of Joshua 24 or Psalms 78 or 105. By nature, the
> credo was always in some sense historical, but its historicality
> was always theological.[57]

At this point one might ask to what extent monotheism can be
considered part of the faith of Israel. It seems clear that Israel's
understanding of God developed over the course of its history. Schmidt
notes that "the first commandment had at first a practical and not a
theoretical aim. It is not intended to teach that there is one and only one
God, creator and upholder of righteousness. [It is] not monotheistic in
presupposition."[58] Bernhard Lang has attempted to briefly sketch the
steps by which Israel came to the more explicit monotheistic faith that
appears in the later stages of the Old Testament. He concludes his
summary as follows:

> With Deutero-Isaiah and the Deuteronomic literature of the
> sixth (and possibly the fifth) century, we reach the end of a
> development which had begun some 300 years before. Now
> Judaism possessed its monotheistic creed, which it bore unal-
> tered through history, to be handed on to Christianity and
> Islam.[59]

Others would want to locate monotheism as at least implicitly present
in the earliest faith of Israel, even if such faith could "for a long time reconcile itself with representations implying the existence of 'other
gods'...."[60] While the views expressed by these and other authors diverge
significantly about the timing of the presence of monotheism in Israel,

nevertheless they are in harmony in affirming its presence and in recognizing at least some degree of development in its being made explicit.
Few would challenge Lang's assertion: "Monotheism is the gift to
mankind of the religion of the Bible."[61]

3. UNITY OF FAITH IN THE OLD TESTAMENT

It is perhaps not without significance that articles about faith in the
various biblical lexica tend not to include a separate heading concerned
with "unity in faith." Indeed, Weiser begins his study of the Old
Testament concept of faith with the remark that the older Israelite
religion was collective in structure, with the result that wealth of usage of
faith language "begins to appear only when the individual breaks free
from the collective bond, and on the basis of his own experience devotes
special attention to the attitude of man to God."[62] This might seem to
imply that faith is more properly speaking the action of an individual and
that it is only with difficulty that one can speak of the faith of a
community.

A different approach is suggested by Martin Buber in his somewhat
controversial book *Two Types of Faith*.[63] Faith has only two basic forms,
writes Buber, the one summed up in the statement "I trust someone,
without being able to offer sufficient reasons for my trust in him"; the
other "I acknowledge a thing to be true, likewise without being able to
give a sufficient reason."[64] For Buber, these two types of faith characterize
the difference between Israelite and Christian faith respectively. In the
first type, a person finds himself in the relationship of faith, primarily as a
member of a community whose covenant with the Unconditioned
includes and determines him within it. In the second, a person is
converted to the truth, primarily as an individual, and community arises
as the joining together of converted individuals.[65] While Buber's
distinction has been criticized for failing to attend to the New Testament
self-understanding of being in a certain continuity with the Old,
nevertheless he does open a path for breaking out of a strictly
individualistic understanding of faith.[66]

Studies are by no means lacking on the sense of community within
the Old Testament and of the individual's relation to community.[67]
Eichrodt sketches the broad outlines of a development from a more
community-oriented mindset on the part of early Israel, rooted in the
general clan and tribal thinking of the communities of the ancient East,
to the more individual-oriented sensitivity which emerges in the course
of the gradual demise of Israel as an independent nation.[68] In both of

these orientations, he comments on the relation between the community and the faith of the individual. In the earlier stage, Israel's predominant communal consciousness and self-understanding as a nation united in covenant with Yahweh had definite implications for the faith of the individual:

> The fellowship with God communicated to the individual in the covenant fits without difficulty into this understanding of the people of God. For that which forms the foundation of a man's relationship with God is not his own limited personal experience but the experience of the national community which bears him. As a member of the nation to which God has revealed himself and given his promises he dares to believe in the relevance of God's power, wisdom and good-ness to his own life also.[69]

Later, during the collapse of the nation as an independent political entity, individualism comes to the fore, heralded in a special way in the words and in the lives of the prophets Jeremiah and Ezekiel.[70] The "astonishing universalism" of post-exilic Deutero-Isaiah opens new, more individualistic conditions for entry into the community:

> The narrow bounds of membership of a common race are here abolished in favour of a unity in faith, and the result is a marked influx of proselytes from heathenism. There could be no clearer assertion that not everyone who has Israelite blood in his veins belongs to the people of the promise, but only the man who appropriates the spiritual inheritance with which Israel is entrusted and proves its worth in his life.[71]

Still there is an unbreakable bond between the faith of the community and the individual, so that, in summary, Eichrodt notes:

> But Old Testament faith knows nothing, in any situation or at any time, of a religious individualism which grants a man a private relationship with God unconnected with the com-munity either in its roots, its realization or its goal. Just as it is the formation of a divine *society* which gives meaning to the divine demand that summons the individual and enlists him in its service, so it is in serving his brethren that the obedience of the one who is called is proved, it is in the

common cultic festivals that his religious life finds its natural expression, and it is toward a perfected people of God that his hope is directed. [72]

The community "remains the mother of the religious life of the individual. For it is the community which provides the context within which revelation, whether past or present, or as yet in the future, must take place."[73]

Carrying this line of thought yet further, some underscore the fact that the community does not merely provide the occasion for the faith of the individual but rather that faith is constitutive of the very essence of the community. Along this line, De Bovis states that faith serves as the tie which binds together the people of God; to be an individual believer at all is merely to be one who has put himself in solidarity with the faith of the community.[74] Similarly, Schmidt sees faith as that which fashioned Israel into one people: "But their decisive inheritance was the Yahwistic faith...; for it was this which led the different groups in the land itself to grow together into a nation. 'Historically, the people of Israel came into existence because their tribes united in the worship of the god Yahweh.'"[75]

If it can be granted that an essential factor drawing and holding Israel together as a community was its faith, that Israel can be properly said to be united in a common faith, the question can be posed as to what that common faith is. In addition to what has been noted above in the discussion of a possible Israelite creed, three lines of inquiry proposed by various Old Testament scholars can prove to be particularly illuminating.

The first is that of Werner Schmidt, who sets for himself the task of determining what is the typical element in Israel's faith.[76] Schmidt begins from the position that, while deeply influenced by neighboring religions, "no similar faith can be found anywhere in the ancient Near East."[77] Israel's faith is unique. Israel never adopted wholesale the religious ideas of her neighbors; there is always a filtering, the use of a certain criterion, according to which elements of surrounding the religious climate are either assimilated or rejected. Schmidt's aim is to delineate this criterion. Furthermore, the faith of Israel can be charted to some degree historically. Schmidt divides his study into four broad chronological periods: nomadic prehistory, the early period after the conquest, the period of monarchy and the late period. Throughout these periods he catalogues different emphases in the way the Old Testament understands God.[78] What is the common thread that runs

through these various faith-depictions of God which appear throughout
Israel's history? Schmidt sees the answer to both of these questions—
about the criterion which distinguishes Israel's faith from that of her
neighbors and about the common thread uniting the various moments
in the Old Testament understanding of God—in the first two commandments of the decalogue (Ex 20,2–6; Dt 5,6–10: "I am the Lord your
God, who brought you out of the land of Egypt, that place of slavery. You
shall not have other gods besides me" and "You shall not carve idols for
yourselves"). Concerning the importance and influence of these
commandments, he notes:

> So the first commandment had far-reaching consequence
> both in word and in substance in history; its voice was heard
> anew in each period. Because it was the basis of and pre-
> served the distinctiveness of Israel, it justifiably determines
> the character of the OT to a large degree.... The history of
> Israel could be written as a history of the first command-
> ment. The effective element in it is its character as a demand.
> It is not an actualized reality simply as such—and in the histo-
> ry of Israel it frequently was not a reality—but it sets a task of
> relating Israel's changing new experiences to the basic
> insight of faith, and so puts reality in motion. So the first
> commandment is not a doctrine uttered once for all and of
> timeless validity, but requires exposition and appropriation
> in changing circumstances. The same is true of the second
> commandment. Faith in the one God is not a situation
> attained by Israel on a single definitive occasion, which is laid
> down by the past for succeeding generations, but a perma-
> nent challenge looking to the future.[79]

Relating these commandments to the two questions which provide the
frame of inquiry for his study, Schmidt remarks:

> First it [the first commandment] distinguishes the faith of the
> OT from neighbouring religions, and secondly it forms the
> criterion by which Israel chose and recast those concepts
> which it made its own from the many in the world around it.
> The first commandment is essentially at work even in places
> in which it is not actually stated. It governs extensive parts of
> the OT, if not even all of them, and thus represents in effect
> the common point of unity, the integrating centre. The OT

tries to speak in such a way of God (and also of man, cf. Ps 16,2; 51,4; [Heb 51,6]; 73,25 et al.) that the first commandment is upheld.... The faith of the OT seeks to meet the challenge of each new situation by measuring it against the first commandment and interpreting it by this. The commandment is a sort of connecting thread or signpost in the understanding of reality, and a criterion in the interpretation of changing human experiences. In the ever varying patterns of history what is seen as vital is to preserve the exclusivity of the faith. In consequence the significance of the first commandment can hardly be overvalued, even when its consequences are by no means obvious beforehand, nor are given once for all, but become clearer only very gradually.[80]

Thus, for Schmidt, that which distinguishes Israel's faith from the religious convictions of all her neighbors and which runs as a connecting thread in her understanding of reality are the commandments: "I am the Lord your God, who brought you out of the land of Egypt, that place of slavery. You shall not have other gods besides me" and "You shall not carve idols for yourselves." They are less doctrines than demands. They determine the character of the Old Testament as a whole and amount to a permanent challenge looking to the future. To the extent that these commandments hold together Israel as a faith community distinct from other religions, they might be seen as the fundamental expression of Israel's common faith.

A second approach can be found in Georg Fohrer's study on the plurality of existential stances (*Daseinshaltungen*) which can be found in the Old Testament.[81] Fohrer is also interested in locating what it is that makes Israel's faith distinct. He is convinced that the specific Dasein-attitude of the Old Testament evolves in contrast to other Dasein-attitudes which it is constrained to oppose. Fohrer begins with faith in the time of Moses. Our knowledge of this faith is sketchy, but it would surely include the conviction that Yahweh should be the only God for the Israelites. This is not yet theoretical monotheism; the existence of other gods for the other peoples seems to be acknowledged. Nor is Yahweh a god limited to a place, a sanctuary. Yahweh is God of a people; his power to aid his people extends beyond geographical limits. Yahweh is a passionate, angry God, a God of righteousness and justice who demands ethical responsibility. He is a warrior God who protects his own. Yahweh inspires unconditioned trust and obedience.

On entry into the land of Canaan, Israel was confronted with the magic Dasein-attitude, whose fundamental conviction is that one can influence and direct the higher powers to help oneself and to hurt others. Safety from the powers of fate and putting those powers at one's own service constitute the typical magical Dasein-attitude. While some in Israel were contaminated by such an approach and adopted elements of the Canaanite Baal religions, an opposing, anti-Canaanite movement looked back with longing to the time before the entrance into the land, to the nomadic ideal. However, such a response, longing for what was no more, could hardly preserve the ancient faith. An adaptation, midway between acceptance of the magical Dasein-attitude and its full-blown rejection in the nomadic ideal, was the development of the cultic Dasein-attitude. While cult, presided over by the priest, was similar to magic in that it sought security through God's help, there were a number of significant differences. While the magician sought his own interest or that of the patron, the priest served the interests of the whole people. The priest was ritually called and installed; the magician learned his métier through some higher power. The cultic Dasein-attitude further developed a legal dimension, which insisted on the unity between faith and ethos. A still further development enters in with the appearance of the national-religious Dasein-attitude. Decisive here is God's election of his people, with strong emphasis on the traditions of the "fathers" and of the coming into the land. One believes oneself safe not only by exercising the cult but also by belonging to the chosen people.

The prophetic Dasein-attitude ushers in the highpoint in the history of Old Testament faith. The prophets call to a new Dasein-attitude in which the experiences, impressions and implications of the Mosaic time live again. It is a call to experience once again Yahweh's awesome essence and holy, decision-challenging will. The prophetic Dasein-attitude is born of a new understanding of God based upon experience—God as filled with holy passion, ready to wipe out all that contradicts his being. Israel is called to respond yes or no to God's being. Yes means faith, love, obedience and trust in the invisible God. Basic to this Dasein-attitude is the experience of the vocation; it always goes back to an experience of revelation, a revelation which challenges the other Dasein-attitudes which had evolved since Israel's entry into the land. The prophetic action overcomes and supersedes the deepest wishes of the magical Dasein-attitude. Prophetic prayer overcomes and fulfills the aspirations of the cultic Dasein-attitude. And the tie with one nation is taken up and passed beyond in the prophetic realization that God is the Lord of all nations. Finally, the various criticisms of "wisdom" found in such writings as Isaiah, Qoheleth and Job serve to deflate that overly optimistic Dasein-attitude which seeks security from following the rules of life.

Fohrer's search for what distinguishes the faith of Israel thus uncovers a plurality of fundamental stances which can be found within the community at differing times and under the force of varying circumstances and influences. His approach brings to light a certain plurality of Dasein-attitudes. But these are clearly not of equal value and import. The prophetic Dasein-attitude marks the highpoint and, perhaps, given the context of Fohrer's concern to locate what is distinctive in Israel's faith, one may say the purity of Israelite belief.

A final approach helpful for considering the question of what constitutes Israel's common faith is the discussion concerning the unity of Old Testament theology.[82] Roland de Vaux, mentioning some eight theologies of the Old Testament published during the years 1930-1960, notes that the authors of those works were deliberately stepping aside from a strict historicism to return to theological concerns. They wanted to systematically organize the material of the Old Testament around its fundamental doctrines.[83] Robert Martin-Achard comments on this organizational function of Old Testament theology: "The theology of the OT attempts to organize the multiformed and sometimes confusing data which Israel's bible contains, works with Israel's faith expressions and, in a certain sense, fashions 'a confession of faith in the second degree,' i.e., *an echo of an echo; a witness based on witnesses.*"[84]

A first instructive observation is that various attempts to organize the complex data of the Old Testament into a coherent theology themselves display a certain diversity. Surveys by Martin-Achard and Hasel offer a convenient illustration of such diversity. Eichrodt (1933) adopts the covenant as the central concept and symbol for securing the unity of biblical faith, not as a "doctrinal concept, with the help of which a complete corpus of dogma can be worked out, but the characteristic *description of a living process*, which was begun at a particular time and at a particular place, in order to reveal a divine reality unique in the whole history of religion."[85] E. Sellin (1936) organizes his Old Testament theology around the holiness of God.[86] Ludwig Köhler (1936) finds the statement "God is the Lord" to be the "backbone of Old Testament theology," while Hans Wildberger (1959) "suggests that 'the central concept of the Old Testament is Israel's election as the people of God.'"[87] The second edition of T. Vriezen's *An Outline of Old Testament Theology* focuses on the concept of "communion" as the essential root, fundamental idea and keystone of the message of the Old Testament.[88]

In various studies between 1968-1972, Georg Fohrer delineates a double concept around which everything may be grouped: the sovereignty of God and the communion between God and human beings.[89] Rudolf Smend (1970) revives Wellhausen's formula, "Yahweh the God of Israel, Israel the people of Yahweh," not so much as a "central concept" but rather as a formula which gives expression to the tension between God and Israel which constitutes the Old Testament's basic theme.[90] For Günther Klein (1970) the kingdom of God is the focus,[91] while Walther Zimmerli (1972) emphasizes the importance of Yahweh's name and sovereignty.[92] Finally, Claus Westermann (1978), drawing upon his studies of creation, refuses to limit the center of the Old Testament to themes such as the covenant or the history of salvation. He proposes a more inclusive guiding principle—all forms of the exchange between God and human beings—as more adequate to the God of the Old Testament, who not only intervenes in history to save but also creates and providentially blesses.[93]

In the midst of these efforts, Gerhard von Rad caused quite a stir when his own *Old Testament Theology* challenged the possibility of identifying a unity to Old Testament theology.[94] In the postscript to the English translation of his study, von Rad states:

> In many respects new territory was then opened up by the important works of Köhler and Eichrodt. The question today is, of course, whether there was then firmly established a system which allows the contents of the Old Testament to be developed in a really pertinent and organic way. And, in spite of the great stimulus which all Old Testament scholars have received from Köhler and Eichrodt, we have to give the answer "No."[95]

Von Rad's argument for this conclusion is that there is a diversity and even a heterogeneity among the voices to be found in the Old Testament. Every new moment of God's saving action in history became the point of departure for further reflection and for creative interpretation. Israel continually lived between promise and fulfillment, imparting to the history of its various witnesses a dynamism which resists unification into any single pattern. No unifying concept can include all of the voices. Von Rad's position has thus been called a focus on salvation history; it wants to carefully preserve the diversity of "theologies" present in the Old Testament and the creative interpretation of the tradition which they represent.

Where does this listing of various views concerning Old Testament theology lead with regard to the question of whether it is possible to delineate a common faith which held Israel together as a community? First of all, the variety represented by the various authors who have attempted to write an Old Testament theology and the caveats by von Rad and others all lead to a certain caution about attempting to state what was the "common faith of Israel." It is clear that a variety of theological points of view are present within the Old Testament and that it is not particularly easy to say precisely which one was dominant. Secondly, there seems to be, at the same time, a rather significant similarity between the various "Old Testament Theologies," including that of von Rad. They all tend to emphasize in more or less compatible ways God, God's relationship with human beings and the actual evolution of that relationship in history. Perhaps Martin-Achard's remark is not far from the mark:

> There are a variety of OT theologies and yet they present a *unified perspective....* No one OT theology alone can express the OT witness exhaustively and permanently. Though there are different OT theologies, the *foundation is the same*: "Yahweh and Israel," but each expresses the content of the OT in its own unique way. The differences between them should not hide the reality of their unity.[96]

Roland de Vaux adds a theological motive for suspecting such an underlying unity. If Old Testament theology is truly a theology, that is, a study done out of a fundamental faith stance that the Bible is the self-revelation of the one God, then one can appropriately presuppose a certain unity to the divine plan of this one God. A theology of the Old Testament cannot be restricted to asking what was Israel's awareness of God in this or that particular circumstance as reflected by this or that particular book; rather it also asks about what God wishes to teach by means of this history, to Israel and also to people today.[97] The task of the biblical theologian is to discover the unity of the plan of the one God.[98]

CONCLUSION

With this our three step approach to faith and its unity in the Old Testament comes to a close. Earlier (page 10) we cited Van der Leeuw's comment to the effect that the "insignificant" people of Israel was responsible for an immense achievement—"the birth of faith." This chapter has explored faith according to the Hebrew Scriptures and can now close with several preliminary conclusions which draw out the significance of the Old Testament presentation of faith for our understanding of unity in faith.

First of all, it is worth pointing out that the entries for the word "faith" in the various biblical lexica list a number of different Hebrew words which convey the meaning of this experience and that those words can each have a variety of nuances. Clearly, then, the vocabulary for faith exhibits a certain fluidity, reflective of the fact that faith is a comprehensive act which engages cognitive, emotional, ethical and existential dimensions of the whole person. When one asks about unity in faith, then, the Old Testament prompts one to acknowledge the rich complexity of this act and to further specify what unity in faith might mean. Is such unity simply a sameness in what one cognitively accepts as true, or does it require also those existential dimensions of trust and obedience? The discussion of terminology suggests that the existential, fiducial, obediential dimension of faith was predominant over the cognitive dimension in the Old Testament.

This becomes clear also when one considers the historical setting and condition of faith (Section 1.B above). Faith is the human response to the covenant, finding its highest expression in the prophet Isaiah who insists on the necessity of believing and trusting in God as the only way of remaining firm (Is 7,9). One might justifiably ask: does the fact that faith is ineradicably rooted in history carry any consequences for unity in faith? How can one understand a community's unity of faith over the course of several centuries? Might not a diachronic consideration of unity in faith suggest parameters for the criteria for recognizing such unity which are wider than those emerging from a merely synchronic consideration of the unity present at any single moment in history?

The second section of this chapter has shown that, while one can contest whether there exists the precise literary form "creed" in the Old Testament as well as the dating and influence of such creeds on the formulation of the Pentateuch or Hexateuch, nevertheless it is indeed possible to locate relatively short summaries which express the fundamental faith of Israel. Some of these professions of faith are one sentence exclamations, such as: "Yahweh brought us out of Egypt" (Ex 20,2; Dt 5,6); "The Lord is greater than all gods" (Ex 18,11); and "The Lord is great" (Ps 55,27). Others, such as the little credo of Dt 26, list some of the principal deeds of God in salvation history. Moreover, the recounting of God's mighty deeds can be adapted to some degree to suit particular circumstances (Neh 9) or to highlight specific themes such as the Davidic monarchy (Ps 78,68–72) or God's creation of the world (Ps 136). Thus one finds a certain freedom with regard to the profession of faith, a freedom which was rooted in the manifold nature of God's saving work and which allowed for the inclusion of additional themes which acknowledged these works. Moreover, the *shema* underscores the fact that Israel's relationship with God was primarily one of love, which included the various ethical and legal specifications to be found in the law.

In addition, the gradual maturing of Israel's understanding of God into monotheism presupposes the possibility that faith grows in understanding. This latter raises again the question of criteria for discerning unity in faith over the course of time. Growth in understanding implies a certain ignorance at the point of departure of such growth, which is superseded by understanding at the terminus ad quem of the growth. If we can say that people living in different times are truly united in the same faith even though those of one age may have more or less of an understanding of that faith than those of another age, then such unity in faith over the course of time would seem to countenance both that ignorance which is the terminus a quo for growth in understanding and that diversity from one stage to another which actually constitutes such growth.

Finally, it is clear that Old Testament faith is the faith of a community; the individual, who may at times be called upon to believe and trust in isolation, nevertheless always presupposes the covenant community between God and the chosen people as the context for faith. Within this faith community, there can be growth from one fundamental existential stance to another; there can also be the presence of several different existential stances at the same time (Fohrer). Still, one can identify certain features of Israel's faith which distinguish her from her neighbors (Schmidt) and which have been sketched out in the various modern attempts to write a "theology of the Old Testament." While these attempts highlight now one, now another aspect of the relationship between God and God's people in history, nevertheless it is precisely the historical playing out of this covenant relationship which seems to bind all of the various Old Testament theologies together.

In seeking for unity in faith today, Christians would do well not to forget these various insights about faith and its unity which come from Abraham and from their other ancestors in the faith (cf. Gal 3 and Heb 11).

Chapter Two
NEW TESTAMENT TERMINOLOGY FOR AND NUANCES CONCERNING FAITH

Moving from the Old Testament to the New, one is confronted with a veritable explosion of material relevant to the topic of faith and its unity. Because this is so, more space will be required to attempt a relatively adequate account of the material relevant to our topic. A first chapter, after some notes concerning the frequency of occurrence of terminology for faith in the New Testament, will sketch in broad outline a few of the principal theologies of faith to be found there and will survey the views of a number of exegetes concerning the relation between faith in the two Testaments. Because the comparison of faith in the Old and New Testaments reveals a distinctively credal tone in the latter, a second chapter will examine some of the many studies concerning the New Testament profession of faith. A third and final chapter will attempt to fairly explore and to offer a reasonably satisfying solution, to the extent that that is possible, to the thorny problem of faith's unity and diversity in the New Testament.

1. SOME INTRODUCTORY NOTES ABOUT TERMINOLOGY

The Greek verb *pisteuô* and noun *pistis* occur each 243 times in the New Testament, not counting the appearances of adverbial and adjectival forms of the root.[1] The combined use of the words "to believe" and "faith" is surpassed only by the use of such nouns as Christ, man, Lord, Jesus and God, and of such verbs as to do, to come/go, to be/become, to have, to have said and to say.[2] Statistically, therefore, the words for believing and faith are among the most prevalent in the entire New Testament. J. Duplacy notes that, while *pistis* and *pisteuô* were rarely used with a religious meaning in Greek literature of the time, one finds a "massive use" of these terms in a specifically religious sense in the New Testament.[3] Moreover, the distribution of these uses shows that

Pauline and Johannine literature are the two sources most concerned with faith.[4]

Bultmann notes that fundamentally the verb *pisteuein* means "to rely on," "to trust," "to believe" and "to entrust or commit oneself," while the noun *pistis* can mean "faithfulness," "trust," "belief" or "faith."[5] At the same time, Joseph Burgess cautions against presupposing that the words for believing and faith have only one meaning in the New Testament:

> ...famous scholars like Schlatter and Bultmann have held that a New Testament pattern exists for the word "faith." But histor-ical investigation proves otherwise. Faith is used in a variety of ways in the New Testament. No single meaning for faith exists because the New Testament was not being asked to define faith. It is not even quite exact to state that faith has a spectrum of meanings in the New Testament, for the metaphor of a spectrum brings too much of the quantitative to bear on the meaning of faith. Qualitative differences are also present.[6]

Burgess concludes that the meaning of faith must be sought from within the total context of the thought of each individual New Testament writer.[7] In fact, the bibliography concerning faith in the New Testament demonstrates an attention to the nuance given by the various authors; particularly one finds extensive lists of studies devoted to Pauline and Johannine depictions of faith.[8]

Finally, one might note that the terminology for faith is, from one point of view, more stabilized in the New Testament than in the Old. Old Testament exegetes tend to discuss a number of different Hebrew words for faith, only one of which was eventually rendered in the Septuagint with the Greek word *pisteuô*. While New Testament authors sometimes use other words to flesh out their specific understanding of faith (such as those associated with "seeing" or "knowing" in John or with "confidence" in Hebrews), still in general the vocabulary is more stable. A similar contrast can be noted in the fact that terms for believing and for faith are relatively infrequent in the Old Testament, while they are among the most often used in the New.

2. NEW TESTAMENT NUANCES CONCERNING FAITH

What then is "faith" according to the New Testament? In light of the comments of Burgess and Duplacy as well as with the approach of much of the relevant bibliography, clearly an adequate response to this question must at least briefly sketch those various nuances which can be discerned within the major blocks of New Testament material. The following outline of faith in the synoptics, the Pauline literature, the Johannine literature, the letter to the Hebrews and other New Testament writings should help to provide a glimpse of the range of meaning associated with faith in the New Testament.

A. The Synoptic Gospels

When one compares the synoptic gospels with the other New Testament writings, the words "to believe" and "faith" occur relatively infrequently.[9] The context for faith in these books is most consistently the encounter with Jesus, an encounter which provides the opportunity for what Christopher Marshall has described as two kinds of faith: kerygmatic and petitionary.[10] *Kerygmatic* faith is the believing acceptance of Jesus' proclamation of the dawning of the Kingdom of God; Jesus' first announcement of this reign calls for a response of conversion and faith (Mk 1,15). Jesus preaches the good news in the presence of all who will listen (Mt 11,3-6; 13,13-15), but not all can understand or accept his message (Mt 13,10-17). Those who hear the word of Jesus and put it into practice (Mt 7,24-27) are Jesus' true disciples (cf Lk 8,20). The mother of Jesus is singled out as blessed because she believed the word of the Lord (Lk 1,45).

Faith in the synoptics is not only this acceptance of the word; it is also a *petitionary* faith, often associated with Jesus' miracles.[11] Many come to Jesus in their need and often their faith is decisive for the subsequent working of a miracle (those carrying the paralytic: Mk 2,3-12 [Mt 9,2-8; Lk 5,18-26]; Jairus and the woman with the hemorrhage: Mk 5,21-43 [Mt 9,18-26; Lk 8,40-56]; the blind man Bartimaeus: Mk 10,46-52 [Mt 20,29-34; Lk 18,35-43; see also Mk 8,22-26]; the centurion whose servant was ill: Mt 8,5-13 [Lk 7,1-10]; two blind men: Mt 9,27-31 [Mt 20,29-34]; the Canaanite woman: Mt 15,21-28).[12] Faith seems to condition the healings. Of the blind men who seek the restoration of their sight, Jesus asks: "Do you believe that I can do this?" And when they respond yes, he answers: "Because of your faith it shall be done to you" (Mt 9,28-29 [Mk 10,52 and par.; Mk 5,34 and par.]). Jesus strongly praises those who have great faith (Mt 8,10 [Lk 7,9; Mt 15,28]). Everything is possible for those who believe (cf Mk 9,23 and Mt 17,20). Faith thus becomes a participation in the power of God; it is mountain-moving faith (Mk 11,23).[13] Marshall adds that faith is the power of those who are without power; the believer whose only refuge is prayer comes to participate in the very transforming power of God.[14]

While the absence of Christological titles in the faith statements of the synoptics may imply that at least a nucleus of these passages derives from a period before Easter, nevertheless faith in these gospels is not unrelated to a fundamental attitude about the person of Jesus.[15] It is not simply belief in the truth of Jesus' message or belief in God's power to perform miracles. Rather faith ties this truth and power specifically to the person and mission of Jesus. While the precise vocabulary of faith is not used in the exchange at Caesarea Philippi, still that scene reflects the Christological undercurrent that one can discern below the surface of the various passages which do speak more directly about faith:

> And Jesus went on with his disciples, to the villages of Caesarea Philippi; and on the way he asked his disciples, "Who do people say that I am?" And they told him, "John the Baptist; and others say, Elijah; and others one of the prophets." And he asked them, "But who do you say that I am?" Peter answered him, "You are the Christ" (Mk 8,27–29).

Such a faith includes both an intellectual dimension, recognizing the identity of Jesus and putting that recognition into words, as well as a personal, existential dimension in which one enters into a relationship with Jesus as his disciple.[16]

B. Pauline Literature

Paul's writings offer the most extensive usage of faith language in the New Testament and have generated a large bibliography of secondary literature.[17] While one could not do justice to all of this material in a brief summary, still it is helpful to underscore a few of the characteristics and nuances found in the Pauline literature.

"I am not ashamed of the gospel," writes Paul to the Romans. "It is the power of God leading everyone who believes in it to salvation, the Jew first, then the Greek. For in the gospel is revealed the justice of God which begins and ends with faith..." (Rom 1,16–17). Here some of the central aspects of Paul's understanding of faith come into relief. First of all, faith is an acceptance of the gospel, a good news which is summarized many times by Paul in terms of the saving death and resurrection of Jesus Christ (see, for example, Rom 1,3–4; 1 Cor 15,3–5).[18]

Paul's mission is to announce this gospel so that the Gentiles might respond to it in obedient faith (Rom 1,5). Some have pointed out that Rom 10,4–17 is a passage in which Paul summarizes his overall view of faith.[19] In this passage faith is an acknowledgment of God's saving action in Christ: "For if you confess with your lips that Jesus is Lord, and believe in your heart that God raised him from the dead, you will be saved" (Rom 10,9). The revelation that God had raised the Lord Jesus from the dead was experienced by Paul in a very dramatic and life-altering way on the road to Damascus (1 Cor 9,1; 15,8; Acts 9,1–19; 22,5–11; 26,12–18). The message of this gospel must be proclaimed to all: "And how can they believe unless they have heard of him? And how can they hear unless there is someone to preach?" (Rom 10,14), for "faith comes through hearing" (Rom 10,17).

A second element comes to the fore when Paul distinguishes faith from works of the Law: the intimate relationship between faith, justification and salvation.[20] Of their own accord, human beings are unable to overcome the power of sin in their lives—"...every mouth is silenced and the whole world stands convicted before God" (Rom 3,19). Who can free human beings from being held under the power of sin and death? God alone, through Jesus Christ (Rom 7,13–25). Thus faith in Christ places one in a new relationship with God; it makes a person righteous, not on the basis of his or her own endeavors but by the grace and activity of God in Christ (2 Cor 3,4–6; Phil 3,9; Eph 2,8–10). Blackman comments: "This is the new insight Paul has contributed on the nature of faith, and it is his chief self-differentiation from Judaism.... This fundamental humility and willingness to depend on God, abandoning self-sufficiency and the effort to make oneself worthy, is faith in the Pauline sense."[21] Paul's most extensive use of the terminology of faith occurs in the letters to the Romans and to the Galatians, both of which are devoted to explaining that justification comes only through faith, not through works of the law. "If justice is available through the law," Paul argues, "then Christ died to no purpose" (Gal 2,21). But that would amount to "another gospel" (Gal 1,6–9); and there is no other gospel—let anyone who proposes another gospel be anathema (Gal 1,8).

A new existence "in Christ" grows out of faith (Gal 2,20; 2 Cor 3,7–18; 5,7; 5,17: "if anyone is in Christ he is a new creation"; 13,5: "living in faith, Christ is in you"). Being in Christ may be described as "being in the Spirit" (Rom 8,1–4.9–17; 1 Cor 12,13; 2 Cor 3,17–18; Gal 3,2–5.14). Faith means freedom (Gal 4,1–5,13); faith draws one into Jesus' own relationship with the Father so that one becomes a child of God (Rom 8,14–17; Gal 3,26; 4,4–7). Faith expresses itself in love (Gal 5,6), which is the fulfillment of the whole law (Gal 5,14). All of these aspects of the new life which faith inaugurates tend to validate Bultmann's comment that: "'Faith' is the acceptance of the *kerygma* not as mere cognizance of it and agreement with it but as that genuine obedience to it which includes new understanding of one's self."[22] As such faith shapes the way a person lives.

Faith is an individualized gift which is assigned in diverse measures to each believer (cf. Rom 12,3). Faith has those traits which characterize growth and life.[23] Faith can be weak (Rom 14,1) or lacking (1 Thess 3,10); it can progress (Phil 1,25) or increase (2 Cor 10,15). While not always using explicitly the vocabulary of faith, Paul prays that his communities may be strengthened and sustained (2 Cor 13,9; Rom 15,13; 1 Thess 3,13; 5,23); he speaks of the need for correction and restoration (Gal 6,1; 1 Cor 1,10ff; 2 Cor 13,11). Such strengthening and correction applies to their life of faith as well.

One eminent element associated with the gift of faith is "knowledge."[24] This knowledge is of the *kerygma* (1 Thess 5,2; Rom 6,3; 2 Cor 5,1; 8,9) as well as of truths which believers draw as consequences (Rom 8,28; 13,11; 14,14; 1 Cor 3,16; 6,2f.9; 15,58). Bultmann adds:

> Ultimately "faith" and "knowledge" are identical as a new understanding of one's self, if Paul can give as the purpose of his apostleship both "to bring about the obedience of faith" (Rom 1:5) and "to give the light of the knowledge of the glory of God in the face of Christ" (II Cor. 4:6; cf. 2:14: "God... who...through us spreads the fragrance of the knowledge of him"). The same conclusion is to be drawn from his saying that he has given up "confidence in the flesh" for the sake of "the surpassing worth of knowing Christ Jesus" and his then proceeding to develop the purpose of "righteousness from God that depends on faith" as this: "that I may know him and the power of his resurrection and may share his sufferings..." (Phil 3:4–10).[25]

The knowledge of faith concerns that true wisdom which can only be known by those who, taught by the Spirit of God, have the "mind of Christ" (1 Cor 2,6–16). This knowledge is imperfect and constantly growing to greater adequacy (1 Cor 13,9–12; Eph 1,17–19; 3,17–19).

The rich texture and depth of Paul's thought on this topic, only possible to sketch out in a general way here, clearly warns against any overly simplistic understanding of faith. Faith accepts the central proclamation of Christ's saving death and resurrection. This acceptance is no mere intellectual recognition, but rather the saving event by which the believer enters into a new form of existence as a child of God, guided and enlightened by the Spirit. While not merely an intellectual act, faith nevertheless imparts a knowledge which is steadily being perfected under the impulse of God's grace.

C. Johannine Literature

John's gospel is written for the express purpose of promoting faith among those who read or hear it (Jn 20,30–31).[26] This aim must be seen within the context of John's predominant theme of revelation: "No one has ever seen God. It is God the only Son, ever at the Father's side, who has revealed him" (Jn 1,18). John presents Jesus as the Word, the self-communication of God who brings light and life, grace and truth (Jn 1,4.14).[27] Within this context of God's active self-revelation, faith is presented as an active response, not as an abstract concept. The verb "to believe" appears ninety-eight times in the gospel of John, the noun "faith" not even once! Faith means the acceptance of the testimony given by Jesus (Jn 3,11.31–33; 8,13–14) and about him (Jn 5,31–40).[28] It means to receive the message which Jesus brings from the Father (Jn 17,8), to accept the truth of his teaching and doctrine (Jn 7,16–17; 8,31–32; 18,37). Faith ultimately focuses on the person of Jesus himself: "Any who did accept him he empowered to become children of God. These are they who believe in his name—who are begotten not by blood, nor by carnal desire, nor by man's willing it, but by God" (Jn 1,12–13; see also 3,15–18; 4,53; 6,44–47; 8,24; 1 Jn 5,1.5).

For John, such faith is the condition for entering eternal life: "I solemnly assure you, the man who hears my word and has faith in him who sent me possesses eternal life. He does not come under condemnation, but has passed from death to life" (Jn 5,24; see also 3,36; 6,35.40.47; 11,25–26; 20,31; 1 Jn 5,1.5.13). These passages understand salvation in terms of eternal life and affirm that faith leads to salvation, unbelief to perdition.[29] Faith is thus decisive with regard to eternal life. Moreover, faith in Jesus determines one's relationship with God: "Whoever believes in Christ believes in the Father (12:44); whoever does not believe in Christ neither sees nor hears the Father (5:37–38). 'To see God' means, in effect, to believe that Christ is in the Father and the Father is in him (10:38; 14:10. 11. 20)."[30]

A number of commentators notice that John is interested in the process by which a person comes to faith.[31] Here the signs play a distinctive role which contrasts to some degree with their role in the synoptic miracle stories. While faith is a precondition for miracles according to the synoptics (Mk 6,6; 9,23; Mt 13,8), in John it appears as a consequence of the various signs, which occasion the gradual coming to and deepening of faith (Jn 4,50–54; 8,30; 9,35–38; 10,42; 11,45–47; 12,9–11).

There is also a strong correlation between faith and knowledge in John. To believe and to know are "almost indistinguishable one from the other,"[32] as for example in cases where they are used of the same object: "we have believed, and have come to know, that you are the Holy One of God" (Jn 6,69) and "we have come to know and to believe in the love God has for us" (1 Jn 4,16; see also Jn 17,8; 8,24.28). Bultmann summarizes the relation between faith and knowledge in John as follows:

> As all knowledge begins with faith, so it abides in faith. Similarly, all faith is to become knowledge. If all knowledge can only be a knowledge of faith, faith comes to itself in knowledge. Knowledge is thus a constitutive element in genuine faith. If one also realizes that the relation of the Son to the Father is never described as a relation of faith, but only of knowledge, it is evident that this interconnection of faith and knowledge describes human faith, which must come to knowledge but which cannot attain to a definitive state of pure gnosis.[33]

Finally, faith affects the conduct of the believer.[34] The person of faith is "in the world" (Jn 13,1; 17,11.15; 1 Jn 4,17) but not "of the world" (15,19; 17,14.16; cf. 17,6). Faith is demonstrated in keeping the commandments (Jn 15,10; 1 Jn 2,3-4; 3,22-24; 5,2), especially the commandment to love one another (Jn 13,34; 15,12). "Beloved, let us love one another because love is of God; everyone who loves is begotten of God and has knowledge of God" (1 Jn 4,7).

D. Hebrews

The letter to the Hebrews calls for a special note because it uses the noun "faith" some thirty-two times, twenty-four of which come in chapter 11 which recalls the faith of many of the famous men and women of the Old Testament and which begins with the well-known description of faith—"Faith is confident assurance concerning what we hope for, conviction about things we do not see" (Heb 11,1).[35] Clearly faith is spoken of here in terms of confidence and hope. The faith of this "cloud of witnesses" (Heb 12,1) is recalled not because they believed in Christ but as an inspiration to endure and remain steadfast in the trust of the God who remains true to his promises (Heb 11,11.17). Because of this Hebrews is a particularly clear example of the point made by some scholars that faith has a variety of meanings in the New Testament, according to the particular concerns of each individual author.[36] One of the principal concerns of the author of the letter to the Hebrews is to encourage the community to endure in the midst of trials and difficul-

ties (12,1–13), to patiently advance in the understanding and practice of
the faith (5,11–6,20). In contrast with many of the other New Testament
writings which place faith within a context of acknowledging Jesus,
Hebrews understands faith as being very similar to hope, patience and
endurance (3,6; 6,11–12; 10,35–11,1; 12,2). Indeed, for Hebrews, Jesus
is not so much the object of faith as the example for believers (12,2).[37]

E. Other New Testament Writings

Acts makes rather extensive use of the language of faith (fifteen
occurrences of the noun and thirty-nine of the verb).[38] While it
sometimes appears in a merely secular sense (the disciples could not
"believe" that Paul had really changed—9,26) and sometimes continues
the synoptic emphasis as confidence in the power to heal (3,16; 14,9),
the predominant use of faith is to describe the response to the preaching
of the message about Jesus Christ and the growth and establishment of
the nascent Christian community (4,4; 5,14; 9,42; 11,17.21; 14,1; 15,5).
Acts emphasizes the unity of mind and of possessions of those who
believed (2,44; 4,32). Faith leads to baptism (8,12.13; 18,8). Particularly
fervent Christians such as Stephen (6,5) and Barnabas (11,24) are said to
be full of the Holy Spirit and of faith. The missionary journeys of Paul
open the "door of faith" to the nations (14,27).

The letter of James might be characterized as an exhortation about
Christian conduct. Faith language is concentrated in a thirteen–verse
passage (2,14–26) which argues that faith must be accompanied by good
works: faith without works is dead (2,17.26). Some commentators see
James' position as irreconcilable with Paul's view of justification by faith
and not by works[39] or even as a direct attack upon Paul.[40] Others have
argued that James' aim of encouraging a faith which expresses itself in a
certain way of living is not meant to address the specific faith-works
dialectic about which Paul teaches.[41] At least one can note that Paul himself would espouse the view that faith should have a positive effect upon
the way in which the believer lives.

Finally, the pastoral letters (1 and 2 Timothy and Titus) reflect the
situation of the second and third generations of Christians, with their
concern for organizing and continuing the community after the death
of the apostles.[42] In this context, faith language tends more and more to
denote doctrine (1 Tim 1,19; 2,7; 4,1; 4,6; 5,12; 6,10; 2 Tim 1,14; 2,18;
3,8)—that sound doctrine which was received from Paul and the other
apostles and which is threatened now by innovative, false teachings (2
Tim 4,1–5). Church structure is seen as a means to protect the faith of
the community.

This brief survey of some of the various ways in which the inspired authors speak of faith demonstrates that it certainly enjoys diverse shades of meaning within the one canon of New Testament literature. The "discipleship" and "trust" connotations of faith in the synoptics emphasize different aspects than those of Paul's understanding of faith as finding salvation through the acceptance of the proclamation of Jesus' death and resurrection. The Johannine faith which is a knowledge opening the believer to a share in eternal life highlights dimensions other than those of the patient, enduring faith of the letter to the Hebrews. Acts of the Apostles, James and the pastoral epistles offer yet other insights into what Christian faith is all about. Clearly there is a richness and depth to the act of believing which allows for a range of expressions and interpretations. This fact, of course, needs to be taken into consideration when one attempts to address the question of what makes for unity in faith. But before turning to that question, some further clarification about Christian faith can be gleaned from the analysis of several authors who have attempted to compare faith as it appears respectively in the Old and the New Testaments and to draw out some distinctive characteristics of New Testament faith.

3. COMPARISON OF FAITH IN THE
OLD TESTAMENT AND THE NEW

Juan Alfaro concludes his lengthy study of the faith terminology of the Bible with the assertion that the notion of faith in the Old and New Testaments is fundamentally identical.[43] To have faith refers to that global response and adherence on the part of the human being to the God who reveals and saves. This global attitude contains a number of elements, which are of varying degrees of importance and visibility in the two Testaments. Fundamentally, it can be described as an obediential attitude which responds to God with *recognition* (the cognitive element which asserts that God has acted in history to save human beings) and *trust* (the fiducial element which confidently hopes that the God who has fulfilled his promises in the past will do so again now for us). The difference between the presentation of faith in the two Testaments lies in what each stresses. The Old Testament stresses trust in the God who fulfills covenant promises; the New Testament places the cognitive element to the fore, the recognition of some new and decisive divine intervention which has now taken place in Jesus Christ. The main reason for this shift in emphasis is the fundamental fact which differentiates the Old from the New Testament—the Christ event itself.

Bultmann, Blackman and De Bovis all agree with Alfaro's general approach of proceeding from a statement about the fundamental continuity between faith in the Old and New Testaments to a determination of the specific differences between the two.[44] For Bultmann, the specific difference in Christian faith-talk is the acceptance of the kerygma about Christ, which entails a definite content:

> ...it is apparent that acknowledgment of Jesus as Lord is intrinsic to Christian faith along with acknowledgment of the miracle of His resurrection, i.e., acceptance of this miracle as true. The two statements constitute an inner unity. The Resurrection is not just a remarkable event. It is the soteriological fact in virtue of which Jesus became the *kurios*. This is self-evident, and other statements confirm it. Naturally, in view of the inner unity, either one of the statements can be made alone, or the event of salvation can be described differently or more explicitly. The totality is always in view.[45]

At the same time, the acceptance of this kerygma entails a personal relationship to Christ. It entails recognizing that the saving events which took place in Christ took place for oneself. The personal relationship that the believer has to Christ is analogous to that which he or she has to God. Herein lies a new element which gives a particular emphasis of cognitive acknowledgment to Christian faith. In the Old Testament, obedience

> ...is directed to the God whose existence is always presupposed. In its original and true sense, however, faith in Jesus Christ is not obedience to a Lord who is known already. Only in faith itself is the existence of this Lord recognised and acknowledged. Faith embraces the conviction that there is this Lord, Jesus Christ, for it. For only in faith does this Lord meet it. It believes on the basis of the kerygma. It can always believe only on the basis of this message. The message is never a mere orientation which can be dispensed with once it is known. It is always the foundation of faith.[46]

Thus, for Bultmann, the distinctiveness of Christian faith, when compared with faith in the Old Testament, lies in its acceptance of the kerygma, the cognizance of a new element in the content of faith, in the *fides quae creditur*. New Testament faith more directly than that of the

Old Testament requires a conversion at its beginning and a continual attention to stand fast and grow in faith.[47] It entails a personal relationship with Christ. Before they were ever called Christians, the community of those who accepted and followed Jesus were simply called "those who believe."[48]

Others also see a definite novelty in the way faith is portrayed in the New Testament. Zimmermann locates two "fresh impulses" which show the "contrast between the idea of faith in the Old Testament and that contained in the New."[49] The first is the conviction that "the time is accomplished," that what had been promised throughout the writings of the Old Testament had come to definitive fulfillment in Jesus Christ. The effort of the earliest community to understand and explain its experience of Jesus precisely in terms of the Old Testament—particularly in the passion narratives—is a clear illustration of this. Secondly, faith is linked directly to conversion (as in Mk 1,15). Unlike the overall tenor of the Old Testament, the New Testament presents faith as a radical turning away from all that is contrary to God and a radical change of mind and heart. André de Bovis also speaks of two distinctive elements of New Testament faith: 1) faith is a personal decision in which one changes one's life to become a follower of Jesus, and 2) faith confronts one with the moment of truth in which one addresses the question of Jesus' identity and professes that he is the Messiah, the way–truth–life, the Lord.[50] For De Bovis, all of the various New Testament writings return to these two dimensions of faith: personal decision which changes one's life and conviction about who Jesus is.

One can discern several common threads in these various attempts to relate the way in which faith is understood in the two Testaments. All see a continuity between the two Testaments in such a way that the New Testament picks up the fundamental aspects of Old Testament faith: the elements more properly called "subjective" in that they refer to the subjectivity of the believer, such as believing, trusting, hoping in God, as well as the more "objective" elements of Israel's credo, such as the conviction that Yahweh alone is God and is actively directing history for the salvation of his people. All see a newness 1) in the proclamation of the definitive saving action by God in history in the fate of Jesus of Nazareth and, consequently, in the proclamation of Jesus' unique identity, as well as 2) in faith's requiring a personal conversion and appropriation of the effects of this definitive saving action in one's own life.

If this assessment is true, it would explain why the New Testament seems to be more "credal" in its understanding of faith than the Old. One may point to a comment by Bernhard Lang in this regard:

The Old Testament message of the uniqueness of God, of
the lordship of Yahweh and of his action in history was not
very often summarized in credal formulas. With the message
of the New Testament it is quite different. The profession of
faith in the risen Jesus, sometimes linked with profession of
faith in the one unique God, is something we encounter in a
bewildering profusion of concise formulas in all the writings
of the New Testament. Right from the start Christianity can
be termed a religion centred on a creed.[51]

If this understanding of the newness of New Testament faith is
fundamentally sound, then it suggests that a consideration of the credal
nature of the New Testament is in no way merely incidental to an
adequate presentation of its view of faith.

CONCLUSION

This opening chapter about faith in the New Testament has
attempted to demonstrate three points. First, we have noted that the
noun "faith" and the verb "to believe" are among the most abundantly
present in the entire New Testament. This suggests that faith is at the
heart of the communities from out of which the twenty-seven books of
the New Testament emerged; faith belongs to the very core of their self-
understanding and to the very essence of the community of disciples
which is the Church. Secondly, faith enjoys a rich polyvalence of meaning, and that from two distinct perspectives. First of all, a number of
blocks of New Testament material can be individuated as presenting a
distinct and roughly homogeneous general understanding of faith: the
synoptic gospels, Pauline literature, Johannine literature and the letter
to the Hebrews (with a few additional points from Acts, James and the
pastorals). Secondly, within each of these blocks, one can find a further
diversification and wealth of meaning, particularly within the Pauline
and Johannine material. This suggests that any view of faith which would
simply reduce it to one of its dimensions would not be entirely true to
the depth of meaning and experience that this concept represents in the
New Testament. Finally, this chapter has documented a rather strong
consensus among well-respected exegetes that the New Testament view
of faith is in substantial continuity with that of the Old Testament and
that its newness lies precisely in the experience and profession of the
unique and definitive salvific event in Jesus Christ. To this distinctive
profession of faith, which largely constitutes the novelty of New
Testament faith in comparison with that of the Old, we now must turn.

Chapter Three
THE NEW TESTAMENT
PROFESSION OF FAITH

Modern interest in the credal content of the New Testament owes no small part of its origin to the discussion of the relation of the Apostles' Creed to the Scriptures, which took place during the latter half of the nineteenth century and the beginning of the twentieth century.[1] The old legend, mentioned in Hippolytus' *Apostolic Tradition* and elaborated in several other patristic texts, asserted that, before setting forth to preach the Christian good news, each of the twelve apostles contributed one of the twelve articles comprising the Apostles' Creed, thus insuring harmony and unity to their mission once they set upon their different paths.[2] Already in the fifteenth century, the fact that the Orthodox representatives at the Council of Florence knew nothing of the Apostles' Creed raised questions about the veracity of the legend.[3] Not only is there no mention of the Apostles' Creed in the New Testament but historical studies attempting to assign it a date place its composition several centuries later.[4] Moreover, the very notion of a creed as a list of the normative articles which identified the essential doctrine of Christians was seen by some as foreign to a free, charismatic expression of faith posited as characteristic of the New Testament.[5]

However, further penetration into the relation of the Creed to the New Testament, while retaining caution against the anachronism of locating in the Scriptures some form of creed which was to be developed only much later, nevertheless drew attention to the fundamentally confessional nature of the New Testament and of the communities within which it was written. As J.N.D. Kelly pointed out in his Early Christian Creeds:

> ...the early Church was from the start a believing, confessing, preaching Church.... Had the Christians of the apostolic age not conceived of themselves as possessing a body of distinctive, consciously held beliefs, they would scarcely have separated

themselves from Judaism and undertaken an immense programme of missionary expansion. Everything goes to show that the infant communities looked upon themselves as the bearers of a unique story of redemption. It was their faith in this gospel which had called them into being, and which they felt obliged to communicate to newcomers. It would have been surprising if they had not given visible expression to it in their preaching as well as in their corporate life and organization.[6]

Kelly's general evaluation of the early Christian community is substantiated by the many studies which have attempted to analyze the confessional, credal character of the various New Testament writings.[7]

A common thread that runs through several of these studies may be captured by an important text from Paul: "For if you confess with your lips that Jesus is Lord, and believe in your heart that God raised him from the dead, you will be saved" (Rom 10,9). Heinrich Schlier points out that this text speaks of a "confessing" *which regards the person of Jesus*, i.e. that he is Lord, and a "believing" *which regards a particular salvation event*, i.e. that God raised Jesus from the dead.[8] This twofold pattern of confessing a name as pertaining to Jesus and of believing in certain salvation events which are accomplished through him is reiterated by other exegetes, in slightly different terms. Thus, taking his cue from the same text of Rom 10,9, Hans Conzelmann speaks of the early faith of Christianity as concerned with the person and the work of Jesus.[9] Pierre Benoit structures his investigation "The Origins of the Apostles' Creed in the New Testament" according to the two categories "kerygma" and "confession of faith," the former concerned with the central deed of the salvific death and resurrection of Jesus and with its preparation and effects, the latter concerned with various titles by which faith in the identity of Jesus was professed.[10] Various passages can be marshalled to illustrate this common proposal that the New Testament focuses its expression of faith in a double confession about the identity of Jesus and about God's saving action in and through him.

1. IDENTIFYING JESUS

"Jesus has many names"—Franz Mussner attributes this expression to Willi Marxsen.[11] While this is amply verified by various studies concerning the titles of Jesus, the literature which examines the New

Testament precisely in terms of its confession of faith tends to focus on three titles: Christ, Lord and Son of God.[12]

A. Christ

The title "Christ" (Messiah), meaning the anointed one, stems from messianic hopes of Israel and needs to be regarded with some caution when applied to Jesus, a point demonstrated by the theme of the "messianic secret" in the gospel of Mark.[13] In Mark, Jesus displays a certain reluctance to be called by this title and corrects his disciples' understanding of it by interpreting it away from the notion of a triumphant, messianic king. Nevertheless, when Peter answers Jesus' question "Who do you say that I am?" with the confession "You are the Christ," Jesus evidently does not refuse this response (Mk 8,29; Lk 9,20; cf. also Mt 16,20 which adds the phrase: "the Son of the living God"). A whole sequence of sentences in the form of "I am...you are...he is...the Christ" runs through the various books of the New Testament. The passion narratives in the synoptics, both in the trial (Mt 26,63–64; Mk 14,61–62; Lk 22,66–68) and in the taunting beneath the cross (Lk 23,35; cf. Mk 16,32), raise the question of whether or not Jesus is the Christ. In John's gospel, Jesus identifies himself to the Samaritan woman as such (4,26) and the question of his identity as the Christ recurs several times (7,26.41; 9,22; 10,24). The motive behind the writing of the fourth gospel is "so that you may believe that Jesus is the Christ, the Son of God" (Jn 20,31), while Mt 1,16 closes its genealogy with the words "who is called the Christ" and Mk 1,1 identifies what is to follow as the "gospel of Jesus Christ." Paul's exchanges with the Jews in Acts are presented as having the scope of demonstrating that "Jesus is the Christ" (9,22; 17,3; 18,5.28). The Pauline literature itself is filled with this designation (266 times in the uncontested letters; 81 times in the deutero-Pauline letters and 32 times in the pastorals).[14] Here "Christ" has become almost a second name for Jesus (e.g. 1 Thess 1,1.4 "Jesus Christ" and 1 Thess 2,14; 5,18 "Christ Jesus") and the explicit use of the word "Christ" precisely as a title is somewhat rare (i.e. Rom 9,5: "...to them belong the patriarchs, and of their race, according to the flesh, is the Christ..."). Finally, the title is used within the polemical context of distinguishing the liar and the antichrist from one who is a child of God in 1 Jn 2,22 ("Who is the liar but he who denies that Jesus is the Christ?") and 1 Jn 5,1 ("Everyone who believes that Jesus is the Christ is a child of God...").

Clearly the confession of Jesus as the Christ was a widespread and important aspect of the faith of the early Christian community. While the meaning of this designation derives from an Old Testament context and would be particularly understandable among Jewish Christians and while the specific Christian connotation of the title in light of the actual mission and fate of Jesus required modification of the inherited meaning, especially in terms of other Old Testament texts which concerned the suffering servant of Yahweh, nevertheless the identification of Jesus as the Christ is not limited to one particular New Testament theology or community. The confession of Jesus as the Christ finds expression throughout the New Testament.

B. Son of God

The designation "Son of God" has precedents not only in the Old Testament but also in the broader religious context before and during the writing of the New Testament.[15] These precedents provide no single, dominant meaning for the title. In the New Testament, however, this designation is often used to convey the absolute and unique identity of Jesus. As with the title "Christ," once again it is used with the verbal construction "you are...he is...," finding in the synoptic gospels its most solemn expression at Jesus' baptism ("You are my beloved son": Mk 1,11; Lk 3,22; Mt 3,17; cf. Jn 1,34) and at his transfiguration ("This is my beloved Son; listen to him": Mk 9,7; Lk 9,35; Mt 17,5; cf. 2 Pet 1,17). Some manuscripts present the expression as part of the title of the gospel of Mark ("the gospel of Jesus Christ, the Son of God" 1,1) and the annunciation narrative in Luke twice so identifies the child who is to be born (Lk 1,32.35). The taunt of Satan in the temptation scenes repeats the phrase "If you are the Son of God..." (Mt 4,3.6; Lk 4,3.9) and demons about to be exorcised acknowledge Jesus' dignity and power under this title (Mk 3,11; 5,7; Lk 4,41; 8,28; Mt 8,29). As Son, Jesus shares an intimate knowledge with the Father (Lk 10,22; Mt 11,27), although not even the Son knows the hour of the end of the world (Mk 13,32). The parable of the vineyard owner who sends his own son to the wicked tenants (Mk 12,1–12 and par) may go back to Jesus himself.[16] Jesus' identity as Son of God appears as a decisive charge in the trial scenes in Mk 14,61 and Mt 26,63, the two gospels in which the centurion standing below the cross after the death of Jesus declares: "Truly this man was the Son of God" (Mk 15,39; Mt 27,54).

Paul declares in Gal 2,22 "I live by faith in the Son of God, who loved me and gave himself for me," adding in the following chapter that all who have faith in Christ Jesus are "sons of God" (Gal 3,26). 2 Cor 1,19 identifies Jesus Christ, "the Son of God," as the focus of the preaching of Paul, Timothy and Silvanus to the Corinthians. Often when speaking about God or about the Father, Paul refers to Jesus as "his son" (1 Thess

1,10; Gal 1,16; 4,4–6; 1 Cor 1,9; Rom 1,3.9; 5,10; 8,3.29.32; Col 1,13). Sometimes this title can carry different nuances even within the authentic writings of the same Paul. In Rom 1,4 Jesus is "designated" [horisthentos] Son of God in power; in Gal 4,4 Jesus is the preexistent son born of a woman under the law, and in 1 Cor 15,28 Jesus is the son to whom all things will be subjected at the end of the age. Jesus' sonship carries a soteriological significance in connection with his death: it is God's own Son whose death reconciles sinners (Rom 5,10; 8,32; Gal 4,4–5; Col 1,13–14; Heb 6,6). For the author of Hebrews, the fact that Jesus is the Son of God confers upon him a special priesthood (4,14; 7,28) and makes him the consummate and definitive revelation of God (1,2).

Nor is the identification of Jesus as the Son of God lacking in the Johannine literature. Both Nathaniel (1,49) and Martha (11,27) explicitly confess Jesus to be such. As Son, everything that Jesus does is in accord with what the Father is doing; as the Father gives life, so too does the Son and to the Son is given the role of judging all people (5,19–26). God's love is shown in that he sent his only begotten Son, that those who believe in him may have eternal life (3,16–18; cf 6,40; 20,31), a theme that is repeated in 1 Jn 4,9; 5,13. At the beginning of the account of the raising of Lazarus (Jn 11,4) and the prayer of Jesus at the Last Supper (Jn 17,1), it is the Son who is about to be glorified by the Father, either in the working of the miracle or in the passion narrative which immediately follows. The scope of the Christian proclamation, according to the prologue of 1 John, is to create fellowship between the proclaimers and the hearers, a fellowship which is "with the Father and with his Son Jesus Christ" (1,3). This theme is developed later in the letter under the specific nuance of confessing or believing that Jesus is the Son of God: "Whoever confesses that Jesus is the Son of God, God abides in him, and he in God" (1 Jn 4,15); "Who is it that overcomes the world but he who believes that Jesus is the Son of God?" (5,5).

Once again, a chain of texts which is striking by its universal presence throughout the New Testament witnesses to the importance of the confession of Jesus as the Son of God for the early Christian community.

C. Lord

The designation "Lord" also carried a range of meanings during the time of the composition of the New Testament, extending from a title given to various deities or to emperors and kings to the designation of the master of a household or of servants. One of the most common meanings was simply that of being the respectful way of addressing a person in authority.[17] As such it was probably used in addressing Jesus in

his capacity as teacher or healer.[18] Von Campenhausen even dismisses it
as an important Christian confession because, unlike the titles "Christ"
which connoted a very special identification of Jesus for believers of
Jewish background and "Son of God" which would have been equally
distinctive for believers of Gentile background, the title "Lord" did little
to distinguish Jesus from the many "lords" of the Greco-Roman world in
which Christianity was born and in the context of which the New
Testament was written.[19]

While these points provide an important caution against mis-
reading the various texts which refer to Jesus as "Lord," nevertheless
many specific verses do point to this title as one of particular importance
for the expression of the faith of the early Christian community. In the
gospels, Luke seems to convey the sense of post-Easter faith in the risen
Lord when he refers to Jesus some eighteen times simply as "the Lord"
(Lk 7,13.17; 10,1.39.41; 11,39; 12,41; 13,15; 17,5.6; 18,6; 19,8.31.34;
22,61 [two times]; 24,3.34). In addition, the title "Lord" is prominent
in the resurrection chapters of the gospel of John (fifteen times in
chapters 20–21, including the confession of Thomas "My Lord and my
God" of 20,28).[20] But the designation of Jesus as Lord takes on
special significance in Acts and the Pauline literature. Peter's Pentecost
proclamation concludes with the words: "Let all the house of Israel
therefore know assuredly that God has made him both Lord and Christ,
this Jesus whom you crucified" (2,36). Later he characterizes the kernel
of the preaching of the early Church as follows: "You know the word
which he sent to Israel, preaching good news of peace by Jesus Christ (he
is Lord of all)" (10,36). Acts presents a community which very early gives
prominence to the "name" of Jesus ("...for there is no other name under
heaven given among men by which we must be saved" 4,12; cf. 2,21;
4,10.30; 5,41) and frequently this name is given as "the Lord Jesus" (4,33;
7,59; 11,20; 15,11; 16,31; 19,13.17; 20,24.35; 21,13) or "the Lord Jesus
Christ" (11,17; 15,26; 20,21; 28,31). Baptism was administered in the
name of the Lord Jesus (8,16; 19,5; see also 2,38; 10,48; 22,16). Acts 2,34
suggests that the application of this title to Jesus stemmed from
reflection upon the opening verse of Psalm 110: "The Lord said to my
lord, sit at my right hand" and that it characterizes Jesus precisely as the
risen Lord who is now exalted at the side of the Father (see 2,32–33;
4,33).

Paul also makes great use of the designation "Lord" for Jesus:
"Lord Jesus" (1 Thess 2,15.19; 3,11.13; 4,1-2; 2 Thess 1,1.2.7.8.12; 2,8;
Rom 14,14; 1 Cor 5,4.5; 16,23; 2 Cor 9,14; 11,31; Phm 5); "Lord Jesus
Christ" (1 Thess 1,1; 5,9.23.28; 2 Thess 2,1.14.16; 3,12.18; Rom 1,7;

5,1.11; 13,14; 15,6.30; 16,18.20; 1 Cor 1,2. 3.7.8.9.10; 6,11; 15,57; 2 Cor
1,2.3.14; 8,9; 13,14; Gal 1,3; 6,14.18; Phil 1,2; 3,20; 4,23; Phm 3.25);
"Jesus Christ our/my Lord" or "Christ Jesus our Lord" (Rom 5,21;
6,23; 7,25; 8,39; 1 Cor 15,31; Phil 3,8). Again Jesus' Lordship is understood within the context of his resurrection (e.g. Rom 1,4; 4,24–25). 2
Cor 4,5 characterizes the ministry of Paul in the following terms: "For
what we preach is not ourselves, but Jesus Christ as Lord, with ourselves
as your servants for Jesus' sake." But what are perhaps most striking are
several passages which highlight the confessional nature of this designation. Rom 10 places the confession of Jesus as Lord as a condition for
salvation: "If you confess with your lips that Jesus is Lord and believe in
your heart that God raised him from the dead, you will be saved" (v. 9).
1 Cor 12,3 repeats a liturgical formula which had been received from
the prior tradition: "no one can say 'Jesus is Lord' except by the Holy
Spirit," a confession the context of which can be further elucidated by
another text from the same letter: "For although there may be so-called
gods in heaven or on earth—as indeed there are many 'gods' and many
'lords'—yet for us there is one God, the Father, from whom are all
things and for whom we exist, and one Lord, Jesus Christ, through
whom are all things and through whom we exist" (1 Cor 8,5–6). And
finally, the liturgical hymn which Paul has incorporated into the text of
his letter to the Philippians reaches a crescendo in the bestowal on
Jesus of the name above every other name: "Jesus Christ as Lord," with
an echo of Is 45,23 suggesting that the same adoration which is there
given to Yahweh is now also to be given to Jesus.[21] These constitute the
clearest New Testament presentation that one of the earliest Christian
"creeds" was the simple formula "Jesus is Lord."[22] Deutero-Pauline literature, while not exhibiting explicit confessional passages proclaiming
Jesus as Lord, continues to make predominant use of "Lord" as a title
for Jesus (Eph 1,2-3.15.17; 3,11; 4,20; 6,23.24; Col 1,3; 2,6; 3,17; 1 Tim
1,2.12; 6,14.15; 2 Tim 1,2). There is also some incidence of the title in
the remaining books of the New Testament (Heb 6,20; 7,14; Jas 1,1; 2,1;
1 Pet 1,3; 2 Pet 1,2.8.16 [a letter which contains the unique expression
"our Lord and Savior Jesus Christ" at 1,11; 2,20 and 3,18; somewhat
similar is Lk 2,11: "a savior, Christ the Lord"]; Jude 17,21.25; Rev 11,8;
22,20.21).

Thus, as with the designations "Christ" and "Son of God," the
evidence suggests that "Lord" was an important element of the
confession of faith of the early Christian communities, especially for
those to whom were addressed Luke-Acts and the Pauline letters. While
each of these titles carries its own particular nuance and may have

enjoyed more or less emphasis in various communities, it seems clear
that the widespread and commonly-held faith of the early community
identified and confessed Jesus as Christ, Son of God and Lord.[23]
Moreover, the compatibility of these designations with each other can
be shown from various passages where the same author places them
together side by side. A striking example is Rom 1,3–4: "...the gospel
concerning his Son, who was descended from David according to the
flesh and designated Son of God in power according to the Spirit of
holiness by his resurrection from the dead, Jesus Christ our Lord...."[24]

2. THE SALVATION EVENT–
JESUS' DEATH AND RESURRECTION

The event of Jesus' resurrection can be called the point of departure for the beginning of the first Christian community, in the sense that
its coming to be would have been quite unthinkable if Jesus' ultimate
fate had been simply that of death on the cross. This fact does not preju-
dice in any negative way the quite distinct question of the relation of the
historical Jesus to the foundation of the Church. In the context of that
discussion it merely points out that what began with Jesus and the community of disciples that he gathered during his earthly life could scarcely
have continued had he not been raised from the dead. The New
Testament evidence shows that this event and faith in it by those who
experienced the same Jesus of history now as the risen Lord, and by
those who believed on the basis of their testimony, was the condition for
the emergence of the earliest Christian community.

A. 1 Cor 15,3–5

The first written expression of this faith in the New Testament is
the famous passage 1 Cor 15,3–5, a passage which appears as a standard
formula which St. Paul explicitly identifies as having been *received* from
the earlier tradition:

> For I delivered to you as of first importance what I also
> received, that Christ died for our sins in accordance with the
> scriptures, that he was buried, that he was raised on the third
> day in accordance with the scriptures, and that he appeared
> to Cephas, then to the twelve.[25]

This passage not only recalls the central event of Jesus' death, burial and
resurrection, but already provides elements of the richness of meaning

that the pre-Pauline community attached to it: it is *Christ* who died, his death being *for our sins*, his death and being raised were *according to the Scriptures* and he *appeared to those who had been with him during his earthly life*, thus confirming a certain continuity between the risen Christ and the Jesus who exercised his ministry in Galilee and Judea.[26] These details serve to underscore that the resurrection was from the beginning understood and interpreted in the light of faith. God's raising of Jesus from the dead is the fundamental article of faith which Paul repeats again and again in his authentic letters (1 Thess 1,10; 4,14; 1 Cor 6,14 and throughout chapter 15; 2 Cor 4,14; 5,15; Gal 1,1; Rom 4,24.25; 6,4.9; 7,4; 8,11.34; 10,9; this raising appears in the form of the noun *anastasis* in Phil 3,10; Rom 1,4; 6,5).

B. *The Sermons in Acts*

A similar focus upon the death and resurrection constitutes the kernel of the early Christian proclamation as presented in the sermons of Peter and Paul in Acts 2,23–24.32.36; 3,14-15; 4,10; 5,30; 10,39–40; 13,28–30.34.[27] These sermons not only proclaim the central event of Jesus' death and resurrection but also contextualize this event by looking to the past and to the future. Looking to the past, they affirm that what happened to Jesus was part of God's plan (2,23; 13,29) which was foretold by the prophets (2,16-21.25–31.34–35; 3,18.21-25; 10,43; 13,27.33.35.40). They mention the ministry of John the Baptist (10,37–38; 13,24–25) as leading up to "mighty works and wonders and signs" which accompanied the earthly ministry of Jesus himself (2,22; 10,37), whom God had anointed with the Holy Spirit and power (10,38). Looking forward from the resurrection, the sermons speak of the appearances of the risen Lord to various disciples (10,40; 13,31) who now serve as witnesses to what has happened (2,32; 3,15; 5,32; 10,39.41–42; 13,31) and upon whom has been poured out the gift of the Holy Spirit (2,17.33; 5,32). To those who believe and convert is offered the forgiveness of sins (3,19; 5,31; 10,42; 13,38). Jesus is now recognized as savior (4,12; 5,31; 13,23), exalted at God's right hand (2,33; 5,31) as Lord and Christ (2,36; 3,18.20; 4,10). Through the power of his name the sick are healed (3,16; 4,9). A striking aspect present in every one of the sermons is the accent on the agency of God in the planning, preparation and execution of the events related (2,22–24.32–36; 3,13.15.18; 4,10; 5,29; 10,34.38.40; 13,17–23.32–33). Faith is directed to the God of Abraham, Isaac and Jacob (3,13.25; cf. 5,29; 13,17) who has brought about the great deeds of salvation which Peter and Paul proclaim.

C. Other New Testament Texts

The centrality of the death and resurrection of Jesus Christ appears also in other New Testament writings, albeit in different ways. One recalls Martin Kähler's dictum that the gospels are merely passion narratives with long introductions.[28] Each gospel account of the passion, death and resurrection of Jesus bears the unique stamp of its author—the use of details and vocabulary serving the particular interests and theological slant of each—and forms an integral part of the story as a whole. This importance is less pronounced in the remaining New Testament writings, although some of these draw out further implications of Christ's death and resurrection for understanding the mystery of God's plan of salvation (1 Pet 3,18–22; Colossians and Ephesians) or Christ's second coming and the end of the world (already prominent in the letters to the Thessalonians and treated again in 2 Peter, Jude, Revelation).

Commenting on these various testimonies to the salvation event in Christ, H. Schlier and P. Benoit both note a surprising homogeneity which emerges from the New Testament witness taken as a whole.[29] It is as if the whole of God's salvation activity in Christ is contained implicitly in the death and resurrection. Reflecting upon this foundational event, the nascent community, at a comparatively early point,[30] drew out various implications: by looking backward to the origins of God's plan of salvation and forward to its final consummation these believers developed expressions of faith which ultimately are not so removed from that which came to be formulated in the Apostles' Creed and other later creeds.[31] In this sense, the Apostles' Creed can be said to be truly "apostolic" in that what it professes is truly in harmony with the fundamental faith of the Church of the apostles.[32] In this sense too, the Creed has a very close relation to the gospel; to some extent it *is* the gospel and forms the shape that the four canonical gospels came to have.[33]

3. OBSERVATIONS CONCERNING NEW TESTAMENT CONFESSIONS OF FAITH

Several observations need to be made at the conclusion to this presentation of various expressions of New Testament faith in terms of the person and the work of Jesus.

A. Faith Expressions about the Salvation Event Are Prior to Those about Identity

First of all, faith in the work, the salvation events that came about in and through Jesus, is chronologically prior to faith which expresses itself in the designation of Jesus by various titles.[34] Because of what happens in Jesus, he comes to be recognized as Christ, Son of God and Lord. Salvation history makes possible insight into the identity of the savior. Thus one may use the word "functional" as distinct from "ontological" to describe the more primordial confession of Christian faith. However, these categories are not mutually exclusive. Heinrich Schlier, who acknowledges the priority of faith in salvation history to faith in the person of Christ, nevertheless states that investigation into the beginnings of the Christological confession in the New Testament tend to confirm a point made by Joseph Ratzinger: "The whole being of Jesus is found in the function of 'for us,' but the function is—for that very reason—also his very being."[35]

B. The Life-Setting Which Gave Rise to the Various Professions

Secondly, the form and content of the various confessional formulae about the work and person of Jesus are markedly influenced by the life of the primitive community. Oscar Cullmann and Pierre Benoit provide largely complementary lists of occasions which naturally called for and so provided the impetus for the development of Christian confessions of faith.[36] Perhaps most prominent among these was baptism. Baptism was administered in the name of the Lord Jesus or of the Trinity (Acts 2,38; 8,16; 10,48; 19,5; 1 Cor 1,13–15; Mt 28,19) and called for a profession of faith in that name (Acts 22,16).[37] 1 Pet 3,18–22, rich in confessional content about the work and identity of Jesus, appears to be a catechesis developed to explain the significance of Christian baptism:

> For Christ also died for sins once for all, the righteous for the unrighteous, that he might bring us to God, being put to death in the flesh but made alive in the spirit; in which he went and preached to the spirits in prison, who formerly did not obey, when God's patience waited in the days of Noah, during the building of the ark, in which a few, that is, eight persons, were saved through water. Baptism, which corresponds to this, now saves you, not as a removal of dirt from the body but as an appeal to God for a clear conscience, through the resurrection of Jesus Christ, who has gone into heaven and is

at the right hand of God, with angels, authorities, and powers
subject to him.

Here we see not so much a confessional formula to be used in baptism
as a catechetical explanation of baptism which expounds certain fundamental elements of Christian faith.[38] Another text which may be seen as
recalling such elements in relation to baptism is that dense passage from
Eph 4,4–6, which reiterates into a driving crescendo the words "one"
and "all": "There is one body and one Spirit, just as you were called to
the one hope that belongs to your call, one Lord, one faith, one baptism,
one God and Father of us all, who is above all and through all and in all."
If the phrase "one body" might refer to that love between Christians
which had just previously been mentioned in verses 2–3, this passage
associates baptism with the triads Father-Lord-Spirit and faith-hope-love,
all of which have the adjective "one." Certainly one can acknowledge
here at the very least a statement which both uses the Christian terms for
the persons of the Trinity within a passage which mentions baptism. Or
again, G. Bornkamm's study of the four uses of the word *omologia* in
Hebrews concludes that three of them refer to the profession of faith
made at baptism and that the content of this confession was presumed
to be so well known to the readers that the author could simply use the
word *omologia* without further specifying its precise content.[39] Finally,
Benoit suggests that the confessions mentioned in Rom 10,9 and 1 Tim
6,12 "could also have a baptismal origin."[40]

In addition to baptism, the overall liturgical life of the community
is another context which called for the development of short formulae
of faith. Here examples include the exclamation "*Marana tha*," "Come
Lord," of 1 Cor 16,22 and Rev 22,30 and possibly "The Lord is at hand"
of Phil 4,5. At times one finds doxologies (1 Tim 1,17; Rom 11,36; 16,27;
Phil 4,20; Jude 25; Rev 5,13; 7,12) and benedictions (2 Cor 13,13–"The
grace of the Lord Jesus Christ, the love of God and the fellowship of the
Holy Spirit be with you all"). Moreover, the stylized introductions which
open many of the letters may derive from a liturgical setting.[41] All
of these liturgical expressions imply aspects of the faith profession of
the community, aspects which are expressed in the particular mode
of invocation, blessing or praise which is characteristic of worship.
Moreover, the New Testament contains a number of hymns or fragments of hymns which were sung in a common prayer setting (cf Col
3,16) and which are characterized by a lyrical, rhythmic, poetical quality
and are often quite dense in confessional content (Phil 2,6–11; Eph
1,3–10; Col 1,15–20; 1 Tim 3,16; perhaps 1 Pet 2,21–24).[42]

In addition to these liturgical moments, other occasions in the life of the early community gave rise to faith confessions. Exorcisms may have been the source of some short formulae (Mk 1,24; 3,11; 5,7; cf. Jas 2,19) as well as miraculous cures (Acts 3,6; 3,13-16; 4,10). Moreover, polemical situations such as arguments with the Jews about the identity of Jesus (Acts 5,27-33.40-42; 18,5-28; 28,17-28) required the sharpening of the confession that Jesus is the Christ. Similar apologetic confrontation with Greek polytheism could lead to the formulation of expressions of faith such as 1 Cor 8,6: "for us there is one God, the Father, from whom all things come and for whom we exist; and there is one Lord, Jesus Christ, through whom all things come and through whom we exist."

Finally, the experience of persecution, referred to in many passages of Acts (8,1-3; 9,1-2; 11,19; 12,1-5; see also the sufferings inflicted upon Paul and his companions in 13,45.50; 14,2.5.19; 17,13; 19,23-41; and the many trial scenes which run throughout the book: 4,3-22; 5,17-40; 16,19-24; 17,5-9; 18,12-17; 21,27-26,32) required that Christians publicly profess their faith. In this context Jesus himself, who "made the good confession" before Pontius Pilate (1 Tim 6,12-16; see also Heb 12,2-3 and the overall theme of perseverance which runs through Hebrews), is seen as the primary example and it is he himself who instructs the disciples that, as his followers, they may expect persecutions and trials (Mk 13,9-13; cf. Mt 10,17-22; Lk 21,12-19; Jn 16,1-4).[43] In particular, Jesus comforts the disciples that they need not worry about what they are to say in such situations. "The Holy Spirit will teach you in that very hour what you ought to say" (Lk 12,11-12; see Mt 10,19-20). This may well be an important context for understanding the confession "Jesus is Lord" from 1 Cor 12,3—"no one can say 'Jesus is Lord' except by the Holy Spirit" (cf Rom 10,9)—a point brought out later in the Martyrdom of Polycarp (VIII,2), when the aged bishop refuses to say "Caesar is Lord" and so accepts his fate as a martyr.[44]

Baptism, catechesis, common worship, exorcism, healing, polemical argumentation, persecution—all of these provided the context and impetus for the formulation of faith by the earliest Christian community. This demonstrates the very important point that there exists an intimate relation between the everyday life of the Church and its common expression of faith.

C. Their Christological Tone

A third comment about the New Testament confessions concerning the work and person of Jesus Christ addresses the Christological tone and content of these confessions. Oscar Cullmann concludes that the earliest

Christian confessions were neither trinitarian nor theological (in the sense of focusing on God) but rather Christological, in the sense of focusing on the present lordship of Jesus Christ.[45] The focus on the person and work of Jesus Christ is "le noyau historique...en même temp le noyau dogmatique" of the earliest Christian confessions of faith.[46] Thus Cullmann would see a formula such as that of 2 Cor 13,13–"The grace of the Lord Jesus Christ and the love of God and the fellowship of the Holy Spirit be with you all"– as expressing the more accurate chronological sequence of the unfolding of Christian faith, because it places the Lord Jesus Christ at the beginning in its enumeration of the divine Persons. The shift from one article to three articles, as represented by the later creeds, indeed altered the most primitive confession,[47] which limited itself to proclaiming Jesus as Lord (1 Cor 12,3) and Son of God (Acts 8,37; Heb 4,14; 1 Jn 4,15) who exercises domination over all things (Phil 2,6–11; 1 Pet 3,22) and over all time: "Jesus Christ is the same yesterday and today and for ever" (Heb 13,8).

A number of scholars have acknowledged Cullmann's point, in the sense that, until the first Christians became aware of any break with Judaism, the focus of their faith and the burden of their proclamation concerned Jesus Christ, risen from the dead, as Son of God and Lord. The monotheistic heritage which they received from Judaism and their awareness of God as Father, Son and Holy Spirit remained somewhat implicit.[48] However, it would hardly be an accurate account of the faith of the earliest Christians to suggest that belief in one God or in the present action and, therefore, reality of the Holy Spirit was not an integral part of their experience and conviction. At the earliest level of New Testament writings (Paul's letters) there is already abundance of reference to God, the Father, and of the action of the Spirit, an evidence which is also present in the proclamations of Acts and which finds ample expression, to varying degrees, in the gospels and in the remaining New Testament writings. The various binitarian and, with less frequency, trinitarian formulae only serve to confirm this. Thus Kelly is quite justified in concluding:

> It was, after all, natural and inevitable that the initial procla-
> mation of the gospel should emphasize the distinctively
> Christian, entirely novel and revolutionary element in the
> divine revelation. But the framework was there. It was always
> presupposed; and the firmness with which it was apprehend-
> ed is evidenced by the extraordinary way in which the binitar-
> ian and Trinitarian patterns wove themselves into the texture
> of early Christian thinking. In due course, with the develop-

ment of catechetical teaching and of more systematic, comprehensive instruction generally, as well as with the evolution of liturgical forms giving fuller expression to the faith, these vital aspects of it came to receive more regular and formal acknowledgement in creeds and semi-credal summaries. But this was not in response to any challenge or prompting from without: it was simply that binitarian and, ultimately, Trinitarian summaries were inevitably, the Christian faith being what it was, more adequate vehicles for conveying its message. The impulse towards their formation came from within, not from without; and at the New Testament stage we can observe the process in full swing, with confessions of all three types coexisting and interacting.[49]

The point here, of course, is that it would fall short of the facts of the case to affirm that the earliest Christian faith was solely Christological. Affirmations focusing upon the work and person of Jesus Christ may well have been chronologically the first Christian proclamations, but these cannot be isolated and, as it were, distilled from that more global and all embracing faith in God, which time and circumstance carried to an explicit profession of faith in the Trinity.[50]

D. The Polemic Against Other Christians

A fourth and final remark concerning the confessions of faith in the work and person of Jesus touches upon a development which appears toward the close of the New Testament period, that is, the polemic profession of faith which is not directed against Jewish or Greek non-believers and still less a positive invitation to non-believers that they might believe, but rather a polemic confession against others who consider themselves Christians.[51] This turn of events, which parallels the emerging struggle within the Christian community about false doctrine and which, as such, encompasses a wider number of New Testament writings, appears precisely under the aegis of the confession of faith in the letters of John.[52] The context is set in 1 Jn 2,18–19:

> Children, it is the last hour; and as you have heard that antichrist is coming, so now many antichrists have come; therefore we know that it is the last hour. They went out from us, but they were not of us; for if they had been of us, they would have continued with us; but they went out, that it might be plain that they all are not of us.

In this context, 1 John produces a series of confessional statements by which to distinguish the true believer from those whose faith does not measure up to "the message which you have heard from the beginning" (1 Jn 3,11). 1 Jn 2,22: "Who is the liar but he who denies that Jesus is the Christ? This is the antichrist, he who denies the Father and the Son." 1 Jn 4,2: "Every spirit which confesses that Jesus Christ has come in the flesh is of God, and every spirit which does not confess Jesus is not of God." 1 Jn 4,15: "Whoever confesses that Jesus is the Son of God, God abides in him, and he in God." 1 Jn 5,1: "Every one who believes that Jesus is the Christ is a child of God...." 1 Jn 5,5: "Who is it that overcomes the world but he who believes that Jesus is the Son of God?" 2 Jn 7: "For many deceivers have gone out into the world, men who will not acknowledge the coming of Jesus Christ in the flesh; such a one is the deceiver and the antichrist."

While some of these confessions are verbally equivalent to earlier ones in Paul, the synoptics, Acts and John (i.e. "Jesus is the Christ," "Jesus is the Son of God"), nevertheless the context shows that the emphasis here is upon the fact that Jesus, the man from Nazareth, is Christ and Son of God. He has "come in the flesh" (1 Jn 4,2; 2 Jn 7), a theme emphasized by the earthy, experiential language of the prologue 1 Jn 1,1–3: "what we have heard...seen with our eyes...looked upon and touched with our hands..." and the reference to blood in 1 Jn 5,6: "This is he who came by water and blood, Jesus Christ, not with the water only but with the water and the blood." Two related points should be noticed here. First, the confession has shifted from a simply positive proclamation about the identity of Jesus to a correct understanding of that proclamation, an understanding which excludes the possibly docetist or gnostic interpretations against which the author is arguing. Secondly, the confessions in the Johannine letters are not directed to those outside of the Christian community, inviting them to faith, but rather their scope is to correct and thereby protect the faith within the community. The confession has become a sort of "rule of faith" for maintaining the community in a correct interpretation of the Christ event.

CONCLUSION

The examination of the confession of faith of the early Christian community provides a wealth of material that is relevant to the question of the Church's unity in faith. Some of these points will be reviewed shortly in the recapitulation of the New Testament material at the end of Chapter Four. But as a general rule, this material suggests that there was a fundamental unity in the faith of the early community. Even when they differ as to the way of expressing this unity, many of the scholars who have examined the precise topic of the New Testament confessions concur in this conclusion.[53] Nevertheless, in the letters of John, one begins to see a diversity even in this area of the confession of faith, a diversity which shows that a global evaluation of the faith of the New Testament community which only acknowledges its unity would not do justice to all of the scriptural evidence. It is this question of the diversity and unity of faith in the New Testament that must now explicitly be addressed.

Chapter Four
DIVERSITY AND UNITY IN FAITH ACCORDING TO THE NEW TESTAMENT

The previous two chapters have sketched out something of the wealth of meaning of the frequently used terminology for faith in the New Testament as well as the rather substantial consensus among scholars concerning a fundamental core profession of faith concerning the person and salvific work of Jesus. To some extent, each of these two previous chapters offers testimony both to unity and to diversity in the New Testament understanding of and presentation of faith. The question of unity and diversity needs now to be quite directly addressed. To what extent does the evidence of the New Testament as a whole justify the affirmation that there is "one faith" (Eph 4,5)? And if this affirmation is true, how is one to understand the rather striking pluriformity which appears throughout the twenty-seven distinct books which collectively make up the Christian Scriptures?

1. DIVERSITY AND ITS INTERPRETATION

One must begin by acknowledging the manifest diversity in the expression of the faith which runs throughout the New Testament. So many studies have been dedicated to providing the evidence for this diversity that a relatively complete review of the details will not be necessary once again here.[1] In general terms, one can point out that, in the New Testament, there are different types of literature (for example, gospels and letters); different purposes for writing (see the prologues to Luke and Acts, John 20,30–31 or the community correcting tone of 1 Corinthians and Galatians), different accounts of events (for example, the different details in the passion and resurrection narratives of the four gospels[2] and in the infancy narratives of Matthew and Luke[3]) and different theological interpretations of the same event (for example, the interpretation of the scene of Jesus walking upon the water in Mk 6,45–52 and Mt 14,22–33).[4]

Indeed, it is probably not wide of the mark to say that the historical-critical method as employed in biblical exegesis has as one of its principal and rightful aims the uncovering of precisely such differences.[5] In light of them, one may speak of various "theologies" respective to the different authors of the New Testament[6] which reflect the varying theological concerns of the different communities addressed by those authors.[7] E.F. Scott's *The Varieties of New Testament Religion* and Hans Conzelmann's *History of Primitive Christianity* outline these differences chronologically, beginning with the earliest, Palestinian-Jewish Christianity right up to that reflected in the latest stratum of New Testament writings, such as the pastoral letters or the Apocalypse.[8] Others, such as Felix Porsch in his *Viele Stimmen–ein Glaube*, list theologies according to the various individual authors of the New Testament.[9] Within this context of various theologies, some commentators further specify diverse "christologies"[10] and "ecclesiologies."[11] Charlot summarizes many of these diversities under the headings of the textual, historical and theological "disunity" of the New Testament.[12]

Helmut Koester offers what may be taken as a valuable first step in understanding all of these differences within the one New Testament, when he notes:

> Christianity did not begin with a particular belief, dogma or creed; nor can one understand the heretical diversifications of early Christianity as aberrations from one original true and orthodox formulation of faith. Rather, Christianity started with a particular historical person, his works and words, his life and death: Jesus of Nazareth. Creed and faith, symbol and dogma are merely the expressions of response to this Jesus of history.[13]

While Koester's comment here about creeds should be taken within the context of what our earlier chapter showed in reference to the prominence and very early presence of the credal material in the New Testament, still his emphasis upon the primacy of the *person* of Jesus and characterization of the various faith expressions as *responses* to this person and his work seems sound, even confirmed by the material in our earlier section.[14] He goes on to point out two principal factors which cause diversification in the response to Jesus: "the different religious and cultural traditions of those who became Christians" and "the bewildering though challenging impact of Jesus' own life, works, words and death."[15] Other writers concur in this fundamental explanation of the diversity. Each New Testament author and each community addressed were enmeshed in quite particular situations. Schlier notes the consequent fragmentary nature of New Testament writings: they were directed to specific needs or sets of circumstances. No author intends to provide an overall, systematic account of Christianity.[16] Giblet adds that each presents, as it were, a fragment, behind which lies the whole of the Christian faith. No one author presumes to present this whole. Indeed, in a sense, each author needs the others.[17]

In light of these causes, one approach in interpreting New Testament diversity is to evaluate it positively, that is, as the expression of complementary insights into the same one Christ event. This approach, optimistic about the faith unity of the New Testament, emphasizes the necessity of carefully examining the causes of the various differences so as to avoid jumping to the conclusion that they represent true differences in faith.[18] Wolfgang Trilling exemplifies this approach in his discussion of the differences found in the four gospels. Each of the evangelists is not so much a chronicler as a personality who proclaims the gospel story; the activity of witness (*marturion*) and proclamation (*kerygma*) allows space for that variety which reflects the personality of each evangelist. According to Trilling, if one makes a distinction between history and salvation history and recognizes the primacy of the salvific meaning of the text over the presentation of historical details, then much of the problem of diversity in the details of the gospels dissolves.[19]

Of course, the outlook would not be so rosy if the variety in the New Testament were to prove to be not simply complementary but rather, at least at times, conflicting. This is, in fact, the conclusion of a number of exegetes. Conzelmann's essay "Was glaubte die frühe Christenheit?" opens with an enumeration of some of the contrasting positions expressed in the New Testament: the contrast between Paul and his disciples, on the one hand, and James, on the other, over the question of the binding nature of the law; the doctrine of justification by faith and Matthew's attitude about the perfection of the law; the differences between the synoptics and John on the earthly life of Jesus along with the virtual absence of any interest in Jesus' life on the part of Paul; the contradictory eschatologies of John's gospel and of the book of Revelation; the difference between Luke's view of salvation history and the typological understanding of Israel in the letter to the Hebrews. "Wo liegt die Einheit?" he exclaims.[20]

A good illustration of the view that underscores the conflicting diversity in the New Testament can be found in Paul Achtemeier's analysis of the texts in Galatians and Acts relevant to the dispute in the early Church about the necessity of observing the law. His historical reconstruction of the sequence of events behind those texts leads him to the conclusion that Acts, which presents the "council" at Jerusalem as having in some way resolved the dispute between Paul and his opponents concerning the need to observe the Law, gives a false account of what actually happened.[21] Achtemeier takes the account in Galatians as the more historically accurate of the two and reconstructs the sequence of events as follows: 1. There was a first meeting of Paul with leaders of the Church in Jerusalem as recounted in Gal 1,18-21, which parallels Acts 9,26-27. 2. A second meeting took place in Jerusalem (Gal 2,1-10) in which all were agreed that the Gentile Christians need not observe the law concerning circumcision; this meeting is recounted in Acts 11,1-18, but Paul's presence is deleted from that account for the purposes of the author of Acts. 3. Peter and Paul go to Antioch. 4. James, alone as head in Jerusalem, holds the council of Acts 15 with its decree in the form of a letter requiring some observance of the law on the part of Gentile Christians (Acts 15,29 and 21,25). 5. In Antioch, Peter and Barnabas accept James' decree, which sparks Paul's vehement condemnation in Gal 2,11-13 and the split between Barnabas and Paul recounted in Acts 15,36-40.[22] The upshot is that Paul ends up isolated and alone, indeed "betrayed" by Peter, who "sided with the emissaries from James and thus committed his prestige to a denial of the validity of Paul's theological position."[23] Paul remains "the one who lost in the struggle to influence the theological mind of the early church."[24] His viewpoint lost out and remained so "for some fourteen centuries,"[25] presumably a reference to the Protestant reformation. Achtemeier's overall conclusion is that

> "...a romantic view of an original unity does not stand up under historical scrutiny.... The evidence in the New Testament is clear: the church, from its beginning, faced problems of division and disunity, with the result that such unity still remains a goal to be achieved in the life of the visible body of Christ."[26] "That early unity existed, and continues to exist, only in the optimistic historical imagination of scholars...."[27]

While these comments are, strictly speaking, about the unity of the Church and not about unity in faith, nevertheless it is clear that the disunity of the Church derives from a disunity in faith. For Paul, it was "the truth of the gospel" (Gal 2,5) which was at stake. Thus Achtemeier's point appears to be that the conflict in interpreting the gospel portrayed in the texts of Galatians and Acts was never resolved and, therefore, we are left with a New Testament which includes two unresolved and conflicting expressions of faith. From this, one could presumably conclude that unity in faith, at least on this particular point of the requirement that Christians observe at least some elements of the law, does not exist in the New Testament.

Other exegetes appear to extend this notion of the presence of conflicts in faith to the New Testament as a whole.[28] H. Koester's approval of Walter Bauer's thesis (in short, that "orthodoxy" is merely the theological position which eventually won out over other equally apostolic traditions which were subsequently branded heretical) at the beginning of his discussion of diverse Christologies which emerged prior to the writing of the gospels suggests that that thesis is substantially valid for the New Testament, and not only for the later two centuries which were the focus of Bauer's *Rechtgläubigkeit und Ketzerei im ältesten Christentum*.[29] Along this line, Käsemann's repeated comment is so often quoted that it may be considered as a classic expression of this viewpoint: "The New Testament canon does not, as such, constitute the foundation of the unity of the Church. On the contrary, as such (that is, in its accessibility to the historian) it provides the basis for the multiplicity of the confessions."[30] James Dunn's conclusion to his *Unity and Diversity in the New Testament* appears a bit more optimistic, when he writes: "In short, the canon of the NT still has a continuing function in that *the NT in all its diversity still bears consistent testimony to the unifying centre*. Its unity canonizes Jesus-the-man-now-exalted as the canon within the canon. Its diversity prevents us from insisting on a larger or different canon within the canon."[31] Nevertheless, the accent in Dunn's position is upon "recognizing how *few* the essentials are and how *wide* must be the range of acceptable liberty."[32]

What then can be said in response to Conzelmann's question: where lies the unity? First of all, one may agree with Käsemann and others that the problem cannot be resolved on a purely historical level.[33] If one is to avoid the conclusion that the New Testament lacks unity in faith, one needs to offer a theological interpretation (thus one enlightened by faith) which does not ignore the results of historical research but which, at the same time, shows how the diversity in faith expressions uncovered by such research emerged and the way in which the early community handled such diversity so as to maintain a certain substantial unity in its faith.

2. ACCOUNTING FOR UNITY AND DIVERSITY
OF FAITH IN THE NEW TESTAMENT

How did diversity in the expression of faith arise? One should begin with the Christian proclamation of the gospel of Jesus Christ. Giblet points out that, for Paul, this gospel was received *from God himself* (Gal 1,15; thus it is the "gospel of God": 1 Thes 2,2.8.9; Rom 1,1) as well as *from the community* (Paul hands on the tradition which he himself received: 1 Cor 15,1–3; 11,23).[34] This gospel must be passed on in words; it cannot prescind from expression in human language ("Now I would remind you, brethren, in what terms I preached to you the gospel" [1 Cor 15,1]). Moreover, Paul passes on the "words of the Lord," which he presents as absolutely worthy of belief (1 Thes 4,15; 1 Cor 7,10), but which he also feels competent to explain or elaborate when necessary in light of new situations (1 Cor 7,12). Thus, while marked by fidelity to what has been received, the handing on of the gospel tradition is no mere mechanical passing on of a record, a handing on of expressions which simply, as it were, photocopy certain events that happened. Rather it is a spoken testimony, which requires a speaker who witnesses to the way in which he himself has been grasped and changed. It is directed out to all people, not just to those of the speaker's same culture or language. It is a speaking which of its very essence both reflects the experience of the speaker and leaves a certain place for the response of the one spoken to. As such, the speaker invites the listener to share in the experience which he presents and to which he testifies. Thus the proclamation of the gospel creates relationships. It invites the one addressed to join together with the evangelist and with all of those who are bound together with him in the same community by faith. A powerful example of this can be seen in the prologue of the first letter of John; "that which we have seen and heard we proclaim also to you, so that you may have fellowship with us" (1,3; see also the purpose of writing the gospel in John 20,31: "that you may believe that Jesus is the Christ, the Son of God, and that believing you may have life in his name"). The gospel is not proclaimed to engender divisions in those who come to hear and accept it. The scope, purpose and dynamism of proclamation is to create unity in faith.

Once this proclamation is received with unreserved faith, a great development begins to unfold. Already at the beginning of 1 Corinthians, Paul writes: "I give thanks to God always for you because of the grace of God which was given you in Christ Jesus, that in every way you were enriched in him with all speech and all knowledge" (1,4–5). Paul goes on to speak of the wisdom into which Christians grow and mature. "But we preach Christ crucified, a stumbling block to Jews and folly to Gentiles; but to those who are called, both Jews and Greeks, Christ the power of God and the wisdom of God" (1 Cor 1,23–24). This theme is further elaborated in 1 Cor 2,6–16, where Paul adds the idea of maturing in the wisdom of Christ:

> Yet among the mature we do impart wisdom, although it is not a wisdom of this age or of the rulers of this age, who are doomed to pass away. But we impart a secret and hidden wisdom of God, which God decreed before the ages for our glorification.... And we impart this in words not taught by human wisdom but taught by the Spirit, interpreting spiritual truths to those who possess the Spirit.... 'For who has known the mind of the Lord so as to instruct him?' But we have the mind of Christ.

The Christian community progresses in a maturing penetration into the message of the gospel. Because of "the depth of the riches and wisdom and knowledge of God" (Rom 11,33) and because now we know imperfectly and only in part (1 Cor 13,9–12), our limited knowledge being conditioned by our earthly state which naturally includes such factors as culture, language and patterns of thought, this penetration will naturally produce many distinct insights which can take a variety of forms of expression. Nevertheless, the dynamism of this growth is toward unity:

> until we all attain to the unity of the faith and of the knowledge of the Son of God, to mature manhood, to the measure of the stature of the fullness of Christ; so that we may no longer be children, tossed to and fro and carried about with every wind of doctrine, by the cunning of men, by their craftiness in deceitful wiles. Rather, speaking the truth in love, we are to grow up in every way into him who is the head, into Christ... (Eph 4,13–15).

One can readily admit that this process of penetration into the mystery of Christ, conditioned as it is not only by the unfathomableness of its object but also by the imperfection and, more positively, the cultural conditionedness of human persons and communities, can lead to expressions of faith which are in tension. The New Testament texts themselves do not hide such tensions. Were that the case, there would be little basis for the extensive literature that has emerged about diversity and the problem of unity in the New Testament. But already in these same biblical texts we see a number of factors which work toward harmonizing this diversity, toward holding it together in a unity of faith. Let us look at a number of these factors.

3. FACTORS FAVORING UNITY IN FAITH

A. *Common Kerygma*

The first factor is the common kerygma about the person and work of Christ which very early took and maintained the forms of the proclamations about the death and resurrection of Jesus and applied to him a number of titles, principal among which were the titles Christ, Son of God and Lord.[35] The fact that insight into God's salvific action in Jesus increased as the Church came to recognize other dimensions of his action and identity, in addition to his saving death and resurrection, does not lead as a necessary conclusion that these other dimensions are incompatible alternative explanations of this salvation action. In a similar way, while it can and must be acknowledged that even such primary titles as Christ, Son of God and Lord can and should be understood in light of the specific and different contexts within which they emerged and may even be designated as more or less meaningful to one or another Christian community depending on its composition (Palestinian Jewish in Jerusalem, Hellenistic Gentile in Corinth, and so forth), such a recognition in no way suffices as an argument that such titles evidence a conflict in faith about Jesus.[36] Indeed, often a single passage written by one author holds together a number of the different dimensions of the salvation event in Jesus (for example, the speeches in Acts proclaim not only the death and resurrection but also relate it to God's saving activity before and after, or a hymn like Phil 2,6-11 places Jesus' death within a broader process of his self-emptying and exaltation). Similarly, often a single passage written by the same author combines in the space of a few verses two or three of the principal titles attributed to Jesus (Rom 1,3-4; Mt 16,16).[37] If single New Testament authors can hold together in a harmonious whole the various dimensions of the Christ event and also various titles which concern his person, it is hardly convincing to postulate a certain incompatibility between those dimensions and those titles as the basis upon which to conclude a fundamental disunity in New Testament faith. One can hardly escape the reasonable conclusion by scholars like Schlier, Benoit, Kelly and others that, in their fundamental confession about the person and work of Jesus, the early Christians enjoyed a certain deep and substantial unity in faith.[38]

B. Dialogue

Secondly, the early Christian community was one in which a lively exchange occurred between the members, precisely on questions of faith. Acts presents a number of scenes in which a party sets out from Jerusalem to visit a new community in another city with the ostensive purpose of assuring unity between Christians (8,14–17: Peter and John to Samaria; 11,22–26: Barnabas to Antioch and Tarsus), as well as several discussions the purpose of which was to clarify and unify the faith (11,1–18: Peter explaining his actions to the circumcision party in Jerusalem; 15,1–21: the council at Jerusalem; 18,24–26: Priscilla and Aquilla's more accurate exposition of the way of God to Apollos). In addition to these indications from Acts, the writing of the letters which eventually became part of the New Testament canon functioned as a means of drawing Christians together in the same faith. Often letters served to correct a nascent misinterpretation, such as Paul's corrections concerning the last day in 1 Thessalonians, concerning the resurrection in 1 Corinthians and concerning the law in Galatians. Similar attempts to convince others that a particular view was mistaken and in that way to promote unity in faith can be found in such sources as Colossians (on Christ's predominance over the angels), James (on faith being expressed in practice) and the letters of John (warning against docetist denials that Jesus Christ had come "in the flesh"). To be sure, all of these examples give evidence of certain tensions threatening to divide the community in its faith. But one must not overlook the fact that these writings represent efforts to protect and foster unity in faith.

Prosper Grech has compiled a brief survey of the arguments concerning various points of faith which are employed by the authors of Galatians, 1 Corinthians, Colossians, Hebrews, 1 and 2 Timothy, Titus, the gospel of John and the Johannine letters.[39] These arguments include appeal to the confirmation by the Holy Spirit, to scripture (which in the New Testament meant the Old Testament), to the words of Jesus, to the writings of the apostles, to the deposit which was from the beginning, to the authority of the apostle and to the worship of the community. While "orthodoxy" is not a New Testament word, these various arguments which are found in the New Testament lead Grech to conclude that orthodoxy is "perseverance in the faith of the apostolic *kerygma* which creates *koinonia* with the Father, the Son and the Church."[40] Such perseverance does not impose a uniformity which eliminates all diversity.

Moreover, discussion between Christians in the New Testament communities produced growth in understanding the meaning of Jesus' person and work and the impact of the Christ event upon how Christians should live. The New Testament itself does not employ the word "heresy" in the way in which it would come to be used in later centuries, but the same idea is conveyed in many passages which, in very urgent terms, warn about unsound doctrine and false teachers. Such unsound doctrine can come about from a denial of the central confessional proclamation concerning Jesus and his work, as in the false doctrine opposed by 1 John. But it also appears as a result of not going along with the growth in understanding on the part of the community as a whole. A good example here would be the question of the law. Paul's argumentation in Galatians and Romans illustrates the way in which the early community advanced in understanding so as to recognize the implications of the Christ event with regard to the observance of the law. In this case, false doctrine amounts to a refusal to advance with the community in accepting the new understanding of these implications. For Paul, such refusal is so serious that it amounts to teaching of "another gospel."

The New Testament community was a community of the word; argumentation and dialogue were everywhere in evidence. They served the purpose of preserving the original confession of faith, of growing into a deeper knowledge of it and of applying it to daily life. Sound doctrine was the purpose and effect of this activity; unsound doctrine either denied the basic kerygma or did not grow with the community as it advanced in understanding the kerygma and its implications. The ample New Testament evidence that the various communities and individuals were active in discussing the faith and in presenting reasons based on commonly recognized authorities so as to draw together believers into a common expression of faith must count primarily not as evidence for division in faith but rather as evidence for the fact that dialogue was a very early and effective means by which the community, guided by the Holy Spirit, was maintained in unity of faith.

C. Charisms and Ministries

A third and closely related factor concerns the role of charisms and ministry in earliest Christianity. The early community was graced with many gifts, but all derived from the same Spirit (1 Cor 12,4). These many gifts frequently are directed to the expression of faith—"To one is given through the Spirit the utterance of wisdom, and to another the utterance of knowledge according to the same Spirit, to another faith by the same

Spirit...to another prophecy, to another the ability to distinguish between spirits, to another various kinds of tongues, to another the interpretation of tongues" (1 Cor 12,8–10). And all "are inspired by one and the same Spirit" (1 Cor 12,11). The purpose and scope of these gifts is not directed toward division in faith. When Paul lists various ministries in 1 Cor 12,28 and Rom 12,6–8, he underscores the fact that they are not in competition, but rather complement each other. Eph 4,11–13 takes this idea a step further by presenting the ministries of apostles, prophets, evangelists, pastors and teachers as working together in positive collaboration to build up the body of Christ "until we all attain to the unity of the faith and of the knowledge of the Son of God."[41] The gifts and ministries were very much directed toward promoting and maintaining the community's unity in faith. If, from an historical point of view, one must conclude that the New Testament communities did not succeed in preserving a substantial unity in faith but rather remained divided by irreconcilable differences in faith, then one must also conclude that this activity of the Holy Spirit in inspiring ministries for the express purpose of building up the one body of Christ was a failure. That would be a very serious conclusion indeed, for it would imply that the human beings who make up the Christian community have the power to thwart and have in fact successfully thwarted the often reiterated New Testament theme of God's will for the unity of the Church.[42] It is difficult to see how this would not amount to a serious lack of faith in the lordship of Jesus Christ over the community of those who believe in him. The unacceptability of these implications justifies a rigorous scrutiny of claims that the diversity evidenced in the New Testament really amounts to irreconcilable differences in faith. It also encourages a great deal of care in evaluating the historical arguments by which an individual exegete claims to demonstrate the existence of irreconcilable differences in faith. If the historical evidence can be explained equally well by an account which does not characterize the diversity in terms of irreconcilability but rather in terms of complementarity, fruitful tension and growth, such an historical explanation would better cohere theologically with the New Testament confession of the Lordship of Jesus Christ and the New Testament witness to his guidance of the Church through the Holy Spirit.

D. Written Texts

A fourth point concerns the composition of the various New Testament writings. First of all, attention to explaining the differences between specific writings can easily conduce to a forgetting of elements which they share in common. Attempts to address the synoptic problem, for example, rightly seek to account for the differences in the way in which Matthew, Mark and Luke relate the same or similar events and teachings. Redaction criticism explains these differences in terms of the distinct theological slant of each author. What sometimes recedes to the background, however, is the fact that there would be no synoptic problem at all were there not a substantial similarity between them.[43] The composition of the synoptics illustrates how at least some New Testament writings were based upon common sources and traditions, including even earlier writings.

Secondly, one may recognize with J. Gnilka that the writing of each of the four gospels represents an attempt to bring together the traditions which the evangelist has gathered from the community into a coherent whole.[44] Each gospel has a certain literary and theological unity,[45] such that the very writing of a gospel presupposes on the part of the evangelist the conviction that the good news about Jesus of Nazereth can be brought together into a coherent whole.

Thirdly, as James Dunn attests, many of the writings of the New Testament "served as *bridge builders or connecting links* between different strands within first-century Christianity."[46] He further suggests that it was precisely this quality which led to their inclusion in the canon. Because of its relevance and quality, the reader is asked to excuse a rather lengthy quotation:

> Thus Matthew and Hebrews served not so much as Jewish Christian party statements, but rather as bridges between a more narrowly conceived Jewish Christianity and a Jewish Christianity much more influenced by Hellenistic thought.... Similarly Mark and Paul seem to be fulfilling a similar function, holding together Gentile Christianity and diaspora Jewish Christianity. To be sure Galatians or II Cor. 10–13 in particular can hardly be called eirenic, but the canonicity of Paul at this point is a function not so much of any one letter (though Romans would most nearly fill the bill) as of the whole Pauline corpus (particularly when the Pastorals are included); for here within these thirteen letters we have embraced the whole sweep of Christianity from apocalyptic enthusiasm to early Catholicism, from deep Jewish sympathies to whole hearted commitment to the Gentiles, from fervent insistence on the immediacy or revelation to complete subserviency to the inherited tradition, etc. Again Acts and John in different ways serve as bridges between the

origins of Christianity and the situations facing Christianity towards the end of the first century—Acts serving as Luke's attempt to hold together the initial enthusiasm of Christianity with the growing influence of early catholicism, and the Johannine writings serving as a bridge between the message given 'from the beginning' and the challenge facing Jewish Christians within the wider oriental-Hellenistic syncretism of the time. Even Revelation can be seen as a bridge in the way it sought to internationalize Jewish apocalypticism, that it might serve as a vehicle for the hopes of all Christians. Perhaps most striking of all, particularly in view of the tensions of second-century Christianity, is the function fulfilled by 1 Peter, in so far as in its theology and traditional authorship it serves to bring Paul and Peter together.[47]

Dunn immediately goes on to caution against interpreting this irenic spirit which characterizes many of the writings of the New Testament in such a way as to obsure the real diversity within Christianity of the first century and within the New Testament writings themselves.[48] Nevertheless, if his characterization in this passage is true, it counts forcefully against concluding that the diverse expressions of faith represented in the New Testament lead to inevitably irreconcilable positions.

This is not to say that it would not be possible to isolate one or another New Testament expression of faith and develop it to a point at which it could no longer be reconciled with the substantial unity of faith represented by the New Testament taken as a whole. Such would be possible; indeed it would be difficult to imagine any later position which intended to be Christian and yet which was discerned by the wider community as falling outside the acceptable boundaries of unity in faith as not claiming to be rooted in the canonical writings of the New Testament. This was frequently the case of the heterodox views battled by Irenaeus, Tertullian and many others in later centuries. But the fact that such isolation is neither necessary nor desirable would seem to be confirmed by this bridge-building trait which characterizes so many of the compositions of the New Testament. This trait leads one to be suspicious about any position which might conclude to a substantial disunity of New Testament faith on the basis of a supposed irreconcilability of the diverse faith expressions found in the early community. Many writings not only presume that these expressions are reconcilable but are themselves efforts to show their harmony.[49]

E. Leadership

A fifth factor of the life of the early Christian community which addresses the diversity of faith expressions in such a way as to foster unity in faith is the distinctive role assigned to Church leaders. While this factor could well be treated under the third factor listed above, the Spirit-inspired gifts and ministries, it merits some discussion on its own for two reasons. First, a number of New Testament writings explicitly connect the fostering of unity in faith with those who serve as leaders within the community. Second, these writings have sometimes been characterized as marking a shift in the thought of the New Testament, a type of deviation away from an earlier and more authentic understanding of the community and its faith.

With regard to the first point, one should advert first of all to the general prevalence of teaching within the New Testament.[50] In Paul's list of the various God-appointed activities in the one body which is the Church (1 Cor 12,28; cf. Rom 12,7), teachers are indicated in the third place after apostles and prophets, and before administrators, which appears several positions later in the list. Thus teachers appear to be distinct from apostles and administrators. Paul emphatically presents himself as an apostle (Gal 1,1; 1 Cor 1,1; 9,1-2; 2 Cor 1,1; 12,11; Rom 1,1; 11,13) and, therefore, if he considered apostles and teachers as separate ministers within the Church, he presumably did not consider himself primarily as a teacher. Nevertheless, he occasionally speaks of his own ministry as "teaching" (1 Cor 4,17; Col 1,28), praises God that the Roman community has been obedient to the "standard of teaching" (Rom 6,17) and encourages them to resist those who create dissensions in opposition to the doctrine which they have been taught (16,17). He is often described as engaged in teaching in Acts (11,26; 15,35; 18,11; 20,20; 21,21; 28,31). As a missionary, traveling from place to place, Paul should not be thought of as a leader of a particular local community, even though he remained for extensive periods of time in some localities (a year and a half in Corinth [Acts 18,11], two years and three months [or three years] in the area around Ephesus [19,10] and "two whole years" in Rome [28,30]).[51] Still Paul must be thought of in some sense as a leader of Christian communities and it is clear that his letters are instances of his teaching in such a way as to promote unity in faith. Paul's teaching is one that argues, pleads and seeks to convince so as to bring his addressees around to accepting what he proposes to be the gospel and its implications.

Acts presents the apostles as teaching (2,42; 4,2 [Peter and John]; 5,21.42). The apostles and elders gather together in Acts 15,6ff. to

discuss the question of the requirement of circumcision and the
observance of the law and in summing up their decision in a letter to the
Christians at Antioch they (15,22) wrote: "It has seemed good to the
Holy Spirit and to us to lay upon you no greater burden than these
necessary things" (15,28). Clearly for the author of Acts, the gathering at
Jerusalem is presented as an exercise on the part of leaders of the
communities of Jerusalem and Antioch (the former having a certain
primacy of authority) for the purpose of effecting unity on a matter
which touched upon the faith.[52] Finally, Paul's address to the elders of
the church in Ephesus (Acts 20,18–35) introduces the idea that the
elders are guardians of the flock, protecting it from the fierce wolves
which will come after Paul's departure (18,28–29).

Matthew may convey the idea of a certain regulative role with
regard to the faith on the part of the leaders of the community in the
promise of the keys which bind and loose to Peter (Mt 16,19), the same
promise being given also to the disciples in general in Mt 18,18. The
eleven are commissioned to teach authoritatively in Mt 28,18–20. 2 Pet
1,20–21 speaks against individual interpretation of the prophecies of
scripture, implying perhaps thereby that interpretation must in some
way be regulated by the Church as a whole. Jude 3–4 speaks of "the faith
which was once delivered to the saints" in the context of warning about
"ungodly persons who...deny our only Master and Lord, Jesus Christ."

But it is especially in the pastoral letters, under the guise of
instructions by an aged Paul to his emissaries Timothy and Titus in the
respective churches of Ephesus and Crete, that this theme of the role of
the leaders of the local church in preserving unity in faith comes to its
clearest and most forceful expression. The pastorals repeat several times
the stock phrase *pistos ho logos* ("this saying is sure": 1 Tim 1,15; 3,1; 4,9; 2
Tim 2,11; Titus 3,8) and emphasize the necessity of "sound doctrine" (1
Tim 1,10; 2 Tim 4,3; Titus 1,9; 2,1). Timothy is exhorted to teach (1 Tim
4,11.13; 2 Tim 4,2), making use of scripture (2 Tim 3,16). Timothy is
told: "Take heed to yourself and to your teaching" (1 Tim 4,16), and
Titus: "But as for you, teach what befits sound doctrine" (Titus 2,1) and
"in your teaching show integrity, gravity, and sound speech that cannot
be censured, so that an opponent may be put to shame" (Titus 2,7). The
context of these exhortations is the appearance of different and
dangerous doctrines which threaten the community's unity in faith (1
Tim 1,3–7; 4,1; 6,3-5; 2 Tim 2,17-19.23; 3,8; 4,3–4; Titus 1,10–11). Some
indeed have made "a shipwreck of their faith" (1 Tim 1,19-20). The role
of leadership in the community and its task of guarding unity in faith is
connected with the gift received at the laying on of hands (1 Tim 4,14; 2

Tim 1,6). Moreover, Paul's representatives are to select others as overseers and deacons, who are trustworthy in the faith and who have the ability to teach (1 Tim 3,2.9; 2 Tim 2,12).

The conclusion which must be drawn from these various texts is that already in the New Testament one begins to see a certain linking of leadership of the community with the responsibility to promote and guard the community's unity of faith, that is, a certain regulatory function with regard to the faith of the community. Bultmann explains this by pointing out that Christianity begins primarily with the proclamation of the word, a proclamation which "at the same time as it brings knowledge of what God has done in Christ...also brings the hearer a new knowledge of himself."[53] This knowledge is both capable of development and stands in need of development, such that the expositions in Galatians and Romans, for example, "have no other purpose than to unfold the knowledge which is the concomitant gift of faith."[54] The proclamation "led inevitably to further thinking, to questions: What theological and christological, cosmological and anthropological consequences necessarily result? Which ones are legitimate deductions? This is the origin of Christian theology."[55] Before long this leads to the problem of right teaching.[56] "In view of the differences in doctrine and of the conflict between them the question necessarily arose *concerning the authority which might determine 'right' doctrine*. To whom could one appeal in a given case for the correctness of one's opinion?"[57] Bultmann states that the community settled upon the apostles as such an authority, although he adds the proviso that this could have occurred only with the disappearance of the first generation of Christians and "when the conflicts of the apostolic period in which Paul had been involved had died away."[58] Moreover, oral tradition could not suffice for such an appeal to the apostles, since already gnosticizing elements, which leaned heavily on such tradition, made it suspect. "But there was a way out of this if one could point to certain persons as authorized bearers of the tradition, and one could. These persons were the congregational officials, *the bishops*, whose appointment, according to common conviction, went back to the apostles. They represent the legitimate 'succession,'" a term which only emerged later in Hegesippus and Irenaeus, although the verb "to succeed" already appears in 1 Clem 44,2.[59]

For Bultmann it is important to note that this development involved a certain shift from faith to orthodoxy. In the very beginning, it was *faith* that distinguished Christians from Jews and unbelievers, not *orthodoxy*. Orthodoxy and heresy arise out of the differences that develop within the Christian community. "In the nature of the case," he adds, "this takes place very early," giving Gal 1,6-9 as an example.[60] For Conzelmann, such a shift alters rather significantly the original New Testament understanding of faith:

> Faith is understood more and more as timeless doctrine, and thus becomes the *fides quae creditur*. As such, it corresponds to the conviction of the truth of this doctrine, the *fides qua creditur*. The original object of faith is the revelation itself, the God who reveals himself. Now the accent shifts in the direction of doctrine about the revelation.[61]

According to Conzelmann, this development entails a change in the understanding of tradition and of the Church. Whereas originally faith meant conviction, now the truth of doctrines which express the faith must be ascertained and guaranteed by the apostolic tradition which is passed on within the Church.[62] This shift marks the emergence of "early Catholicism."[63]

James Dunn opens his informative chapter entitled "Early Catholicism" with the question: "To what extent are the features which characterize catholic Christianity from the (late) second century already present in the NT?"[64] After tracing the history of the discussion surrounding this expression up to the one who has contributed the most to the debate in recent decades, Ernst Käsemann, he suggests three main features of early Catholicism—the fading of the parousia hope, increasing institutionalization and the crystallization of the faith into set forms—and seeks to determine the extent to which these features can be found in the New Testament. He shows that, while appearing rather late, each of these features, in varying degrees, can be located in an historical overview of the New Testament writings. This finding is not particularly new; Bultmann, Conzelmann, Käsemann and others had already noticed in their own respective lines of research a similar presence of these elements. Dunn also points out that, while the New Testament includes cautions about potential exaggerations in the other three strains of first-century Christianity which he examines (Jewish, Hellenistic and Apocalyptic), such caution is not explicit concerning early Catholicism.[65] He suggests that early Catholicism might also be capable of heretical expression and asks whether it would not have been better had the New Testament explicitly recognized this as well.[66]

One can readily admit that the delay of the parousia, the institutional organization of the community and the concern about the truth of doctrine can each be exaggerated in such a way as to obscure other important testimonies of the New Testament, attention to which serves to place each of those themes in a wider and more adequate context. Indeed, the opponents of "early Catholicism" seem to have in mind precisely such an exaggeration and thus tend to portray it as contradicting earlier, more authentic themes.[67] But is such a contradiction inevitable? And did these later developments, for which the New Testament gives historical evidence, in fact contradict the more original view of the faith, of the Church and of its unity in faith?

Dunn's chapter on early Catholicism begins not only with the question about whether certain features of the Church in the second century can be located in the New Testament, a question to which his careful investigation provides a qualified "yes." He adds several further questions.

> Was catholicism...a falling away from the primeval purity and simplicity of the first century?...was it simply the natural unfolding of what had belonged to the essence of Christianity from the first? Or does the answer lie somewhere in between?—perhaps in a decisive development (or several such) during the first century; perhaps in the dominance of one view over others towards the end of the first century; perhaps in the slow coming together of different elements into a coherent whole which had more lasting power than alternative views and structures; perhaps by way of reaction to other first-century developments.[68]

He does not expressly endorse one of the many options that are suggested by these questions, although a sentence from his final chapter suggests something of his ultimate conclusion regarding early Catholicism:

> Alternatively, the diverse developments of the NT are somewhat like a series of branches (to be sure often intertwined) growing out of the trunk of the unifying centre, with *nothing in the NT itself* to justify the claim that only the branch of early catholicism should become the main (far less normative) line of growth.[69]

One familiar with the discussion of unity and diversity in the New Testament, upon hearing the phrase "nothing in the NT itself," would find it difficult not to be reminded of Käsemann's comment, cited several pages earlier by Dunn himself, that the New Testament canon as such (that is, in its accessibility to the historian) provides the basis for the multiplicity of the confessions. Might that not be the full significance of Dunn's conclusion? On the basis of historical evidence alone, one cannot finally judge the legitimacy of the developments which appear in the New Testament with regard to the role of leadership in regulating the community's unity in faith and which have been discussed under the title of "early Catholicism."

In the end, historical investigation must be complemented by theological interpretation. This is what Käsemann does in considering unity in faith. Only the believer, led by the Spirit and listening to the Word, can say what is the gospel which brings unity to the New Testament.[70] But the same method which allows one to identify the gospel may also be applied to the question of interpreting the developments in the New Testament. In faith, led by the Spirit and listening to the Word, the Church can discern that, according to the New Testament witness, the Spirit leads not just individuals but is at work within the whole community. The Spirit guides the community into oneness of faith by many means, such as the reception of common credal formulas, the entering into dialogue about contested issues, the exercise of charisms and ministries which foster unity and the composition of the writings which came to be accepted into the canon. In addition to these means, the Spirit also guides the community in organizing itself in such a way that, precisely as a community, precisely in a corporate way, it can maintain its unity in faith. Thus faith can identify the legitimacy of the emergence of leadership with a regulative and normative role in discerning the Church's unity in faith. In faith, one can discern the Spirit behind this development. History alone cannot make such a discernment.

This does not mean that such a discernment is based on "blind faith"—faith functioning as a deus ex machina solution to an otherwise insoluble problem. On the contrary, it rests on important themes of the New Testament itself, such as God's will for the unity of the Church, God's control of salvation history, the Lordship of Jesus over the community and the animation and guidance of the whole body of God's people through history by the Holy Spirit. Indeed the ecclesiological themes that the Church is the Body of Christ, the People of God, the Temple of the Holy Spirit, cohere much more soundly with an understanding of unity in faith which recognizes its corporate dimension and organizational means provided by God for maintaining that corporate dimension than does an explanation of unity in faith which, in the end, must resort to the discernment of the individual

Christian and which leaves wide room for diversities in faith which are not merely complementary but even conflicting. This line of argument calls for a serious questioning of the way in which Dunn speaks of the unity of the Church and, in particular, of early Catholicism in the conclusion of his *Unity and Diversity in the New Testament*. There he states that to accept the ecclesiological developments represented by early Catholicism as normative for the life of the Church amounts to an arbitrary restriction to only one strand of the New Testament. It is to narrow the canon, to make the norm for canonicity that which is only one part of the canon; it is to fail to respect the canonical diversity of Christianity.[71] This sounds good. Who would wish to or be presumptuous enough to restrict the Word of God? But what his presentation tacitly eliminates is a theological interpretation of the New Testament which, fully respecting the historical diversities in emerging forms of Church order and expressions of faith and diverse models of the relation between the two, at the same time does not see this diversity as simply a sequence or enumeration of various strands, each of which can serve equally well as the basis for a particular form of Christianity, but rather as the progressive movement of God's one people under the guidance of the Holy Spirit. To characterize the emergence of the role of Church leadership in regulating the community's unity in faith as an arbitrary restriction of the diversity canonized by the New Testament is only possible if one a priori excludes the theological interpretation which discerns that emergence as being the work of the Holy Spirit. The fact that such a theological interpretation cannot be based upon historical research alone does not make it unscientific; it is fully capable of acknowledging and integrating all that has and can be established through such research. What would appear arbitrary and unscientific, on the other hand, would be the a priori exclusion of such a theological interpretation. This is what does not seem to ring true in the conclusion of Dunn's otherwise excellent study. In the end, he seems to suggest that the fine historical research which he has presented about unity and diversity in the New Testament pits the canon against the theological interpretation that the emergence of a normative teaching ministry in the Church was the work of the Holy Spirit. But historical research on its own is not sufficient to resolve this theological issue. Moreover, there are good theological motives, based ultimately upon God's will for the unity of the Church and of the present Lordship of Jesus over the Church through the activity of the Holy Spirit, which support just such an interpretation.

SUMMARY OF CHAPTER FOUR

One may sum up this discussion of unity and diversity in faith according to the New Testament in the following way. One can certainly verify the presence of diversity in the expression of faith in the New Testament. Such diversity would become problematic for unity in faith to the extent that it would amount to irreconcilable differences in faith. In order to argue that there is a substantial unity in faith, an attempt was made to explain the way in which the proclamation and growth in knowledge of faith led to an inevitable diversification of expression, elements of which could indeed be in tension. However, five factors were described which together serve as dynamic forces toward preserving unity in faith: commonly held credal statements, dialogue, charisms and ministries, the composition of the New Testament canonical books, and the development of a regulative role on the part of leaders of the Church with regard to questions of conflict in faith. These factors worked together in such a way that, while there was diversity and even tension in the early Christian community, these tensions were able to be held together and one can with some confidence affirm that the New Testament Church enjoyed a rather substantial unity in faith. The tensions did not tear the Church apart into distinct communities which were divided from one another in faith but rather were able to be reconciled and made complementary by the various forces acting for unity in faith which were effective in the life of the community as a whole.

BRIEF RECAPITULATION OF
THE NEW TESTAMENT MATERIAL

The theme of faith in the New Testament is a rich and multi-faceted topic, which both challenges and rewards the one who tries to come to grips with it. We have explored this topic from a number of angles: its terminology, various nuances and distinctiveness vis-à-vis faith in the Old Testament (Chapter Two), its expression in confessional and credal formulas (Chapter Three) and its unity in diversity (Chapter Four). While the implications of the biblical and patristic material for the way we understand unity in faith will be set forth in more developed form in Part Three, it is perhaps useful at this stage to briefly recapitulate a few relevant points from these last three chapters on the New Testament, in a way similar to the summary which appeared at the end of Chapter One about the Old Testament.

First of all, one is immediately struck by the massive use of the terminology for faith in the New Testament, especially when compared with its use in the Old Testament. When taken together, the nearly five hundred occurrences of the noun "*pistis*" (faith, belief) and of the verb "*pisteuein*" (to believe) indicate a preoccupation with faith which runs through virtually every New Testament book and certainly through each of the major blocks of material. It is a preoccupation which one finds at the earliest strata of New Testament literature and which perdures right through to the latest. This points to the ineradicable place of faith within the Christian community. The community is of its very nature a community of faith. Faith defines the community; it is a constitutive factor in its identity. And because of this, the unity of the Church necessarily includes as one of its most essential characteristics unity in faith. This means that Church unity cannot be adequately conceived along the lines of a free association of people with like minded goals or a loose federation of communities dedicated, for example, to bettering humankind. Because faith is so essential to the community reflected in the pages of the New Testament, Church unity would not be that unity mandated and sanctioned by the New Testament if it were not a profound unity in faith.

Secondly, the wealth of passages, rich both in their occurrence and in their content, which speak of faith demonstrate that, for the New Testament, faith cannot be reduced to one simple description or definition. The faith which is trust in Jesus who heals in the synoptic gospels should not be emphasized to the point of giving short shrift to or of obscuring the faith which is reflected in Paul's powerful statement from the letter to the Romans: "If you confess with your lips that Jesus is Lord and believe in your heart that God raised him from the dead, you will be saved" (10,9). Or again, as this very verse so nicely illustrates, the existential faith which confesses Jesus as savior and Lord and which entrusts one's destiny to him cannot be opposed to a doctrinal faith which assents to some rather specific truths about God's presence in the activity and in the very person of Jesus. These various dimensions form part of a whole. It therefore seems reasonable to expect that unity in faith should reflect this multi-dimensionality of faith. If this is so, then a view of faith unity which would focus only upon the acceptance of Jesus as one's personal Lord and savior, highlighting thus the existential, fiducial aspect of faith, but paying little or no attention to doctrinal harmony about Jesus' identity as both human and divine or about the whole range of doctrinal and moral truths which are part of Christian faith would be insufficient. At the same time, an understanding of unity in faith which focused entirely upon doctrine and gave no place to what joins together people who have committed their lives to Christ and who know and love the triune God by means of prayer and Christian discipleship would clearly be a truncated view from the perspective of the New Testament. Both aspects need to be prized; neither taken for granted. One wonders whether tensions and misunderstandings within the ecumenical movement might not sometimes stem from insufficient attention to the global integrity of faith. How can all of the dimensions of faith be valued adequately in terms of their contribution to effecting unity in faith? A clearer answer to this question could well open the path to further insight into the degree to which Christians are already united in faith, as well as provide direction for ways in which such unity could be further enhanced.

Third, it seems quite clear that the most modest and surely unchallengeable result of the many studies concerning whether or not the New Testament may be said to contain a creed is the conclusion that Christian faith is of its essence confessional. Whatever else it entails, the act of faith includes also the profession of a number of truths. The believer becomes a member of the community of believers precisely by sharing with that community certain fundamental truths about Christ and his salvific work, along with the implications of this kernel as they may come to be expressed in further doctrinal or moral teachings. Christian faith, right from the beginning, makes a claim to truth which is most serious and to which it remains committed, even to the point of martyrdom. In this the Church merely follows its Lord, whose words and actions constituted a claim which could not be tolerated by some of the religious leaders of his day and which consequently led to his condemnation and death. In this way, "right doctrine" or "orthodoxy" is to some extent inevitably and necessarily part of Christian faith. Conzelmann's statement, therefore, that, with the appearance of "early Catholicism," the Christian community passed from faith to orthodoxy is unfortunate and misleading. Perhaps, because of unhappy historical connotations, the word "orthodoxy" may not be the best; it is not, after all, a biblical term. Still, right from the very beginning and throughout every strand of the New Testament, Christian faith entails such confessions as: "Jesus is risen"; "You are the Christ, the Son of the living God." One cannot legitimately make use of the valid results of historical-critical research, which show a considerable degree of diversity in the New Testament, to conclude that somehow Christian faith allows room for mutually contradictory statements or that to insist upon this or that particular truth as an expression of sound and "orthodox" doctrine is somehow a falling away from the more primitive and pure conception of Christian faith. Still less should one throw out what is implied in the word "orthodoxy" (that is, the firm adherence to sound and true doctrine) in the name of a supposedly more sophisticated sensitivity to the pluralism inherent in history and culture. Such positions misguidedly exaggerate what is of value in the historical sensitivity which is rightly such an important aspect of biblical and theological research today. They unnecessarily throw out the baby with the bath water. In an attempt to be true to history they negate what would seem to be one of the most clearly established facts about the communities of the New Testament: the strongly confessional nature of their faith.

Fourth, not a few of the scholars who have studied the New Testament confessions of faith concur in stating that a variety of identifiable aspects of the life of the primitive community provide the *Sitz im Leben* within which the various credal formulas emerged. These features of community life include catechesis and baptismal preparation, liturgy, mission, public profession of faith on the occasion of persecution and martyrdom and opposition to incipient error. These constitute natural occasions for the formulation of expressions of faith which are common to the community as a whole and which thus also foster unity in faith. In the New Testament, these situations provided the occasion for the formulation of the short creed-like confessions which can be found therein. From this one may perhaps extrapolate a general rule about unity in faith. The more that communities are united in catechesis, liturgy, mission, witness and official teaching, the more they will tend to be one in professing the same faith. The less they share in these normal and necessary activities in the ongoing life of the Church, the less they will tend to be united in faith. If the New Testament can be taken as a model, one of the more urgent and promising tasks for the contemporary ecumenical movement in fostering unity in faith would be to maximize what they may share in the content and structure of their catechesis, liturgy, mission, witness and official teaching. This does not mean that legitimate diversity would be flattened into uniformity. It merely acknowledges that one of the most powerful forces for fostering shared faith is shared life.

Fifth, with regard to the precise topic of the legitimate diversity which does not disturb unity in faith and which indeed may be understood as expressing more fully the catholicity of the Church, one may readily agree with and even conclude that the New Testament itself supports Oscar Cullmann's famous dictum: uniformity is a sin against the Holy Spirit. Cullmann's point is only a restatement of Paul's basic ecclesiological position in 1 Cor 12–14, where he combines a pneumatological appreciation of the one source of the variety of gifts and charisms with the image of a body with one head and many members, all in order to argue that diversity and unity enjoy a fundamental compatibility within the Church. Chapter Four argued that the question of unity and diversity in faith needs to be considered within the context of the historicity of the Church as the pilgrim People of God. The New Testament can serve as an illustration of this. There can be no question that the gospel message, the kerygma as that may be located in various short summaries, was proclaimed to create unity. The earliest believers and evangelists did not preach with the intention of creating mutually exclusive Christian communities. But as the preached word is accepted and assimilated, as individuals and communities over the course of time reflect upon the deeper significance of the Christ event and upon its implications for their lives, naturally a host of diversities make their appearance. Such diversity is based upon the richness of the mystery contemplated and upon the wealth of intellectual, cultural and emotional qualities of the subjects who lovingly contemplate and bring their reflections to expression. This double wealth constitutes, along with the universal will of God to save all human beings in Christ (cf. 1 Tim 2,4–5) through the working of the Holy Spirit (cf. Rom 8,9–17), the root of the catholicity of the Church. Among the diversities in expression of faith which naturally emerge over the course of history, many are fully compatible and they may be considered as pure gain. However, some are in tension or even contradict each other. Within this concrete situation of the Church as a pilgrim people moving through time, a number of factors which make up part of the life of the community serve as tools for sorting out differences and for maintaining unity in faith. The New Testament contains at least five such factors: the kerygma (Creed), dialogue, charisms, Scriptures and leadership. Perhaps others could be added. Be that as it may, these considerations suggest that unity of faith, at least as that is realized over the course of time, should be considered as a process involving a number of factors. To say this does not amount to denying that unity in faith also entails, for example, the common adherence to a doctrinal definition concerning some particular point, such as the decision that Jesus is "of the same nature" as the Father, taught by the Council of Nicea. Rather, it simply acknowledges that an authoritative intervention such as a definition by an ecumenical council is part of this ongoing process. Unity in faith over the course of history is not to be achieved so much by compiling an exhaustive list of doctrines that everybody can agree to on a given occasion. Rather it requires that all of the communities united together in the full communion which is the one Church of Christ throughout the world accept and participate in those principal factors which not only make for unity in faith at the present moment but which also serve to safeguard and foster that unity in the future as new insights and reflections continue to flesh out in an ever more perfect way the catholicity of the faith of Christ's Church.

PART TWO:
FAITH AND ITS UNITY ACCORDING TO THE PATRISTIC LITERATURE

While a study of the teaching of the Scriptures about faith and its unity is a formidable task, moving on to a consideration of this theme in the writings of the ecclesiastical authors of the first few centuries of Church history could seem almost impossible. Anyone familiar with the various standard collections of patristic texts (Migne's *Patrologia greca/latina, Die griechischen christlichen Schriftsteller, Corpus scriptorum christianorum orientalium, Corpus scriptorum ecclesiasticorum latinorum, Corpus Christianorum. Series greca/latina* and *Sources chrétiennes*, to mention only the most important and well known) knows that they contain hundreds of volumes. It would be naive indeed to suppose that any one individual could master such a vast amount of material. Moreover, given such a wide range of types of literature (letters, apologies, controversial works criticizing other Christian thinkers, commentaries on the Scriptures, expositions of specific doctrines or of the Creed, ecclesiastical histories, conciliar decrees, liturgical texts and so forth) written over a period of several hundred years, one could expect that the notion of faith and its unity might well take on a variety of shades of meaning and undergo a certain degree of development. As such, even at the outset one would have good reason to suspect that there is no single patristic answer to questions such as "what is faith?" and "how is one to understand unity in faith?" Thus the task which we now take up, that is, a survey of those patristic writers who have made the more important contributions to understanding faith and its unity, is quite formidable.

Fortunately, a number of careful studies which attempt to trace the major lines of the patristic doctrine about faith have already appeared and can be used as a solid point of departure for a fresh return to the original sources.[1] Moreover, standard instruments such as Quasten's Patrology and Rouët de Journel's Enchiridion patristicum are furnished with indices which offer further useful assistance.[2] With such fine secondary sources as guides, the task of inquiring into the patristic doctrine of faith and its unity draws much more into the range of what can be done.

The various surveys of patristic teaching about the specific topic of faith proceed chronologically and, while including comments about a large number of writers, tend to concentrate on about fifteen prominent figures. Usually one begins with a brief discussion of faith in the earliest writings from the apostolic fathers. From then on, the principal characters are Justin, Irenaeus, Tertullian, Clement of Alexandria, Origen, Cyril of Jerusalem, Hilary of Poitier, the Cappadocians (Basil, Gregory of Nazianzus and Gregory of Nyssa), John Chrysostom, Ambrose, Augustine and Theodoret.[3] Moreover, even among these more prominent contributors to our understanding of the topic "faith," not all are equal. Among Eastern writers, Clement of Alexandria and Origen usually receive the most extensive comment; among those of the West, Augustine.

A chronological procedure will be followed here as well. The opening chapter (Chapter Five) will focus upon the principal authors relative to our theme of faith and its unity in the period before the first ecumenical council, held at Nicea in 325. After Nicea, the volume of patristic literature increases dramatically. It will be treated in two steps, with separate chapters dedicated to the principal authors who wrote respectively in Greek (Chapter Six) and Latin (Chapter Seven).

Chapter Five
FAITH AND ITS UNITY
ACCORDING TO PRE-NICEAN WRITERS

This chapter will treat seven authors, each with his own uniqueness but also to some extent representative of a specific type of literature. Clement of Rome and Ignatius of Antioch represent that earliest group of post-New Testament writers who are commonly grouped together under the title "apostolic fathers." Writing at the turn of the first century, they are without a yet commonly recognized New Testament and they offer a glimpse of the tensions and divisions which threatened their communities, the earliest about which we know after those in the New Testament itself, as well as the way in which they saw faith as exercising a role in keeping their communities united. Justin Martyr represents a new type of literature—early Christian apologetic—which attempted to show the reasonability of Christian faith in the face of objections posed to it by the Jewish and Greek context into which Christianity was attempting to find a place. Irenaeus and Tertullian, of the late second to early third centuries, are among the first and most forceful to point out the danger of and argue against "heresy," especially that of various groups of "gnostics." Their writings offer insight into the ecclesial nature of faith, its apostolicity and the way in which it binds the Church together, differentiating those who by faith may be said to truly belong to the churches in succession to the apostles from those who have been led astray, particularly by philosophical and mystical speculation. Finally, Clement of Alexandria and Origen are the first to sketch out systematic presentations of Christian faith, harmonizing faith and reason in such a way that they have been thought of as among the first theologians, properly so called. As a general rule, the methodological procedure in this and in the following two chapters concerning the patristic literature will be to treat each author in question, first, with regard to his understanding of faith and, second, with regard to any insights he may offer which are relevant to unity in faith.

1. CLEMENT OF ROME

Clement of Rome's *Letter to the Corinthians* (usually dated around the year 96) has no section devoted precisely to developing the theme of faith, but does make a number of points which, taken together, allow one to glimpse its meaning for this very early author.[1] The aim of the letter is to encourage the Corinthians to return to unity among themselves (51-59), a unity strained because some members of the community rejected those who were serving in roles of leadership (13-15 and 44). Thus the virtues of humility, submission and accepting correction are prominent themes of the letter (16-18, 28-32, 37-38), along with some passages stating that the origins of the ministries of leadership can be traced back through the apostles to Christ and, ultimately, to God (42 and 44).

It is interesting that the cause of division in the Corinthinian community is not presented as a lack of unity in faith in the doctrinal sense of that term. There is no hint of false or heretical doctrines here. Nevertheless, faith in the sense of a humble and submissive attitude toward God and toward God's will is proposed as an important element of the solution which the divisions in Corinth call for. Right from the opening of his letter, Clement states that, in the past, the Corinthians have been known for "the excellence and constancy of your faith" (1 [Funk, 98])[2] but that, with the outbreak of division caused by envy, "the eye of faith has grown dim" (3 [Funk, 102]; Staniforth, 24). He proposes the faith of Abraham (10) and Rahab (12) from the Old Testament and that of Peter and Paul (5) from the New as examples for the Corinthinians in this moment of crisis. The faith of these heroes of the past illustrates humble obedience and hospitality in the case of Abraham and Rahab; it is the opposite of that jealousy and envy which led to the persecution of Peter and Paul and which now was causing the divisions among the Corinthians. Thus faith is understood as a way of living, an attitude of humility and submission (28-32), of love (48); it is an aspect of the life of virtue (60). One is called to live in faith (34) and truth (60) and to be a "faithful" person (62). At the same time, faith is a gift (35 and 64). Faith alone justifies: "...we are not justified by ourselves...but by that faith through which alone Almighty God has justified all men since the beginning of time" (32 [Funk, 138-140]; Staniforth, 39). At the same time, faith must be accompanied by efforts to live a virtuous life (33-36).

Clement does not emphasize the noetic dimension of faith, but some texts hint at his sense that acceptance of truth claims is also part of faith. Thus, paragraphs 23-27 provide an argument for the credibility of the resurrection, implying that Christian faith entails the affirmation of cognitive truths relative to the raising of Jesus from the dead. Paragraphs 19–22 call upon a stoic theory of the harmony of creation to bolster the reasonability of Clement's appeal for peace within the Corinthian community.[3] This noetic dimension, entailing understanding and even vision, is beautifully expressed in 36:

> Through Him [Jesus Christ] we can look up to the highest heaven and see, as in a glass, the peerless perfection of the face of God. Through Him the eyes of our hearts are opened, and our dim and clouded understanding unfolds like a flower to the light; for through Him the Lord permits us to taste the wisdom of eternity (Funk, 144-146; Staniforth, 42).[4]

The fact that these important and distinctive dimensions of faith can be recognized in Clement's passing references to it suggests that the richness of faith, inherited from the Scriptures, continues as part of the Christian awareness right from the earliest post-biblical writings.

2. IGNATIUS OF ANTIOCH

Ignatius of Antioch, in his seven letters written on the journey toward martyrdom in Rome (usually dated 107), is, like Clement of Rome, intensely interested in the unity of the communities he addresses.[5] His own community of Antioch in Syria had suffered from divisions, and only in his last three letters, written from Troas, does it become clear that Ignatius has learned of the return of peace there (Phil 10, Sym 11, Poly 7). For Ignatius, the greatest threat to unity is false doctrine, which he condemns with great frequency and vehemence (Eph 6; 8–10; 16–17; Mag 8; Trall 6; Phil 3; Smy 4; Poly 3). In particular he writes against a type of Christian-Judaism which would require observance of the law (Mag 10) and against docetism which denies the reality of Jesus' suffering, death and resurrection (Trall 8–10; Smy 1–3). Faith then clearly includes for Ignatius a certain doctrinal content. This content is in the line of Pauline tradition in that it focuses upon the centrality of the death and resurrection of Jesus (Eph 20; Mag 9; Trall 2; Phil 8-9; Smy 7).[6] Unity in faith (Eph 20) requires professing the same doctrine. For Ignatius, the principal way of maintaining unity in faith is to remain united with the bishop (Eph 2; 6; Mag 6; 13; Phil 1; Smy 9). A striking combination of musical metaphors is employed to convey this unity:

...your justly respected clergy, who are a credit to God, are attuned to their bishop like the strings of a harp, and the result is a hymn of praise to Jesus Christ from minds that are in unison, and affections that are in harmony. Pray, then, come and join this choir, every one of you; let there be a whole symphony of minds in concert; take the tone all together from God, and sing aloud to the Father with one voice through Jesus Christ, so that He may hear you and know by your good works that you are indeed members of His Son's Body. A completely united front will help to keep you in constant communion with God (Eph 4 [Funk, 216]; Staniforth, 76).

Ignatius encourages obedience to the bishop and clergy so that "with undivided minds" the community can "share in the one common breaking of bread" (Eph 20 [Funk, 230]; Staniforth, 82). "...let me urge upon you the need for godly unanimity in everything you do" (Mag 6 [Funk, 234]; Staniforth, 88).

Although doctrinal unity appears to be a principal aspect of Ignatius' thought about faith, at least two other dimensions are also unmistakably present. First, faith is a way of living. Ignatius writes of the "deeds of faith" which are not possible to the unbeliever any more than "deeds of unbelief" are possible to the believer (Eph 8 [Funk, 220]; Staniforth, 78). Faith and love are frequently mentioned together (Eph 1; 9; 14; Mag 1; 13; Trall 8; Phil 11; Smy 1; 6; 13). In Eph 14, he writes:

Given a thorough-going faith and love for Jesus Christ, there is nothing in all this that will not be obvious to you; for life begins and ends with those two qualities. Faith is the beginning, and love is the end; and the union of the two together is God. All that makes for a soul's perfection follows in their train, for nobody who professes faith will commit sin, and nobody who possesses love can feel hatred (Funk, 224; Staniforth, 79–80).

In addition to this faith which is a way of life and of love, one might point out a second and related theme: faith as mystical knowledge. This comes through when Ignatius speaks of growth in faith, such as in Eph 3, where he writes that he is only a "beginner in discipleship" and of his need for "lessons in faith and admonishment and patience and toleration" (Funk, 217; Staniforth, 76). He states that the Trallians are "still in your infancy," adding:

> Even I myself, for all my chains and for all my ability to
> comprehend celestial secrets and angelic hierarchies and the
> dispositions of the heavenly powers, and much else both seen
> and unseen, am not yet on that account a real disciple. (Trall
> 5 [Funk, 246]; Staniforth, 96).

This sense of mystical knowledge and union takes on the nuance of
"indwelling" in Eph 15:

> Whatever we do, then, let it be done as though He Himself
> were dwelling within us, we being as it were His temples and
> He within us as their God. For in fact that is literally the case;
> and in proportion as we rightly love Him, so it will become
> clear to our eyes ([Funk, 224–226]; Staniforth, 80).

It is within this context that Ignatius' second name—Theophorus, God-
bearer—finds its full relevance. Indeed all Christians are God-bearers
and Christ-bearers (Eph 9).[7] Perhaps one can see the fullest expression
of this mysticism which is part of Ignatius' faith in his letter to the
Romans, with its many inspiring passages expressing eagerness to experience martyrdom for Christ.

Here again, then, in Ignatius of Antioch we find a writer from the
earliest generations of the Church who, while not expounding at length
precisely upon the topic of faith, nevertheless has provided an open win-
dow for the contemporary researcher, which reveals already at the
beginning of the second century a doctrinal understanding of faith
upon which the unity of the community depended. Also Ignatius
witnesses to a deep relationship between faith and life in the practice of
charity as well as a faith which grows into mystical union with God.

3. JUSTIN MARTYR

When one turns from writers like Clement and Ignatius to the
apologists of the second century, including such figures as Justin Martyr
(c. 165), Tatian (post 172?) and Athenagoras (c. 177), the most striking
contrast which immediately appears as a general trait and which deeply
colors the way in which they take up the more specific topic of faith is
the fact that these authors are not addressing a Christian community.
Because of this very different context, what they say concerning faith has
a new tone and content quite different from what one finds in the apostolic fathers. Primarily this newness centers around what might be called

the theme of the credibility of Christian faith. Justin Martyr may serve as
a suitable example of this.

Justin's principal works are his *First Apology*, addressed rather
grandly to the emperor, his sons, the Senate and the whole people of
Rome, and his *Dialogue with Trypho, a Jew.*[8] The first work begins as an
appeal for justice on behalf of Christians, attempting to refute charges of
atheism and immorality against them and to explain the reasonableness
of their faith (for example, the credibility of the resurrection [*Apology*,
19]). Justin also describes some aspects of Christian life and worship
(obedience to civil authorities [17]; continence [29]; celebration of the
sacraments, of the eucharist and weekly worship [55–57]). Faith is
presented largely in the context of conviction: "And we have been
taught, and are convinced, and do believe..." (*Apology*, 10 [PL 6, 340];
ANF I, 165; see also 17 and 18) that Jesus is the Christ and the Son of
God (*Apology*, 40: "...the Spirit of prophecy...foretold the conspiracy
which was formed against Christ by Herod...; and how He should be
believed on by men of every race; and how God calls Him His Son..." [PL
6, 389]; ANF I, 176; see also *Apology* 53 and 54). By far, Justin gives the
largest space in his argument on behalf of the credibility of Christian
faith to the fulfillment of Old Testament prophecies (chapters 30–50
and scattered texts throughout). But he also discusses Christianity by
making reference to Plato and other philosophers and poets (18 and
59–60) and to classical Greco-Roman religion (9 and 20–26). In the
Apology, faith is understood as belief in God as revealed in Jesus Christ:

> For, impelled by the desire of the eternal and pure life, we
> seek the abode that is with God, the Father and Creator of
> all, and hasten to confess our faith, persuaded and convinced
> as we are that they who have proved to God by their works
> that they followed Him, and loved to abide with Him where
> there is no sin to cause disturbance, can obtain these things.
> This, then, to speak shortly, is what we expect and have
> learned from Christ, and teach (8 [PL 6, 337]; ANF I, 165).

Faith acknowledges the salvific deeds of Christ's passion and resurrection, which were foretold by the prophets (40–42, 52–53 and 55).
Faith confesses that Christ is the King of glory, Son of man (51) and Son
of God (54). It is in the *Apology* (46) that one finds the often referred to
teaching that the logos was in the world before Christ.[9]

The *Dialogue with Trypho* is Justin's longest work (142 chapters)
and takes the form of a dialogue in the Platonic style between the author

and Trypho, a "Hebrew of the circumcision," who is accompanied by a band of followers. Trypho happens upon Justin one day as he is walking in the countryside, in the customary garb of a philosopher, and initiates the dialogue for the purpose of hearing something profitable. The exchange begins with Justin's retelling of his conversion to Christianity after having pursued the truth in the teachings of the philosophers, a conversion that was sparked by his chance meeting with a Christian sage who pointed out some of the perplexities of Greek philosophy and the superiority of the divinely inspired teaching of the prophets. When Trypho responds that, in his view, Christianity is a groundless invention (*Dialogue*, 8), the dialogue takes off in a series of exchanges in which Justin responds to various Jewish objections to Christianity and shows various ways in which the Old Testament texts should be interpreted as referring to Christ.

In this context, faith for Justin means accepting the Christian message, something that the Jews have not done and so are called "children who have no faith" (chapters 27 [PL 6, 533]; ANF I, 208; and 123 [PL 6, 761]; ANF I, 261):

> ...and along with Abraham we shall inherit the holy land, when we shall receive the inheritance for an endless eternity, being children of Abraham through the like faith. For as he believed the voice of God, and it was imputed to him for righteousness, in like manner we, having believed God's voice spoken by the apostles of Christ, and promulgated to us by the prophets, have renounced even to death all the things of the world. Accordingly, He promises to him a nation of similar faith, God-fearing, righteous, and delighting the Father; but it is not you, "in whom is no faith" (chapter 119 [PL 6, 753]; ANF I, 259).

This text, appearing toward the end of the book, indicates the dynamic that runs throughout, that is, the contrast between Justin and Trypho, between Christians and Jews, with regard to their respective acceptance of Jesus as Christ and Son of God and acknowledgment of his saving death and resurrection which was foretold by the prophets. "I shall prove to you as you stand here that we have not believed empty fables, or words without any foundation, but words filled with the power of God..." (9 [PL 6, 493]; ANF I, 199). Thus the focus is on Jesus Christ. Numerous texts from the Old Testament are produced to show that he is the Son of man foretold by Daniel (31 and 76), the priest-forever mentioned in Psalm 109 (33 and 83), the one born of a Virgin according to Isaiah 7 (63, 66, 68, 71 and 75), that various Old Testament titles point to his divinity (126–128) and that he is therefore rightly worshiped by Christians (38). Special emphasis is given to prophecies which foretold his suffering (12, 32, 38, 39, 52–53 and 89) which was for our salvation (95), as well as to Old Testament symbols and predictions concerning the cross (86, 89–91 and 94–99).

In summary, the *Dialogue* amounts to a Christian interpretation of the Old Testament, presented as being in contrast with the faulty interpretation of Trypho and his teachers (9 and 29). One can correctly interpret the Scriptures only in the Holy Spirit (92). Because of this heavily Christological concentration upon the identity of Jesus as Christ and Son of God and upon his salvific death and resurrection, Lührmann rightly points out a strongly Pauline flavor in Justin's understanding of faith.[10] This includes as well a strong link between faith and salvation (28–29 and 44–45).

Given the overall thrust of Justin's writing as an apology addressed to those who are not Christians, it is not surprising that the unity of the Church in one faith is not a predominant theme for him. Nevertheless, one finds a few passages in which Justin comments on divisions of faith within the Christian community. In the *Apology* 58, he mentions Marcion as one who denies that God is the maker of all things "and that the Christ predicted by the prophets is His Son" (PL 6, 416; ANF I, 182). Justin adds that those who seduce men from God and Christ are devils. In the *Dialogue*, he notes a positive effect that follows from the emergence of erroneous doctrines:

> The fact that there are such men confessing themselves to be
> Christians, and admitting the crucified Jesus to be both Lord
> and Christ, yet not teaching His doctrines, but those of the
> spirits of error, causes us who are disciples of the true and
> pure doctrine of Jesus Christ, to be more faithful and stead-
> fast in the hope announced by Him (*Dialogue*, 35 [PL 6, 549];
> ANF I, 212).

Justin turns the presence of such divisions in faith to his advantage, recalling that Jesus himself foretold that there would be "false Christs" and "false apostles," once again demonstrating the truth of Christianity by means of an argument based upon the fulfillment of prophecy. Be that as it may, it is clear that, for Justin, some ways of expressing

Christian faith can be called true, others erroneous. The unity of Christians in faith falls squarely upon the question of doctrine.

4. IRENAEUS

With Irenaeus (end of the second century), we return to writings which are directed to those within the Christian community. The two complete works of his which we have are of unequal length and scope. *Adversus haereses* (c. 180) is a rather massive effort in five books to catalogue the various heresies, mainly gnostic, which led up to the Valentinianism which was current at the time of Irenaeus (Book I), to refute them (Book II) and to offer the true Christian doctrine which has passed down from the apostles and which is contained in the teachings of the Lord and of the various books of the New Testament (Books III-V).[11] Irenaeus appears to want to underline the contrast between the succession of the heretics (AH I,31,3), beginning from Simon Magus (Acts 8,9–24), the father of all heretics (AH III, Prologue; see I,23,2), on the one hand, and the succession of the apostles which passed on down through the churches which they founded (AH III,3,1–4), on the other. Irenaeus' other complete work, the *Proof of the Apostolic Preaching* (probably written some time after AH), is much shorter, a kind of a compendium of Christian teaching at the end of the second century, based primarily on a Christian interpretation of the Old Testament.[12] What can these two works tell us about Irenaeus' understanding of Christian faith and of its unity?

While neither of them includes a direct treatment of faith as such, from the nature of these texts it is quite clear that faith concerns a specific doctrinal content. *Adversus haereses* begins with the words: "Inasmuch as certain men have set the truth aside..." (AH I, Prologue [SC 264, 18]; ANF I, 315). Its purpose is to refute the so-called knowledge of the gnostics by means of a correct interpretation of the Scriptures and arguments based upon reason. The purpose of the *Proof* is both to confirm the faith of his brother Marcianus and to help him to "confound all those who hold false views...and [to] expound what we have to say in its integrity and purity" (*Proof* 1 [SC 62, 28]; Smith 47). Within this context, some of the particular traits of Irenaeus' view of faith are his emphasis upon an all-encompassing view of salvation history. God the creator is none other than the one whom Jesus Christ calls Father (AH II,1-2; II,9,1). God's action on behalf of human salvation extends back to the time of Adam (AH III, 23), includes the covenants with Adam, Noah and Moses and the definitive covenant established in Jesus Christ (AH III,11,8), and reaches its culmination in the recapitulation of all things in Christ (AH III,21,10; III,22,1; V,21,1).[13] Moreover, as Lührmann points out, Irenaeus was the first Christian writer to have at his disposal and make use of a relatively complete New Testament; he had a keen sense that the apostolic tradition was in accord with the New Testament; and he spoke of a *regula fidei* which resulted from this harmony.[14] These particular resources and emphases, along with the fact that Irenaeus' writings are principally concerned with refuting false doctrine and expounding true doctrine, give his understanding of faith a particularly doctrinal tone.

Nevertheless, it should be added that Irenaeus touches upon other aspects of faith as well. In the tradition that stems from Paul and is present also in Clement and Justin, Irenaeus sees a continuity, even an identity (AH IV,21,1), between the faith of Abraham and that of Christians.[15] Abraham is justified by faith. Thus faith is connected with a stance toward God which introduces the believer into the realm of salvation (AH IV,37,5). Still, even here, there is something of the idea of accepting a certain doctrinal content since, according to Irenaeus, the prophets and righteous individuals of the Old Testament had foreknowledge of Christ through the inspiration of the Holy Spirit and awaited his coming (AH III,21,4). Another element of Irenaeus' view of faith is the assertion that human knowledge of God is necessarily limited (AH II,28,1–3). One of the failures of the heretics is their presumption in desiring and claiming to know things that are hidden in God and which even the Son did not claim to know (AH II,28,6–8). Furthermore, Irenaeus is aware that human freedom is intimately engaged in the act of faith (AH IV,37,5). Faith is a human act, not predetermined, as the doctrines of some of the gnostics claimed. Finally, Irenaeus may be the first Christian writer to employ a text from the Septuagint—Is 7,9—which later would become very significant in patristic thought about the nature of faith: "Unless you believe, you shall not understand" (*Proof* 3 [SC 62, 31]).[16]

Thus while Irenaeus did not devote a work to analyzing the act of faith as such, still it is clear that he recognizes something of the multivalence which also characterizes it in Scripture and in other Christian writings: faith accepts a determinate doctrinal content but must modestly acknowledge the limits which encompass such doctrine; faith engages freedom and, as in the paradigmatic case of Abraham, it is intimately bound with justification and salvation.

But it is when we consider the precise theme of "unity in faith" that Irenaeus provides some of the most striking texts in the whole of patristic literature. In light of the focus of the present book, the following passage deserves to be cited at length:

1. The Church, though dispersed throughout the whole world, even to the ends of the earth, has received from the apostles and their disciples this faith: [She believes] in one God, the Father Almighty, Maker of heaven and earth, and the sea, and all things that are in them; and in one Christ Jesus, the Son of God, who became incarnate for our salvation; and in the Holy Spirit, who proclaimed through the prophets the dispensations of God, and the advents, and the birth from a virgin, and the passion, and the resurrection from the dead, and the ascension into heaven in the flesh of the beloved Christ Jesus, our Lord, and His [future] manifestation from heaven in the glory of the Father "to gather all things in one," and to raise up anew all flesh of the whole human race, in order that to Christ Jesus, our Lord, and God, and Saviour, and King, according to the will of the invisible Father, "every knee should bow, of things in heaven, and things in earth, and things under the earth, and that every tongue should confess" to Him, and that he should execute just judgment towards all; that He may send "spiritual wickednesses," and the angels who transgressed and became apostates, together with the ungodly, and unrighteous, and wicked, and profane among men, into everlasting fire; but may, in the exercise of His grace, confer immortality on the righteous, and holy, and those who have kept His commandments, and have persevered in His love, some from the beginning [of their Christian course], and others from [the date of] their repentance, and may surround them with everlasting glory.

2. As I have already observed, the Church, having received this preaching and this faith, although scattered throughout the whole world, yet, as if occupying but one house, carefully preserves it. She also believes these points [of doctrine] just as if she had but one soul, and one and the same heart, and she proclaims them, and teaches them, and hands them down, with perfect harmony, as if she possessed only one mouth. For, although the languages of the world are dissimilar, yet the import of the tradition is one and the same. For the Churches which have been planted in Germany do not believe or hand down anything different, nor do those in Spain, nor those in Gaul, nor those in the East, nor those in Egypt, nor

those in Libya, nor those which have been established in the central regions of the world. But as the sun, that creature of God, is one and the same throughout the whole world, so also the preaching of the truth shineth everywhere, and enlightens all men that are willing to come to a knowledge of the truth. Nor will any one of the rulers in the Churches, however highly gifted he may be in point of eloquence, teach doctrines different from these (for no one is greater than the Master); nor, on the other hand, will he who is deficient in power of expression inflict injury on the tradition. For the faith being ever one and the same, neither does one who is able at great length to discourse regarding it, make any addition to it, nor does one, who can say but little, diminish it. (AH I,10,1–2 [SC 264, 154–161]; ANF I, 330–331).

Here we see not only a summary of many fundamental points of Christian belief as they will be contained in the various creeds (AH III,10,1)[17] and given a normatively fixed formulation in the Creed of Niceo-Constantinople,[18] but also the profound unity of the Christian confession of faith. Though scattered everywhere, the Church remains as if "occupying but one house," believing "as if she had but one soul, and one and the same heart." Commenting on the response given to the apostles in the preaching at the beginning of Acts and specifically glossing Acts 4,24–30 ("And when they heard it [the account of the release of the apostles by the chief priests and elders], they lifted their voices together to God and said, 'Sovereign Lord...'"), Irenaeus writes:

These [are the] voices of the Church from which every Church had its origin; these are the voices of the metropolis of the citizens of the new covenant; these are the voices of the apostles; these are voices of the disciples of the Lord, the truly perfect, who, after the assumption of the Lord, were perfected by the Spirit and called upon the God who made heaven, and earth, and the sea,—who was announced by the prophets,—and Jesus Christ His Son, whom God anointed, and who knew no other [God] (AH III,12,5 [SC 211, 196-197]; ANF I,431).

These originating voices continue down through the ages so as to constitute a harmony of voices among believers. Irenaeus adds that the voices of Valentinus and of Marcion do not blend in with this harmony.

Where does the problem of division in faith originate? For Irenaeus, false doctrines arise from the presumptuous claim to know too much (AH II,28,1-9); it stems from various philosophical and cosmological speculations, as typified by the doctrines of the gnostics, which have little to do with and which even contradict the originating voices of faith of the first Christians. One response by Irenaeus is to attempt to show the absurdity of the reasoning of the various heretics (see, for example, AH II,3-8, which raises various objections, on the grounds of sound thinking, to gnostic views about creation). But what is perhaps an even more dangerous source of false doctrine is the misinterpretation of Scripture. The Valentinians pervert the Scriptures (AH I,8-9); others do the same (AH I,18-19; AH II,10,1-2; AH II,20-24 and many other places). Irenaeus goes on to suggest a method for interpreting Scripture, making use of the more clear and straightforward passages in order to understand the parables and other passages which are open to a variety of interpretations (AH II,27,1-3).

> If, therefore, according to the rule which I have stated, we leave some questions in the hands of God, we shall both preserve our faith uninjured, and shall continue without danger; and all Scripture, which has been given to us by God, shall be found by us perfectly consistent; and the parables shall harmonize with those passages which are perfectly plain; and those statements the meaning of which is clear, shall serve to explain the parables; and through the many diversified utterances [of Scripture] there shall be heard one harmonious melody in us, praising in hymns that God who created all things. (AH II,28,3 [SC 294, 276-277]; ANF I, 400).

But Irenaeus' principal means for avoiding false doctrine is to believe that teaching which is found in the ancient churches established by the apostles and whose succession in ministerial leadership can be established. "We have learned from none others the plan of our salvation, than from those through whom the Gospel has come down to us, which they did at one time proclaim in public, and, at a later period, by the will of God, handed down to us in the Scriptures, to be the ground and pillar of our faith" (AH III,1,1 [SC 211, 20-21]; ANF I, 414). He proceeds to mention those whom he considers as the apostolic sources of the four gospels: Matthew, Peter (for the gospel of Mark), Paul (for the gospel of Luke) and John (AH III,1,1), adding: "If any one does not agree to these truths [contained in the gospels], he despises the companions of the Lord; nay more, he despises Christ Himself the Lord; yea, he despises the Father also, and stands self-condemned, resisting and opposing his own salvation, as is the case with all heretics" (AH III,1,2 [SC 211, 24-25]; ANF I, 415). For Irenaeus, even if the apostles had not left us any writings (AH III,4,1),[19] we can still follow their doctrine because we know the churches which they established: "and we are in a position to reckon up those who were by the apostles instituted bishops in the Churches, and [to demonstrate] the succession of these men to our own times; those who neither taught nor knew of anything like what these [heretics] rave about" (AH III,3,1 [SC 211, 30-31]; ANF I, 415). To avoid the tediousness of reporting the successions of all the apostolic churches, Irenaeus limits himself to reporting that of "the very great, the very ancient, and universally known Church founded and organized at Rome by the two most glorious apostles, Peter and Paul," adding that it is necessary "that every Church should agree with this Church" (AH III,3,2 [SC 211, 32-33]; ANF I, 415) and providing a list of bishops from Linus down to the time in which Irenaeus was writing (AH III,3,3).[20] These texts point out the profound connection in the mind of Irenaeus between unity of faith and what may be termed its apostolic ecclesiality, that is, its being maintained in the churches of apostolic origin under the guidance of a succession of leaders which originated with the apostles themselves.[21]

5. TERTULLIAN

Of Tertullian (c. 155-220) Johannes Quasten writes: "Forever a fighter, he knew no relenting towards his enemies, whether pagans, Jews, heretics, or later on, Catholics. All his writings are polemic."[22] This statement signals a complexity that one encounters in understanding the views of Tertullian, that is, at a particular point (c. 205-207)[23] he became a Montanist, with the result that his later writings exhibit a certain criticism toward the "institutional" Church which is not present in his earlier ones. What weight should be assigned to his writings as a Montanist? In addition, he was the first of the major patristic authors to write principally in Latin, because of which there is a certain fluidity in the Latin terminology which he employs to speak about faith.[24] Moreover, Tertullian was by profession a lawyer, a fact which explains the argumentative style and even the literary form (i.e. *The Prescription of Heretics*) of many of his works. He had a deep knowledge of Greek and Latin literature, philosophy and law and displayed a passionate commitment to the truth.[25]

Of Tertullian's many works,[26] none is directed specifically to explaining the act of faith or what might be called its epistemological status. Some hints can be gleaned from a work such as the *Apology*, which, in chapter 17, speaks of a type of knowledge of God on the basis of God's works and on the basis of the testimony of the soul. Chapter 18 proceeds to speak of "an ampler and more authoritative knowledge" of God and of his counsels contained within written revelation, which was set down by individuals "abundantly endowed with the Holy Spirit" (CSEL 69, 46; ANF III, 32). Tertullian adds: "Whoever gives ear will find God in them; whoever takes pains to understand, will be compelled to believe."[27] Thus faith is related to hearing.[28] Escribano-Alberca sees in these texts from chapters 17–18 of the *Apology* a cosmological and anthropological knowledge of God upon which faith adds a further dimension.[29] Still, as Escribano-Alberca himself admits, there is a degree of dualism in Tertullian's view of truth, which ultimately sees philosophy as the source of heresies ("Miserable Aristotle!...What indeed has Athens to do with Jerusalem? What concord is there between the Academy and the Church? What between heretics and Christians?" [*The Prescription of Heretics* 7; CCL 1, 192-193; ANF III, 246]). One who has faith needs no more: "With our faith, we desire no further belief. For this is our praiseworthy faith, that there is nothing which we ought to believe besides" (*Prescription* 7; CCL 1, 193; ANF III, 246). Tertullian even seems to move toward attributing a degree of irrationality to faith in *On the Flesh of Christ* 5: "And the Son of God died; it is by all means to be believed, because it is absurd. And He was buried, and rose again; the fact is certain, because it is impossible" (CCL 2, 881; ANF III, 525).

That Tertullian also views faith as a prerequisite for salvation may be drawn from his discussion of the relation between faith and baptism in *De baptismo* 13 (CSEL 20, 212-213; ANF III, 675–676). Here he responds to the view that, since Abraham pleased God not by means of the sacrament of water but by that of faith, baptism by water is not necessary. Tertullian responds that, prior to Christ's birth, passion and resurrection, salvation was obtained by "naked faith," but since the time of Jesus' command to baptize the nations (Mt 28,19) and his teaching that all must be born again of water and the Holy Spirit (Jn 3,5), baptism is necessary, as various texts from Acts illustrate (Acts 9,18; 22,10; 22,8). Later, in *De baptismo* 16 (CSEL 20, 214; ANF III, 677) Tertullian notes that another baptism, that of martyrdom, can take the place of water-baptism. The important point for our discussion is not so much Tertullian's insistence on the necessity, after the explicit command of Christ, of some form of baptism for salvation, but rather that his overall argument posits such baptism as additional to the "bare faith" which sufficed for Abraham. Whether in the case of Abraham or in that of a baptized Christian, faith is always presupposed as a requirement for salvation. Hence faith is not simply a question of accepting what God has revealed, but has an existential, soteriological dimension as well. Rounding off this more existential aspect, one should note that, for Tertullian, faith becomes stronger in times of fasting and persecution (*Concerning Flight in Persecution* 1 [CSEL 76, 17–19]); it has no fear before persecution (*Ibid.* 14 [CSEL 76, 42–43]) and, in the face of martyrdom, despises ordinary human necessities such as the preservation of life (*The chaplet* 11 [CCL 2, 1056–1058]). Faith is closely related to patience (*Concerning patience* 6 [CSEL 47, 10–11], where comparison is made with Abraham); one's faith is reflected in the quality of one's conduct (*The Prescription of Heretics* 41 [CCL 1, 222]).

But, in addition to these epistemological or soteriological considerations, Tertullian's view of faith is predominantly focused on its doctrinal truth. The reader cannot but be struck by this in the strongly argumentative tone of his writings. Here at least two points should be made. First of all, Tertullian refers repeatedly to the "regula fidei" (*The Prescription of Heretics* 13 [CCL 1, 197]; *Against Marcion* IV, 36 [CSEL 47, 546-547]; *Against Praxeas* 3 [CSEL 47, 230]; *Concerning the Veiling of Virgins* 1 [CSEL 76, 79]), which is a short summary of the main doctrines which comprise Christian faith. The following text may serve as an illustration.

> Now, with regard to this rule of faith—that we may from this point acknowledge what it is which we defend—it is, you must know, that which prescribes the belief that there is one only God, and that He is none other than the Creator of the world, who produced all things out of nothing through His own Word, first of all sent forth; that this Word is called His Son, and, under the name of God, was seen "in diverse manners" by the patriarchs, heard at all times in the prophets, at last brought down by the Spirit and Power of the Father into the Virgin Mary, was made flesh in her womb, and, being born of her, went forth as Jesus Christ; thenceforth He preached the new law and the new promise of the kingdom of heaven, worked miracles; having been crucified, He rose again the third day; (then) having ascended into the heavens, He sat at the right hand of the Father; sent instead of Himself the Power of the Holy Ghost to lead such as believe; will

come with glory to take the saints to the enjoyment of ever-lasting life and of the heavenly promises, and to condemn the wicked to everlasting fire, after the resurrection of both these classes shall have happened, together with the restoration of their flesh. This rule, as it will be proved, was taught by Christ, and raises amongst ourselves no other questions than those which heresies introduce, and which make men heretics (*Prescription* 13 [CCL 1, 197–198]; ANF III, 249).

In addition to and in contrast with the Trinitarian structure which one notes here, other summaries by Tertullian exhibit a binitarian form. This, along with the various wordings used in respective *regulae*, points to a certain fluidity in style and content in the way in which Tertullian conceived the *regula fidei*. Quasten summarizes Tertullian's presentation of the *regula fidei as* a "creed-like summary of the faith that corresponds very nearly to the baptismal symbol quoted by Hippolytus of Rome in his *Apostolic Tradition* of A.D. 217."[30]

Secondly, this faith was delivered to the Church by Christ through the apostles. This point is developed in *The Prescription of Heretics*, chapters 19 and following. The problem that Tertullian is confronting here is the fact that all of those whom he describes as heretics often make use of the Scriptures to argue for the validity of their position. Tertullian uses a legal procedure common within Roman law[31] to argue that one need not engage the heretics on the precise interpretation of Scripture because Scripture has been entrusted to a particular community of believers and, consequently, the heretics, being separated from that group, have no claim to interpret and base an argument upon Scripture.

Our appeal, therefore, must not be made to the Scriptures; nor must controversy be admitted on points in which the victory will either be impossible, or uncertain, or not certain enough....the natural order of things would require that this point should be first proposed, which is now the only one which we must discuss: "With whom lies that very faith to which the Scriptures belong? From what and through whom, and when, and to whom, has been handed down that rule, by which men become Christians?" For wherever it shall be manifest that the true Christian rule and faith shall be, there will likewise be the true Scriptures and expositions thereof, and all the Christian traditions (19 [CCL 1, 201]; ANF III, 251–252).

The subsequent chapter (20) proceeds to answer the questions posed in the above citation.

> Christ Jesus our Lord...did, whilst he lived on earth, Himself declare what He was, what He had been, what the Father's will was which He was administering, what the duty of man was which He was prescribing; (and this declaration He made,) either openly to the people, or privately to His disciples, of whom He had chosen the twelve chief ones to be at His side, and whom He destined to be the teachers of the nations. Accordingly, after one of these had been struck off, He commanded the eleven others on His departure to the Father, to "go and teach all nations, who were to be baptized into the Father, and into the Son, and into the Holy Ghost." Immediately, therefore so did the apostles, whom this designation indicates as "the sent." Having, on the authority of a prophecy, which occurs in a psalm of David, chosen Matthias by lot as the twelfth, into the place of Judas, they obtained the promised power of the Holy Ghost for the gift of miracles and of utterance; and after first bearing witness to the faith in Jesus Christ throughout Judaea, and founding churches (there), they next went forth into the world and preached the same doctrine of the same faith to the nations. They then in like manner founded churches in every city, from which all the other churches, one after another, derived the tradition of the faith, and the seeds of doctrine, and are every day deriving them, that they may become churches. Indeed, it is on this account only that they will be able to deem themselves apostolic, as being the offspring of apostolic churches. Every sort of thing must necessarily revert to its original for its classification. Therefore the churches, although they are so many and so great, comprise but the one primitive church, (founded) by the apostles, from which they all (spring). In this way all are primitive, and all are apostolic, whilst they are all proved to be one, in (unbroken) unity, by their peaceful communion, and title of brotherhood, and bond of hospitality,—privileges which no other rule directs than the one tradition of the selfsame mystery (CCL 1, 201–202; ANF III, 252).

From this Tertullian concludes that only the apostles whom Christ sent should be believed about the Christian faith, along with those churches which were founded by the apostles. "...those moulds and original sources of the faith must be reckoned for truth, as undoubtedly containing that which the (said) churches received from the apostles, the apostles from Christ, Christ from God. Whereas all doctrine must be prejudged as false which savours of contrariety to the truth of the churches and apostles of Christ and God" (21 [CCL 1, 202–203]; ANF III, 252). Which churches are to be considered apostolic? All those churches which profess the same doctrine which is professed in the churches founded by the apostles: "We hold communion with the apostolic churches because our doctrine is in no respect different from theirs" (21 [CCL 1, 203]; ANF III, 252–253).

Tertullian proceeds in the following chapters to respond to such objections as that the apostles did not sufficiently teach the truth that was handed on to them (22 [CCL 1, 33–35]), that they were imperfect and divided in their teaching (23–25 [CCL 1, 204–207]), that they held back the whole truth, reserving some of it for special friends (26 [CCL 1, 207–208]) and that their churches were unfaithful in passing it on (27 [CCL 1, 208–209]). His argument reaches a kind of crescendo in chapter 28, where Tertullian satirically taunts that, even if one supposes that the Holy Spirit should have failed in his office of leading the churches into the truth (Jn 14,26), "is it likely that so many churches, and they so great, should have gone astray into one and the same faith?...When, however, that which is deposited among many is found to be one and the same, it is not the result of error but of tradition. Can any one, then, be reckless enough to say that they were in error who handed on the tradition?" (28 [CCL 1, 209]; ANF III, 256). Underlying Tertullian's rhetoric here one glimpses the deep unity which he posits between the role of the Holy Spirit, on the one hand, and the faithful, unified handing on (tradition) of Christian faith, on the other.

Chapter 32 issues a challenge to his opponents to demonstrate that their churches are truly apostolic: "Let them produce the original records of their churches; let them unfold the roll of their bishops running down in due succession from the beginning in such a manner that that first bishop of theirs shall be able to show for his ordainer and predecessor some one of the apostles or of apostolic men,—a man, moreover, who continued steadfast with the apostles. For this is the manner in which the apostolic churches transmit their registers..." (32 [CCL 1, 212]; ANF III, 258). There follows a brief reference to the succession of leaders in the churches of Smyrna and Rome. But even if these opponents should try to contrive such a succession, he retorts, they would be proved wrong by the fact that their doctrine is so different from that of the apostles.

For their very doctrine, after comparison with that of the apostles, will declare, by its own diversity and contrariety, that it had for its author neither an apostle nor an apostolic man; because, as the apostles would never have taught things which were self-contradictory, so the apostolic men would not have inculcated teaching different from the apostles unless they who received their instruction from the apostles went and preached in a contrary manner. To this test, therefore will they be submitted for proof by those churches, who, although they derive not their founder from apostles or apostolic men (as being of much later date, for they are in fact being founded daily), yet, since they agree in the same faith, they are accounted as not less apostolic because they are akin in doctrine [*pro consanguinitate doctrinae*] (32 [CCL 1, 213]; ANF III, 258).

Finally, in Chapter 37, Tertullian applies all of this to the original question of who has the legal right to interpret the Scriptures.

Since this is the case,...heretics ought not to be allowed to challenge an appeal to the Scriptures.... and it may be very fairly said to them,...."As you are none of mine, what have you to do with what is mine? Indeed, Marcion, by what right do you hew my wood? By whose permission, Valentinus, are you diverting the streams of my fountain?...This (I say) is my property. I have long possessed it; I possessed it before you. I hold sure title-deeds from the original owners themselves, to whom the estate belonged. I am the heir of the apostles. Just as they carefully prepared their will and testament, and committed it to a trust, and adjured (the trustees to be faithful to their charge), even so do I hold it" (37 [CCL 1, 217–218]; ANF III, 261).

It is clear from this series of texts that, for Tertullian, faith concerns a specific doctrinal content, such as can be expressed in a short summary of the type of the *regulae* which he refers to on several occasions. Moreover, this faith has been placed in the hands of the apostolic churches. At least three comments are appropriate in this regard. First of all, for Tertullian there is a profound unity in the faith of all the apostolic churches. This unity is not only for him an evident fact which can be empirically verified by consulting with the churches of apostolic origin. It is also based upon the very notion of a tradition guided by the Holy Spirit. Secondly, this harmony is related to the apostles and to the churches that they founded. It is derived from a succession in leadership, as is attested to in Tertullian's use of the registers of leaders going back to the apostles. Yet, for Tertullian, it would appear that the decisive criterion is not that of leadership but rather that of faith. Even those recent churches which cannot trace a line of leaders back to the apostles are genuinely "apostolic" by virtue of a certain *consanguinitas doctrinae*. This accent leaves open the development in Tertullian's later Montanist writings of a view of the Church "of the Spirit" which can be contrasted with "the Church which consists of a number of bishops."[32] Finally, like Irenaeus before him, Tertullian even more forcefully rejects the interpretations of Scripture offered by his opponents, the "heretics." He is doubtful that mere arguing about the way Scripture is to be interpreted will produce thoroughly satisfying results. Rather, the interpretations of those who have not maintained continuity with the apostolic churches can and should be rejected *a priori*. Where the faith of the apostles is present, there also is the correct interpretation of Scripture. And this is to be found in the apostolic Church.

In his earlier writings, this Church is that which can show its line of descent from the apostles, although it includes also more recent churches which maintain consanguinity of doctrine with those churches and, hence, with the faith of the apostles. His later writings loosen and, indeed, seem to repudiate the connection between apostolicity and the churches which can establish their ministerial succession from the time of the apostles. Thus Tertullian's later, Montanist position does not seem to be entirely consistent with the argument in *The Prescription of Heretics*. His later de-emphasis and even scorn of ministerial succession could harmonize with the view that it is ultimately doctrinal consanguinity which is decisive for apostolicity. However, *The Prescription of Heretics* does not tend to admit any ultimate opposition between doctrinal consanguinity and ministerial succession.

6. CLEMENT OF ALEXANDRIA

If one considers Clement of Alexandria (c. 150 - c. 216) alongside of Irenaeus and Tertullian, who, roughly speaking, might be classified as his contemporaries, Clement stands out as offering a very different view of faith. The tone is strikingly less polemical and antagonistic than that which one finds in these other two writers, especially in Tertullian, although the purpose of Irenaeus' *Adversus haereses* almost necessarily carries with it a certain polemical tone as well. Clement instead, while he takes several occasions to reject the errors of certain gnostics, especially Valentinus and Basilides, nevertheless spends relatively little time combating the views of others. Indeed, the very word "gnostic" represents a perfection of the human person for Clement; faith is positively related to gnosis. Philosophy is evaluated as containing many elements of truth (*Exhortation* VI,67–72; *Stromata* I, chapters V-VII, XVII and XX) which can serve as resources for a more educated faith, one which goes beyond "naked faith" (*Stromata* I,IX,43,1) to a faith which is developed and enhanced by culture and reflection. Clement's writings themselves might serve as an illustration of this enhancement, so rich are they in knowledge of the philosophy, history, literature and religious thought of the ancient world.

Clement's surviving works are almost entirely limited to three interrelated writings: the *Exhortation to the Greeks* (one book of 12 chapters), the *Instructor* (three books of 13, 13 and 12 chapters respectively), and the *Stromata* or *Miscellanies* in eight books of various lengths.[33] These three writings form something of a complete whole in that the *Exhortation* invites its readers to initial conversion to the Christian faith; the *Instructor* discusses growth in faith and in *gnosis* under the tutelage of the Word (*Logos*) and includes a great many practical guidelines for daily life concerning such matters as eating, drinking, bathing and so forth; and the *Stromata* intends "to furnish the materials for the construction of a true gnosis, a Christian philosophy, on the basis of faith, and to lead on to this higher knowledge those who, by the discipline of the Paedagogus, had been trained for it."[34]

Something of the positive tone of Clement's presentation of faith in its relation to the perfection of the individual can be gleaned from the beautiful fifth and sixth chapters of the first book of the *Instructor*, which delights in the childlike quality which characterizes Christianity. Clement begins by noting that pedagogy concerns the formation or education (*'agogê*) of children (*paídôn*). "It remains for us to consider the children whom Scripture points to; then to give the paedogogue charge of them. We are the children" (*Instructor* I,V,12,1 [SC 70, 133]; ANF II, 212). He proceeds to link together a chain of New Testament texts which either call the followers of Jesus children or which praise children (Jn 21,4: "Children, have you any fish?"; Mt 19,14: "Let the children come to me...; for to such belongs the kingdom of heaven"; Mt 18,3–4: "unless you turn and become like children, you will never enter the kingdom of heaven. Whoever humbles himself like this child, he is the greatest in the kingdom of heaven"; Mt 21,16: "Out of the mouths of babes and sucklings thou hast brought perfect praise" [= Ps 8,2]; Jn 13,33: "Little children, yet a little while I am with you"; Mt 11,16-17: "But to what shall I compare this generation? It is like children sitting in the market places..."; Mt 25,33: "lambs"; Mt 10,16: "innocent as doves"; Mt 23,37: "O Jerusalem.... How often would I have gathered your children together as a hen gathers her brood under her wings....")." The Christian is like a child who is brought up into maturity under the guidance of Christ.

> We, then, who are infants, no longer roll on the ground, nor creep on the earth like serpents as before, crawling with the whole body about senseless lusts; but, stretching upwards in soul, loosed from the world and our sins, touching the earth on tiptoe so as to appear to be in the world, we pursue holy wisdom, although this seems folly to those whose wits are whetted for wickedness. Rightly, then, are those called children who know Him who is God alone as their Father, who are simple, and infants, and guileless... (*Instructor* I,V,16,3-17 [SC 70, 140-141]; ANF II, 213).

Whoever follows the command of Christ to take no thought of the needs of tomorrow but rather depends on the Father alone is in reality a child of God. This puts the Christian in a continual state of learning: "For so is the truth, that perfection is with the Lord, who is always teaching, and infancy and childishness with us, who are always learning" (*Instructor* I,V,17,3 [SC 70, 142-143]; ANF II, 213). Clement brings his meditation on childhood to a close reflecting on Isaiah's prophecy to the effect that the promised savior is spoken of as a child: "For to us a child is born, to us a son is given..." (Is 9,6). "O the great God! O the perfect child! The Son in the Father, and the Father in the Son. And how shall not the discipline of this child be perfect, which extends to all, leading as a schoolmaster us as children, who are His little ones? He has stretched forth to us those hands of His that are conspicuously worthy of trust (*pepisteuménas*; hence the SC translation puts it: 'l'object de notre pleine foi.')" (*Instructor* I,V,24,3 [SC 70, 152-155]; ANF II, 215).

Chapter Six of Book One of the *Instructor* continues to develop this theme of the growth of the Christian as an infant or as a child, but becomes more explicit in using the terminology of faith.

> For instruction leads to faith, and faith with baptism is trained by the Holy Spirit. For that faith is the one universal salvation of humanity, and that there is the same equality

before the righteous and loving God, and the same
fellowship between Him and all, the apostle most clearly
showed, speaking to the following effect: "Before faith came,
we were kept under the law, shut up unto the faith which
should afterwards be revealed, so that the law became our
schoolmaster to bring us to Christ, that we might be justified
by faith; but after that faith is come, we are no longer under a
schoolmaster" (Gal 3,23–25).... "For ye are all the children of
God through faith in Christ Jesus" (Gal 3,26). (*Instructor*
I,VI,30,2–31,1 [SC 70, 166–167]; ANF II, 217).

These reflections upon childhood, along with the many texts from
Chapters Five and Six of Book One of the *Instructor* concerned with
growing into an ever more mature faith, already indicate some of the
themes of what has been called Clement's masterpiece about faith, Book
Two of the *Stromata*. Here several of the already classic scriptural passages about faith are recalled: Hab 2,4–"the righteous shall live by faith";
Is 7,9–"If you will not believe surely you shall not be established" [LXX:
"neither shall you understand"]; Heb 11,1–2.6–"Now faith is the assurance of things hoped for, the conviction of things not seen. For by it the
men of old received divine approval.... And without faith it is impossible
to please him. For whoever would draw near to God must believe that he
exists and that he rewards those who seek him." Within the context of
these texts, Clement notes that faith "is a voluntary preconception, the
assent of piety" [*prolypsis hekousios, theosebeias synkatathesis*] (*Stromata*
II,II,8,4 [SC 38, 38]; ANF II, 349). Faith is a foundation for knowledge
(II,II,9,3). It cannot be demonstrated, and yet it is more sure than any
rational demonstration since it is nothing other than the acceptance of
the very voice of God (II,II,9,6). Because of this, faith is a gift, a grace
(II,IV,14,3), which bestows new eyes, new ears and a new heart
(II,IV,15,3). Faith can be said to be more important than and the criterion of knowledge (*gnosis*) (II,IV,15,5); and yet at the same time *pistis*
becomes *gnosis* and *gnosis* is rooted in *pistis* (II,IV,16,2). Faith is proleptic
(II,IV,17,3); it is an anticipatory knowledge which leads to growth into
further love (II,VI,30,3) and *gnosis* or knowledge (II,VI,31,1). Faith is the
support of the truth (II,VI,31,3).

Faith is thus necessary both for salvation and for growth into
more perfect knowledge. In the latter sense, it is the condition for the
possibility of true gnosticism which, it must be remembered, is nothing
but the maturation of the Christian life (II,XI,48,1–52,7): "The Gnostic
is therefore fixed by faith" (II,XI,51,3 [SC 38, 75]; ANF II, 359). This,

then, is a view of faith which attempts to root itself in Scripture but also search for what is useful in Greek philosophy, particularly insofar as the latter reflects upon the Logos. It is a view of faith which emphasizes its dynamic character, leading to growth not only into greater knowledge but into all of the virtues; faith is the basis of all the virtues.[35]

What might all of this be able to say to the question of unity in faith? Clement does not seem to have texts which speak about this topic with that kind of directness that one finds in Irenaeus or Tertullian. Because of his emphasis upon the reality of maturing and growing in faith, one might surmise that his view presupposes at least a degree of diversity in faith which would distinguish one who is less mature in faith from one who has arrived at greater maturity. Still, one passage about such growth explicitly states:

> And writing to the Ephesians, [Paul] has unfolded in the clearest manner the point in question, speaking to the following effect: "Till we all attain to the unity of the faith, and of the knowledge of God, to a perfect man, to the measure of the stature of the fulness of Christ: that we be no longer children, tossed to and fro by every wind of doctrine, by the craft of men, by their cunning in stratagems of deceit; but, speaking the truth in love, may grow up to Him in all things."—saying these things [for] the edification of the body of Christ, who is the head and man, the only one perfect in righteousness; and we who are children guarding against the blasts of heresies, which blow [to inflate us with pride]; and not putting our trust in fathers who teach us otherwise, are then made perfect when we are the church, having received Christ the head (*Instructor* I,V,18,3–4 [SC 70, 142–145]; ANF II, 213).

Evidently, for Clement, growth leads to "unity in faith" and to the rejection of the various "blasts of heresies." The last four chapters of Book VII of the *Stromata* take up again the question of heresies. Chapter XV attempts to respond to the objection of Greeks and Jews that the divisions among Christians damage their credibility and so absolve one from the need to take Christianity seriously. Clement responds that the Lord himself had predicted that there would be weeds among the wheat. Still one can distinguish between the two in that those Christians are to be believed who "in no way transgress the canon of the Church. And especially do we keep our profession in the most important points, while they traverse it" (*Stromata* VII,XV; PG 9, 525–526A; ANF II, 549). The following chapter (XVI; PG 9, 529–546) turns to the correct interpretation of Scriptures as an important means for distinguishing truth from heresy. Heretics are characterized as those who have "spurned the ecclesiastical tradition," ceasing to be "of God and to remain faithful to the Lord." In their interpretation, they fail to take the whole into consideration but rather select ambiguous passages and draw out their own opinions from them. In Chapter XVII (PG 9, 545–554), Clement has recourse to the argument from antiquity as a counter to the various doctrines of the heretics. This leads to the following passage on the unity of the Church:

> ...it is evident, from the high antiquity and perfect truth of the Church, that these later heresies, and those yet subsequent to them in time, were new inventions falsified [from the truth]. From what has been said, then, it is my opinion that the true Church, that which is really ancient, is one, and that in it those who according to God's purpose are just, are enrolled. For from the very reason that God is one, and the Lord one, that which is in the highest degree honourable is lauded in consequence of its singleness, being an imitation of the one first principle. In the nature of the One, then, is associated in a joint heritage the one Church, which they strive to cut asunder into many sects. Therefore in substance and idea, in origin, in pre-eminence, we say that the ancient and Catholic Church is alone, collecting as it does into the unity of the one faith...which results from the peculiar Testaments, or rather the one Testament in different times by the will of the one God, through one Lord—those already ordained, whom God predestinated, knowing before the foundation of the world that they would be righteous (PG 9, 551–552; ANF II, 555).

In summary, one might point out that Clement is obviously convinced of the unity of the Church in one faith. Heresies are later inventions which falsify the truth and threaten to break the Church into many factions. But by and large Clement's attention focuses not so much upon the overcoming of divisions in faith. His more characteristic contribution to Christian thought about faith emphasizes the positive theme of the ability to grow in faith and the complementarity between faith and reason.

7. ORIGEN

Origen is one of the most prolific and influential writers, not only of the early third century in which he lived, but of the entire patristic period. The sheer volume of his output is quite astounding: Eusebius of Caesarea, an admirer, compiled a list of some 2000 titles and Jerome, depending on Eusebius, lists 800 of Origen's works.[36] This vast output was facilitated by the fact that wealthy friends supplied Origen with a number of stenographers and copyists who put into writing his various lectures at Alexandria and Caesarea, where he was at the head of the Christian catechetical schools from 203–231 and from 231–254, respectively.[37] His writings are usually grouped into several broad categories: 1) textual criticism, especially the *Hexapla*, a work which lined up in parallel columns the Hebrew text of the Old Testament, a Greek paraphrase and four Greek translations; 2) exegetical works which included commentaries and homilies on many books of the Bible, among the more famous being those on the gospels of Matthew and John; 3) apologetical treatises, the most extensive and famous being his *Contra Celsum*, written toward the end of his life as a refutation of a virulently anti-Christian work by that author under the title of *True Discourse*; 4) dogmatic writings, especially the *De principiis* (*Peri archon*), which has been hailed as the first systematic work of Christian theology[38] and which hence has sometimes gained for Origen the title of "father of Christian theology"; and 5) practical writings, such as his commentary on the Lord's prayer, the first to appear in Christian literature and the beginning of a long line of similar commentaries, or his *Exhortation to martyrdom*.

While much of Origen's work has not survived, partially because of the condemnation of fifteen of his doctrines by the Synod of Constantinople in 543 and his later being listed among the heretics by the Fifth General Council in 553, nevertheless that which remains fills many volumes of the standard patristic collections such as Migne's *Patrologia greca*, *Die griechischen christlichen Schriftsteller* and *Sources chrétiennes*. Our observations here about Origen's doctrine of faith will be guided by authoritative commentators who have focused their study in a special way upon Origen and on the specific theme of the patristic doctrine concerning faith.

Origen appears to have been less enthusiastic about the positive values of Greek philosophy than was his predecessor as head of the school at Alexandria, Clement.[39] This may be in part explained by the fact that he was born into a Christian family and was nourished from his youth on study of the Scriptures, unlike Clement whose path to

Christianity was preceded by formative years seeking wisdom in Greek philosophy and culture.[40] Escribano-Alberca begins his account of Origen's doctrine of faith, the longest single section in his survey of patristic thought on this theme, with a section on the Word of Scripture as the origin of faith.[41] Commenting on Moses' response to Yahweh in Ex 4,10: "Oh, my Lord, I am not eloquent...," Origen notes that the greatest of human eloquence is dumb, when compared with that of the Logos.[42] Against the gnostic tendencies of the time to separate the Old and New Testaments, Origen emphasizes that it is the same Word which inspires and speaks through both.[43] This Word is bread to be eaten for the nourishment of the soul.[44] Origen applies the image of the "faithful and true" one who rides on a white horse (Apoc 19,11) to the relation between the Logos and the words and letters of Scripture; the latter bear the Word who is thus accessible, hearable, by means of Scripture.[45]

Origen points out that the wells in Genesis 24 and 29, where the patriarchs met their wives, are figures of the Scriptures; by familiarity with the Scriptures an intimate union or spiritual marriage comes about between the soul and the Word.[46] Origen is very aware of the progressive nature of this relationship with the Word. The sense of growth toward greater knowledge and intimacy is highlighted by his distinction between simple faith and seeing faith or *gnosis*. Origen's notion of simple faith finds expression in his defense against the charge of Celsus that Christianity is credulous (*Contra Celsus* I,9–13 [SC 132, 96–113]). Origen responds that there is as much investigation and reasoning about difficult doctrines and passages in Scripture among Christians as among the adherents of any religion or philosophy. Nevertheless, the simple faith of those who have neither the time nor the disposition to inquire into complex arguments is not to be despised. Simple faith is part of God's merciful plan, which gives access to the benefits of knowledge of the truth and of conversion of the moral life to a vast array of people. Moreover, faith is the initial point of departure for entering into any philosophy and, indeed, for the many normal human activities such as undertaking a voyage, getting married or planning a business venture. When faith is so necessary for all human endeavors, how much more reasonable it is to have faith in the word of God (*Contra Celsum* I,10–11 [SC 132, 102–107]).

Having defended the value and utility of simple faith, however, Origen is clear that a faith which is developed by reasoning, which attains to knowledge of God by means of the wisdom of God (*Contra Celsum* I,13 [SC 132, 110–113]), is preferable to simple faith (cf. *Contra Celsum* V,20 [SC 147, 62–63]). He writes of this growth in the following words:

But when the Word of God says, "No man knoweth the Father but the Son, and he to whomsoever the Son will reveal Him," He declares that no one can know God but by the help of divine grace coming from above, with a certain divine inspiration. Indeed, it is reasonable to suppose that the knowledge of God is beyond the reach of human nature, from which stem the many errors into which men have fallen in their views of God. It is, then, through the goodness and love of God to mankind, and by a marvellous exercise of divine grace to those whom He saw in His foreknowledge, and knew that they would walk worthy of Him [that he] made Himself known to them.... In whatever part of the world he [a Christian] is, he prays; but he rises above the universe, "shutting the eyes of sense, and raising upwards the eyes of the soul." And he stops not at the vault of heaven; but passing in thought beyond the heavens, under the guidance of the Spirit of God, and having thus as it were gone beyond the visible universe, he offers prayers to God. But he prays for no trivial blessings, for he has learnt from Jesus to seek for nothing small or mean, that is, sensible objects, but to ask only for what is great and truly divine; and these things God grants to us, to lead us to that blessedness which is found only with Him through His Son, the Word, who is God (*Contra Celsum* VII,44 [SC 150, 116–121]).[47]

For Origen, simple faith, although it is both reasonable and laudable, is clearly not the final, more perfect state of knowledge which has become possible in Christ. Aided by God's grace the eyes of the soul are raised upward, piercing the heavens and resulting in a passage from blindness to sight.

For every one who sees with the eyes of his soul serves the Divine Being in no other way than in that which leads him ever to have regard to the Creator of all, to address his prayers to Him alone, and to do all things as in the sight of God, who sees us altogether, even to our thoughts. Our earnest desire then is both to see for ourselves, and to be leaders of the blind, to bring them to the Word of God, that He may take away from their minds the blindness of ignorance. And if our actions are worthy of Him who taught His disciples, "Ye are the light of the world," and of the

Word, who says, "The light shineth in darkness," then we shall give wisdom to those who are without it, and we shall instruct the ignorant [and teach the infants] (*Contra Celsum* VII,51 [SC 150, 134–137]; ANF IV, 632).

Damien van den Eynde has compiled a brief list of texts from Origen which convey a sense of two levels of the knowledge of God: faith and *gnosis*, simple faith and faith par excellence, "preaching" and "doctrine," simple teachings and those which are more difficult and more elevated, the instruction given to beginners and those beautiful and sublime doctrines destined for the perfect.[48] Initial faith in the preaching of the Church, based upon the message of the Scriptures, is always the necessary point of departure for further growth.[49] The *gnosis* into which the more perfect grow is above all an understanding of the mysteries of the Scriptures, which, written under the inspiration of God, are worthy of their author and thus contain an immeasurable wealth of wisdom, especially when understood in their spiritual sense. *Gnosis*, according to Origen, "is essentially a divine illumination, a religious knowledge which has faith as its point of departure and ecstasy as its goal."[50] The degree to which this doctrine—i.e. that simple faith is far surpassed by the *gnosis* of those who are more perfect—is akin to the gnostic heresies of the early Church is disputed among scholars. J. Lebreton sees here a rather dangerous elitism, while Van den Eynde points out various texts in which Origen explicitly distances himself from the various well-known gnostics of the early Church.[51] In any case, it is clear that for Origen faith begins a growth into further knowledge. This growth is conditioned not only by study and reflection but also by growth in moral perfection.[52]

What can be said about unity in faith according to Origen? While the various secondary sources concerning the patristic doctrine of faith do not indicate specific texts from Origen on the Church's unity in faith, a number of passages do shed light on what he might say about this topic. One appears at the beginning of the first book of his *De principiis* (I,Preface,2):

Since many, however, of those who profess to believe in Christ differ from each other, not only in small and trifling matters, but also on subjects of the highest importance, as, e.g., regarding God, or the Lord Jesus Christ, or the Holy Spirit; and not only regarding these, but also regarding others which are created existences, viz., the powers and the holy virtues; it seems on that account necessary first of all to fix a definite limit and to lay down an unmistakeable rule regarding each one of these, and then to pass to the investigation of other points. For as we ceased to seek for truth (notwithstanding the professions of many among Greeks and Barbarians to make it known) among all who claimed it for erroneous opinions, after we had come to believe that Christ was the Son of God, and were persuaded that we must learn it from Himself; so, seeing there are many who think they hold the opinions of Christ, and yet some of these think differently from their predecessors, yet as the teaching of the Church, transmitted in orderly succession from the apostles, and remaining in the Churches to the present day, is still preserved, that alone is to be accepted as truth which differs in no respect from ecclesiastical and apostolical tradition (SC 252, 78–79; ANF IV, 239).

Here one sees a clear acknowledgment of the existence of unacceptable differences among those who claim to be Christians and recourse to what had been handed on from the apostles as a criterion for limiting such diversity. The paragraph (*De principiis* I,Preface,3) which follows the text cited above asserts that the apostles delivered with utmost clearness certain doctrines which were necessary for everyone, even those who are dull, leaving, however, the grounds within their statements for further understanding by those who are led by the gifts of the Holy Spirit to attain it. *De principiis* I,Preface,4–8, proceeds to list the teachings which the apostles clearly handed on to the Church:

> *section 4*—three paragraphs devoted respectively to the
> Father, Jesus Christ and the Holy Spirit;
> *section 5*—the immortality and freedom of the human soul;
> *section 6*—concerning the devil and his angels;
> *section 7*—on the creation of the world;
> *section 8*—on the inspiration and spiritual sense of the Scriptures.

Throughout these sections, Origen repeatedly makes reference to the fact that these doctrines are "taught throughout the Churches" and are "the teaching of the Church" or "part of the Church's teaching." Several points about unity in faith are clear from these remarks. First of all, unity is to be found in the teachings which come from the apostles and which continue to be taught within the Church. Second, this unity is based upon a series of relatively precise doctrines which are held by all. Third, such unity leaves room for some diversity, particularly that between those who have greater understanding by means of the gifts of the Holy Spirit and those who have less.

Because of the Trinitarian structure of section 4, one might ask about the possible relation of Origen's list of essential doctrines to the early creeds which were emerging in connection with baptism. His enumeration of articles is somewhat free, as can be seen in his adding, as part of the teaching which is to be found in the Church, such doctrines as the immortality of the soul, human freedom, angels and devils—doctrinal material which one does not find in the early creeds. Moreover, some points often mentioned in the creeds—the risen Jesus seated at the right hand of the Father, his coming in glory as judge at the end of time, the holy Church—are absent from Origen's enumeration. Thus it would appear that Origen never actually quoted a baptismal creed as such.[53]

This text from the preface of Book I of *De principiis* is but one of several in which the same kind of listing of essential articles of faith can be found. Others include the *Commentary on St. John* XXXII,16,187–189 (SC 385, 268–269), the *Commentary on St. Matthew*, ser. 33 (PG 13, 1643D–1644B and GCS 38, 61) and *In Ep. ad Tit.* (PG 14, 1303C–1306A). The text from the *Commentary on St. John* appears within the context of interpreting the phrase "all faith" (*pasan ten pistin*; cf. 1 Cor 13,2: "and if I have all faith so as to remove mountains"). Interpreting this expression as meaning completeness of faith, Origen proceeds to give examples of a faith which would lack certain fundamental elements, such as believing in Jesus but not that one and the same God was God of both the Old and New Testaments or believing that Jesus suffered under Pontius Pilate but not that he was born of the Virgin Mary and the Holy Spirit and so forth. Such a believer would lack a fundamental article of the faith (*pisteos kephalaio*). The text in the *Commentary on St. Matthew* follows the mention of individuals or groups who were generally considered by the patristic writings to be heretics: Marcion, Basilides, the Valentinians, the Apellians and the Ophites. Those who, unlike these aforementioned who have fallen away from the truth, wish not to dissent from the public and manifest articles of faith (*de publicis quidem et manifestis capitulis*) will adhere to the Trinitarian structured list of doctrines, which Origen then proceeds to list. These examples suffice to show that a certain body of fundamental doctrines, believed by the Church as a whole, formed a criterion on the basis of which Origen identified those who did not hold such doctrines as heretics.

The theme of heresy is taken up in a somewhat different context in *De principiis* IV,I,9, where Origen speaks of the cause of heresy as rooted in a misinterpretation of the Scriptures, deriving principally from a lack of understanding Scripture's spiritual sense. In contrast to the false interpretations of the heretics, Origen proposes to spell out the suitable method of interpretation for those "who cling to the standard (*kanonos*) of the heavenly Church of Jesus Christ according to the succession of the apostles" (SC 268, 300–301; ANF IV, 357). He proceeds to recount the mysterious depth of Scripture, spelling out the threefold sense which is to be there found. But the relevant point for the present discussion is Origen's insistence that correct interpretation is related to "the rule (*kanon*) of the heavenly Church of Jesus Christ transmitted by the succession of the apostles." The Word of God as given in Scripture is without a doubt the point of departure for so much of what Origen says about knowledge of God in faith and *gnosis*. But he sees a deep tie between this word and the Church which has been charged to preach the gospel to every creature.[54] Girod concludes his brief summary of the relation between Church and scripture according to Origen with the words: "The Scripture is indeed the book in which Origen learned everything. But, for him, it cannot be read except within the Church."[55]

In summary, we find in Origen a strong statement that faith and knowledge are ultimately based upon the revealed Word, in contrast to which all human speech is mute. But once this Word is received in faith, a fruitful reflection leading to knowledge and holiness takes off. Origen gives the ecclesial and apostolic tradition a decisive role in the fostering of unity in faith. At several points he provides a list of clear, fundamental doctrines which all must accept. In addition Origen attributes the Church's unity or division in faith to respectively correct or mistaken ways of interpreting the scriptures.

CONCLUSION

This chapter has considered seven authors writing during the period from 100 to 250. One is struck by the wealth of different reflections about faith, conditioned largely by the strikingly diverse situations within which each author wrote. Clement of Rome and Ignatius of Antioch were concerned with faith's place in healing divisions within specific local communities. Justin sought to render Christian faith credible within the context of Jewish and Greek objections. Irenaeus and Tertullian attempted to preserve the traditional Christian doctrines of faith against the speculations of the gnostics. And Clement of Alexandria and Origen tried to harmonize faith with reason so as to guide their readers to that fruitful knowledge of revelation which is part of Christian maturity.

Common to all of these authors is an awareness of the multi-dimensionality of faith, particularly in that it incorporates both doctrinal and existential aspects. One notices in Western writers such as Irenaeus and Tertullian a general tendency toward a negative evaluation of reason's ability to express faith, while Clement of Alexandria and Origen tend to evaluate reason more positively. Various positions about the relation of scriptural interpretation to faith are in evidence: for Justin, biblical interpretation centering on the fulfillment of prophecy can show the reasonability of Christian faith; for Irenaeus and Tertullian, heretical interpretations are rejected a priori because their proponents lack appropriate apostolic credentials; for Clement of Alexandria and Origen allegorical and mystical interpretation leads to the higher Christian life, nourished by the depth of the wisdom contained in God's Word. While all of the authors studied hold that the Church is and ought to be one and that its unity includes unity in faith, this theme appears more prominently in Ignatius of Antioch, Irenaeus and Tertullian than in the two Clements, Justin and Origen. Still, a common thread is to grant to the Church and its leaders a significant role in fostering unity in faith.

We will return again to some of the specific contributions of these early writers concerning faith and its unity in the final chapter. But the scene is about to change rather dramatically with the civil recognition of Christianity and the appearance, within the very bosom of the great Church, of the monumental Trinitarian and Christological controversies which dominated the fourth and early fifth centuries. To some of the principal figures in these momentous developments we must now turn.

Chapter Six
FAITH AND ITS UNITY IN EASTERN PATRISTIC WRITERS AFTER NICEA

Origen died around the year 255. The latter half of the third century was a relatively quiet period in patristic writing,[1] which would explode again into the intense literary activity which Quasten calls the "golden age of ecclesiastical literature" after the Edict of Milan by Constantine in 314, which officially tolerated the practice of Christianity within the Roman empire.[2] The large amount of material which resulted from this "explosion" is too extensive to be treated in a single chapter. For this reason, the present chapter will limit itself to a number of the principal fathers who wrote in Greek: Athanasius, Cyril of Jerusalem, the Cappadocians (Basil, Gregory of Nazianzus and Gregory of Nyssa), John Chrysostom, Cyril of Alexandria and Theodoret of Cyrus. The following chapter will analyze the contributions to our theme of three major authors who wrote in Latin: Hilary of Poitier, Ambrose of Milan and Augustine of Hippo.

As will soon be seen, the problems of maintaining unity in faith, posed from within the Christian community first by Arianism and later by Nestorianism, exercised a dominant influence upon those who were writing in the Greek-speaking areas of Christianity during the fourth and fifth centuries. This will profoundly affect what they write about faith, although in most cases one also finds interesting reflections about faith which are not directly related to these two great doctrinal controversies.

1. ATHANASIUS

J.A. Möhler's famous study of this prominent patristic figure, active as a bishop and leading proponent of the doctrine of Nicea during the stormy period between the first two ecumenical councils, was entitled simply *Athanasius the Great*.[3] Athanasius was esteemed and translated by John Henry Newman during the revival of patristic studies in England in the mid-nineteenth century and Quasten notes that he was called "the father of orthodoxy" by the Greek Church.[4] In light of such high regard, it is rather surprising that the surveys concerning the patristic doctrine of faith, which have served as a principal point of departure for the research underlying the present book, make so little mention of him.[5] How can this be explained?

The fundamental reason lies in the fact that Athanasius (295–373) was not interested in analyzing and describing "faith" as such but rather in defending correct doctrine. For him, "faith" is roughly equivalent to sound doctrine.[6] He opens his early *Discourse against the Greeks* by proposing to "set forth a few points of the faith" (PG 25, 3–4; LNPF IV, 4), thereby implying that he understands "faith" along the lines of the all-encompassing sum total of Christian doctrine. In his *Discourses against the Arians* (1,2 and 3,27 [PG 26, 13–14 and 381–382]), faith is presented as the opposite of the heretical teachings of the Arians. His *Letter to Serapion* (1,28 [PG 26, 593–594]) attributes as the motive of all his efforts the aim of substantiating "the very tradition, teaching, and faith of the Catholic Church from the beginning, which the Lord gave, the Apostles preached, and the Fathers kept."[7] Even the spurious works which at one time or another had been attributed to Athanasius and whose titles suggest a substantial treatment of faith, such as *Sermo major de fide* (PG 26, 1263–1294) and *Expositio fidei* (PG 25, 199–208), consider faith as an ensemble of doctrines. Because of this concentration upon correct doctrine, Athanasius' writings, while quite useful in bringing into relief various dimensions of specific Christian teachings, offer less material directly relevant to the precise topic of the present book—the meaning of faith and of its unity. Nevertheless, a few points from the writings and activities of the "father of orthodoxy" are of interest for our present theme and should be briefly mentioned.

First of all, Athanasius may be viewed as a transitional figure, whose writings represent a certain shift in focus which occurred in patristic literature with the advent of Arianism and the beginning of the ecumenical councils. This transition can be glimpsed when one compares his *Discourse against the Greeks* and its companion work *Discourse on the Incarnation of the Word*, probably written in 318,[8] with most of his later writings. The former treatises argue against the idolatry of the Greeks and the unbelief of the Jews in a way that reminds one of the earlier apologetical works of Justin, Clement of Alexandria or Origen. In contrast, after the first ecumenical council of Nicea in 325, at which

Athanasius was present as the then thirty year old deacon and secretary to Bishop Alexander of Alexandria, his writings become devoted almost entirely to the controversy within the Christian community which raged around the correct understanding of Christ and the Trinity. In contrast with Irenaeus or Tertullian, who at the end of the second century appealed to such principles as apostolic succession to dismiss the authority of those against whom they argued, Athanasius struggled against the views of individuals such as Arius who enjoyed considerable ecclesiastical and civil recognition. Such support from Church and state leaders for Arius was strong enough to lead to the deposition of Athanasius from the see of Alexandria five times!

This change in context required a different method of theological argumentation. Athanasius could not simply call into question the authority of those whom he opposed; he needed to marshall careful argumentation and biblical interpretation to demonstrate the correctness of his views. Scripture remains his fundamental source and basis for sound doctrine. Athanasius' Thirty-ninth *Festal Letter* (PG 26, 1177–1178 and 1437–1438) presents for the first time our list of twenty-seven books of the New Testament as those which alone can be considered canonical.[9] Yet, at the same time Athanasius argues for the legitimacy and necessity of non-scriptural terminology in expounding and defending correct doctrine. Thus his *Letter on the Decrees of the Council of Nicea* (PG 25, 415–476; LNPF IV, 150–172) attempts to show that the non-biblical word "homoousious" is consonant with the understanding of Christ found in Scripture as well as in the writings of many earlier ecclesiastical writers.[10] In all of this one can see that the unity in faith which Athanasius promoted is based upon conformity with Scripture and tradition as well as an appropriate use of new terminology which is developed to handle difficulties which may arise in the course of time.

In addition to his use of Scripture, tradition and reason, Athanasius stands as a witness to several other, even more transparently ecclesial means to counter heresy and thus to foster the unity of the Church in the true faith. Three deserve specific mention: emphasis upon the authority of the Council of Nicea, letters to other bishops and appeal to the bishop of Rome. The first of these is very apparent throughout Athanasius' writings and may be verified by perusing the already mentioned *Letter on the Decrees of the Council of Nicea*. With regard to the second—epistolatory contact with other bishops—not only do the letters written to all the bishops of the world (PG 25, 221–240; LNPF IV, 91–96) and to the bishops of Egypt (PG 25, 537–594; LNPF IV, 222–235) on the occasion of two of his depositions from the see of Alexandria serve as witness to this, but so do many letters written to individual bishops on specific questions, usually in connection with one or another aspect of Arianism.[11] Finally, the *Apology against the Arians* (PG 25, 247–410; LNPF IV, 97–147) contains documentation concerning the support which Athanasius solicited and received from Pope Julius and a synod held in Rome in the year 341. These references reveal Athanasius' conviction about the important role that bishops, councils and the pope play in fostering correct doctrine and thereby also the Church's unity in faith.

2. CYRIL OF JERUSALEM

A second writer from this period who has an important contribution to make with regard to the topic of faith and the Church's unity in faith is St. Cyril of Jerusalem (315–387). Cyril was not prolific. In addition to his short "Sermon on the Paralytic," "Letter to Constantius" and several fragments, Cyril's principal contribution to patristic literature is his "Lenten Catechesis," a series of twenty-four lectures given during Lent and Easter week around 350 to those who were baptized that year in the church of the Holy Sepulchre in Jerusalem.[12] The Catechesis is divided into an introductory lecture (Procatechesis), which exhorts the listeners to enter wholeheartedly into the final step of the catechumenate which they are now beginning; eighteen lectures, which speak of repentance, baptism and faith and which give an explanation of the Creed used in Jerusalem; and five lectures (the mystagogical catechesis) given immediately after Easter, which explain the sacraments of baptism, chrismation and the eucharist.[13] The text appears to be a transcription of the actual oral catecheses themselves, able to include, therefore, such dramatic touches as directing the hearer's gaze toward the hill of Golgotha as Cyril recalls that after only an hour of faith the good thief was granted eternal life (V,10) or as he expounds the meaning of Jesus' saving death (see XIII,4). The lectures constitute a unique treasure in that they provide a picture from the mid-fourth century Jerusalem community both of the celebration of the liturgy and the sacraments as well as of the explanation of the faith given to those about to be received into the community of believers. Several points relevant to the theme of faith and its unity should be noticed.

First of all, lecture V is dedicated specifically to the topic of faith. Cyril notes that to be transferred from the rank of catechumens to that of the faithful is a great dignity granted by the Lord; it brings one into communion with Jesus (V,1; quoting 1 Cor 1,9). The believer is truly wealthy, even though he be poor (V,2). Simply from the point of view of daily human activities, a certain common "faith" is indispensable, for example, that type of trusting faith needed when entering into a marriage or planting crops or undertaking a voyage by sea (V,3). How much more reasonable it is, therefore, to embrace that true faith, without which it is impossible to please God (V,4; quoting Heb 11,6). Here Cyril enlists a favorite patristic text—Is 7,9: "If you will not believe, you shall not understand"—to argue that it is only faith which allows one to understand virtues and vices for what they are, thus making possible a life pleasing to God. Abraham is pointed to as an example of trusting in God's promises (V,5-6), as well as Peter, whose walking upon the water (Mt 14,29-32) illustrates the power of faith (V,7). The faith of believers can also have a salutary effect upon others, as in the case of the paralytic (Mt 9,2-6) or of Lazarus (Jn 11,34-40), whom Jesus healed and restored to life in response to the faith of their friends and family (V,8-9). There are two kinds of faith for Cyril: dogmatic faith which assents to truths and which thereby allows one to pass from death to life (V,10) and the special gift of faith which enables one to perform works which are beyond merely human power, the faith that can move mountains (V,11; citing Mt 17,20). Finally, the most important doctrinal points, all of which are confirmed by the Scriptures, have been collected into a summary by the Church and are now handed on to the catechumens for their knowledge and as a protection against the false doctrines of the heretics.

> In learning and professing the faith, embrace and guard that only which is now delivered to you by the Church, and confirmed by all the Scriptures. For since not everyone has both the education and the leisure required to read and know the Scriptures, to prevent the soul perishing from ignorance, we sum up the whole doctrine of the faith in a few lines. This summary I wish you to commit to memory, word for word, and to repeat among yourselves with all zeal, not writing it on paper, but engraving it by memory on the heart....For not according to men's pleasure have the articles of faith been composed, but the most important points collected from the Scriptures make up one complete teaching of the faith (V,12 [PG 33, 519-522]; McCauley, 146)....Guard them with care else by chance the enemy may despoil those who have grown remiss, or some heretic may pervert the traditions entrusted to you (V,13 [PG 33, 523-524]; McCauley, 147).

Here one should notice the relation between the Scriptures and the summary of doctrine handed on in the catechesis before baptism. For Cyril, this doctrine is none other than that which is found in Scripture; his method throughout all of the catecheses consists in a demonstration of the truth of doctrine on the basis of biblical testimony.[14] Secondly, the Church is presented as capable of summing up the whole of Christian doctrine in a few lines, which in turn has a formative influence upon the faith of the individuals about to receive baptism—they learn this summary by heart. Finally, the faith which is learned by catechumens serves as a safeguard against false doctrines proffered by the "enemy" or by "some heretic." In a rather concise way, these sentences reveal the interrelation between Scripture, Church, the individual and unity in faith (which in this case is implied in caution about the "perversions" of heresy).

Thus lecture V constitutes a marvelous description of faith. It is an act of trust in God (as in the case of Abraham and Peter) as well as the acceptance of doctrine based upon Scripture. Faith allows one to please God and leads to salvation. It engages both the individual and the community. Faith is the grace-enabled act of the individual, who places trust in God and engraves the summary of doctrine upon his heart. At the same time, the Church discerns the content of this doctrine and presents it to the neophyte who is then formed in the faith. It is interesting to notice that Cyril speaks about the relation between faith and life everlasting when he comments upon "dogmatic faith":

> Dogmatic faith involves an assent to some truth; and this truly profits the soul, as the Lord says: "He who hears my words, and believes him who sent me, has life everlasting; and does not come to judgment." ...For, if you believe that Jesus Christ is Lord, and that God raised Him from the dead, you will be saved and translated into paradise by Him who brought the robber into paradise. Doubt not that this is possible; for He who here on holy Golgotha saved the robber after a single hour of faith will save you also when you believe (V,10 [PG 33, 517–518]; McCauley, 145).

For Cyril, clearly, any opposition between saving faith and faith in doctrine is out of the question; such an opposition would contradict the testimony of Scripture.

Stepping back from Lecture V and taking a view of the Catechesis as a whole, several further points should be made. First of all, the importance of Scripture in Cyril's Catechesis must be underscored. Lecture IV, a preliminary summary of the principal Christian doctrines which is intended to introduce the catechumens into the subject matter which they will consider at greater length in the course of the subsequent Lenten lectures, closes with several paragraphs about the Scriptures (IV,33–37). In addition to the legend about the miraculous translation of the Hebrew Scriptures into Greek (IV,34), here one finds a list of the canonical books of the Old and New Testaments, prefaced by the following remark: "Study earnestly only those books which we read openly in Church. For far wiser and more devout than yourself were the Apostles and the ancient bishops, the rulers of the Church, who handed down these books" (IV,35 [PG 33, 497–498]; McCauley, 136). Clearly Cyril sees an intimate relation between Scripture and Church here, in that the Church can discern which books make up the inspired canon.

Secondly, the catecheses not only expound in a positive way the principal points of Christian faith, showing them to be rooted in Scripture, but also they negatively argue against various false views of heretics, Jews, Samaritans and Gentiles (Protocatechesis, 10). The danger of these various viewpoints is noted in a general way throughout Lecture IV and elaborated with greater specificity in Lecture VI with regard to the correct doctrine about God, Lecture XII concerning the incarnation, Lecture XV on interpretations of Christ's second coming and Lecture XVI about the Holy Spirit. What strikes one about these warnings is the fact that Cyril is here preparing catechumens for baptism. We are not dealing here, as it were, with a debate among professional theologians but rather with the necessary formation of those who wish to enter the community of the faithful. Catechesis, therefore, both expounds the faith and distinguishes from it those doctrines or interpretations which are incompatible with communion in the same faith. The obvious presupposition of Cyril's procedure here is that communion in faith is partially a result of the Church's catechesis.

Third, the Creed as a summary of those principal doctrines contained in Scripture is an important tool in such catechesis. Such a credal summary appears in Cyril as a kind of practical necessity, since an exhaustive study of all of Scripture is not possible for most individuals. This led to the development of a particular literary genre, of which Cyril's Lectures are among the first, that is, a commentary or explanation of the Creed, usually written with a view to catechesis. J.N.D. Kelly's "Introduction" to Rufinus' commentary on the Apostles' Creed begins its list of those who used this literary form with Cyril of Jerusalem (referring to the Catechetical Lectures, especially nos. VI to XVIII) and adds the names of Gelasius of Caesarea (d. 395), Niceta of Remesiana (c. 385–415), Ambrose of Milan (c. 339–397) and Augustine of Hippo (354-

430) to that of Tyrannius Rufinus (c. 345–410) as among those who followed Cyril in writing such a work.[15] Thus we see here in Cyril's
Catechetical Lectures the beginning of a "tradition" of writing expositions of the Creed, a tradition which expresses the conviction of a number of patristic writers that faith can be presented in a summary form
which expresses the essential doctrine of the Scriptures and that the
unity of the Church in the same faith is brought about in part by the formation of those who wish to become Christians in the correct understanding of this summary.

3. BASIL THE GREAT

> Almost the whole East, most honorable Father (and by the
> East I mean the regions from Illyricum to Egypt), is being
> shaken by a mighty storm and flood. The old heresy sown by
> Arius, the enemy of truth, is now shamelessly springing up,
> like a bitter root that yields deadly fruit, and is finally prevail-
> ing. For, as a result of calumny and abuse, the champions of
> sound faith in each diocese have been banished from the
> Church, and the control of affairs has been handed over to
> those who are leading captive the souls of purest faith
> (Epistola 70 [PG 32, 433–434]).[16]

So writes St. Basil the Great (c. 330–379) in the year 371 to an unnamed
addressee, who is generally considered to be Pope Damasus (pope from
366–384).[17] The struggle for the acceptance of the orthodox faith as
defined by the first ecumenical Council of Nicea in 325 against Arius is
the overarching context for considering St. Basil's comments about
faith. Basil not only appealed to Pope Damasus that he visit the East to
help combat the spread of Arianism, finally overcome only by the first
Council of Constantinople (381) with the support of the emperor
Theodosius, but also requested that St. Athanasius of Alexandria write a
circular letter to all the bishops encouraging communion in the same
faith (Letter 82). The struggle against erroneous doctrines recurs repeatedly in Basil's letters and is echoed also in his short essay *Concerning
Faith* and in his work entitled *Morals*.[18] For Basil, the Creed accepted by
Nicea is an important tool for promoting unity in faith:

> Therefore, let us seek for nothing more, but hold out to
> the brethren who wish to be united with us the Creed of
> Nicaea; and, if they agree with it, let us require further that

they must not say that the Holy Spirit is a creature, nor be in communion with those who say it. But, I think that we should demand nothing beyond this. In fact, I am convinced that by a longer association and an experience together without strife, even if it should be necessary to add more for the purpose of explanation, the Lord who makes all things work together unto good for those who love Him will grant it (Letter 113 [PG 32, 527–528]; Way I, 240).

Indeed, in several letters concerned with the unity of the Church in one faith, Basil quotes either entirely (Letters 125 and 140) or in part (Letters 128 and 159) the words of the Nicene Creed. Nevertheless, it is clear that the Creed of Nicea is not considered by Basil as the final and wholly adequate statement of Christian faith. Letters 125, 140 and 159 note that questions about the divinity of the Holy Spirit had not yet appeared at the time of Nicea, with the result that the third article of its Creed simply states "[We believe]...in the Holy Spirit." As in Letter 113 cited above, Basil felt it necessary to add a more explicit confession about the divinity of the Holy Spirit, something which would be done by Constantinople I two years after Basil's death. Still, he was very cautious about what could be added to the Creed, as is reflected in his comments in Letter 258, 2, to Bishop Epiphanius:

> ...we are not able to add anything at all to the Nicene Creed, not the slightest thing, except the glorification of the Holy Spirit, because our Fathers made mention of this part curso-rily, since at that time no inquiry had yet been stirred up regarding it.... We are aware that, when we shall once disturb the simplicity of the Creed we shall find no limit to our words, since the arguments will always lead us on farther, and we shall confuse the souls of the simpler folks by the introduction of strange material (PG 32, 949–950; Way II, 218–219).

One might conclude that the Creed is a practical necessity for maintaining unity in faith according to Basil. It can be augmented and refined in the course of time, as the Church living together in communion under the guidance of God may come to see fit. But this should be done with great caution, especially because of the pastoral risk of causing confusion.

In addition to his concern for the unity of the Church in the same faith, Basil's writings include several comments about the nature of faith as such, particularly in his short work *Concerning Faith*, which, as he himself states, is written within the more serene context of positively describing faith and its essential content and not of attempting to refute false opinions. Faith is rooted in listening to and accepting what is said in Scripture:

> Now, then, faith is a whole-hearted assent to aural doctrine with full conviction of the truth of what is publicly taught by the grace of God....But, if "the Lord is faithful in all his words" (Ps 144,13) and "All his commandments are faithful, confirmed for ever and ever, made in truth and equity" (Ps 110,8), to delete anything that is written down or to interpolate anything not written amounts to open defection from the faith and makes the offender liable to a charge of contempt. For our Lord Jesus Christ says: "My sheep hear my voice" (Jn 10,27), and, before this, He had said: "But a stranger they follow not but fly from him because they know not the voice of strangers" (Jn 10,5). And the Apostle, using a human parallel, more strongly forbids adding to or removing anything from Holy Writ in the following words: "yet a man's testament if it be confirmed, no man despiseth nor addeth to it" (Gal 3,15; *De fide* 1 [PG 31, 677–680]; Wagner, 59).

This acceptance of God's Word in Scripture is also conveyed in Rule Eight of *The Morals*: "That we must neither doubt nor hesitate respecting the words of the Lord, but be fully persuaded that every word of God is true and possible even if nature rebel; for therein is the test of faith." (PG 31, 711–712; Wagner, 81).[19]

What is the relation between faith and knowledge? In *Concerning Faith* Basil notes that it is suitable, especially in defending the faith against those who would despise it, to make use of arguments not based upon Scripture. Human knowledge can contribute to the act of faith, for example, by showing from the evidence of creation that there is a creator. This knowledge can serve as a kind of preamble to accepting in faith the word revealed by the creator (so Letter 235). Nevertheless, the object of faith and of worship is God, who is ultimately incomprehensible; human beings can know that God is but not what God's substance is (Letter 234). Thus Basil writes:

It is impossible to express in one word or one concept, or to grasp with the mind at all, the majesty and glory of God, which is unutterable and incomprehensible, and the Holy Scripture, although for the most part employing words in current use, speaks obscurely "as through a glass" even to the clean of heart. The beholding face to face and the perfect knowledge have been promised to those who are accounted worthy in the life to come....Holy Writ contains a store of knowledge as limitless as is the incapacity of human nature to grasp in this life the meaning of the holy mysteries. Even though more knowledge is always being acquired by everyone, it will ever fall short in all things of its rightful completeness until the time when that which is perfect being come, that which is in part will be done away [with]. (*Concerning Faith* 2-3 [PG 31, 681-684]; Wagner, 60-62).

After these partly apophatic, partly eschatological reflections upon the limits of human knowledge of God, Basil proceeds to a short, dense and thoroughly Trinitarian summary of the content of Christian faith (*Concerning Faith* 4 [PG 31, 685-688]: Wagner, 63-65). In contrast to what is taught by false prophets, this faith is the "tradition that we have received"; in adhering to it, "...we shall walk according to the rule of the saints, 'built upon the foundation of the apostles and prophets, Jesus Christ, our Lord himself being the chief cornerstone...'" (*Concerning Faith* 5 [PG 31, 689-690]; Wagner, 67). This reference to Christ and the apostles recurs in the introductory line to Chapter Three of Rule Twelve of *The Morals*: "That we should observe everything without exception which has been handed down by the Lord through the Gospel and the Apostles" (PG 31, 723-724; Wagner, 90).[20] Thus for Basil Christian faith focuses upon the Trinity. It accepts revelation as this has been delivered in the Scriptures and through Jesus and the apostles. Human knowledge and faith are not in opposition, but our present understanding of God is conditioned by human finitude and by our pilgrim state.

4. GREGORY OF NAZIANZUS

Gregory of Nazianzus (c. 330-390) is not particularly noted for any work which discusses directly the act of faith per se, as that might be distinguished from faith's content. But a perusal of his writings is particularly illuminative when considering the question of unity in faith. This is principally because he played a very unique role at the precise moment in which the Church definitively rejected Arianism and various other Christological and Trinitarian misinterpretations of revelation as contained in Scripture and irrevocably affirmed the orthodox interpretation of the Council of Nicea. In many ways, Gregory of Nazianzus was the man of the hour in this crucial moment. His writings, which fall into the three classifications of discourses, letters and poems, all contain valuable information and argumentation relative to these important events, but the ones upon which we will focus here are several of the discourses.[21]

This literary form is itself illuminative for the topic of unity in faith, for it consists in a public lecture, following upon the rules of rhetoric which Gregory had learned in the course of his classical education in Athens, which aims at convincing an audience to adopt a particular point of view or course of action. He employed it to great effect in Constantinople, which was predominantly Arian due to a succession of Arian emperors, when he arrived in 379 to become the bishop of those Christians loyal to Nicea. His eloquence in many discourses delivered during the short period of just three years (379–381), particularly the five so-called "theological discourses" which carefully argue on behalf of the orthodox doctrine of the Trinity and which won for him the epithet "Gregory the theologian," was an important factor in bringing the city back to the doctrine of Nicea. Quasten notes that, in Byzantine times, Gregory was called "the Christian Demosthenes," adding that "he is beyond doubt one of the greatest orators of Christian antiquity and surpasses his friend Basil in his command of the resources of Hellenistic rhetoric."[22]

The scope of his discourses was not only to invite his listeners to reject error and to embrace truth, but to create peace within the Christian community as well. Three of them are specifically devoted to the topic of peace (6 [PG 35, 721–752], 22 [SC 270, 218–259] and 23 [SC 270, 280–311]); another concerns the role of bishops and theologians in teaching within the Church (20 [SC 270, 56–85]) and yet another is devoted to moderation in disputes (32 [SC 318, 82–155]). Gregory notes that the body of Christ is one, obviously employing the image used by Paul in 1 Cor 12, 12–27 (Discourse 6, chapter 1 [PG 35, 721–722]); all who belong to it have become one mouth and one voice (*cheilos hen kai phone mia*; Discourse 23, chapter 4 [SC 270, 286]). They should be of one mind in matters of faith, having the same inspiration and the same breath (*hen empneomenous, hen pneovtas*; Discourse 23, chapter 12 [SC 270, 306]). On several occasions Gregory repeats that much of the divisiveness among Christians has not originated from differences in faith

(Discourse 6, chapter 11 [PG 35, 735-738]; 22, chapters 11-12 [SC 270, 242-247]; 23, chapters 3-4 [SC 270, 284-287]). Rather they are based upon love of power or wealth, jealousy, hate and pride (Discourse 22, chapter 5 [SC 270, 228-229]). Discourse 22 notes the incoherence of this state of affairs with the fact that Christianity is the religion of charity (chapter 4 [SC 270, 226-227]); division is like a madness which no medicine can cure for the sick person continues to harm himself (chapter 7 [SC 270, 234-235]; see also Discourse 32, chapter 4 [SC 318, 90-91]). Moreover, it is absurd to accept the command from the Lord to forgive seventy times seven times and to continue to fight with one another; absurd to believe "Blessed are the peacemakers" and continue to make enemies (chapter 15 [SC 270, 254-255]).

Discourse 32 offers Gregory's view of the reason underlying much Christian division and what can contribute much to its cure. The cause of the trouble is in Christians themselves; individuals of ardent and noble character rush rashly into speculation about God (chapter 3 [SC 318, 88-89]) with the result that there are many parties with many differing views of Christ and of the Holy Spirit (chapter 5 [SC 318, 92-95]). Ardor for Christianity is not governed by knowledge; faith drifts in many directions, like a ship without a pilot (chapter 5 [SC 318, 94-95]). Christians need, instead, to follow the "royal road" of moderation, the mean between laziness or indifference about faith, on the one hand, and an ardor which is reckless, on the other (chapter 6 [SC 318, 96-97]). Just as order governs the whole universe (chapters 7-9 [SC 318, 98-105]) and is the "mother and security of all beings" (chapter 10 [SC 318, 104-105]), so too must order reign in the Church, which is but one body of members with different roles and functions. All are equal in value, but not all have equal functions (*isotimias en tois anisois*; chapter 10 [SC 318, 106-107]). Developing this Pauline image (chapters 11-12 [SC 318, 108-113]), Gregory notes that, while it is a wonderful service to teach, there is less danger in listening (chapter 13 [SC 318, 112-113]). Because of the many difficulties and obscurities which attend speaking about the divine, knowing when to be silent is a gift from God (chapter 14 [SC 318, 114-115]). Gregory enlists the examples of Moses and of Paul (chapters 15-16 [SC 318, 116-121]). Although these two played such an important role in handing on the Law and the gospel, nevertheless Moses only glimpsed the back of God passing by (Ex 33,18-20; SC 318, 118-119) and Paul taught that here we see only as in a mirror, darkly, and longed for when he would see face to face (1 Cor 13,12; SC 318, 116-117). Who are contemporary believers to pretend a knowledge greater than these heroes of the past? Or consider Christ's action of selecting only a few of the apostles to go with him to the top of Mount Tabor or further with him into the garden of Gethsemane. This caused no bitterness among the others (chapter 18 [SC 318, 124-125]). What is needed is humility, recognizing and listening to the word of those within the community who have been entrusted with the role of leadership (chapter 19 [SC 318, 124-127]). Wisdom means to know oneself and therefore to moderately forego speculation about the nature of the unbegotten Father, about the call of the only-begotten Son and about the glory and the power of the Holy Spirit. The foundations of faith, such as the profession of the Trinity (cf. also chapter 5 [SC 318, 94-95]) and that Jesus is Lord and that God raised him from the dead (Rom 10,9), are sufficient (chapters 20-25 [SC 318, 126-139]). Justification comes not through agility in argumentation (chapter 22 [SC 318, 132-133]) but only through faith (chapter 25 [SC 318, 138-139]). Gregory praises the faith of the simple, unlearned believer (chapters 25-27 [SC 318, 137-145]), counsels against ambition (chapter 28 [SC 318, 144-147]) and praises humility (chapter 29 [SC 318, 146-149]). One should be slow to condemn and, in confronting those who hold erroneous doctrines, employ that gentleness which can maximize the possibility of retaining each brother (chapters 29-31 [SC 318, 146-151]). Prudence should govern the selection of what the young are given to read as well as who may be allowed to speak in the assembly (chapter 32 [SC 318, 150-153]). There are many ways to salvation; not everyone need take up the more subtle questions about God, but each should approach God by one's way of living (chapter 33 [SC 318, 152-55]).

For all of his irenicism and for all of the weight he gives to following the leaders of the Church, it is clear that Gregory was not and would not accept being in peaceful communion with all of the various Christians and bishops of his day. The crucial issue which he continually returns to in the various Discourses as decisive for the unity of the Church is correct doctrine about the Trinity. For uniting Christians, nothing is more important than consensus (*symphonia*), nothing more detrimental than diversity (*diaphonia*) about the doctrine of God (Discourse 6, chapter 12 [PG 35, 737-738]). True piety is only this: to adore the Father, the Son and the Holy Spirit, the divinity and power both one and three; being united in this, Christians should then come to the same mind on the other points which divide them (Discourse 22, chapter 12 [SC 270, 242-245]). The reference to "other points" (*kai t'alla homonoesomen*; which the SC edition renders "mettons-nous d'accord aussi sur le reste" [245]) would seem to imply that Gregory does not see the profession of faith in the Trinity as a sort of minimum standard by which all Christians would be united but more along the lines of a condition sine qua non which leads to a wide-ranging harmony in faith.

Gregory of Nazianzus used eloquent discourses to convince divided Christians to come together in a common faith. He was remarkably successful, when one thinks of the change which occurred in Constantinople over the period of only three years, culminating in the second ecumenical council which confirmed the orthodoxy of what Nicea had taught some fifty-five years earlier. His effectiveness as a bishop within his own diocese and in collaboration with other bishops in an ecumenical council might serve to illustrate and confirm his teaching about the importance of the role of leadership within the Church. Pastoral guidance and exhortation by those charged with leadership was in his case a powerful force for promoting and maintaining the unity of the faith of the Church.

Nevertheless, Gregory himself realized that exhortation and pastoral guidance alone would not necessarily be the most powerful means toward unity in faith. He admits as much by closing his Discourse 37, which was delivered in the presence of the emperor Theodosius shortly before the latter decreed that all Christians in his realm must adhere to the doctrine of Nicea,[23] with the comment: "My word of argument on behalf of the Trinity will have not so much power as your edict" (chapter 23 [SC 318, 316–317]). His own efforts, however, illustrate that discourse (perhaps one may prefer to say today "dialogue") and Church order, along with humility, modesty, charity and self-criticism (on the last of these, see Discourse 23, chapter 4 [SC 270, 286–287]), can effectively foster and maintain unity in faith.

5. GREGORY OF NYSSA

Quasten notes that, while Gregory of Nyssa (c. 335–394) was not an outstanding administrator like Basil or an attractive preacher like Gregory of Nazianzus, he was the most gifted of the Cappadocians as a speculative theologian and mystic.[24] His *Oratio catechetica magna* has been hailed as the first attempt since the *De principiis* of Origen to compile a systematic account of Christianity.[25] Gregory of Nyssa also receives a good deal of attention from Escribano-Alberca in his monograph about faith and knowledge of God in the *Handbuch der Dogmengeschichte*.[26] This is so even though Escribano-Alberca concurs with the judgment of W. Völker that "faith" is not a technically precise term in the writings of Gregory and that it can convey a variety of meanings.[27] The reason for this interest derives principally from the scope of Escribano-Alberca's

monograph, which attempts to examine faith precisely under the rubric
of "knowledge of God." In this context, Gregory of Nyssa marks a turning
point from earlier Eastern fathers such as Clement of Alexandria and
Origen in his stepping aside from a more positive assessment of the
capacity of human beings to know God.

This is sharply brought out in Gregory's commentary on the sixth
beatitude: "Blessed are the pure of heart, for they shall see God," where
he writes:

> The Divine Nature, whatever It may be in Itself, surpasses
> every mental concept. For It is altogether inaccessible to rea-
> soning and conjecture, nor has there been found any human
> faculty capable of perceiving the incomprensible; for we can-
> not devise a means of understanding inconceivable things.
> Therefore the great Apostle calls His ways *unsearchable*,
> meaning by this that the way that leads to the knowledge of
> the Divine Essence is inaccessible to thought. That is to say,
> none of those who have passed through life before us has
> made known to the intelligence so much as a trace by which
> might be known what is above knowledge.[28]

But this does not mean that human beings have no way to know God.
Indeed the point of the beatitude under consideration is the promise by
Jesus that the pure of heart will "see God." Gregory states that one way of
knowing God is the path of learning through analogy something of the
creator by means of what he has created, knowing the artist through his
works. But, for Gregory, the beatitude "Blessed are the pure of heart"
concerns yet a deeper knowledge. Since the human being is made in the
image of God, he or she may come to know God through this image, if it
in turn has been purified and returned from any corruptions of sin to its
more original state. Under such conditions, to know oneself allows one
to see the archetype in the image. This is the knowledge promised in the
beatitude, not a knowledge which is contemplation of that "Nature
which is above the universe."

> But since the promise of seeing God has a twofold meaning,
> on the one hand, that of knowing the Nature that is above
> the universe, on the other, that of being united to Him
> through purity of life, we must say that the voice of the Saints
> declares the former mode of contemplation to be impossi-
> ble, whereas the second is promised to human nature in Our

Lord's present teaching, *Blessed are the clean of heart, for they shall see God* (PG 44, 1273–1274 B-C; Graef, 151).

J. Daniélou sees this as a significant turning point away from *gnosis*, from that speculation on the divine nature which came naturally to Clement of Alexandria and Origen.[29] There are two paths to knowing God: symbolic knowledge, by means of reflection upon the visible world, and mystical knowledge, the experience of the presence of God by means of grace, which is a knowledge of love, accessible to all Christians who are united in the darkness of faith to God present in the soul.[30]

This theme of faith as a knowledge of God in darkness is nicely captured in one of the final passages of *The Life of Moses*:

> For when you conquer all enemies (the Egyptian, the Amalekite, the Idumaean, the Midianite), cross the water, are enlightened by the cloud, are sweetened by the wood, drink from the rock, taste of the food from above, make your ascent up the mountain through purity and sanctity; and when you arrive there, you are instructed in the divine mystery by the sound of the trumpets, and in impenetrable darkness draw near to God by your faith, and there are taught the mysteries of the tabernacle and the dignity of the priesthood (II,315).[31]

In this context, Gregory's Sixth Homily on the Canticle of Canticles, commenting on Song 3,1 ("On my bed at night I sought him whom my heart loves—I sought him but I did not find him"), states that words or concepts are a kind of impediment to "finding" God.[32] Because of this sense of breaking beyond the barriers of human limitation, Gregory's understanding of faith is at times almost interchangeable with his view of "hope."[33]

Alongside these points which move in the direction of a mysticism of darkness, the *Oratio catechetica magna*, being more of a down to earth introduction of the faith intended for use in explaining Christian doctrine to those who have not yet accepted it, adds several of Gregory's further convictions about faith. First of all, in responding to the question as to why redemption has not been brought about for all human beings, his response is that faith must be free (31 [PG 45, 77–78 C-D]). Elsewise to believe could not be thought of as praiseworthy or virtuous. Moreover, faith is absolutely necessary for that rebirth about which Jesus speaks with Nicodemus in the gospel of John (in Jn 3,6; see *Oratio catechetica magna*

39–40 [PG 45, 101–106]). What is quite interesting here is the connection which Gregory makes between *doctrinal* faith and the possibility of rebirth. Whoever believes that the Trinity is uncreated can be reborn into eternal life; whoever falsely believes that there is some aspect of creatureliness in the Trinity and is baptized into such a faith is not reborn to eternal life. For like begets like; the eternal cannot be begotten from the creaturely (PG 45, 99–100 B-C).

This would seem to supply an important nuance to Gregory's view of the mystic ascent to God through faith which has been elaborated above. The fact that ultimate union with God breaks beyond concepts does not mean that "what" one believes is a matter of indifference. In *The Life of Moses* or the *Homilies on the Canticle of Canticles* Gregory seems to be speaking about the ultimate goal of faith, a certain union in darkness which is possible for the individual who has progressed in a life of virtue. In the *Oratio catechetica magna*, he is speaking of the very beginnings of the life of faith and here rebirth itself is not possible if one does not believe in the divinity of the Son and of the Holy Spirit.

This provides a point of entry for considering unity in faith for Gregory. The journey which tends toward mystical union with God begins in that common faith which affirms the divinity of the Trinity. Gregory's one work which carries the title "De fide" (the *Ad Simplicium*; PG 45, 136–145) is simply a brief defense of Trinitarian faith, largely along the lines which gained expression at Constantinople I. Such a faith, which is the condition for the possibility of rebirth according to the *Oratio catechetica magna*, is the principal topic of the various dogmatic works attributed to Gregory, most of which are somewhat polemical in tone insofar as they argue against the various Trinitarian heresies of the time. One of these, the *Contra Eunomium*, Book II, begins with a description of the historical origins of this faith in Christ:

> The faith of Christians, which has been preached by the disciples to all the peoples of the whole world in accord with the command of the Lord, is neither from men nor through men but through our Lord Jesus Christ, who is the Word of God, and life, and light, and truth, and God, and Wisdom, and all of these by nature.... But convinced that the true God appeared in the flesh, we believe to be true only that mystery of piety which was handed on through this Word our God, who spoke through his own Apostles....We believe therefore that faith which the Lord expounded to his disciples, saying thus: *Go, teach all nations, baptizing them in the name of the*

Father, and of the Son and of the Holy Spirit. This is the word of mystery, in which our nature is transformed into what is better by a supernatural generation, while it is reformed from the corruptible to the incorruptible, from the old human nature into his image who in the beginning created us in the divine likeness.[34]

The rootedness of faith in the acceptance of what Christ revealed to the apostles and what continued to be handed on by them explains why, for Gregory, the doctrine of Christian faith is no human creation. It explains also the importance of the Scriptures in Gregory's theology. One example of this is his *De Spiritu sancto. Adversus Pneumatomachos Macedonianos* 3 (PG 45, 1303-1304 C-D), where he notes that he has nothing new to say, only that which has already been written in the divinely inspired writings. Thus there is a kind of doctrinal unity in faith which goes back through the Scriptures and the apostles to Word of God himself. All Christians should be united in the one faith which is the acceptance of the revelation of God. This is the underlying motivation behind Gregory's arguing so strenuously against those who did not accept Christ's message or understand it in a way which faithfully mirrored its full Trinitarian meaning.

6. JOHN CHRYSOSTOM

"Where is the wise man? Where is the scribe?" (1 Cor 1,20-21). Commenting on these words of St. Paul, John Chrysostom asks rhetorically what philosopher or what expert in Jewish tradition has saved us and made known the truth, to which he replies: "Not one. It was the fisherman's work, the whole of it." He adds:

It remains that where God's wisdom is, there is no longer need of man's....now we need no more reasonings, but faith alone. For to believe on Him that was crucified and buried, and to be fully persuaded that this Person Himself both rose again and sat down on high, this needeth not wisdom, nor reasonings, but faith. For the Apostles themselves came in not by wisdom, but by faith, and surpassed the heathen wise men in wisdom and loftiness.... For this transcends all human understanding.[35]

Chrysostom loved to contrast the superior wisdom of even the most unlettered believer to the foolishness of even the most learned unbeliever. In his Sermons on the Statues, delivered not long after his ordination to the priesthood and partially responsible for establishing his fame as an orator,[36] he challenges his listeners to question the simplest Christian peasant, working in the fields around Antioch, about God's existence, about creation and providence and about the sufficiency and reward of a virtuous life, and to compare the response with the confusions of the philosophers concerning the same topics. The former, though he may be illiterate, enjoys clear and true convictions concerning these things and compares to the latter, though highly educated, as a prudent adult compares to a little child (*Ad populum Antiochenum*, Homilia 19,1 [PG 49, 189–190]).[37] In another place, he draws the obvious conclusion from this state of affairs:

> It is then a sign of a weak, little, and pitiful mind not to believe. And so when they make faith a charge against us, let us make wont of faith a charge against them in return....For as believing belongs to a lofty and high-born soul, so disbelieving doth to a most unreasonable and worthless one, and such as is sunken drowsily into the senselessness of brutes.[38]

John Chrysostom (c. 347–407), born to a Christian family, was baptized as a young adult and, after several years as an ascetic, was ordained a deacon (381) and a priest (386) in the great patriarchical city of Antioch. For twelve years he had the duty of preaching in the principal church there (386–397), until he was chosen to succeed Nectarius, the patriarch of Constantinople, in 397. Because of conflicts with other ecclesiastical leaders and, especially, with the empress Eudoxia, he was exiled to Cucusus in 404 and, having been banished to a still more distant city at the eastern end of the Black Sea, died during the journey in 407.[39]

The large majority of his extensive writings, so many of which were preserved because of their beauty, sound doctrine and popularity (volumes 47–64 in Migne's *Patrologia greca*), is comprised of sermons, characterized by the rhetorical and exhortatory style of such a literary genre. Because Chrysostom had the custom of preaching sequences of sermons on particular books of the Bible (Genesis, Psalms, Isaiah, Matthew, John, Acts, Hebrews and the entire Pauline corpus), his hundreds of sermons group together into large cohesive collections. The result is that one finds more doctrinal or exegetical comprehensiveness in his writing than one might expect from a collection of homilies, each of which, while differing somewhat in length, per force had to be short enough to be delivered to a group at one sitting. Nevertheless, it is true that Chrysostom's overall viewpoint on any particular topic has the quality of being scattered among many individual sermons. Rarely, as in the case of his famous book on the priesthood, did he compose a work which in a more or less systematic way addressed a particular theme.[40] This is true also with regard to his teaching about faith.[41]

As the contrast presented above between the believer and the philosopher illustrates, faith for John Chrysostom is a kind of wisdom or knowledge, though this must be nuanced by what he says about the limitations of human knowledge. Commenting on John 1,5 ("The light shines in the darkness"), he notes, "This light becomes present through faith, and when present, it subsequently shines with great abundance upon him who receives it; if you provide a pure life for it, it will remain continuously dwelling within you."[42] Faith allows one to see in a new way. Addressing those about to be baptized on the meaning of the name "the faithful," he says:

> We faithful have believed in things which our bodily eyes cannot see. These things are great and frightening and go beyond our nature. Neither reflection nor human reason will be able to discover and explain these things; only the teaching of faith understands them well. Therefore, God has made for us two kinds of eyes: those of the flesh and those of faith.[43]

The eyes of faith see what is hidden beneath the externals which are grasped by the senses (*In Matthaeum*, Homilia LXXXII, on Mt 26,35 [PG 58, 743] concerning the eucharist; on the eyes of faith see also *In Apostolicum dictum: Hoc autem scitote* [PG 56, 271] and *De verbis Apostoli: Habentes eumdem Spiritum* I [PG 51, 275]). The difference between a believer and an unbeliever is like that between a person who can read and one who cannot. Looking at a letter, the one who cannot read sees merely ink and paper; the one who can goes beyond these impressions, recalling the voice of his absent friend speaking to him by means of these external things (*In Epistolam I ad Corinthios*, Homilia VII,1-2 on 1 Cor 2,7 [PG 61, 55-56]). Faith also allows the believer to view the past in a more accurate way. Believers today can understand the event of Jesus' crucifixion more accurately than some of those who stood at the very foot of the cross (*In epistolam ad Galatas*, 3,1 [PG 61, 648-649] and *In Apostolicum dictum: Hoc autem scitote*, 1-2 [PG 56, 271-272]). Furthermore, faith regards the future in a new light; it looks to the things that are yet only hoped for (*In epistolam ad Hebraeos*, Homilia XXI on

Heb 11,1 [PG 63, 151]). It is the faith which looks to the future in hope which enables Christians to commit their lives to Christ and to accept even suffering and death should these result from their commitment (*Ad Theodorum lapsum* II [PG 47, 314-315]; *In Acta Apostolorum*, Homilia LI [PG 60, 356]; *In Acta Apostolorum*, Homilia X [PG 60, 89]; *In epistolam ad Romanos*, Homilia XIV [PG 60, 532]; *In epistolam II ad Corinthios* [PG 61, 461]). St. Paul is a magnificent example of how faith makes Christian liberty invincible in the face of persecution. When they imprisoned him, Paul's captors certainly had no intention of bestowing an honor upon him. Yet to the eyes of faith, these very captors, even against their explicit intention, by placing Paul in chains ended up crowning him in glory (*In epistolam ad Colossenses*, Homilia X, on Col 4,4 [PG 62, 371]).

While Chrysostom uses the metaphor of "seeing" to convey that wisdom which distinguishes believers from unbelievers, the "word" is perhaps an even more important vehicle for his understanding of faith. Faith comes from hearing (*In epistolam ad Romanos*, Homilia XVIII on Rom 10,16-17 [PG 60, 573-574]; see also *In epistolam II ad Corinthios*, Homilia V on 2 Cor 2,17 [PG 61, 431] and *In epistolam I ad Thessalonicenses*, Homilia III on 1 Thess 2,13 [PG 62, 407]). God has spoken to human beings, from the beginning in person (*In Genesin*, Homilia II on Gen 1,1 [PG 53, 27-28]), later through the prophets and finally through his Son (*In epistolam ad Hebraeos*, Homilia I on Heb 1,1 [PG 63, 14-15]). What is heard is the word, which is contained in the Scriptures, which in turn have been inspired by the Holy Spirit (*In Genesin*, Homilia XXI on Gen 5,1-2 [PG 53, 175-176]; *In epistolam II ad Timotheum*, Homilia IX on 2 Tim 3,16 [PG 62, 650]). Scripture is like a letter sent from God (*In Genesin*, Homilia II on Gen 1,1 [PG 53, 28]; *In epistolam ad Galatas* on Gal 1,9 [PG 61, 624]). Chrysostom takes Jesus' parable which closes with Abraham's response to the rich man—"If they do not hear Moses and the prophets, neither will they be convinced if someone should rise from the dead" (Lk 16,31)—as meaning that, according to Jesus himself, the credibility of the Scriptures as the Word of God is greater even than that of one who came back from the grave (*In epistolam ad Galatas* on Gal 1,9 [PG 61, 624]). This estimation of Scripture as the Word of God which should be accepted in faith is constantly reaffirmed by the very theological method of John Chrysostom. All of his writings take as their point of departure the authority of the biblical Word of God. Indeed they are fundamentally commentaries upon this Word and applications of it to daily life.

What does one "know" by means of the Word? According to Boularand, one could sketch in broad outline the content of faith for

Chrysostom in terms of two groups of truths.[44] The first group derives from the material proper to the Old Testament: the existence and general attributes of God (uniqueness, infinity, incorporality, goodness, power); creation and, in particular, human nature in the image and likeness of God; divine providence and retribution. These truths can be known by reason, although the usefulness of accepting them in faith on the basis of the word of God is brought out by the contrast between the uneducated believer and the educated unbeliever.[45]

The second group of truths is comprised of those great mysteries of the New Testament, which, wholly inaccessible to reason, are only available to faith. At the heart of these mysteries is the fact that God became a human being, was crucified and raised for our salvation. This essentially was the message announced by Gabriel to the Virgin and by the prophets and the apostles to the whole world (*In epistolam I ad Corinthinos*, Homilia XXXVIII on 1 Cor 15,1 [PG 61, 323]; *In Acta Apostolorum*, Homilia I on Acts 1,5 [PG 60, 21]). The truth of these mysteries concerns human salvation, which was the purpose of all of Christ's actions, particularly of his death on the cross (*In Joannem*, Homilia XXVII on Jn 3,16 [PG 59, 160]; *In Genesin*, Homilia XXVIII on Gen 9,17 [PG 53, 256]; *In epistolam ad Ephesios*, Homilia I on Eph 1,5 [PG 62, 13]; *In Joannem*, Homilia XLV on Jn 6,38 [PG 59, 255]; *In epistolam ad Romanos*, Homilia VII on Rom 3,25 [PG 60, 444]; *In epistolam II ad Corinthios*, Homilia III on 2 Cor 1,20 [PG 61, 410]; *In epistolam ad Galatas* on Gal 1,3–5 [PG 61, 617]). The mystery of the economy of universal salvation through the cross of Jesus Christ, the incarnate Son of God, unfolds into a double object of faith: the mystery of God as Trinity and the mystery of redemption.

Concerning the mystery of God as Trinity, Chrysostom's two series of sermons *On the Incomprehensible Nature of God* (PG 48, 701–812) develop the idea that no one knows God except God and that what we know of the Trinity is what has been revealed in the incarnate Word (see also *In Joannem*, Homilia XV on Jn 1,18 [PG 59, 98–99] and *In epistolam ad Romanos*, Homilia XIX on Rom 11,33–34 [PG 60, 593]). In these sermons Chrysostom criticizes the more radical party of the Arians, the followers of Eunomius known as the Anomoeans, precisely because they claim to know God as God knows himself. This amounts to a blasphemous arrogance which in effect reduces the ineffable mystery of God to the limits of human reason. Clearly, what leads to the heresies against which Chrysostom argues is a certain misuse of reason which makes exaggerated claims in "explaining" the mystery of God. Concerning the mystery of redemption—the Father's eternal design to welcome sinful human beings again into friendship through the incarnation and death on the cross of his only Son, to make them adopted children, uniting them all without distinction of race in the risen Christ by the gift of the Holy Spirit in baptism, with a view to granting them a share in his glorious inheritance, eternal life, which is to know the only true God and Jesus Christ whom he has sent (Jn 17,3)—all of this is a mysterious wisdom which is contrary to the wisdom of the present age.[46] Why, in discussing the plan of redemption in Christ, does St. Paul speak of a hidden and secret wisdom in 1 Cor 2,7? Because no one, not even the angels and archangels, could have ever imagined these wonders before the event (see *In epistolam 1 ad Corinthinos*, Homilia VII on 1 Cor 2,7 [PG 61, 55]).

The transcendence of these mysteries above human reason and made known only by the revelation contained in the New Testament makes clear the utter necessity of faith.

> In all circumstances, beloved, we need faith—faith, the mother of virtues, the medicine of salvation—without it we cannot grasp any teachings on sublime matters. But [those who are without faith] are like people trying to cross the sea without a ship. These are able to swim for a while by using hands and feet, but when they have gone farther out they are soon swamped by the waves. So, also, those who have recourse to their own reasoning before accepting any knowledge are inviting shipwreck, even as Paul says: "who have made shipwreck of the faith" (*In Joannem*, Homilia XXXIII [PG 59, 187-188]; Goggin I, 322).[47]

Not only is faith necessary, but reason tends toward confusion:

> Now, nothing makes one so dizzy as human reasoning, which says everything from an earthly point of view, and does not allow illumination to come from above. Earthly reasoning is covered with mud. Therefore, we have need of streams from above, so that, when the mud has fallen away, whatever part of the reason is pure may be carried on high and may be thoroughly imbued with the lessons taught there (*In Joannem*, Homilia XXIV [PG 59, 147]; Goggin I, 240).[48]

Because of this, Chrysostom recognizes a certain element of receptivity in faith (*In epistolam ad Romanos*, Homilia II on Rom 1,17 [PG 60, 409]).

Faith is obedience (*In Matthaeum*, Homilia VII,1 [PG 57, 81–84] and *In Matthaeum*, Homilia XIV,2 [PG 57, 219]). It accepts without hesitation (*In epistolam I Timotheum*, Homilia I on 1 Tim 1,4 [PG 62, 506–507]); it does not scrutinize what is taught (*In epistolam ad Romanos*, Homilia I on Rom 1,5 [PG 60, 398]). Whatever God has said and done, we should simply believe and obey (*In epistolam ad Romanos*, Homilia XVIII on Rom 10,16–17 [PG 60, 573–574]). The apostles have been sent out only to proclaim what they have heard from the master, not to add something of their own (*In epistolam ad Romanos*, Homilia I on Rom 1,5 [PG 60, 398]) and it is not for us disciples to judge these teachers, but simply to believe (*In epistolam ad Galatas* on Gal 1,8 [PG 61, 625]).

The receptivity of faith provides the context for John Chrysostom's understanding of the relationship between faith and the Church. In the first *Baptismal Instruction*, Chrysostom writes:

> You must also keep this truth firmly fixed in your minds, that the Holy Spirit is of the same dignity as the Father and the Son. Christ said to His disciples: Go, therefore, and make disciples of all nations, baptizing them in the name of the Father, and of the Son, and of the Holy Spirit. Did you see the exactness with which Christ makes profession of this truth? Did you see how unambiguous His instruction is? Let no one hereafter disturb your mind by bringing the searchings of his own reason into the Church's dogmas as he tries to confuse beliefs that are correct and sound. Avoid the companionship of such people as you would avoid drugs which could destroy you....Such is the strictness we wish you to show in regard to the dogmas of the Church, and we desire you to keep them fast fixed in your minds (*Baptismal Instruction* 1, paragraphs 23–25 [SC 50, 120–121]; Harkins, 32).

Thus there is a handing on from Christ to the apostles to the Church. The apostles have transmitted the gospel without additions, just as they received it from God, through Christ in the Holy Spirit, and the Church has conserved their doctrine without alteration (*In epistolam II ad Corinthios*, Homilia V on 2 Cor 2,17 [PG 61, 431]; *In epistolam ad Galatas* on Gal 1,6 [PG 61, 622]; *In Acta Apostolorum*, Homilia I on Acts 1,1–2 [PG 60, 16–17]; *In epistolam I ad Corinthios*, Homilia I on 1 Cor 1,1-3 [PG 61, 12-13]). This explains Chrysostom's insistence upon holding fast to the doctrines of the Church. Commenting upon Peter's confession of faith in

Mt 16,16, he states that the faith of this confession is the rock upon which Christ builds his Church, adding:

> For the Father gave Peter the revelation of the Son and the Son committed to him the dissemination of knowledge of the Father and of Himself throughout the whole world, giving to a mortal man all power in heaven. For He who extended the Church through the whole earth and showed it more powerful than the heavens, saying "the heavens and the earth will pass away but my words will not pass away" (Mt 24,35), gave the keys to Peter (*In Matthaeum*, Homilia LIV on Mt 16,13–23 [PG 58, 534–535]).[49]

Chrysostom explicitly states that the faith is one; it is the same in all who truly believe. Nevertheless there can be a certain diversity among believers, insofar as some are more or less studious or capable (*In epistolam I ad Corinthios*, Homilia IX on 1 Cor 3,16 [PG 61, 78]). In one of his sermons at which some people from the countryside were present, Chrysostom addressed his Greek speaking audience with the words: "Do not consider their barbarian tongue but look to their mind, which has been molded by sound doctrine. For what is the benefit of speaking the same tongue if there is a division of minds? And what harm is there in speaking different tongues when there is a unison of faith?"[50]

Finally, one should add that, for St. John Chrysostom, faith must be made manifest in the way one lives (*Ad populum Antiochenum* V,5–6 [PG 49, 77]; *In Matthaeum*, Homilia LXIV, 4 [PG 58, 614]). It is not only a matter of wisdom or vision or hearing. Justification is by faith alone (*In epistolam ad Romanos*, Homilia VIII,2 [PG 60, 456–457]); it is a gift, a grace (*In Joannem*, Homilia LI on Jn 7,37–44 [PG 59, 285]). At the same time, faith without works is dead (*In Matthaeum*, Homilia XXIV,1 [PG 57, 321–322]; *In epistolam ad Ephesios*, Homilia IV, 3 [PG 62, 34–35]). *Baptismal Instructions* 2,17 (SC 50, 143) and 4,31 (SC 50, 198) speak of a contract between new Christians and the master, a contract which is written in faith. Commenting on the parable of the vine and the branches, Chrysostom notes that it is by faith that the believer is united to Christ, just as the branch is united to the vine; faith thus gives access to the powerful life flowing from Christ (*In Joannem*, Homilia LXXVI,1 on Jn 14,31–15,10 [PG 59, 411]). Perhaps John Chrysostom's thought on faith might be summed up by what he calls the "dignity" of faith. In Homily 46 on the gospel of John, he writes:

The Prophet foretold this of old, prophesying in the words: 'They all shall be taught of God.' Do you see the high dignity of faith? And do you see how he predicted that they were going to learn, not from men, nor through a man, but through God Himself? (*In Joannem*, Homilia XLVI,1 on Jn 6,45 [PG 59, 285]; Goggin I, 463-464).

7. CYRIL OF ALEXANDRIA

Like Athanasius, the most illustrious of his predecessors as bishop of Alexandria, Cyril (d. 444) figured prominently in one of the most important Christological controversies of the early Church—in his case, the dispute surrounding the condemnation of Nestorius by the third ecumenical council, held at Ephesus in 431. Also like Athanasius, Cyril receives but scant treatment in surveys concerning the patristic doctrine of faith.[51] His writings, filling ten volumes of Migne's *Patrologia graeca* (vols. 68–77), include biblical commentaries, an apology against the emperor Julian the Apostate, various letters and, especially, polemical writings against Arianism and Nestorianism.

Cyril's role of being the forceful protagonist of the victorious position in one of the most difficult and agitated doctrinal controversies of the early Church doubtless determined the way in which he understood faith. Christian faith is, first and foremost, the doctrinal truth which has been received by means of the tradition of the Church and which was being threatened by the errors of Arius and Nestorius. Cyril was passionately devoted to the truth of Christian faith. His great desire was "to work, live and die for faith in Christ" (*Letter 10* [PG 77, 69–70 and 78]); he expressed his willingness to suffer any injury, "if only the faith might remain whole and safeguarded" (*Letter 9* [PG 77, 61–62]). Cyril understood the faith as having been delivered to the Churches from the apostles (*Letter 1* [PG 77, 13–14]), adding that we must guard and defend this faith which has been given to us by the Holy Spirit in the Scriptures and was passed on by the famous fathers gathered at Nicea (*Letter 55* [PG 77, 291–294]). In keeping with this, most of his writings are concerned with defending correct doctrine, first in opposition to Arius, in which case Cyril's work closely follows that of Athanasius, and later in opposition to Nestorius, a context which called for the development of Cyril's specific contribution to the Christological and Trinitarian doctrine of the Church and which remains his principal endowment to Christian thought. These most important of Cyril's contributions are not the specific concern of the present study and, therefore, should not be explored here. However, as one might expect, such a significant theologian and pastor is not without some relevant insights about faith and its unity and to a few of these we now briefly turn.

While Cyril's controversial and dogmatic writings understand faith primarily in its doctrinal sense, his other writings show an awareness of some of its further dimensions. For example, his commentary on Isaiah 7,9 ("Unless you believe you will not understand [stand firm]")—that verse so popular among patristic writers as a point of departure for commenting upon faith—applies this text to the correct understanding of the Word/Logos of God (*In Isaiam IV* [PG 70, 199–200]). This application underscores one of what might be called the "subjective" dimensions of the act of faith, that is, that faith enables the subject to interpret correctly and leads to understanding, an idea so dear to Cyril's contemporary, St. Augustine. Or again, the commentary on Heb 11,1 ("Now faith is the assurance of things hoped for, the conviction of things not seen") emphasizes the certainty and surety of faith in contrast with all wavering (*In epistolam ad Hebraeos*, XI,1 [PG 74, 989–990]). Here Cyril is touching upon the epistemological status of the act of faith. When one turns to the *Apology against Julian* (PG 76, 503–1058), one sees a Cyril who may be compared to those many other ecclesiastical writers who defended Christianity against the criticisms of Hellenism and who, in the process, bring into clearer relief the specific quality and nature of Christian faith. The emperor Julian the Apostate, in his criticism of the "Nazarenes," argues that the true path to wisdom lies in the religious and cultural achievements of Greece and Rome and that the ascetic, cultic and theurgic practices of Hellenic religion and philosophy led to a kind of enlightenment and communion with the gods. Commenting on Cyril's response to this, William J. Malley writes:

> St. Cyril's vision, of course, was entirely opposed to this conception of salvific wisdom. A person can only attain divine wisdom through faith in Christ and by his initiation into the Church through baptism....true wisdom is found in the Sacred Scriptures interpreted through the divine gift of the Spirit. This enlightenment enables the wise man to live a life of moral purity in imitation of Jesus of Nazareth, the prototype of every wise man.[52]

This summary by Malley shows that, for Cyril, faith is intimately connected with wisdom, with initiation into the Church and with living a good moral life, dimensions which could be forgotten if one only considers Cyril's more predominant trait with regard to faith, his passion for orthodox doctrine.

Nevertheless, this interest in the integrity and orthodoxy of doctrine does offer some insight into the precise topic of unity in faith. It is clear that Cyril of Alexandria is one of the most vibrant witnesses that unity in faith means professing the same doctrine concerning such issues as the unity of humanity and divinity in Jesus Christ and the implications of this unity for the fittingness of calling Mary the Mother of God. Unity in faith cannot be satisfied by a common acceptance of rather vague or general doctrinal principles. Doctrine must be true to the reality of God and of Christ and as such it is necessary for the believer to stand firm for true doctrine. Doctrinal indifferentism is absolutely foreign to the patristic literature as a whole and perhaps no single writer brings this into sharper focus than Cyril of Alexandria.

Within this context, it is useful to draw attention to two further points. First of all, Cyril was convinced that the Church was both capable and obliged to do all in its power to insure unity in faith, to the extent that this is possible with the help of the Holy Spirit. His writings and letters addressed to other bishops, to emperors and to monks show an awareness of the participation of many segments of the community in this promotion of unity in faith. In particular, councils serve as privileged means to foster such unity. His early Trinitarian writings against Arius show a conviction about the legitimacy and effectiveness of the Council of Nicea in expressing that doctrine about the Trinity which can and should unite the Church. His central role at the Council of Ephesus witnesses to this conviction still more. Within this context of Cyril's obviously positive appraisal of the effectiveness of councils as tools for maintaining unity in faith, one should add that he perceived no contradiction or tension between this and, on the other hand, appeal for a pronouncement on the part of the bishop of Rome. Indeed, it was precisely the positive endorsement of Cyril's views by Pope Celestine I and a Roman synod in 430 which prompted Cyril to compose and call upon Nestorius to accept the twelve anathemas which were eventually at the center of the discussion at the Council of Ephesus. The point to be underscored here is that Cyril's writings and actions reflect the conviction that interventions by councils and by the bishop of Rome were effective means for maintaining the Church's unity in faith and that, moreover, these means were not seen as in any way incompatible or in conflict.[53]

Secondly, the conflict with Nestorius convinced Cyril that a decisive criterion for correctly interpreting either the Scriptures or previous doctrinal decisions by councils, such as those contained in the Creed of Nicea, was agreement with the broad consensus of earlier patristic literature. As Quasten comments: "It is certainly his merit that from now on Patristic testimony stands with Scriptural as authority in theological argumentation. In his trinitarian works, he intends to sum up in a systematic presentation the teaching of the Church Fathers."[54] The question of interpretation had always been a major dimension of the doctrinal controversies which tended to divide the Christian community right from the beginning. Irenaeus and Tertullian had recourse to the apostolic foundation of particular churches and the legitimate succession of their pastors as means for discerning who was qualified to provide a valid interpretation of Scripture. Much later, an author such as Augustine would find a decisive turning point on his road to conversion in the discovery that the Scriptures could be explained in a reasonable way. He himself would provide a list of rules for correct interpretation. Cyril makes explicit the principle that agreement with the broad consensus of the patristic writers is a reliable sign of sound interpretation. In his second and third letters to Nestorius (*Letter 4* [PG 77, 45–46] and *Letter 17* [PG 77, 119–120]), he argues that we can determine whether we are holding steadfast to the faith (cf. 2 Cor 13,5) by testing our doctrines in the light of theirs. This principle of interpretation was adopted by the Council of Ephesus in making its judgment upon Nestorius and has remained a classical procedure for theological argumentation, particularly in the East.

8. THEODORET OF CYRUS

Quasten calls Theodoret "one of the most successful writers of the Eastern Church" and "the last great theologian of Antioch."[55] His success is based to some degree on the wide range of areas in which he was able to contribute; his writings include exegetical, apologetic, dogmatic and historical books, as well as sermons and letters. Another trait, this one even more distinctive of Theodoret when compared to the other writers who appear in the present survey, is the fact that several of his works were composed in defense of someone condemned as a heretic, Nestorius, and in criticism both of St. Cyril of Alexandria and of the Council of Ephesus, whose champion Cyril was. Given such circumstances, perhaps it is useful to seek a balanced context for considering this writer in the opening paragraph of John Henry Newman's brief biography, entitled significantly "Trials of Theodoret."

It was the happy lot of Chrysostom to live in the lull between those fierce doctrinal tempests, which from time to time swept over the face of early Christendom: it was the great misfortune of Theodoret to pass his life under their wildest fury. Hence it has come to pass that, while Chrysostom is a Saint all over the world, Theodoret has the responsibility of acts which have forfeited for him that ecumenical dignity. He was betrayed into great errors of judgment, as even Popes have been betrayed; but, like Popes, without thereby committing himself to any heresy. In the great controversy of his day he was carried away by private, party, national feeling; but he was a great Bishop and writer notwithstanding. Yes, a great and holy Bishop; nor is there anything in his life, as it has come down to us, to forbid our saying that he was as genuine a Saint even as those whose names are in the calendar. Cyril, his antagonist, has not the burden of his ecclesiastical mistakes, but neither has he the merit of his recorded good works. Nor indeed is Theodoret without honorary title in the Church's hagiology: for he has ever been known as "the Blessed Theodoret." And this at least he had in common with St. Chrysostom, that both of them were deposed from their episcopal rank by a Council, both appealed to the Holy See, and by the Holy See both were cleared and restored to their ecclesiastical dignities.[56]

The interest of this intriguing figure from the first half of the fifth century for our topic of faith and its unity falls principally along two lines. First of all, Theodoret wrote one of the last great defenses of Christianity against the then-fading Hellenism of his day. The first book of this apology is concerned with the charge that Christianity is unreasonable because it requires one to place faith in its principal doctrines, which cannot be demonstrated from reason. This provides the opportunity for an explicit discussion of the nature of faith. Secondly, the positions which Theodoret took during what Newman, above, called the "wildest fury" of the "fierce doctrinal tempests" of the early Church invite some reflection upon the unity in faith of the Christian community.

The *Therapy for the Hellenic Illnesses* (*Hellenikon Therapeutike Pathematon* or, in the Latin, *Graecarum affectionum curatio*) probably was written shortly before the Council of Ephesus.[57] For some time, it had been suggested that Theodoret was writing his "therapy" as a rejoinder to Julian the Apostate's *Against the Galilaeans* (363), wherein the latter describes Christianity as an illness, Christians needing to be pitied rather than hated.[58] While Theodoret's *Therapy* is clearly not a detailed response to Julian,[59] its overall theme of treating Hellenism as an illness shows just how far Christianity had gone in replacing the once dominant Greco-Roman religion. It is comprised of twelve books, the first (1) devoted to defending faith, followed by five which concern doctrinal topics (2, creation and the Trinity; 3, angels and demons; 4, the material cosmos; 5, anthropology; and 6, providence, culminating with the incarnation), with the remaining six (7-12) being largely a contrast of various Hellenic and Christian practices, showing the superiority of the latter.

Theodoret's method is to demonstrate the truth of Christianity by means of Greek philosophy, a procedure which he compares to the bees extracting what is sweet from various flowers and leaving the bitter behind (I,124-126 [SC 57.1, 135-136]) or, again, to doctors who prepare medicines by making use of poisons, leaving aside what is harmful and manipulating the rest so as to provide a curative drug (I,127 [SC 57.1, 136]). To this effect, the *Therapy* cites nearly one hundred different works of Greek philosophers, poets and historians in about 340 passages.[60]

What does Theodoret say of faith in this study? Given the apologetic context, he does not attempt a description of faith which would presuppose that his hearer accepted the truth of revelation and thus, also, what revelation may contribute to one's understanding of faith. Rather, Theodoret wishes to "justify" faith on the basis of the teaching of the Greek philosophers and poets. His first line of argument is that the philosophers themselves require faith from their disciples. Pythagoras demanded that his followers remain silent for their first five years as his disciples (I,55 [SC 57.1, 119]) and the mere fact that "Pythagoras said so" was to be given more weight than any other evidence (I,56 [SC 57.1, 119]). Similarly, Plato encourages us to believe the poets, even though they do not provide proof for what they say (I,58-61 [SC 57.1, 120-121]). For Theodoret this means that the opponents of Christianity are struck down by their own arrows (I,54 [SC 57.1, 119]). Indeed, accepting in faith the revelation of the God of the universe is certainly more reasonable than accepting the word of poets and philosophers (I,57 and 69 [SC 57.1, 119-120 and 122]).

In pointing out the inconsistency of criticizing Christianity for requiring faith but failing to criticize Hellenic writers for doing the same, Theodoret is not trying to undercut the latter so much as to bring to light the necessity of some kind of faith for any sort of learning. Whether with regard to such elementary points as the alphabet (I,94 [SC

57.1, 128]) or advanced disciplines such as geometry and astronomy (I,95–96 [SC 57.1, 129]) or even controversial issues such as the size of the sun (I,97–98 [SC 57.1, 129]), one must place an initial faith in the teacher, if one is to truly advance in knowledge (see I,107 [SC 57.1, 131]). Faith and knowledge are thus closely related and may be said to need each other (I,92 [SC 57.1, 128]); faith comes first, knowledge follows (I,116 [SC 57.1, 133–134]). In response to the critics of Christianity one must say that it is truly absurd to maintain that in all other areas the teacher knows and the disciple must place faith in him, except in the sole case of divine teaching, where the order would be reversed and knowledge must be made to precede faith (I,108 [SC 57.1, 131]).

In paragraphs 70–79 of Book I, Theodoret relates the necessity of faith to the object which Christians seek to know—realities of which there are not clear, visible images (I,72–77 [SC 57.1, 123–124]), indeed "divine things": "We need understanding eyes (*noeron ommaton*) to grasp intelligible things and, just as we need eyes of the body to contemplate visible things, so it is clear that we need faith for initiation into divine things" (I,78 [SC 57.1, 124]). These "eyes of faith" are as close as Theodoret comes in his *Therapy* to that quality of faith which is beyond a simple act of trust in a teacher and instead connotes an ability to see and to comprehend, which had appeared in a number of the earlier ecclesiastical writers (for example, Gregory of Nyssa or John Chrysostom) and which is conveyed by the modern notion of "sensus fidei." Later, he provides a definition of faith: "In our view, faith is a willing acceptance by the soul, the contemplation of a reality which is not seen; it is a stance toward that which is and a grasp of the invisible in harmony with our nature; it is an unambiguous disposition rooted in the souls of those who possess it" (I,91 [SC 57.1, 128]; see also I,107 [SC 57.1, 131]). The fact that Theodoret largely limits his defense of faith to the argument of its universal use and utility is no doubt a result of the quite limited aims of the *Therapy* as an apologetic work. He ends Book One with the words: "Now that you know how necessary faith is, apply to yourselves the silence of Pythagoras; listen tranquilly to our exposé, accepting with faith what we will tell you. Be assured that in this way you will rapidly acquire the truth" (I,128 [SC 57.1, 136]).

Of course, Theodoret's understanding of faith in the opening book and, indeed, throughout the *Therapy for the Hellenic Illnesses* is largely determined by the apologetic scope of that work.[61] Thus it considers primarily the cognitive dimension of faith, justifying faith within the forum of knowing by means of reason. To leave the discussion

of Theodoret's view of faith there would not do him justice. Several
other important themes which concern the salvific, existential aspect of
faith are present in his various exegetical works. Thus faith is what
"justifies" Abraham (*In Genesin*, Interrogatio 68 [PG 80, 177–178]) and
"saves" Rahab (*In Ruth*, Interrogatio 1 [PG 80, 519–520]). Salvation is
the fruit of faith (*In Isaiam* 7,9 and 10,23 [PG 81, 275–276 and
309–310]), a theme which naturally finds expression in Theodoret's
comments on St. Paul's letter to the Romans (*Interpretatio epistulam ad
Romanos*, 3,27–30 and 4,4 [PG 82, 85–86 and 87–88]). Faith is intimately
related to grace (*Interpretatio epistulam ad Philippenses* 1,7 [PG 82,
561–562]); it is a gift of the Holy Spirit (*Interpretatio epistulam ad Ephesios*,
1,13 [PG 82, 513–514]). At the same time these affirmations need to be
complemented by Theodoret's view that faith must find expression in a
life of virtue (*In Genesin*, Interrogatio 68 [PG 80, 177–178]; *In psalmos*
48,1 [PG 80, 1217–1218]); it must be joined to practice (*In Ezechielis
prophetiam* 47,6–7 [PG 81, 1241–1242]). He repeats several times that
faith alone, unaccompanied by good deeds, does not suffice for
salvation (*In Isaiam* 1,23 [PG 81, 231–232] and *Interpretatio epistulam ad
Titum* 3,8 [PG 82, 869–870]). These texts illustrate that, for Theodoret, a
purely intellectual understanding does not adequately reflect the full
reality of faith.

With regard to unity in faith, a comment on Eph 4,5–6 ("there is
one Lord, one faith, one baptism"; PG 82, 533–534) states that it is
fitting that there should be concord (*symphonia, homononia*) among
believers. Theodoret does not elaborate upon this idea to any length.[62]
Certainly one may observe that the vicissitudes surrounding his
involvement in the Councils of Ephesus and Chalcedon show that there
was often a good deal more discord than concord among believers, even
among those who would eventually recognize each other as falling
within the boundaries of sharing the same faith. At Ephesus and for a
considerable time after the reconciliation between Cyril of Alexandria
and John of Antioch, Theodoret refused to condemn Nestorius and
even had to be required to do so twenty years later during the Council of
Chalcedon so as to gain acceptance from the other bishops there
present.[63] Moreover, one hundred years after Chalcedon, the next
ecumenical council, Constantinople II (553), felt it necessary to
condemn several of Theodoret's dogmatic treatises written against Cyril
and the Council of Ephesus and in defense of Theodore of Mopsuestia
and Nestorius.[64] Yet, as Newman noted, history has not judged
Theodoret among the "heretics." It would seem that there is something
to be gleaned from all of this with regard to the topic of unity in faith.

First of all, condemnations, while themselves being rather clear, can veil a number of issues which lurk in the background. The discussions which lead up to such condemnations may be forgotten with the passage of time. The unambiguous denunciation of Nestorius may appear obviously correct today in a way that hides the dangerous tendencies in the Alexandrian theology of those who spearheaded that denunciation. Theodoret was suspicious of the Alexandrian stress on the unity of Christ. This was his theological motive for defending Nestorius' inadequate and erroneous attempt to maintain the unconfused duality of the natures of Christ. He suspected a hidden "monophysitism" in Alexandrine Christology, already reflected in the earlier mistakes about the unity of Christ proposed by Apollinaris and later to come to more explicit expression in the doctrine of Eutyches. While the Alexandrian leader Cyril himself avoids the mistaken understanding of Christ associated with monophysitism (see the formula of union, probably written by Theodoret [!], and the letter of Cyril to John of Antioch),[65] the fact that his successor at Alexandria, Dioscorus, supported the monophysite Eutyches and that much of the Egyptian church did not accept the decisions of Chalcedon, resulting in a break in communion which continues to the present day, would seem to suggest that Theodoret was fundamentally justified in being suspicious of Alexandrian Christology. He was probably right in fearing certain of its emphases; but his intervention to counter these was not careful enough. To do so by defending Nestorius was surely a mistake.

In the next chapter, we will see a similar witness to the rather complex nature of the issues which can be at stake in doctrinal discussions, when we consider Hilary of Poitier's "defense" of bishops who resisted Nicea, not because they followed Arius but because they feared that Nicea's definition opened the way for a Sabellian monarchianism. Thus in both of the major doctrines in question during the first four ecumenical councils (the Trinity for Nicea I and Constantinople I and Christology for Ephesus and Chalcedon), there was what might be called an "orthodox" resistance to the conciliar decisions based upon legitimate fears (of monarchianism, as we shall see, in the first case and of monophysitism here in the second). The "one faith" which the councils eventually came to recognize and sanction was a faith which incorporated the legitimate caveats of the loyal opposition. It was a faith which acknowledged that the Son was homoousios with the Father without thereby collapsing the three persons into one. It was a faith that professed Mary to be Theotokos without thereby collapsing the humanity and divinity of Jesus Christ into one nature. Theodoret's refusal to condemn Nestorius' theology at Ephesus and his willingness to do so at Chalcedon twenty years later illustrates the complexity of the issues involved in the most fundamental mysteries of Christian faith. This patristic testimony to the high degree of subtlety surrounding decisions concerning the faith and, therefore, concerning also the unity of the Church in the faith should not be forgotten. The "trials" of "Blessed" Theodoret, several of whose unnamed works were and remain condemned by the fifth ecumenical council, stand as a witness to this subtlety as well as a call to use great care in approaching the topic of identifying that boundary line beyond which one is no longer properly within the communion of the one faith.

CONCLUSION

The eight authors surveyed in this chapter covering the period which stems roughly from 300 to 450 are strikingly original and profound in their theology and in the specific contributions they make to a deeper understanding of faith and its unity. Three of them—Cyril of Jerusalem, Basil and Theodoret—produced short treatises specifically addressing the nature of faith. All of them were strongly influenced by the great Trinitarian and Christological controversies which raged in their time, although John Chrysostom was something of an exception to the extent that he lived and wrote in the period after the demise of Arianism and before Nestorianism saw the light of day. Because of this context, the doctrinal, cognitive side of faith is present in all of these authors; indeed it is the dominant aspect in writers such as Athanasius and Cyril of Alexandria. Yet many passages recognize the existential and salvific dimensions of faith and a writer like Gregory of Nyssa describes faith as opening a path of mystical ascent and union with God which is otherwise quite beyond human capabilities. With regard to reason, one notices a rather widespread caution, typified by the view of Basil and Gregory of Nazianzus that the presumptuous misuse of reason lay at the root of many of the doctrinal errors of the day or the view of John Chrysostom that the most unlearned believer is wiser by far than the most educated unbeliever.

The Word of God in Scripture is seen as the firm foundation of the Church's doctrines of faith by Cyril of Jerusalem, Basil, John Chrysostom and Theodoret, who all relate the credibility of Scripture to the authority of God. In this way, as well as in the more epistemological considerations of Theodoret in his apology against the ills of Hellenism, the theme of authority takes its place in the discussion of faith. Cyril of

Jerusalem notes that the Creed is a distillation of biblical doctrine, making accessible in kernel the whole of Christian faith, even to those who have not the time, talent or inclination for a life of study. For Athanasius, Basil and Cyril of Alexandria, the Creed of Nicea is the standard of correct faith. Unity in faith is generally seen by these writers as related to various means which the Church uses to maintain and insure such unity: the pastoral ministry of bishops (Gregory of Nazianzus), councils (virtually all of the authors), appeal to the bishop of Rome (Athanasius, Basil, Cyril of Alexandria) and appeal to the consensus of the holy writers of the past (Athanasius, Cyril of Alexandria).

So much solid and nourishing doctrine appears in these great authors from the East. Before integrating it into some overall conclusions about unity in faith in our concluding chapter, we now turn to one final series of investigations to find out what was happening in the West.

Chapter Seven
FAITH AND ITS UNITY
IN POST-NICEAN LATIN WRITERS

The battles concerning Arianism in the life of the Eastern Church during the fourth century could not but have an impact on the West, even though there the danger of becoming Arian was more due to imposition by Arian civil authorities than by any sincere adherence on the part of the faithful or their pastors. In addition, the number of prominent writers is somewhat less than in the East. The present chapter will explore the thought on faith and its unity in three of the principal figures who dominate Latin patrology in the fourth and early fifth centuries: Hilary of Poitier, Ambrose of Milan and Augustine of Hippo.

1. HILARY OF POITIER

Hilary of Poitier (c. 315–387) has been praised as the Athanasius of the West because of his efforts to counter and reverse the spread of Arianism in the middle of the fourth century.[1] He is somewhat unique among the Latin fathers in that, because of his support of Athanasius, he was exiled for several years (356–360) to the East (Phrygia), where he had the opportunity to familiarize himself in detail with the issues in the Christological (and the beginnings of the pneumatological) controversies which caused such division among the bishops there.[2] His *De Trinitate*, the first Western book of its completeness and length about the Trinity, was written during his exile and represents a detailed refutation of the fundamental positions of the Arians as well as an exposition and defense of the doctrine proclaimed by Nicea.[3] Thus his activity and interests can be compared with that of his contemporaries Basil, Gregory of Nazianzus and Gregory of Nyssa.

With regard to the precise topic of faith, A. Gardeil noted that all the elements for a "complete tract on faith" can be found in the topical index to Hilary's works which appears at the end of Volume 10 of

Migne's *Patrologia Latina*.[4] Hilary used the word "faith" with exceptional frequency. A. Peñamaría compiled a remarkably detailed list of more than 1,300 occurrences of the word, which he divided into over 100 different usages: for example, faith as affirming, following, seeking, rejecting; faith of the apostles, of the saints, of the Church; faith related to justification, to salvation and to a holy life; metaphors for faith such as sight, hearing, fire, way, harbor, defense, food; faith as simplicity and trust; faith in relation to reason and knowledge; the growth and decline of faith; the unity of faith; and so forth.[5] Yet for all of this, according to Peñamaría, nowhere in his writings does Hilary provide "a theology of faith."[6] Without going into the very detailed exposition which an exhaustive treatment of the topic would require, what follows will attempt to highlight some of the more salient features of Hilary's understanding of faith with a view toward the guiding theme of the present book, unity in faith.

An initial insight can be gleaned from Hilary's comments about his own conversion to Christianity, found at the beginning of *De Trinitate*. Seeking to live a virtuous life (I,2 [CCL 62, 2]) and to know the author of the gift of life (I,3 [CCL 62, 3]), he eventually stumbled on the books of Moses and the prophets, revealing God the creator who identified himself with the words "I am who am" (Ex 3,15; I,5 [CCL 62, 4–5]). Seeking to further know this God and also troubled by anxiety about the finitude of his own human life, Hilary explored the writings of the New Testament (I,10 [CCL 62, 9–10], where he quotes in full the prologue of the gospel of John). He then relates:

> ...the Word of God became flesh in order that through God the Word made flesh, the flesh might be elevated to God the Word.... My soul, therefore, gladly accepted this doctrine of the divine revelation: to proceed through the flesh to God, to be called to a new birth by faith, to be permitted by his power to obtain a heavenly regeneration. In all this it sees the solicitude of its Father and Creator, nor does it believe that it would be annihilated by Him through whom it had been brought from nothingness to this very thing that it is. All of this is beyond the range of the human mind because reason [is] incapable of grasping the ordinary teachings of heavenly wisdom... (I,11–12 [CCL 62, 9–10]).[7]

Hilary adds that his soul refused to give up his newfound belief because it could not completely understand it, but rather remembered "that it would be able to understand if it believed" (I,12 [CCL 62, 12]; McKenna, 13). This is a first important aspect of faith for Hilary: that it is directed toward what cannot be comprehended. Addressing his opponents, he writes: "You declare that faith serves no purpose if there is nothing that can be comprehended. On the contrary, faith proclaims that this is its purpose: to know that it cannot comprehend that for which it is seeking" (II,11 [CCL 62, 49]; McKenna, 45–46).

Such knowledge of what is beyond human comprehension is possible because God reveals it: "...let us concede to God the knowledge about Himself, and let us humbly submit to His words with reverent awe. For He is a competent witness for Himself who is not known except by Himself" (I,18 [CCL 62, 19]; McKenna, 18; see also III,20 [CCL 62, 90–92] and VI,17 [CCL 62, 215]). Thus, what one believes is not the product of arbitrary choice, but is based upon the meaning of what has been spoken (VII,33 [CCL 62, 300–301]); one enters into faith not by questioning, but by following (*In Matthaeum* 7,10 [PL 9, 957]). This submission brings a certain clarity, as was exemplified by St. Paul's teaching of the faith:

> He did not abandon us to the vague and misleading speculations of an undefined doctrine, or expose the minds of men to uncertain theories, but limited the freedom of our intellect and will through the barriers he himself had constructed and set up against them, so that he did not allow us to be wise except in those things that he had preached, since it is forbidden to believe in any other way than in accordance with the clear-cut definitions of the unchangeable faith (*De Trinitate* XI,1 [CCL 62A, 529]; McKenna, 459).

This helps also to explain the role of Scripture in Hilary's view of faith. His discovery of the truth was at one and the same time a discovery of the Scriptures. His argument against the Arians in *De Trinitate* leans heavily upon Scripture, showing that Arius and his followers misinterpret the biblical texts (I,30 and 32 [CCL 62, 28-29 and 30-31]) or even wish to correct the Word of God: "Oh, the measureless shame of human folly and insolence for not only finding fault with God by not believing His own statements about Himself but even condemning Him by correcting them!" (VI,17 [CCL 62, 215]; McKenna, 185). Hilary finds great significance in the fact that Paul's proclamation of the death and resurrection of Christ in 1 Cor 15,3–8 includes the phrase "according to the Scriptures":

While he did not disregard our feeble thoughts and the slanders against the faith that might perplex us, he only added this conclusion "according to the Scriptures," to his teaching about the death and the resurrection, in order that we might not become helpless because we were tossed about by the wind of useless disputes or hampered by the absurd subtleties of unsound opinions. The untarnished faith would always be called back to this harbor of its own true religion so that it would believe and confess the death of Jesus Christ, the Son of God and the Son of Man, "according to the Scriptures." Thus a God-fearing assurance was placed at our disposal in the struggle against a degrading doctrine, since we are to believe that Christ Jesus died and rose again just as it is written about Him (X,67 [CCL 62A, 521–522]; McKenna, 452).

In *De Trinitate* there are two principal causes which lay at the root of heresy: the misuse of reason and the misinterpretation of Scripture. The arguments of the book are all directed toward countering these two causes.

The fact that faith is the acceptance of God's self-manifestation as recorded in Scripture, thus entailing a knowledge which is beyond what is known simply by reason, implies that there should be no hesitation or doubt in believing (*In Matthaeum* 7,10 [PL 9, 957]; *De Trinitate* X,68–69 [CCL 62A, 523–524]). Hilary interprets Rom 10,8–9 ("The word is near you, on your lips and in your heart") as implying "an unquestioning acceptance of the true faith in our thinking as well as in our speaking" (*De Trinitate* X,70). There should be no distance between the mind and the lips:

It is piety not to doubt; it is justice to believe; and it is salvation to confess. Salvation consists in not being lost amid uncertainties, in not being aroused to foolish talk, in not engaging in any kind of debate about the attributes of God, in not fixing limits for His power, in not searching anew for the causes of the inscrutable mysteries, in confessing the Lord Jesus, and in believing that God raised Him from the dead.... Hence, faith is in simplicity, justice is in faith, and piety is in the confession. God does not call us to the blessed life by means of difficult questions, nor does He lure us on by the various categories of oratorical eloquence. Eternal happiness is obtained completely and easily by believing that God raised Jesus from the dead by confessing that He Himself is the Lord (X,70 [CCL 62A, 525-526]; McKenna, 455-456).

This does not imply for Hilary that faith is divorced from reason. While one needs to guard against the speculations of philosophy (*De Trinitate* I,13 [CCL 62, 12-14]; XII,20 [CCL 62A, 593]) and recognize the limits of human knowledge (*De Trinitate* I,19 [CCL 62, 19]), nevertheless, faith leads to an understanding (*De Trinitate* I,12 and 22 [CCL 62, 12 and 20-21]) and even requires the support of learning so that it can stand fast in times of adversity (*De Trinitate* XII,20 [CCL 62A, 593-594]). Faith knows the mysteries of the kingdom (*In Matthaeum* 13,2 [PL 9, 993]); it can progress and become more perfect (*In Matthaeum* 4,21 [PL 9, 939]).

Hilary shares a number of the convictions about faith which are also expressed by other patristic writers. Abraham is the father of all believers ("*princeps fidei et timoris Dei,*" *In Psalmos* 127,7 [PL 9, 707]; *In Matthaeum* 2,3 [PL 9, 925-926]) and faith is intimately related to justification (*De Trinitate* 10,68-69 [CCL 62A, 523-524]; *In Matthaeum* 31,10-11 [PL 9, 1069-1070]). Faith is God's gift (*De Trinitate* VI,37 [CCL 62, 242]) and, at the same time, engages human freedom (*In Matthaeum* 10,17 and 30,3 [PL 9, 972 and 1065-1066]) and can be spoken of as meritorious (*De Trinitate* VI,33 and 47 [CCL 62, 236 and 252]). Faith should be reflected in a life of holiness (*In Psalmos* 144,17 [PL 9, 862]). Faith brings salvation (*In Matthaeum* 7,4 [PL 9, 995]) and immortality (*De Trinitate* VI,48 [CCL 62, 253]). In general terms one might characterize faith simply as the human side of that relationship which is the covenant (communion) between God and human beings.[8]

This faith is the foundation of the Church (*De Trinitate* VI,37 [CCL 62, 241]). Hilary likes to repeat Paul's teaching (Eph 4,4-6) that there is one Spirit, one hope, one Lord, one faith, one baptism, one God and Father of us all (*De Trinitate* VIII,40 [CCL 62, 353-354]; XI,1-2 [CCL 62A, 529-531]). He links the unity of the faith with the unity of the Church in a particularly forceful way:

It may well be that there is another faith if there are other keys to the kingdom of heaven. It may be that there is another faith, if there will be another Church against which the gates of hell shall not prevail. There may be another faith, if there will be another apostleship that binds and looses in heaven that which has been bound and loosed by it on earth. There may be another faith, if there is a Christ, other than He who is, who will be proclaimed as the Son of God. But, if this faith alone which confesses Christ as the Son of God merited for Peter the glory of all the beatitudes, then that faith which will confess Him rather as a creature made from nothing, since it has not received the keys of the kingdom of heaven, is outside of the faith and power of the Apostle, and is not that Church and does not belong to Christ (*De Trinitate* VI,38 [CCL 62, 243–244]; McKenna, 209).

This passage binds tightly together faith, the Church and Christ. To have "another faith" is to be "outside of" the Church and Christ. In another place, Hilary states whoever alters the faith no longer has faith (*Contra Constantium* 24 [PL 10; 600]).

Furthermore, the references to the apostleship and to Peter in this passage echo other passages from Hilary. The Church's doctrine is that which was preached by the apostles (*De Trinitate* I,2 [CCL 62, 23]); it is based on the testimony (*De Trinitate* I,34 [CCL 62, 33]) and the authority (*De Trinitate* I,36 [CCL 62, 35]) "of the apostles and the gospels." Commenting on Mt 9,36–10,1, where Jesus has pity on the crowd because they are like sheep without a shepherd, Hilary states that Jesus then calls to himself the twelve to give them authority to cast out unclean spirits and to heal in order to show that all the laborers in the harvest must have their origin in the apostles (*In Matthaeum* 10,2 [PL 9, 967]).[9] Knowledge of God and of the profundity of evangelical doctrine comes from the light of the preaching of the apostles (*In Matthaeum* 10,17 [PL 9, 972]). Those who receive the apostles receive Christ and those who receive Christ receive God, commenting on Mt 10,40, so that by a succession of graces (*ordo gratiarum*) to receive the apostles is to receive God (*In Matthaeum* 10,27 [PL 9, 978]). Despite their weakness (*De Trinitate* VI,52 [CCL 62, 257–258] even speaks of their weakness in faith at the moment of Christ's crucifixion and death), the apostles were destined to become foundations and pillars of the churches (*In Psalmos* 67,10 [PL 9, 450]).

The reference to Peter in the text quoted at length above (*De Trinitate* VI,38 [CCL 62, 243-244]) is also developed in Hilary's other writings. Commenting on Peter's confession in Mt 16,16, he writes:

And the confession of Peter obtained the reward of which it was fully worthy, for in the man he saw the Son of God.

> Blessed is he and praised because he extended his vision to
> see beyond his human eyes, regarding not that which was of
> flesh and blood but catching sight of the Son of God by
> revelation of the Father, judged worthy to be the first to
> recognize that which in Christ was of God. O happy he who,
> in the giving of his new name, is foundation of the Church,
> worthy stone on which is built she who breaks the laws of hell,
> the gates of Tartarus and all the prisons of death. O blessed
> doorkeeper of heaven, to whose decision is entrusted the
> keys of access to eternity, whose judgment on earth is taken
> beforehand as authority in heaven, so that what is bound or
> loosed on earth receives also in heaven the condition of that
> same state (*In Matthaeum* 16,7 [PL 9, 1009-1010]).

De Trinitate makes several references to the confession of faith by Peter
(VI,20 and 36 [CCL 62, 219 and 239]), adding that he "amid the silence
of all the Apostles, recognized the Son of God by the revelation of the
Father, for this is beyond the limits of human weakness, and deserved
the supereminent glory by the confession of his blessed faith" (VI,37
[CCL 62, 242]; McKenna, 207-208). These words indicate a certain
priority of Peter among the apostles. Thus, for Hilary, the faith is one
and is entrusted to the one Church; the apostles and Peter played a
foundational role in witnessing to this one faith.

A final reflection on unity in faith may be drawn from Hilary's
De synodis (PL 10, 479-546), which is particularly interesting because
of its irenic purpose.[10] Hilary's aim in this book was to present to
the bishops of the West various Creeds from Eastern councils which
had been held during the years 341-357, so as to convince them that not
all Eastern bishops who had some reluctance about Nicea's term
"*homoousios*" were Arians. Indeed many of the "homoiousian" Creeds
(for "*homoiousios*" instead of "*homoousios*") contained clear rejections of
the Arian view that the Son was a creature. What one sees here is the
recognition that tensions over the appropriateness of a particular word
for expressing the faith do not necessarily imply a real division in faith.
Hilary tried to understand the fears about monarchianism which the
word "*homoousios*" connoted for some of the bishops of the East and,
recognizing their orthodoxy vis-à-vis the more serious threat of
Arianism, consequently sought to reconcile their view with that of
bishops in the West. This shows a spirit which, while passionately
committed to the truth, sought to listen more attentively and
understand more accurately the views of others whose position seemed

different from his own, with the result that he judged some such differences to be more a matter of terminology than of faith. Hilary thus is an example of one whose devotion to truth did not exclude reconciliation; indeed, it required it.

2. AMBROSE OF MILAN

From the biography written by his secretary Paulinus, we learn of Ambrose's great reluctance to accept election as bishop of Milan in 374.[11] Had he not accepted, the Western Church would likely have been deprived of one of its more illustrious doctors. In light of the scope of the present book, it is particularly interesting that his election as bishop seems to have resulted from the situation of a community being divided in faith. Those who adhered to the decisions of the Council of Nicea (325), on the one hand, and those who followed the Arian views of the recently deceased bishop Auxentius, on the other, were unable to agree about who should succeed him. When Ambrose, in his capacity as a civil official, intervened to maintain order, he was unanimously chosen, even though still a catechumen and therefore he first had to be baptized before he could become bishop.

Ambrose was born sometime in the decade of the 330's (the precise year is not known) and died in 397. His literary output spanned the twenty year period from 377–397 and can be roughly divided into two halves on either side of the years 385–387. His later writings show more knowledge of Origen, a predeliction for the Canticle of Canticles and more influence of neoplatonic thought.[12] Ambrose's works may be classified under the categories exegetical (by far the largest group, including commentaries, of varying length, especially on aspects of the book of Genesis, on several psalms and, his longest work, on the gospel of Luke), ascetical-mystical (on the duties of ministers and, especially, on virginity), dogmatic (arguing against various heresies and expounding sound doctrine concerning the Trinity, Christ and the Holy Spirit) as well as some sermons, letters and hymns.

Of all the fathers of the Church Ambrose was perhaps the most influential in secular or public affairs.[13] He was a confidant to the young emperor Gratian, whose request for further information about the doctrinal disputes revolving around the Arian, Sabellian and Macedonian heresies led to the writing of Ambrose's dogmatic works entitled De fide (CSEL 78, 1–307) and De Spiritu sancto (CSEL 79, 5–222).[14] His dealings with other emperors (Valentinian II and Theodosius) and empresses (Justina), and his efforts to insure that new bishops to vacant sees would not be Arian, underscore the active role he played in trying to influence the life of the Church in his time.[15] No small amount of literature about Ambrose concerns his thought and impact in the area of relations between Church and State.[16]

Ambrose's understanding of faith cannot be sought simply in his work having that title (*De fide*), the five books of which almost exclusively consider faith as correct doctrine. This emphasis is understandable in a work executed for the precise purpose of defending certain truths against the "impious" views of Arius and others. But the description of faith as doctrine appears to be undergirded by a more fundamental conception, deriving from Philo of Alexandria, which sees faith as a virtue and, indeed, as "the root of all virtues" (*De Cain et Abel* II, 28 [CSEL 32.1, 402]; see also *De Abraham* I,5,32 [CSEL 32.1, 526–527]; and *De paradiso* 13,64 [CSEL 32.1, 324]).[17] Faith concerns the whole of a person's experience, as the example of Abraham shows, whose entire life was changed and indeed often afflicted by various trials on account of his answer to God's call and promise (cf. *De Abraham* I,8,66 [CSEL 32.1, 545–546]).

Ambrose uses a wide range of images to convey this sense of the global impact of faith upon the life of the believer. He compares coming to faith with childbirth, the joy of the new life of the believer more than compensating for the pains of labor (*Explanatio super psalmum XXXV* 28 [CSEL 64, 69]; cf. *De interpellatione Job et David* I,15 [CSEL 32.2, 220]). Faith is like a rock within each believer, upon which he builds his dwelling place (*Expositio evangelii secundum Lucam* VI, 98 [CSEL 32.4, 275]). Ambrose compares the tables of stone upon which the finger of the Lord wrote the Law and which Moses dashed to the ground when he discovered the idolatry of the Israelites (Ex 32,19) with the hearts of those upon which the finger of the Holy Spirit inscribes the faith. "If faith fails, the tablet of your heart is broken" (*De Spiritu sancto* III, 14 [CSEL 79, 156]; Deferrari, 159). The woman who suffered from a hemorrhage for twelve years and who came up behind Jesus in the midst of a pressing crowd to touch the hem of his garment (Lk 8,42–48) is an image of one who has faith.

> Christ is touched by faith, by faith Christ is seen. He is not touched by the body, not seen with the eyes. For no one sees who seeing does not see; no one hears who does not understand that which he hears; no one touches unless he touches with faith [faithfully, *fideliter*].... If we too want to be healed,

let us touch the hem of Christ's garment with faith. (*Expositio evangelii secundum Lucam* VI,57–58 [CSEL 32.4, 255]).[18]

The sense of faith as entailing an intimate contact with Christ is developed in Ambrose's use of the bride-bridegroom theme, drawn from the Canticle of Canticles, to describe the relation between the Lord and the individual soul.

> "Come, come." The repetition is good because, whether present or absent, you ought to be present to the Lord your God and to please Him. Come when you are present, come when you are absent, although you are still in the body—for to me all those are present whose faith is with me.... And so, "Come, come, my bride; you will come, yes come safely, from the source, which is faith. She comes, yes comes safely, from the earth, and comes safely, who comes to Christ. She comes with the merit of faith and the glory of works that shine like Sanir and Hermon..." (*De Isaac vel anima* 47 [CSEL 32.1, 671–672]).[19]

Obviously, to think of faith merely as an intellectual assent to truths would fall quite short of what Ambrose understands by that word. It is an all encompassing attitude toward and response to God which determines a person's life. Faith is very close to devotion.[20]

Ambrose adds other such "existential" dimensions to his overall presentation of faith. Faith entails growth and transformation, like the mustard seed (Lk 13,19) which becomes a large tree giving shelter to many birds (cf. *Expositio evangelii secundum Lucam* VII,176–186 [CSEL 32.4, 360-366]). Here he also relates faith to the kingdom of heaven: since both faith and the kingdom are compared to a mustard seed; "thus he who has faith, has the kingdom of heaven; and the kingdom of heaven is within us, just as faith is within us" (177 [CSEL 32.4, 361]). Justification comes from faith. As in the case of Abraham, justification is on account of a faith which promptly believes God and does not wait for rational explanations (*De Abraham* I,21 [CSEL 32.1, 516–517]). Faith, not the law, renders people just (*Contra Auxentium* 24 [CSEL 82.3, 97-98]);[21] indeed, the fact that Zechariah is struck dumb at hearing the announcement of the birth of his son symbolizes the silencing of the dispensation of the Law (*Expositio evangelii secundum Lucam* I,39–42 [CSEL 32.4, 35–38]). Faith bears fruit in a virtuous life (*Expositio evangelii secundum Lucam* VII,118 [CSEL 32.4, 332]) and the virtues practiced by those without faith fail to produce their proper fruit (*Explanatio super psalmum* 141 [CSEL 64, 35]). Moreover, to believe without performing the works of faith is to squander one's inheritance just like the prodigal son (*De penitentia* II,15 [CSEL 73, 170]). Whoever enters the Church with faith and good works becomes a member of the heavenly city which comes down from heaven (Apoc 21,2) and whose walls are made of living stones (1 Pet 2,5; so *De apologia David* I,83 [CSEL 32.2, 353]).

When one turns to Ambrose's specifically dogmatic works, one finds that the rich existential meaning of faith which is outlined above is not foreign to but in fact includes a cognitive and doctrinal dimension. Commenting upon Jn 17,3 ("Eternal life is this: to know you, the only true God, and him whom you have sent, Jesus Christ"), Ambrose points out that, just as the Scriptures do not separate the Father from the Son, so neither can we if we hope to receive the reward of eternal life (*De fide* V,17 [CSEL 78, 223]; cf. V, 69 [CSEL 78, 242–243]).[22] Thus Christianity entails a certain knowing (*cognitio*), the content of which the Arians, for example, have come to deny because of their questions and interpretations (*De fide* V,16 [CSEL 78, 222]). Ambrose concludes Book III of *De fide* with a reflection upon the martyrdom of Stephen, who, at the moment of his death, looks up and sees the heavens opening and the Son of man standing at the right hand of God (Acts 7,56). The one for whom the heavens are opened sees Jesus at God's right hand; the one who has closed the eyes of his mind does not. Then, shifting the metaphor, he adds that the heavens will be open for those who confess that Jesus is at God's right hand but will be closed to those who have a different faith (cf. *De fide* III,138 [CSEL 78, 157]).

Because he is convinced that Christian faith gives a true knowledge of God, Ambrose is able to vigorously argue against doctrinal positions which differ from the Trinitarian and Christological decisions of the Council of Nicea (325) as well as against the faulty pneumatology which would be condemned by Constantinople I (381).[23] His argumentation usually amounts to an explanation of the Scriptures, particularly a response to the interpretations of problematic texts upon which the various heresies built their positions.[24] In this he continues a practice which is very common in the anti-heretical writings of many of the fathers. All of that said, however, one needs to bear in mind that, for Ambrose, such knowledge through faith remains modest. The Trinity can still be called "incomprehensible and inexpressible" (*De fide* IV,91 [CSEL 78, 188]).[25] According to Ernst Dassmann, the knowing which Ambrose has in mind is not so much an understanding as an acceptance, a holding firm and confessing.[26] It is truly knowledge, but knowledge only accessible to faith. Here Ambrose has recourse to Is 7,9, so often cited by patristic writers for the purpose of explaining the relation between faith and knowing: "O man, it is beyond you to know the depth of wisdom; it is sufficient for you that you believe. 'For if you do not believe, neither will you understand'" (*De interpellatione Iob et David* I,29 [CSEL 32.2, 230]).[27]

Within this context one should place Ambrose's comments about philosophy. Philosophers are often more concerned about the subtleties of argumentation than about the consideration of the truth: "For this is the glory of dialecticians, if they seem to overpower and refute the truth with words. On the other hand, the definition of faith is that truth not words be weighed. Finally, the simple truth of the fishermen excludes the words of philosophers" (*De incarnatione dominicae sacramento* 89 [CSEL 79, 268]; cf. *De fide* I,84).[28] This is not meant to set up faith in opposition to reason. Referring to the prologue to Luke's gospel, in which Luke states that it is his intention to add his own account to those many already in circulation about "the things which have been accomplished among us" (Lk 1,1), Ambrose notes that the gospel has expanded throughout the whole world, enlightening the minds of believers and strengthening their hearts. The truth of the gospel can be discerned only by the intellect and thus one can attribute a certain reasonability to faith (cf. *Expositio evangelii secundum Lucam* I,4 [CSEL 32.4, 12]). Nevertheless excessive questioning about the doctrines of faith can easily lead one into error, as it had in the case of the Arians: "These, indeed, place all the power of their poisons in dialectical discussion which, according to the definition of the philosophers, has no constructive power but seeks to tear down. But God was not pleased to save his people through dialectic; for the kingdom of God is in simplicity of faith and not in contentions with words" (*De fide* I,42 [CSEL 78, 17–18]).[29]

How might all of this relate to the unity of the Church in faith? First of all, for Ambrose, faith is the "foundation of the Church" (*De incarnationis dominicae sacramento* 34 [CSEL 79, 240]), a foundation which draws together into one heart and one mind (Acts 4,32) people from every nation ("*in unum mente et studio convenerunt*": *Explanatio super psalmum XLVII*, 7–8 [CSEL 64, 351–352]; see also *De Isaac vel anima* 59 [CSEL 32.1, 683]). Faith unites the Church (*Contra Auxentium* 24 [CSEL 82.3, 98]). No doubt this is because faith comes from hearing: "...whoever believes, hears and he hears so that he might believe; whoever does not believe does not hear, but neither wants nor is able to hear lest he believe" (*De fide* II,132 [CSEL 78, 103]). In this regard, the apostles play a very important role. They are the ministers of the divine Word; what they have heard and seen they pass on to others (cf. *Expositio evangelii secundum Lucam* I,5–9 [CSEL 32.4, 12–17]). This transmission is effective: "But we also have seen through John; we have looked with our eyes through the apostles; we too have examined with the finger of Thomas" (Ibid., V,96 [CSEL 32.4, 220]). The apostles thus are "sowers of the faith" (Ibid., V,44 [CSEL 32.4, 199]; VII,59 [CSEL 32.4, 306]). As such they may be spoken of as "foundations" of the Church (Ibid., II,87 [CSEL 32.4, 91]; cf. Eph 2,20), as twelve doors through which the nations may enter (*Expositio Psalmi CXVIII* XXII,37 [CSEL 62, 506]) and, along with the prophets and teachers, as a tower to protect the peace of the vineyard (*Hexameron* III,50 [CSEL 32.1, 92–93]).

Among the apostles, Ambrose recognizes for Peter a special place.

> This, then, is Peter, who has replied for the rest of the Apostles; rather, before the rest of men. And so he is called the foundation, because he knows how to preserve not only his own but the common foundation. Christ agreed with him; the Father revealed it to him. For he who speaks of the true generation of the Father, received it from the Father, did not receive it from the flesh. Faith, then, is the foundation of the Church, for it was not said of Peter's flesh, but of his faith, that "the gates of hell shall not prevail against it." But his confession of faith conquered hell. And this confession did not shut out one heresy, for, since the Church like a good ship is often buffeted by many waves, the foundation of the Church should prevail against all heresies *(De incarnationis dominicae sacramento* 33–34 [CSEL 79, 239–240]; Deferrari, 231).

The commentary on Luke's account of the profession of faith at Caesarea also finds a special importance in the fact that Peter was the first to believe, adding that his faith was decisive and firm, without hesitation and, therefore, a model for all believers (cf. *Expositio evangelii secundum Lucam* VI,93–98 [CSEL 32.4, 272–275]). Ambrose regularly returns to the idea that Jesus founds his Church upon Peter, calling him the "foundation" of the Church (Ibid., IV,68–70 [CSEL 32.4, 174–175]; *De fide* IV,56 [CSEL 78, 176–177]; *De Spiritu sancto* II,158 [CSEL 79, 149]; *De virginitate* 105 [PL 16,292–293]). Moreover, he sees the denial by

Peter (Lk 22,54–60), his tears of repentance (Lk 22,61–62) and his triple profession of love (Jn 21,15–19) as a trial which prepared Peter to undertake the task of pastoring the flock of Christ (*Expositio evangelii secundum Lucam* X,72–92 and 173–179 [CSEL 32.4, 483–490 and 522–526]; *De fide* V,2–4 [CSEL 78, 217]).[30]

Precisely what conclusion can be drawn from this material about Peter has been the object of quite contrasting opinions and need not divert us into a more specific study here.[31] What is clear is that Ambrose sees the Church as united in faith and that its faith is rooted in and to some extent mediated by the apostles, the sowers of faith, among whom Peter exercised a particular role as the one who first professed the faith, for whom the Lord prayed (cf. *De fide* IV,56 [CSEL 78, 176]) and to whom the Lord gave a special pastoral responsibility. In addition to these conduits of the faith from the original group of Jesus' followers, Ambrose also sees an important role for those who later exercise leadership within the Church. Thus in *De fide* V,7–15 (CSEL 78, 218–222), one finds a digression about Ambrose's own duty and task, which he shares with all other priests and bishops, to speak much (*prolixioris sermonis*) so as to "build upon the foundation of the faith" (8). That bishops have a preeminent role in making decisions which regard the faith is expressed in *Epistula* XXI to the Emperor Valentinian II, which contains the often quoted line: "But if we examine the context of holy Scripture or of times past, who will deny that in a matter of faith, in a matter, I say, of faith, bishops usually judge Christian emperors; not emperors bishops" (CSEL 82.3, 76).[32] This rather courageous statement to the emperor is given within the context of general remarks which tend to disparage the voice of the laity in dealing with questions of faith. However, in the same letter, Ambrose states that he "rightfully despises" the council held in Rimini, which differed from the faith of Nicea and during which, according to Ambrose, pressure from pro-Arian civil authorities coerced the bishops to act contrary to their better judgment. Indeed, many of those whom Ambrose called heretics had been ordained as bishops, so that in *De paenitentia* I,7 (CSEL 73, 122), we find the clarification that not all who seem to be bishops are authentic (*veri sacerdotes*); heresies cannot in principle have authentic ministers. Thus Ambrose gives a very important role to the apostles and to Peter as well as to bishops and even the Church of Rome with regard to their excercising a special role in preserving the unity of the Church in the faith. At the same time, he was aware that the mere fact of being ordained or of gathering together in a "council" did not guarantee that bishops would necessarily teach authentic doctrine.

3. AUGUSTINE OF HIPPO

Plumbing the mind of St. Augustine on faith and its unity both demands an unusual effort and delivers an unusual reward. This is so not only because of the immensity of what he has written and what has been written about him, but also because the themes of faith and of the unity of the Church touched his life in a very personal way.[33]

Faith, its intellectual integrity and existential necessity were deeply enmeshed in the great pursuit of wisdom which culminated in Augustine's conversion, the struggle leading up to which is so dramatically unfolded in the early books of the *Confessions*.[34] At the climax of that story, after Augustine reads Paul's words exhorting the Romans to put off rioting and drunkenness and to put on the Lord Jesus Christ (13,13–14), a great peace comes over him. The text continues:

> Before shutting the book I put my finger or some other marker in the place and told Alypius what had happened. By now my face was perfectly calm. And Alypius in his turn told me what had been going on in himself, and which I knew nothing about. He asked to see the passage which I had read. I showed him and he went on further than the part I had read, nor did I know the words which followed. They were these: *Him that is weak in the faith, receive.* He applied this to himself and told me so (CSEL 33, 195).[35]

It is most fitting that this account of Augustine's conversion should include a reference to faith, albeit in this case to the "weak faith" of Alypius. For it was precisely the problem of faith, of having to accept Catholic doctrines on the basis of authority and not as established by reason, which sidetracked Augustine to a nine year sojourn among the Manichaeans.[36] This seminal experience of his life as a believer, that is, of having struggled with the problem of the intellectual acceptability of faith, provided the stimulus for writing a number of books about faith over the course of the years: *The Advantage of Believing* (written in the year 391, roughly five years after the scene of his conversion described above), *Faith and the Creed* (393), *The Christian Combat* (a rewriting of *Faith and the Creed* for those whose knowledge of Latin was weak, 397), *On Faith in Things Unseen* (399), *Faith and Works* (413), and *Faith, Hope and Charity* (421).[37] In addition to these books which are more or less directly concerned with analyzing or describing faith, Augustine takes up the theme more tangentially in many other books, sermons and letters.

The unity of the Church, on the other hand, became a particular focus for Augustine within the context of his long struggle against the Donatists in North Africa. Here the issue was not so much faith as such but rather the nature of the Church as inclusive of both saints and sinners, and of that universal unity which Augustine refers to as the *catholica* in contrast with the mere *pars Donati*.[38] While the precise theme of "unity in faith" does not appear as the immediate focus in his writings about Donatism, the presupposition of these writings, as indeed of all of his many polemical writings, is that those against whom he is writing (principally Manichaeans, Donatists, Pelagians and Arians) are divided from the unity of the whole Church, the catholica, because of a lack of unity in *faith*.

Thus faith and its unity were themes to which Augustine energetically devoted his attention in a wide range of varying contexts.

One probably cannot obtain a sense of the meaning and importance of faith for Augustine if one does not try to appreciate the supposed opposition between faith and reason of which he was convinced from the age of nineteen until his estrangement from Manichaeanism at the age of twenty-eight. Faith seemed to be credulity. It seemed to require accepting something as true without a reasonable basis for such acceptance. The Manichaeans promised to establish their doctrines by reason, without exacting any sacrificium intellectus. Because of this epistemological context, one may say that, in addition to whatever moral and spiritual aspects it entailed, Augustine's conversion was also highly intellectual. It consisted of a twofold change of mind: a growing disillusionment with the "purely reasonable" doctrinal explanations of the Manichaeans and a gradual acceptance that it can be reasonable to believe after all. Augustine recounts this change most directly in *The Advantage of Believing* and the *Confessions*.[39]

Regarding his disillusion with the Manichaeans, Augustine notes that they were "more fluent and eloquent in refuting others than they were strong and sure in proving their own beliefs," adding: "But because they disputed widely and vigorously for a long time and in much detail over the errors of the unlearned—something which I learned too late was very easy for anyone of average learning—we thought that we should necessarily retain whatever they implanted in us of their own doctrine, since we met no other with which we might be satisfied" (*Advantage* I,2 [CSEL 25, 5]; Meagher, 393). Increasingly finding that his perplexities about Manichaean doctrine received no satisfying explanation, Augustine placed high hopes in meeting a certain Faustus, who enjoyed an exceptional reputation for intelligence. A lovely passage in the *Confessions* V,6 recounts:

> For the other Manichees whom I met and who failed to pro-
> duce any answers to the questions I was raising on these
> subjects were always putting forward his name and promis-
> ing me that as soon as Faustus arrived and I was able to dis-
> cuss matters with him, all these difficulties of mine,
> together with any more weighty questions that I might care
> to ask, would be very easily dealt with and very lucidly
> explained. Well, he did arrive, and I found him a charming
> man with a very pleasant choice of words; he came out with
> exactly the same things as the others are always saying, but
> he did it much more elegantly. However, my thirst could
> not be relieved by expensive drinking vessels and a well-
> dressed waiter. My ears were full already of this stuff, and
> the arguments themselves did not appear to me to be any
> better simply because they were better expressed; elo-
> quence did not make them true; nor could I consider the
> soul wise because the face was attractive and the words well
> chosen. And as to those who promised me so much of him,
> they were not good judges of things (CSEL 33, 96; Warner,
> 96).

Augustine's disappointment with the empty eloquence of Faustus was for him the last straw which definitively broke his adherence to Manichaeanism.

At the same time, it was accompanied by a more positive insight, which would open the way for his drawing close to the Catholic Church: that it could be reasonable to believe. For one thing, human life would be impossible were one to doubt everything which one could not establish by reason alone.

> I considered what a countless number of things there were
> which I believed though I had not seen them and had not
> been present when they had taken place—so many historical
> events, so many facts about countries and cities which I had
> never seen, so many things told me by friends, by doctors, by
> one man or another man—and unless we believed these
> things, we should get nothing done at all in this life. Then in
> particular I considered how fixed and unalterable was the

belief I held that I was the son of a particular father and mother, a thing which I could not possibly know unless I had believed it on the word of others (*Confessions* VI,5 [CSEL 33, 120]; Warner, 117; see also *Advantage* XI,25–XII,26 [CSEL 25, 31-34]).[40]

If belief is for all practical purposes inevitable, are human beings necessarily condemned to credulity? Augustine's way out of this dilemma (either credulity or practical inactivity) is to distinguish between belief and opinion. Belief involves the acceptance of the testimony of another whom one has good reason to regard as trustworthy; opinion, on the other hand, is thinking that one knows that of which one is actually ignorant.[41] It is the latter—opinion—which is open to the charge of credulity. Belief, instead, can and must be distinguished from credulity in that it is reasonable, based upon the trustworthiness of the one who is believed.[42] Augustine sums up these epistemological reflections as follows: "What we understand, accordingly, we owe to reason; what we believe, to authority; and what we have an opinion on, to error" (Advantage XI,25 [CSEL 25, 32;]; Meagher, 425).

The crucial question becomes therefore: Is there an authority which one has good reason to believe? This is precisely the way in which reflection upon faith led Augustine to the question of authority. He writes: "...I thought that the truth lay in no wise hidden except in the way it should be sought, and that this same way would have to be taken from some divine authority. It remained to find out what that authority was..." (*Advantage* VIII,20 [CSEL 25, 25]; Meagher, 416).43 If belief is nothing other than the acceptance of the teaching of an authority and if there can be sound reasons in favor of such acceptance, then the opposition between belief and reason is overcome. One is not faced with the dilemma of choosing either faith or reason. Faith and reason are of one piece. What one knows by reason is complemented and enhanced by what one believes; what one believes is penetrated and becomes more deeply comprehended by means of reason. This means that faith and reason are not to be considered as mutually exclusive alternatives, which was precisely the way Augustine had considered them when he cast his lot with the Manichaeans.

"...what we believe [we owe] to authority..." (*Advantage* XI,25 [CSEL 25, 32]; Meagher, 425). This correlation between authority and faith is reinforced when Augustine reflects upon the temporal priority which both enjoy in relation to reason.

We are guided in a twofold way, by authority and by reason. In time, authority has the prior place; in matter, reason.... Thus it follows that to those desiring to learn the great and hidden good it is authority which opens the door. And whoever enters by it and, leaving doubt behind, follows the precepts for a truly good life, and has been made receptive to teaching by them, will at length learn how pre-eminently possessed of reason those things are which he pursued before he saw their reason, and what that reason itself is, which, now that he is made steadfast and equal to his task in the cradle of authority, he now follows and comprehends... (*De Ordine* II,9,26 [CSEL 63, 165]; Przywara, 54).

This image of authority as a cradle is complemented by another—the shade provided by the boughs of a tree: "The order of nature is such that, when we learn anything, authority precedes reason.... And because the minds of men are obscured by the habitual darkness of sin and evil which enshrouds them and, as a consequence, lack the clarity of perception proper to reason, it has been beneficially provided that the dazzled eye be led into the light of truth beneath the boughs of authority" (*The Way of the Catholic Church* I,2,3 [CSEL 90,5]).[44] Augustine's point is that the weakness of human understanding in coming to know the truth of the things of God, a weakness which may be compared to infancy or to having eyes which are only accustomed to seeing in the shadows, implies the need for the aid of authority in coming to grasp what is true. For this reason, he concludes: "there is no sounder principle in the Catholic Church than that authority should precede reason" (*The Way of the Catholic Church* I,25,47 [CSEL 90, 52]; Gallagher & Gallagher, 39). This same temporal priority is also attributed to *faith* vis-á-vis reason (see *Contra Faustum* XVI,8 [CSEL 25, 446–447] and *De vera religione* 14 [CSEL 77, 20], both of which emphasize that Christians first believe on the basis of sound authority and only later pose questions which lead to fuller understanding).

Nevertheless, it is important to notice that there is also a certain priority to reason: "In time, authority has the prior place; in matter, reason..." (*De Ordine* II,9,26 [CSEL 63, 165]; Przywara, 54). This priority takes two forms. First, as has been indicated above, faith can be regarded as reasonable at all only and precisely because a particular authority can be individuated as worthy of trust and belief. Reason indicates whom one should believe (cf. *De vera religione* XXIV,45 [CSEL 77B, 32]), thereby rendering faith reasonable. Augustine does not tire of pointing out reasons for believing the authority of the Church, placing special weight on the improbable fact that, despite its apparently humble origins, it had spread throughout the known world: "Now, does this seem vain or unsubstantial to you, and do you think that it is either a little or no divine miracle that all mankind runs its course in the name of the One crucified?" (*On Faith in Things Unseen* IV,7 [CCL 46, 11]; Deferrari & McDonald, 461; see also *Advantage* XIV,31–XVII,35 [CSEL 25, 38–46]; *Confessions* VI,11 [CSEL 33, 133–134]; *The Way of the Catholic Church* I,7,12 [CSEL 90, 14]; *De catechizandis rudibus* VI,10 [CCL 46, 130–131];[45] *Epistula 137* IV,15–16 [CSEL 44, 117-121];[46] *Civitas Dei* XXII,5-6 [CSEL 40.2, 588–594]).

Secondly and more importantly, reason enjoys a certain priority insofar as faith is seen as a first step which leads to understanding: "For faith is understanding's step, and understanding is faith's reward" (*Serm. [de Script. Nov. Test.]* CXXVI i,1 [PL 38,698]; ii,3 [PL 38,699]; Przywara, 52). "We believed that we might know; for if we wished first to know and then to believe, we should not be able either to know or to believe" (*In Joannis Evangelium* XXVII, 9 [CCL 36, 274]; Przywara, 58). Thus to a certain extent, faith needs to be overcome, to be gone beyond. At the opening of his work *Faith and the Creed*, Augustine speaks of those "possessed of spiritual insight," who "have been found worthy not only to embrace and believe the Catholic faith as set forth in the words of the Creed, but also to possess a knowledge and understanding of it, being further aided by enlightenment from the Lord. For it is written: 'Unless you believe, you shall not understand'" (*Faith and the Creed* I,1 [CSEL 41, 4; Russell I, 316). Thus a certain progression is possible: "what before was only believed begins to be clearly understood" (*The Christian Combat* XIII,14 [CSEL 41, 117]; Russell II, 331).

As these texts indicate, such growth in understanding can obviously happen to some degree in the present life. But it requires a certain humility. A magnificent passage in which Augustine speaks about his reading of St. Paul addresses this point of the attitude required for growth in understanding.

So I most greedily seized upon the venerable writings of your spirit and in particular the works of the apostle Paul.... I discovered that everything in the Platonists which I had found true was expressed here, but it was expressed to the glory of your grace; so that whoever sees should not *so glory as if he had not received*—received, indeed, not only what he sees but also the power to see it; for what hath he, which he hath not

received. I found too that one is not only instructed so as to
see you, who are the same forever, but also so as to grow
strong enough to lay hold on you, and he who cannot see you
for the distance, may yet walk along the road by which he will
arrive and see you and lay hold on you.... None of this is found
in the books of the Platonists. Their pages make no mention
of the face and look of pity, the tears of confession, your
sacrifice—a troubled spirit, a broken and contrite heart, the
salvation of the people, *the bridal city, the earnest of the Holy
Ghost, the cup of our redemption....* They are too proud to *learn of
Him, because He is meek and lowly of heart; for these things hast
Thou hid from the wise and prudent and hast revealed them unto
babes....* In marvelous ways these things grew and fixed
themselves in the depths of my being as I read that *least of Thy
apostles,* and had meditated upon your works and had
trembled (*Confessions* VII,21 [CSEL 33, 166-168]; Warner,
157–159).

In this connection Augustine comments from time to time upon
Scripture passages such as "Blessed are the pure in heart, for they shall
see God" (Mt 5,8) or "[the Holy Spirit] cleansed their hearts by faith"
(Acts 15,9), explaining them as referring to that purification which is
prerequisite to enjoying the vision of God (*In Ps. CIX* 8 [CCL 40, 1608]; *In
Ps. XCVII* 3 [CSEL 39, 1373-1374]). His early work, *The Magnitude of the
Soul,* includes a catalogue of the "seven degrees" of the soul's greatness.[47]
While the first two degrees discuss the soul (the principle of life) as
enjoyed also by plants and animals, degrees three through seven read as a
kind of itinerary of the human soul to God, in which gradual purification
leads to its resting in God, as if in a dwelling place (*Magnitude* XXXIII,70-
76 [CSEL 89, 217-225]).[48] This progression is captured in a brief text
from *Faith, Hope and Charity* I,5 (CCL 46, 50; Peebles, 371):

> Now the mind, once it has been imbued with the beginning
> of faith (which works through charity), tends through good
> living to attain unto sight, whereby the righteous and pure of
> heart know that ineffable beauty whose full vision is supreme
> happiness.... We begin in faith; we achieve by sight. This is
> the sum-total of the whole doctrine.

Such heady optimism about knowing God must be tempered by the
sober realism of passages such as that in his later work, *The Retractations,*

concerning his early discussion of faith and knowledge in *The Advantage of Believing*. Looking back, Augustine now cautions modesty with regard to the claim and extent of human knowledge of God in this life. The context is a statement from the *Advantage* which distinguished those who have already found the truth from those who are still seeking. Augustine recalls the text from St. Paul: "For now we see in a mirror dimly, but then face to face. Now I know in part; then I shall understand fully, even as I have been fully understood" (1 Cor 13,12), to support his main point: "For in this life, knowledge, however extensive, does not constitute complete happiness, because that part of it which is unknown is by far incomparably greater" (*Retractations* XIII,2 [CSEL 36, 66]; Bogan, 60). This eschatological backdrop is never forgotten by Augustine, as a few further texts illustrate. "For what we are seeking at His behest, that we shall find upon His manifesting it to us Himself, so far as these things can be found in this life.... We must believe that they are perceived and grasped more clearly and perfectly...by all good and religious men after their present life" (*De libero arbitrio* II,ii,6 [CSEL 74, 41–42]).[49] Or again:

> For even now He is in us and we in Him. Only, now we believe this, but then we shall also know. Although even now we know by faith, but then we shall know by beholding....For now, He hath loved us to the end that we should believe and keep the commandment of faith; but then, He will love us to the end that we may see, and in seeing receive the reward of our faith. For even now we love by believing in that which we shall hereafter see; but then we shall love by seeing that which we now believe (*In Joannis Evangelium* LXXV,4 and 5 [CCL 36, 516 and 517]; Przywara, 60).

Thus Augustine never loses sight of the limits of knowledge of God in this life.[50]

To these general characteristics of faith must be added several additional points. First of all, Augustine clearly relates faith to the Creed and to doctrine. Of the six books we have listed above as explicitly dedicated to a discussion of faith, three are little more than commentaries on the Creed (*Faith and the Creed, The Christian Combat* and *Faith, Hope and Charity*). The first of these begins with a passage which reveals the importance of "truths" or doctrines in Augustine's conception of faith.

As expressed in the Creed, the Catholic faith is familiar to believers who have learned it by heart in as few words as the subject permits. In this way the truths to be believed are framed in few words for the benefit of those who have been born again in Christ, for beginners and young ones whose faith has not yet been made strong by a careful training in the spiritual meaning of the divine Scriptures. This faith is to be expounded to them at greater length as they advance and rise to the heights of divine knowledge along the sure path of humility and charity (*Faith and the Creed* I,1 [CSEL 41, 3-4]; Russell I, 315-316).[51]

Augustine immediately goes on to note that "underneath these few words of the Creed,...most heretics have attempted to conceal their poisonous wares" (*Faith and the Creed* I,1 [CSEL 41, 4]; Russell I, 316). The three books which are commentaries upon the Creed include both a positive exposition of orthodox doctrine as well as a refutation of heretical positions. The presupposition of such a procedure is, of course, that Christianity entails a certain body of doctrine which can to some extent be understood and from which alternative doctrines presenting themselves as Christian can be distinguished and shown to be erroneous. Moreover, Augustine also repeats the patristic tradition to the effect that heresy is permitted by God because its refutation can serve to benefit the Church (with reference to 1 Cor 11,19; in *On Faith in Things Unseen* VII,10 [CCL 46, 18]; *Civitas Dei* XVI,2 [CSEL 40.2, 124–127]; XVIII,51 [CSEL 40.2, 351–354]).

Secondly, following the Scriptures, Augustine understands faith as closely associated with justification and salvation.

The fact that "the just man lives by faith" (Hab 2,4; Gal 3,2) is a matter of Scripture as well as a truth corroborated by the very weighty authority of apostolic tradition. And since this faith requires of us the service of both heart and tongue, we must be mindful both of justice and salvation, for the Apostle says: "With the heart a man believes unto justice, and with the mouth profession of faith is made unto salvation" (Rom 10,10) (*Faith and the Creed* I,1 [CSEL 41, 3]; Russell I, 315).

Magnus Löhrer, in his analysis of faith in the early writings of Augustine, sees a crucial advance in the latter's understanding when he begins to consider faith not simply from the problematic of the relation between faith and reason but also from within that of the relation between grace and freedom.[52] Faith is an act of God, the effect of God's grace. In a passage attempting to explain why the miracles which occur so often in the gospels do not seem to take place anymore, Augustine speaks of the change which today occurs in the life of so many individual believers throughout the world as more wonderful than the miracles recounted in Scripture.

> For as the soul is better than the body, so is the health of the soul a better thing than the health of the body. The blind body doth not now open its eyes by a miracle of the Lord, but the blinded heart openeth its eyes to the word of the Lord. The mortal corpse doth not now rise from the dead, but the soul which lay dead in a living body doth rise again. The deaf ears of the body are not now opened, but how many have the ears of their heart closed, which yet fly open at the penetrating word of God, so that they believe who did not believe, and they live well who lived evilly, and they obey who obeyed not, and we say, "Such a man is become a believer"; and we wonder when we hear of them we had known as hardened (*Serm. [de Scrip. N.T.]* LXXXVIII, 3, 3; [PL 38, 540]; Przywara, 47).

In his work *De spiritu et littera*, Augustine explains that faith is surely a voluntary action, yet one that is only possible precisely because God acts upon a person in such a way that "the very will by which we believe is reckoned as a gift of God" (XXXIV,60 [CSEL 60, 220]; see also, XXXI,54 [CSEL 60, 211]).[53] "...faith itself is not to be attributed to the human free will...nor to any antecedent merits...; but we must confess it as a free gift of God,...because we read in the same Epistle: 'God hath divided to every one the measure of faith' Rom 12.3" (*Epistula CXCIV* iii,9 [CSEL 57, 183]).[54]

That faith is intimately connected with justification and salvation and may be thought of almost as a miracle of God's grace is not unrelated to yet a further clarification by Augustine—that faith should always be bound together with an effort to live a good life. The aim of *Faith and Works* is to respond to possible misunderstandings which could flow from the insight that faith is a gift and work of God. In particular, Augustine wishes to respond to three points: that avowed sinners who express no desire to change their lives can be baptized (I,1–VI,8 [CSEL 41, 35–44]), that only doctrine need to be taught prior to baptism and teachings regarding the moral life can be left to later (VI,9-XIII,20 [CSEL 41,

44–61]) and that ultimately the baptized will be saved regardless of whether or not they reform their lives (XIV,21–XXVI,48 [CSEL 41, 61-95]).[55] His method is to marshall many New Testament texts which insist on the need for conversion (for example, Mt 18,15–18), for putting on the "new man" (for example, Col 3,9–10) and for avoiding actions which will exclude one from the kingdom of God (for example, 1 Cor 6,9–10).

One can conclude this sketch of Augustine's view of faith by pointing out how positively he conceives of it. Faith brings health to the person; it is like a healing medicine. Recalling his state when he still withheld belief, Augustine writes:

> By believing I might have been cured, so that the sight of my mind would be clearer and might be somehow or other directed toward your truth which is the same forever and in no point fails. But it was the same with me as with a man who, having once had a bad doctor, is afraid to trusting himself even to a good one. So it was with the health of my soul which could not possibly be cured except by believing, but refused to be cured for fear of believing something false (*Confessions* VI,4 [CSEL 33, 119–120]; Warner, 117).

This text associates once again faith with sight. In any number of places Augustine writes of the "eyes of faith": "...when faith acts in its own sphere, reason, following after, finds something of what faith was seeking.... For faith has its own eyes with which it sees, so to speak, that what it does not yet see is true...."[56] Within this very positive outlook one must situate Augustine's repeated reference to that scripture text which inspired many patristic writers in their reflection upon faith: "Unless you believe, you will not stand firm/understand" (Is 7,9).[57] For Augustine, this passage from Isaiah means that faith is a necessary point of departure for knowledge of the things of God: believe so that you may understand (crede ut intelligas).[58]

Turning to the topic of unity in faith, Augustine's thought must be approached in a rather indirect and circumspect way since, while many of his writings directly examine faith and its content, the precise theme of unity in faith is more a subject which Augustine presupposes than one upon which he reflects explicitly. He is convinced of and thoroughly committed to the universal unity of the Church. Unity in faith is one of the principal components of this unity. The greatest evidence of Augustine's conviction that the Church is and must be one in faith is the overwhelming predominance of what might be called, although the word has a rather negative connotation today, the polemical nature of much of his writings.[59] Many texts could serve to illustrate this, but perhaps a brief glance at the aptly titled *The Christian Combat* (= *De agone christiano*) will suffice.

As noted above, this text takes the basic form of a commentary upon the Creed. But what is most striking is that it is not a positive elaboration or presentation of the various individual articles comprising the Creed but rather a refutation of the errors which had been proposed by various heretics in connection with each of the single articles. Augustine launches the work with a reflection upon 2 Tim 4,7-8: "I have fought the good fight, I have finished the race, I have kept the faith. Henceforth there is laid up for me the crown of righteousness." The adversary over whom Paul is victorious in *keeping the faith*, explains Augustine, is none other than the Devil (I,1 [CSEL 41, 102]). The various heretics are represented as proposing diabolical doctrines, which are "blasphemies against Almighty God" (IV,4 [CSEL 41, 105]).[60] Augustine's purpose in this book is to assist his readers to "keep the faith" after the example of St. Paul and, therefore, also to be able to await a similar crown of victory. Within this context, one of the most striking features of the book is the literary device employed throughout the actual commentary on the Creed (XIV,16–XXXII,34 [CSEL 41, 119–37]) of beginning each chapter with the words: "Let us not heed those who say...." Time and again Augustine explains, usually by means of rational argument but sometimes by reference to Scripture, why various heretical doctrines are erroneous.

Reason, of course, is not the only tool to which Augustine has recourse in arguing on behalf of those positions which constitute true doctrine and in the acceptance of which the whole Church enjoys unity of faith. Given what has been noted earlier on the essential interrelation between faith and authority in Augustine's thought, he is quite consistent in giving authority a principal role in the maintenance of unity in faith. We have already seen that, for him, faith is not credulity because it is not unreasonable to place trust in an authority which reason recommends as credible. Now just such an authority is the Catholic, universal Church (as distinct from the various heretical *partes*; see above pages 175 and 178-179). But it would be a mistake to limit Augustine's designation of the credible authorities upon which unity of faith is based simply to the Church. In several densely packed pages about Augustine's theological method, A. Trapè lists both Scripture and Tradition along with the Church as those "authorities" to which his theology had constant recourse.[61]

Trapè rightly points out that Augustine's conversion was marked by a prolonged and serious study of the Scriptures, made possible partly by his ability to see that the perplexities which had plagued him about the apparent contradictions in Scripture could be resolved with the proper interpretation (cf. *Confessions* V,14 [CSEL 33, 111]).[62] This affirmation of the authority of Scripture is attested to both by the fact that Augustine produced many hundreds of pages of commentary and sermons upon various books of the Bible (most especially upon Genesis, Psalms and John) as well as by the fact that many of his "systematic" works begin with a synthesis of the biblical doctrine relevant to the question at hand (for example, Books I–IV of *De Trinitate* [CCL 50, 27–205]). Nevertheless, Scripture cannot simply be thought of as a self-sufficient authority, especially as a force for maintaining unity in faith, for there always remains the delicate problem of its correct interpretation. The close of the first book of *Christian Instruction* (I, 36,40–40,44 [CSEL 80, 30–33]) comments upon the danger of faulty interpretation and notes that all correct interpretation should lead to the practice of the virtues. Augustine goes so far as to say that "a man who relies upon faith, hope, and charity and resolutely holds fast to them does not need the Scriptures, except to teach others" (I,39,43 [CSEL 80, 32]; Gavigan, 59). What is the proper disposition required for reading the Scriptures? "...when anyone recognizes that 'the end of the precept is charity from a pure heart and a good conscience and faith unfeigned,' and proposes to refer his whole comprehension of Sacred Scriptures to these three virtues [faith, hope and charity], he may approach the interpretation of those books fearlessly" (I,40,44 [CSEL 80, 33]; Gavigan, 60). These comments point out a certain primacy of virtue over the mere knowledge of the various details of Scripture. But, beyond this and more directly related to the topic of unity in faith, Augustine notes that heresy or division in faith is often based upon the misinterpretation of Scripture (see, for example, *The Christian Combat* XXVII,29 [CSEL 41, 129]; *Christian Instruction* III,2,3 [CSEL 80, 80]). This problem of misinterpretation means that, for Augustine, a simplistic approach to the authority of Scripture, without an acknowledgment of the need for careful attention to the question of proper interpretation, would never be sufficient.

Augustine also refers to the authority of tradition, not only in incidental ways, such as the reference to the "weighty authority of apostolic tradition" which we have seen above concerning justification by faith (*Faith and the Creed* I,1 on page 182 above), but also as a general principle underlying the belief and practice of the Church. In *De baptismo*

(II,12 [CSEL 51, 187]; V,31 [CSEL 51, 289]) he speaks of the many
customs which are found neither in Scripture nor in the decisions of the
councils but which nevertheless have been handed on and are observed
"per universam ecclesiam." The baptism of infants, the practice of not
rebaptizing heretics, various liturgical practices and fasts are examples of
such traditions for Augustine. Their universal acceptance or catholicity is
the sign of their authenticity and apostolicity.[63] Moreover, it is precisely
when he speaks of tradition that Augustine offers one of his clearest
statements about unity in faith as well as about that diversity which such
unity can include. The context is an attempt to mediate between the
claims of those who uphold various practices within the Church on the
basis of the traditions handed down by apostles:

> But, if the answer is made that James taught this at Jerusalem,
> and John at Ephesus, as Peter did at Rome, namely that one
> should fast on Saturday, but that the other lands fell away from
> this teaching, while Rome remained steadfast; and if the other
> side retorts that it was rather certain localities in the west,
> including Rome, which did not hold the tradition of the
> Apostles, while the lands of the east, where the Gospel was
> first preached, remained firm without any variation in the
> tradition handed down by all the Apostles as well as by Peter
> himself, namely that one should not fast on Saturday, then this
> is an interminable quarrel, begetting contention and endless
> argument. Let there be one faith of the universal Church,
> which is spread abroad everywhere, just as within the Church
> among the members, even if that same unity of faith is
> manifested by diverse practices, what is true in the faith is
> nowise hindered by that diversity. 'All the glory of the king's
> daughter is within.' But, those observances which are differ-
> ently practised are prefigured by her garment, of which it is
> said: 'In golden borders, clothed round about with varieties.'
> Let that garment also be so varied by diverse observances, but
> not so as to be rent by contradiction and controversy (*Epistula
> XXXVI*, 22 [CSEL 34, 51–52]); Parsons I, 157-158).

Obviously, Augustine does not understand unity in faith as eliminating
the variety of colors in the garment of the Church, the king's daughter
here in his comment upon Psalm 45,14–15.
    In addition to the authority of Scripture and Tradition, the voice of
the Church carries an important weight, particularly in maintaining unity

in faith. Secondary sources are fond of repeating the rather forceful statement which almost seems to place the authority of the Church above that of Scripture: "For my part, I should not believe the gospel except as moved by the authority of the Catholic Church" (*Contra epistulam... fundamenti*, 5 [CSEL 25, 197]).[64] This assertion needs to be nuanced by its context, which is a refutation of the Manichaean claim that Manes can properly be called an apostle, given various indications within the New Testament as to the identity of an apostle. Within this precise context Augustine retorts: you ask me to believe that Manes is an apostle on the basis of the Scriptures but I only know which books make up the Scriptures by means of the authority of the Church, the same authority which has also denied that Manes can be considered an apostle. Thus, Augustine's primary argument here is to point to a logical inconsistency in the argument of the Manichaeans. Nevertheless, while it would not be entirely proper to see here a subordination of the authority of Scripture to that of the Church, this comment does presuppose that the authority of the Church is indispensable for interpreting Scripture and for resolving even that most basic question of which books are to be considered as the inspired Word of God.[65]

The authority of the Church is indispensable in other ways as well. It transmits and interprets the tradition (*Letter* 54,1 [CSEL 34, 159]; *De baptismo* II,7,12 [CSEL 51, 187]);[66] it opposes heresies (*De baptismo* II,4,5 [CSEL 51, 48-49]); it establishes the *regula fidei* (*Christian Instruction* III,2,2 [CSEL 80, 79]).[67] One can always rest secure if one remains with the Church, no matter what difficulty arises (*De baptismo* III,2,2 [CSEL 51, 197-198]). In the final remarkable section of a letter to the Donatists, Augustine expresses this confidence in the Church by means of the unusual ploy of applying Jesus' condemnation of the scribes and Pharisees ("observe whatever they tell you, but not what they do"—Mt 23,3) to leaders within the Church. After mentioning that the Church, spread abroad through the nations, tolerates within its midst weeds among the wheat and chaff mixed with the good grain, that its nets of the word and the sacraments enclose both good and bad fish, Augustine adds:

> For this reason the Lord strengthened the patience of His servants by these and other parables, to prevent them from thinking that their virtue would be defiled by contact with wicked men, and thus, through human and vain dissensions, they should lose the little ones, or these should perish. The heavenly Master went so far in forewarning them that He

even warned His people against bad rulers, lest, on their account, the saving chair of doctrine should be forsaken, in which even the wicked are forced to utter truth; for the words they speak come not from themselves but from God, and He has placed the teaching of truth upon the chair of unity (*Epistula CV* [CSEL 34, 609]; Parsons II, 210).

The reason for Augustine's optimism in this letter that human weakness cannot destroy the virtue or the doctrine of the Church lies in his association of the Church with Christ. This same *Epistula CV* includes an incredible sequence opening with the words: "In the Scriptures we have learned Christ; in the Scriptures we have learned the Church. We both possess the Scriptures; why do we not both hold to Christ and the Church in them? Where we recognize Him of whom the Apostle said: 'To Abraham were the promises made and to his seed. He saith not: and to his seeds, as of many, but of one: and to thy seed, which is Christ' (Gal 3,16); there we also recognize the Church of which God said to Abraham: 'In thy seed shall all nations be blessed' (Gen 22,18)" (CSEL 34, 605; Parsons II, 206). Augustine proceeds to comment upon fourteen Old Testament texts, as having both a Christological and an ecclesiological interpretation. It is clear that Augustine's confidence about "the saving chair of doctrine" and "the chair of unity," which immediately follows at the close of *Epistula CV*, is directly rooted in his confidence in Christ. Indeed, his conviction about the authority of the Church must be carried back ultimately to the more fundamental conviction about the authority of Christ. Already at the close of the very first of his works that have come down to us, Augustine states: "I am sure that I shall never depart from the authority of Christ; for I find no other more reliable" (*Contra Academicos* III,20,43 [CSEL 63, 80]).[68]

This confidence about the authority of the Church, considered as a universal unity, is expressed in another famous text, particularly dear to John Henry Newman: "Wherefore securely the whole world judges that they are not good who cut themselves off from the whole into one particular part" (*Contra epistulam Parmeniani* III, 24 [CSEL 51, 131]).[69] This principle—*securus iudicat orbis terrarum*—appears here within the context of a work which argues against those who would divide themselves from the whole for the purpose of a purer Christian community. Such a self-segregation amounts to a rash act of pride in Augustine's view (*Contra epistulam Parmeniani* III, 24 and 28 [CSEL 51, 129–131 and 136]).

Emphasis upon the universality of the Church led also to a positive understanding of the ministry of the bishop of Rome.[70] *Epistula XLIII* addresses one of the principal events surrounding the origin of the Donatist division, the Donatist charge that the ordination of Caecilan as bishop of Carthage in 311 was invalid because it was conferred by Felix of Aptunga, who allegedly had betrayed his faith out of fear during the last of the great persecutions which began under Diocletian. Augustine counters that Caecilan was united by pastoral letters to the Church of Rome, "where the primacy of the apostolic chair has always flourished" (*Epistula XLIII*, 7 [CSEL 34, 90]). Thus, acknowledgment by Rome sufficed for Augustine to counter any doubt about the legitimacy of Caecilan. Also he speaks of the primacy of the apostolic see in this connection. Another anti-Donatist letter produces a list of all of the bishops of Rome beginning with Peter down to Anastasius, pope in the year 400 when the letter was written, noting that this list included no one who shared the various Donatist doctrines (*Epistula* LIII, 2 [CSEL 34, 153-154]). Finally, one may refer to the famous sermon of September 23, 417, concerning Pelagianism (*Sermo CXXXI* [PL 38,734]). Augustine notes that two local councils held in North Africa, one at Carthage and one at Milevius, had rejected Pelagianism and had sent their proceedings to the apostolic see (*ad sedem apostolicam*). Both had received in reply a rescript from Rome validating their decisions. Then appear the famous words: "*causa finita est.*" According to Pierre Batiffol, this phrase was later expanded to become the aphorism: "*Roma locuta est, causa finita est*"—a phrase which Batiffol himself considers an impoverishment with respect to the original context, because it lacks the reference to the interplay between a decision by a local synod and its confirmation by the apostolic see which was explicitly mentioned in the original sermon. Regardless of one's eventual opinion regarding the aphorism, it is clear that Augustine's phrase "*causa finita est*" reflects his view that the Roman Church is to be considered an arbiter in controversies concerning the doctrine of the faith, as in the case of the Pelagian controversy.[71]

It has been a long and arduous task to work through so many Augustinian texts which are relevant to understanding his thought on faith and its unity, nor at the end of that labor can one breezily claim to have done a wholly adequate job of it. As a kind of preliminary summary, one may say that Augustine integrates into his own very personal synthesis many of the themes concerning faith and its unity which find expression in other patristic writers. Producing more books devoted explicitly to this topic than any other author of the early Church, he offers the most penetrating systematic account of faith which had appeared up until his time. He thought through the relation between faith, reason and authority in a way which, even today, can be neglected by anyone who wishes to study this theme only at the risk of missing some of faith's most salient features. What is perhaps most engaging about Augustine's theoretical and epistemological reflections concerning faith is the fact that they originated not in serene speculation but in his own compelling struggle to believe. In this he can surely speak to people of today.

CONCLUSION

Hilary, Ambrose and Augustine are three great patristic writers who were all caught up in the struggles of their times to maintain unity in faith. In the cases of Hilary and Ambrose, this contact was largely limited to stemming the spread of Arianism in the West. While Augustine enters into the fray of the Arian controversy in his masterpiece on the Trinity and in some of his last writings, he devotes many other works to opposing Manicheanism, Donatism and Pelagianism. All of this confirms that for these three Latin fathers, faith was certainly understood as including the acceptance of correct doctrine. But, as we have seen, it also includes much more. Hilary offers a rich collection of images to convey the manifold dimensions of the existential side of faith; Ambrose sees faith as the fountain of all the virtues; Augustine as the salubrious medicine which brings healing to the soul. All three root their faith in acceptance of the Word of God in Scripture; all three offer a balanced view of reason which is both attentive to its potentialities and cautious about its limitations and weaknesses. Concerning unity in faith, each explicitly refers to the action of the Church as working to achieve this goal. Hilary gives the most explicit discussion of the role of councils. All three develop the role of Peter and of the bishop of Rome as important points of reference for unity in faith to a degree which had not otherwise been seen in patristic literature, even when one recalls the important comments of writers such as Irenaeus, John Chrysostom and Cyril of Alexandria in this regard.

Having now come to the end of our survey of biblical and patristic material relevant to understanding faith and its unity, it is time to move on to the task of synthesizing and drawing out some implications which may be useful for us today.

PART THREE:
IMPLICATIONS OF THE INVESTIGATION

Chapter Eight
TOWARD A BIBLICAL AND PATRISTIC UNDERSTANDING OF UNITY IN FAITH

The aim of the preceding chapters has been from the start a rather ambitious one: to discover what the Bible and the patristic literature have to say about faith and its unity. It soon became apparent not only that the theme of faith is taken up quite often in these two sources but also that each source contains a variety of voices and has led to the production of a rather extensive secondary literature. The intention of the previous seven chapters has been to let these voices be heard again anew, at times by leaning more heavily on secondary studies, but always with the aim of allowing the original thought to emerge. It goes without saying—but it is only honest to admit the point frankly and explicitly—that the survey presented in the preceding chapters is not and, given the extent of the relevant material, probably can never be exhaustively complete. Nevertheless, one can hope that the principal voices in this wide ranging chorus and their dominant melodies have been given expression.

The aim of this final chapter is both easier and more difficult to accomplish than what has gone before. It is easier, in that we will limit our reflections to that material which has already been introduced and cease, for the time being, from pursuing the many new trails which continually open up before the researcher in the fields of biblical and patristic literature. It is more difficult, in that the varied material which has been introduced up to this point must now be brought into some manageable synthesis or framework without, in the process, reducing it to a sequence of shallow least common denominators.

Finally, this closing chapter must focus more directly upon the precise topic of unity in faith. Logically and methodologically it was necessary throughout the earlier investigative chapters to explore the material potentially relevant to unity in faith only after asking what faith as such means for the particular author in question. Here, after having now devoted considerable attention in the preceding pages to describing faith as such, the precise question of unity in faith must become the principal focus of attention.

1. UNITY IN FAITH AS A NEW QUESTION

One should begin by noting that, in general, the biblical and patristic texts which speak explicitly about faith—that is, those texts which use the precise terminology "faith" and "to believe"—tend not to focus upon the *unity* of faith.[1] This point can be illustrated, first of all, by recalling what we have found in Part One, dedicated to the Bible. The Old Testament texts which actually use the terminology of faith (*'âman, batah,* and so forth) help us to sketch out the basic meaning of this act in terms of having trust and confidence in God's promise, in responding to the covenant by obeying the directives laid out in the Law and, ultimately, in accepting some truths about God, such as that there is only one God and that Yahweh who redeems Israel is also the creator of the universe. When one attempts to raise the question of an Old Testament creed or of the unity of the faith in the Old Testament, one is drawn inexorably to secondary sources—to the analyses of various twentieth century exegetes, such as von Rad or Noth concerning the "credo" of the Old Testament[2] or such as Schmidt, Fohrer, Köhler, Eichrodt, Vriezen, Zimmerli, Westermann and, once again, von Rad regarding the characteristic trait or theology of the Old Testament.[3] This suggests that the question of unity in faith requires a stepping back from the more immediate lived experience of faith; it requires seeking an answer to a question which, at least in the majority of texts which speak of faith, the Old Testament itself did not pose. Unity of faith is much more a presupposition of the Old Testament than an object of explicit reflection.

The same can be said about the New Testament. Here the terminology of faith and explicit reflection about the various dimensions of faith is much more prominent than in the Old Testament. Nevertheless the standard studies about faith in the New Testament spend very little time, usually no time at all, upon the topic of *unity in faith*. This reflects the actual text of the New Testament itself, where, while the terminology for faith is among the most frequently repeated, occurring hundreds of times, the precise expression "unity of faith" occurs only once (!), in Eph 4,13.[4] Thus one is again forced to have recourse to predominantly secondary studies, especially upon the question of the unity and diversity to be found within the respective theologies of the various writings of the New Testament.[5] The question of unity in faith cannot be answered sim-

BIBLICAL AND PATRISTIC UNDERSTANDING OF UNITY IN FAITH   197

ply on the basis of an exegesis of various New Testament texts which speak of faith. Rather one must step back from the specific texts and pose a question about them which the original authors did not intend to address explicitly.

This same point applies as well to much of what has been surveyed in Part Two, concerning the patristic literature. One can locate a few texts which directly reflect upon unity in faith—one recalls, for example, Irenaeus' beautiful image of the one voice, repeated in all the languages of the earth, in harmony with the voice of the original community (*Adversus haereses* III, 10,2 and 12,5). But such texts are rather rare. Most patristic passages which directly speak of faith consider it within one of two contexts: its relation to reason and its relation to justification and sanctification. In the first context one finds not only apologetic works, such as those by Justin (*Apology* and *Dialogue with Trypho*) or Theodoret (*Therapy for the Greeks*), which attempt to "justify" Christian faith before those who do not believe, but also efforts to show the intellectual acceptability of faith in a way that can satisfy believers as well, as, for example, in some texts by Augustine (*The Advantage of Believing*). In this context, one may also place the various reflections which address respectively the positive role of reason in coming to a greater knowledge of what is accepted in faith (here one thinks especially of Clement of Alexandria and Origen, although many others, including Augustine, can also be added) as well as the negative propensity by which reason, in seeking to explain the revealed mysteries, can lead into error and heresy (here one recalls Tertullian, Hilary, Gregory of Nyssa and John Chrysostom, among others).

The second context—that of the relation between faith and justification and/or salvation—emphasizes the transformation of life which faith brings about. Whether it be the humility described by Clement of Rome or the fountain of all virtues noted by Clement of Alexandria and Ambrose, whether the faith that can move mountains which Cyril of Jerusalem distinguished from "dogmatic faith" or the wisdom of the good life practiced by the simplest believing peasant which John Chrysostom praised so highly, whether the faith which is the doorway to eternal life for Hilary or the grace dependent faith which Augustine argues must be accompanied by good works—by means of all of these reflections the various patristic writers develop the ways in which faith brings about a new mode of being on the part of the believer. Faith is the healing medicine of which Augustine speaks so eloquently in his *Confessions*, the miracle by which persons continue to be made whole, now not in body but more wonderfully in soul and spirit.

Instead, when one asks about the thought of these writers on the topic of unity in faith, one must either seek guidance in the secondary literature, which is usually rather sparse on this precise theme, or approach the primary sources in a roundabout way, not so much asking what they say about unity in faith but rather inquiring into their views about such themes as the contrast between the faith of the Church and that of the various heretics or the entrusting of revelation to the Church. Along the former line, there is certainly a tremendous amount of "anti-heretical" material among the writings of the Fathers of the Church. The prevalence of this type of literature presupposes at least two convictions which, therefore, can be said to be common to the authors who penned these polemical works. One such presupposition is that, whatever life-transformative aspects it entails and whatever their relative importance or even preeminence, faith also includes some clear doctrinal content, the acceptance of which is "non-negotiable" in the sense that the community cannot acquiesce in maintaining communion with those whose views on some particular issues contradict the doctrinal convictions which are believed to have been handed on from the beginning and which form the perennial faith of the community. In this way, secondly, these polemical works also presume that the Church is and should be one in faith. These presuppositions concerning the doctrinal content of faith and concerning the unity of the Church in believing this content remain, however, largely undeveloped pre-suppositions. They need to be elaborated in an explicit way. Nor do they exhaust the patristic contribution to understanding unity in faith.

What is important to note here is the fact that neither the Bible nor the patristic literature has focused in a direct way upon the topic of unity in faith. One simply does not find many books or treatises or even developed passages which, on the basis of an understanding of the nature of faith, proceed to address the further question "what then does it mean to be united in faith?" This does not mean that the authors of the Scriptures and patristic literature did not believe that the Church is one in faith. Just the opposite is the case. Everywhere unity in faith is presupposed as an essential trait of the community.[6] Nowhere can one point to writings which encourage division in faith or which find as normal and acceptable a state of affairs in which the beliefs and actions of some Christians are contradicted by those of others. The presupposition always remains unity. But the precise characteristics of this unity in faith are not explicitly developed.

This realization is already a valuable result of the study of faith in the Scriptures and the patristic literature. If it is true that our most authoritative documents from the past more presuppose unity in faith than reflect upon it explicitly, then we should not expect from them a completely clear and developed account of what it means to be united in faith. This occasions the further question: how clear and developed an account of unity in faith has the Christian community ever produced? The very divisions which emerged at the close of the period whose writings are studied in this book (that is, which emerged after the Councils of Ephesus and Chalcedon), as well as those divisions which occurred later over the course of many centuries, serve as a rather ironic witness to the perennial conviction that the Church must be one in faith. If Christians had not presupposed that unity in faith is essential for the life of a united community they never would have separated from each other for reasons of doctrinal incompatibility. But how explicitly has this presupposition been developed? One may wonder and even suspect that, in an ecumenical age when so much hope and effort is being poured into the reestablishment of unity among Christians, one of the special and unique tasks of the Church is a deeper reflection upon precisely what it means to be one in faith. This new context of seeking unity focuses attention more directly upon the nature of unity in faith than was likely in earlier ages, when the interest focused more upon preserving and accurately expressing the revelation given by Christ through the apostolic Church and handed on to us by our forebears in faith. This latter task of preservation and expression, of course, must always remain a primary work of the Church. And yet it does not exhaust that work. In an age which has a particular vocation to foster the healing of divisions in faith, the Church's work includes the task of understanding more adequately the precise theme of unity in faith so as to better promote any factors which foster it. If this is so, a vital task for today will be not simply to repeat what one finds in the Scriptures and the patristic literature about faith and its unity. In addition, on the basis of the witness that one finds there, one must attempt to "render an account" of the *unity* in faith that we seek—an especially appropriate response in our time to that call for ongoing reflection which 1 Peter 3,15 encourages when it asks Christians to always be ready to give an account of the hope that is in them.

That is the task which we hope to begin in the remaining pages of this chapter. Are there *elements* present in the material we have already seen which can bring into focus various characteristics of unity in faith? What do the Bible and the patristic literature say quite directly about faith and more indirectly about its unity which can help us to understand more clearly what it means to be one in faith? If we are able to draw out such characteristics or essential traits of unity in faith, we will be in a much better position to seek it with greater perspicacity—not simply to grope forward in the dark rather blindly—and to recognize with greater surety the moment of arrival when that has finally been reached.

2. BIBLICAL AND PATRISTIC FOUNDATIONS FOR UNDERSTANDING UNITY IN FAITH

A. Insights Common to the Bible and the Patristic Literature Which Derive from the Nature of Faith

    i. The Polyvalence of Faith. A first point regards the nature of faith and enjoys that rare advantage of being supported almost universally by every author we have studied, whether from the Old Testament or the New, whether from the pre-Nicene or post-Nicene patristic writers, either of the East or of the West. Faith is almost always presented as a complex and multi-dimensional action or state, which engages the whole human person, mind, heart and will. This finds expression already in the Old Testament, at the very "birth of faith" to use Van der Leeuw's expression, where a variety of terms are needed for conveying the meaning of this action or state.[7] In the New Testament, while the vocabulary of faith appears more stable,[8] not only can one discern a number of distinct "theologies of faith" (Paul, John, Hebrews and so forth) but even within any single author the meaning of faith is polyvalent.[9] Paul jumps out as an obvious example, for whom faith is both assent to and confession of the truth of the gospel—that Christ has died for our sins and been raised from the dead according to the Scriptures (1 Cor 15,3-5)—as well as God's gratuitous means of justification (Rom 4-5); faith can be contrasted with the law (Gal 2-3), but at the same time is said to work itself out in love (Gal 5,6). This same polyvalence appears throughout the patristic literature as well. Even those whose discussions of faith appear in a predominantly apologetic context (Justin, Theodoret) or within a confrontation with the "heretics" (Irenaeus, Tertullian) or in works which seek to provide an epistemological justification for faith (at times, Augustine), all include a variety of descriptions of faith which touch upon its relation to salvation or justification or a virtuous life or growth in knowledge and love of God.[10]

    Virtually no one among the biblical and patristic authors reduces faith to only one of its dimensions. Might this not suggest that unity in faith also needs to be conceived in such a way as to avoid reducing faith to merely one of its dimensions? This can be proposed even though it might be objected immediately that at least many of the patristic writers, if not some from the New Testament as well, seem to make agreement even in quite precise doctrinal formulations a *sine qua non* of unity in faith.[11] But if faith really includes, along with the acceptance of particular truths which are revealed by God and which one cannot simply deduce from reason, also the very personal response to God in trust and self-donation, would not an adequate conception of unity in faith need to take into account quite explicitly these more existential and personal dimensions of faith? Those who freely commit their whole selves to God, offering the full submission of intellect and will to the God who reveals, are surely united in a faith which cannot be described solely in terms of intellectual assent.[12]

ii. The Historicity of Faith. A second point which has an important connection to this first stems from a theme which appeared in our discussion of the Old Testament view of faith, but which resonates with a number of other themes found in the New Testament and the patristic literature as well. This is the observation that faith is "historical" in the sense that it is not simply a once and for all promise of covenant faithfulness or acceptance of a list of doctrines, but rather a relationship lived out in the context of the ebb and flow of daily life.[13] As history, faith moves. It was a teaching dear to the scholastic theologians of the high middle ages that faith can never rest; its very epistemological state is such that it always is agitated to move on to greater knowledge and love.[14] What the scholastics deduced from epistemology, the people of God, already in the Old Testament, lived in their own religious experience. The historicity of faith both implies and is demonstrated by the fact of *growth in faith*—and this in all of the dimensions of faith, not only the existential dimensions of trust and self-donation in response to God but also in the noetic dimensions of knowledge of God and right doctrine reflective of revealed truth. Monotheism itself, so fundamental a principle of the religion of the Bible, emerges only gradually, as the Old Testament exegetes now demonstrate to the peaceful acceptance of both the scholarly and the ecclesial community.[15]

This second point relates in an important way to the first, which concerned the need to conceive unity in faith in terms which do not reduce it simply to one dimension, for example, that of acceptance of doctrinal formulations. For this second point—the fact that faith is lived in history and characterized by growth—recognizes and, in a general way, accounts for the emergence and growth of doctrine. Faith as histo-

ry highlights the fact that the various dimensions of faith are not in isolation from one another. It is the ongoing relationship with God which
moves on to ever new ways of living out the faith and of formulating
believed truths. This progress of faith through time is characterized by
advance into greater holiness and deeper knowledge of God. Here one
recalls the many beautiful scriptural and patristic passages which speak
of maturing and becoming more perfect in faith (for example, Eph 4,11-
15, or various passages in Clement of Alexandria, Origen and Gregory
of Nyssa).[16] But the history of faith would seem to caution that time can
also bring corruption or forgetfulness (hence that recurrent patristic
theme of the need to remain faithful to the tradition, including both life
and doctrine, that has been handed on from the beginning).[17]

Of course, the greatest temptation for those who wish to
understand faith in an historically sensitive way is to proceed to the
invalid conclusion of historical relativism: there is no revealed truth
which perdures through time and which one firmly grasps and affirms
in faith. One of the clearest indications of the unacceptability of such a
conclusion is the deeply confessional nature of the New Testament
doctrine of faith.[18] Faith may be said to be historically relative and
historically conditioned, in the sense that the way in which this
relationship with God is lived and the formulas in which its doctrinal
content is given expression will occur within a certain range of historical
coordinates (time, place, language, culture and so forth). Faith so lived
and formulated can only be adequately understood if one seeks to
understand these coordinates. But it is an invalid conclusion about
faith's historicity to jump beyond these cautious assertions to the
unjustifiable position that what was once a virtuous living of faith no
longer is so, that what was once a true doctrinal formulation now is false.
Historical sensitivity in no way necessarily leads to historical relativism.
In fact, it should lead to just the opposite. An historically sensitive
investigation of this or that particular moment in the history of faith can
give access to values and truths which are perennial, which illuminate
life today as well.

If one of the essential dimensions of faith is its historicity, a
conception of unity in faith will be more adequate to the extent that
it succeeds in incorporating such historicity. This means that it is likely
that one should understand unity in faith as a state of affairs which is
always in need of being maintained, fostered and achieved anew in
history. Like faith itself, unity in faith may be considered as an essential
possession or trait of the Church. At the same time, the Church cannot
rest from the effort to maintain and grow in faith unity. This must always

be worked at. Unity in faith can thus be seen as both a gift and a task, as a possession and a project. This means further that the task of promoting unity in faith is not primarily an historical accident which results from various unfortunate divisions for which we must repent. While it is true that divided communities must attempt to reestablish full communion in cooperation with grace and according to the will of Christ, it nevertheless remains the case that, even if these divisions had never taken place or even if one could rejoice that all Christian communities were in full communion today, the task of fostering unity in faith would remain.

A very delicate and sensitive application of the principle that faith is historical concerns unity in faith regarding doctrines which divided communities, in isolation from one another, have come to recognize as part of God's revealed truth. Such doctrines may appear foreign or even false to those individuals and communities who, by reason of the anomalous situation of division, did not participate in the faith history which led to the recognition and reception of such doctrines as part of the Word of God revealed in Scripture and Tradition. The historicity of faith suggests that such doctrines will have to be contemplated again together by communities hoping to arrive at full communion in faith, so that the historical steps which made possible their recognition in the first place can be reexamined and shared by all. Such a new and shared reflection upon revelation would presumably and hopefully offer opportunity for growth in faith on the part of all the participants.

iii. Faith and Creed. A third characteristic of faith which can have some important consequences for the way in which we understand unity in faith is the propensity of faith to find expression in short summaries or creeds. The topic of the nature and development of creeds, in particular of those two which enjoy wide acceptance and use among Christians today—the Apostles' Creed and the Niceo-Constantinopolitan Creed—is not one that could be treated in this book. That would require a separate study of its own, to which already many works have been devoted.[19] However, by limiting oneself simply to the Old and New Testaments, insofar as they may be said to contain or make use of credal material, along with a number of commentaries upon or reflections about creeds which one can locate in the patristic literature, some valuable points begin to come into relief.

First of all, whether or not the precise word "creed" is the best or most appropriate word to describe the phenomenon, both Testaments contain short summaries which attempt to concisely express a number of the most essential truths of faith. At times, such as in von Rad's thesis about the origin of the Hexateuch, such summaries are posited as the point of departure giving the basic parameters within which evolved the more elaborate and detailed story which we today have as the final text of the Scripture. In this regard, the description by Schlier, Kelly and others of the relation between the early Christian confession of faith and the eventual text of the New Testament is quite similar to that of von Rad, in that it places a relatively short confession, taking different forms but including roughly the same essential elements, as one of the points of departure for the writing of the New Testament.[20] The relation between Scripture and creed would be explained by several of the Fathers of the Church in terms of the creed being a kind of short synthesis of all which is contained in the Bible. Such a short summary is seen by the fathers as eminently useful to the Church for such moments as baptism, when an individual is required to profess in a concise form the whole of the faith of the community. Its usefulness also devolves from the fact that not all in the Church have the time or inclination or talent to devote themselves to an exhaustive study of Scripture. For many if not for all Christians, an absolutely exhaustive profession explicitly mentioning all doctrinal truths known by the Church is a practical impossibility. Thus, the emergence of short formulas of faith, at least as can be deduced from some patristic voices, stems from both the need for a comprehensive profession of faith and, at the same time, a recognition that not every aspect of revealed truth can or need be explicitly mentioned in such a profession.[21]

A striking finding of research concerning a possible Old Testament credo is the pluriformity which characteristizes the various texts which may be considered as short professions of faith. From the "short historical credo" of Dt 26 which emphasizes the liberation from slavery in Egypt and the bestowal of the promised land to formulas which emphasize other themes such as the covenant, the royal house of David, God as creator and so forth, the situation in which Israel found itself led quite naturally to the inclusion of and emphasis upon different aspects of its faith in the various short summaries which emerged in the course of its history. Such a fluidity can be noted in the New Testament as well, where reflection on the work and person of Jesus led to the formulation of confessions employing various titles (Messiah, Son of God, Lord), forms (binitarian, Trinitarian) and conceptions of the salvation action accomplished by God in Jesus. At the same time, the rejection and even "anathematizing" of some ways of speaking about Jesus or of presenting the gospel (for example, 1 Jn 2,22; 1 Cor 16,22; Gal 1,8–9; on unacceptable behavior, see 1 Cor 5,1–2) shows that the community felt obliged to set limits to such diversity.

The patristic era also offers a plurality of creeds, as the opening section of Denzinger's *Enchiridion symbolorum* testifies.[22] In the writings which we have examined, it is clear that after the first ecumenical Council of Nicea in 325, which devised a Creed with the precise purpose of expressing the authentic doctrine that Christ was of the same nature (*homoousios*) as the Father, authors such as Basil and Gregory of Nazianzus in the East or Hilary and Ambrose in the West looked upon this Creed as a measure of orthodoxy and as a means of fostering unity in faith. This use of the Creed led to an insistence upon not altering any of its hard-won phrases, with the result that the fluidity or pluriformity which one finds in surveying earlier symbols gradually is replaced by a rather careful and universal adherence to a formula whose terms are fixed. Yet even here, our study pointed out that Basil, who was a great proponent of maintaining the doctrine and wording of the Creed of Nicea, could at the same time encourage an expansion of its final section so as to explicitly respond to those who, only in the period after Nicea, had begun to question or deny the divinity of the Holy Spirit.[23] Thus he stands as a witness that, given the new exigencies of a later period, the Creed, which, according to Basil, as a general rule should be carefully preserved without changes or additions, may nevertheless require some expansion. Another rather fascinating witness both to the need for a fixed creed as an instrument of unity in faith and, at the same time, of a benign reading of a number of creeds produced by "semi-Arian" Eastern councils of the mid-fourth century is Hilary's *De synodis*.[24] Hilary's advocacy of the Creed of Nicea as an important formula around which the whole Church should be united in the faith cannot be doubted. At the same time, he could see that at least some of the hesitancy with regard to the word *homoousios* stemmed not from a desire to deny the divinity of Jesus but from a fear of obscuring or denying the threeness of the divine persons. Thus, even in a critical period when precise formulation was becoming more fixed as a means to promote and ensure unity in faith, a strong proponent of this process was nevertheless able to recognize the same faith expressed in different terms.

A final point emerging from our study of the creeds is the fact that their appearance and function as expressions of faith was intimately related to the overall, daily life of the community. This theme needs to be developed at greater length than has been done in the present book. Here it emerged most directly during the consideration of the credal material present in the New Testament.[25] Analysts such as Cullmann and

Benoit show that short summaries of faith were needed by the early Church for a number of common experiences within the day to day life of the community, such as the baptism of new members, catechesis, the celebration of the liturgy, healings and exorcisms, discussions about correct doctrine and the profession of membership in the community in the face of persecution. The New Testament material suggests that a variety of situations in daily life occasion and require the framing of short summaries of the essential truths which unite the community in faith. This same trait of being situated in daily life was hinted at also in our treatment of the Old Testament, where the various candidates for "creeds" were seen as having their natural setting in liturgical services (such as the annual thanksgiving for the harvest in the case of Dt 26,3–10).[26] At the other end of the time spectrum we have surveyed, the patristic literature offers any number of examples of commentaries on the Creed as a means of forming Christians into a common acceptance of the doctrine outlined in the Creed.[27] Here examples include not only commentaries directed to neophytes (such as Cyril of Jerusalem's *Catechetical Instructions* or Augustine's *The Christian Combat*) but also expositions presented before a group of bishops gathered in council (Augustine's *Faith and the Creed*). A point which seems derivable from this evidence is that common life, shared in a number of different activities such as liturgy, catechesis, theology, mission and so forth, is the natural condition which leads to the framing of short summaries of the faith which unite the community. If this is so, it suggests that full unity in faith should not be conceived as that condition without which no sharing of ecclesial life is possible. To conceive the path toward Church unity in such a sequence could well preclude the possibility of arriving at unity in faith and, consequently, of arriving at full unity. The relation between shared life and the emergence of creeds suggests, instead, that divided communities, even before having healed their divisions completely, need to share as much as possible in ecclesial activities such as worship, formation, study and mission. As would seem to be implied from what we know of the emergence and function of short summaries of faith in the Scriptures and the patristic literature, the experience of shared life should lead to greater unity in faith.

B. Insights Common to the Bible and the Patristic Literature about Unity in Faith

The first part of this chapter argued that biblical and patristic literature focus predominantly upon faith and not upon its unity. To find out what this literature has to say about *unity* in faith, one usually has to step back and reflect upon the implications or presuppositions of what is said about faith. The previous three sections have followed this general observation. They have considered three characteristics which qualify faith as such—its multi-dimensionality, its historicity and its capability of being expressed in creeds—and then proceeded to draw out some consequences which follow from each of these characteristics for unity in faith. However, the examination of each source considered in the earlier chapters of this book—the Old and New Testaments and each individual patristic writer—also uncovered some indications which directly address the precise topic of unity in faith. It is to this material which we now turn.

The discussion of unity in faith in the Old Testament led to consideration of the characteristic belief, attitude or theology which may be said to unify the Old Testament and to distinguish the faith which it represents from that of neighboring religious communities.[28] What emerged from the secondary literature was a series of attempts either to present a theory which accounts for what is distinctive about the faith of Israel or to fashion a synthesis—an Old Testament theology—which brings into a harmonious whole the various elements present in the many books and in the long story of salvation history which underlies them. These various attempts are all directed toward expressing, to the extent that it is possible, the unity of faith of the Old Testament. Moreover, one can discern a degree of similarity among such theories. For example, the identification of the distinctiveness of Israel's faith in terms of the first two commandments of the decalogue (Schmidt), on the one hand, need not appear in sharp contrast but rather quite in harmony with the unification of the various themes of the Old Testament under the heading of the covenant (Eichrodt), on the other hand.

Still, the very plurality of these efforts by a variety of individual scholars searching for a unifying principle or systematic framework after the fact, as it were, unable simply to point to an obvious unity which is evident to all but rather needing to read the scriptures anew precisely with an eye toward discerning what holds them together—all of this suggests that the unity of a canon of books written by so many different authors from within very different historical and cultural circumstances is a unity which can be discerned only by the community as a whole. The "library" which is the Bible contains too much for a single mind to sum it all up or unify it in such a convincing and insuperable way that additional summaries are no longer needed or desirable. The unity of faith which the Old Testament represents probably cannot be summarized *definitively*. Each summary bears within it the seeds for contemplation which make possible further attempts to understand more fully and to express more adequately the coherence of the whole. This may point to a general principle with regard to unity in faith: any synthesis which tries to account for all of the richness contained in "the deposit of the faith" will, at least in the pilgrim state of this earthly life, remain provisional. This could imply that important instruments for fostering comprehensive unity in faith, such as catechisms, for example, will always stand in need of futher explanation. Common acceptance of a catechism could be a very important expression of unity in faith as well as a tool for maintaining and growing in such unity. But such a synthesis could not be thought of as the last word in presenting a unified and comprehensive view of the faith. This comment would apply even more to syntheses offered by single exegetes or theologians.

The very phenomenon of discerning a group of writings as being inspired by God and as forming part of a "canon of Sacred Scripture" is a phenomenon which presupposes a certain underlying conviction that the writings so discerned do not contradict one another.[29] Indeed, to believe in a canon of scripture at all is in itself an act of faith in the unity of God and of God's Word. The fact that the precise details leading to the discernment of the canon as we know it are shrouded within the long history during which some individual writings gradually gained wide acceptance while others eventually did not suggests again that it is only the community as a whole over the course of history that is capable of discerning the unity of faith which the canon represents.[30]

This point that the discernment of a canon of Scripture pre-supposes a unity in faith among the various writings recognized as belonging to the canon applies, of course, to both Testaments. But the New Testament taken on its own provokes some further reflections that may prove to be yet more significant for understanding unity in faith. Composed in what, relatively speaking, is a much shorter time frame and characterized by a view of faith which is sharply more confessional than that of the Old Testament, the New Testament writings much more quickly and explicitly reveal the problem of unity and diversity in faith. Thus, although somewhat anachronistic since the more common meaning of such terms appears only later, it would be possible to write in a credible way about "orthodoxy" or "heresy" according to the New Testament; one could hardly say the same about the Old Testament.[31]

It is generally accepted, almost to the point of being considered a truism, that the New Testament presents the reader with a certain amount of diversity, according to the respective approaches of the various individual authors. In Chapter Four we argued that the presence of what might be called diverse theologies within the New Testament as well as the potential tension between them and, moreover, the evidence of actual discord within the community should not be construed as leading inexorably to the conclusion that the New Testament depicts a Church that is more divided than united in faith. Such diversity can be understood as the natural result of the proclamation of the good news about Jesus Christ in a variety of cultural contexts, each having distinct concerns and conceptualities within which this message can be received. But the proclamation of the gospel intended from the start to create communion in faith, not division. The inevitable differences and even tensions resulting from the dissemination of the Word were not simply left to evolve into full blown divisions within the community. Instead, a number of factors constantly worked toward the reconciliation of divisive tendencies and the harmonization of diverse views into a whole, the parts of which are not mutually contradictory.[32] These factors included: short formulas of faith such as the credal material (which can be found in virtually all of the major blocks of the New Testament), frank discussion among believers (as is evidenced in Acts and in various letters), charisms bestowed by the one Spirit for the service of unity (as attested in 1 Corinthians 12–14 and Ephesians 4), recourse to the Scriptures along with the later discernment of conciliatory books as part of the New Testament canon (one recalls Dunn's list of the conciliatory aspects of many New Testament books) and, finally, the guidance of leaders who made the conscious effort to maintain unity in faith (as suggested by Acts 15 and the pastoral letters).

The point to notice here is that unity of faith according to the New Testament is the result of effort and of collaboration with the grace of the Holy Spirit on the part of the whole Church. It is not simply a once and for all established characteristic which Christ bestowed upon the Church as the point of departure for its life. One may say that unity in faith is always realized and continues to be realized as part of the process of the ongoing life of the Church. Unity in faith occurs not primarily by means of a once and for all acceptance of a list of doctrines but much more by means of participation in a process through which the Church continually advances into the fullness of truth under the guidance of the Holy Spirit.

The New Testament presents the factors listed above as forces favoring unity in faith. The patristic literature takes this inheritance as its point of departure and develops it. Just as the problem of division in faith becomes even more explicit and sharpened when one moves into the patristic literature, where various bodies of doctrine oppose one another and some come to be identified as heresies, so too the factors favoring unity become more clearly individuated. Most of all, one needs to underscore the explicit and continued reference to the Church and to its ongoing life under the leadership of its pastors as the overall means for maintaining unity in faith. For Irenaeus, the faith is entrusted to the apostolic Churches.[33] Tertullian says the same for the Scriptures; only the Church has the right to interpret them.[34] Clement of Alexandria speaks about the "canon" of the Church as the norm regulating the faith and Origen compiles a list of the more important points of doctrine which are handed on in the Church.[35] Cyril of Jerusalem says that it is the Church which has the ability to distill the Creed from the scriptures, thereby extracting their essence.[36] Gregory of Nazianzus sees order within the Church as the condition of its unity in faith.[37] Gregory of Nyssa sees the faith of Christians as coming from God through Christ to the apostles and thereby to the Church.[38] Faith is the foundation of the Church for Hilary and Ambrose;[39] John Chrysostom[40] and Augustine[41] both stress that the faith and the Scriptures have been entrusted to the Church.

How does the Church serve as a means for fostering unity in faith? In examining the New Testament we noted five elements within the life of the Church and which promote unity. These elements are all reaffirmed to one degree or another by various patristic authors. The unifying force of the *short summaries of faith* may be seen both in Basil's promotion of the Creed of Nicea as an instrument of orthodoxy[42] and in its use for the catechetical formation of new Christians by Cyril of Jerusalem and Augustine.[43] The healthy *dialogue and exchange of views* which one finds in the New Testament is only intensified, sometimes moving more in the direction of simply condemning errors rather than that of attempting to win the other party over to what one believes to be true. Even here, however, much of the "polemical" literature flowing from the pens of the fathers attempted to convince, employing arguments based upon reason and upon a congenial interpretation of Scripture.[44] The sense that the *gifts and charisms* of the Holy Spirit are guiding the Church toward the truth is captured by Tertullian's retort that only such guidance could account for the fact that so many churches from all over the world are united in faith, in contrast with the more localized heretical groups.[45] *Scripture* is the primary authority employed by the various patristic writers in explaining the faith and in arguing against errors, as verifiable by a simple perusal of the works of virtually every author of that period. And finally, beginning already with Clement of Rome and Ignatius, there is constant recourse to those charged with *the leadership of the community*, starting with the apostles, as a principal means promoting unity in faith.

Patristic thought relative to these various factors serving unity in faith does not simply repeat what is already to be found in the New Testament. The progressive experience of working for unity in faith brings new applications of the above factors as well as more developed insight into some of them. For example, the use of short faith summaries which one finds in the New Testament may be seen as a forebear of the more elaborate *regula fidei* proposed by Irenaeus and Tertullian for the purpose of indicating the unifying core of Christian doctrine[46] or even of the baptismal creeds which developed in yet another context, that of the liturgy.[47] Later, Nicea's use of a credal formula to proclaim the doctrine of the divinity of Christ is a further ecclesial and doctrinal application of the Creed, somewhat different from its earlier use as the concise expression of the beliefs of the Church which one was required to accept upon admission to the community of faith at baptism. Other factors favoring unity which come into sharper relief in the patristic period are: the weight of tradition (one recalls the explicit reference to its authority in Tertullian, Clement of Alexandria, Basil and Augustine),[48] the common biblical and doctrinal interpretations of the fathers (Cyril of Alexandria is usually considered the key proponent of this factor),[49] the deliberations and decisions of regional and ecumenical councils (Basil, Hilary and Theodoret are but a few witnesses to their role in fostering unity in faith)[50] and, finally, recourse to primatial sees, particularly that of Rome (Irenaeus, Hilary, Ambrose, John Chrysostom and Augustine write of Peter and/or the Church at Rome as a force for unity in faith; Athanasius, Basil and Cyril of Alexandria seek the intervention of the bishop of Rome in the midst of doctrinal crises in the East).[51] All of these may be seen as further specifications of that constellation of factors already discernible in germ in the New Testament.

Looking back over all of this material concerning unity in faith from the wide range of biblical and patristic literature, it is difficult to escape the conclusion that unity in faith, while a) definitely entailing a certain degree of doctrinal unanimity, is at the same time b) a product of an ongoing and seemingly unending process, to which contribute many factors of the life of the Church. Both of these points are important. First of all, doctrinal harmony is decisive for unity in faith. At times one catches an irenic note in one or another author which acknowledges the "good faith" of the one in error and thus does not "excommunicate" him or her, as in St. Paul's vigorous exhortations about the resurrection in 1 Corinthians 15 or about salvation by faith in Galatians.[52] Both issues are vitally important for Paul and yet he does not consider those to whom he is writing as irremediably lost to error and cut off from the community; instead he seeks to win them over. In a similar way, Augustine illustrates an attitude common among many of the patristic writers. While his rhetoric against the Manicheans could often be quite sharp, nevertheless his *Against the Epistle Called the Fundamental* explicitly notes that his aim is not the destruction but the recovery of those against whom he is arguing. He states that one may hold an erroneous view more from thoughtlessness than from malice.[53] Still, these examples of recognizing a certain common ground (may one even say common ground in some of the existential dimensions of faith such as acceptance of Jesus as one's savior or a trustful, obediential attitude toward God?) in no way diminish the decisiveness of doctrinal harmony. Paul may have accepted the Corinthians as his sisters and brothers in Christ, but it appears certain that he did so in the expectation that they come around to believe that Jesus was raised from the dead. Augustine was convinced that the doctrines of the Manicheans were of Church-divisive significance. One simply cannot peruse the material from the biblical and patristic authors without acknowledging their conviction that doctrinal agreement is an essential and decisive aspect of that unity in faith which should, in their mind, characterize the Church.

At the same time, if one steps back from the debates and struggles about particular doctrinal agreements and takes a larger view, if one does not miss the forest for the trees, as it were, it seems evident that doctrinal agreement is an ongoing task for the Church. It is not a once and for all achievement. If this is so, then it follows that one of the most important aspects of reestablishing unity in faith among Christian communities which are presently divided will have to be the sharing of those factors which foster unity in an ongoing way. For unity in faith is never simply an "achievement," in the sense of a moment in which rather perfect and universal accord could somehow be accomplished and verified. Surely there are moments of "achievement," such as in the case of a decision by an ecumenical council concerning a hitherto controversial doctrinal issue. But even in such a solemn and historically verifiable case, the conciliar decision is but the point of arrival in a journey of faith and becomes immediately the point of departure for the active reception of the doctrine which has thus become understood in a deeper way.

C. Further Patristic Developments

A final section about unity in faith concerns those new developments which only appear in the post-biblical period with the advent of patristic literature. These writings grapple with the problem of unity in faith in a more explicit way than do the Scriptures themselves. As symptomatic of this difference, one may observe that the word "orthodoxy" never appears in the New Testament. The word was, for all practical purposes, a creation of the Church of the patristic era, gaining frequency of use only in the authors who wrote after the Council of Nicea and especially in the orient, where eventually a feast of orthodoxy was established in the liturgical cycle. It may indeed be the case that the fathers of the Church were more concerned about "orthodoxy" than about "unity in faith." As we have indicated above, their interest was primarily to determine and defend correct doctrine, rather than to theorize about what makes for unity in faith, a task which the Church today, however, in the present ecumenical age may not avoid. But in determining and defending correct doctrine, the patristic authors were drawn naturally to make use of and thereby also to test the relative merits of reason, Scripture and ministerial authority as means to promote the acceptance of such doctrine. By reflecting upon their use and their evaluation of these three factors it is possible to learn yet more about unity in faith.

i. Reason. The first point that strikes one about human reason is that the patristic literature contains rather strongly contrasting evaluations of its usefulness for understanding Christian revelation and doctrine. One recalls the forcefully negative voices of Tertullian ("What has Athens to do with Jerusalem?"),[54] of Hilary (shocked at the shamelessness of heretics who claim to understand so much that they would even correct the word of God)[55] and of John Chrysostom (for whom the mud of reason needs to be washed away with the cleansing waters of faith).[56] Gregory of Nazianzus holds up the humility of St. Paul, who was taken up to the seventh heaven but who claimed to know here on earth only "in a mirror darkly," as an encouragement that his contemporaries not engage in philosophical speculations which could lead them away from a humble acceptance of sound teaching.[57] Irenaeus, Hilary, Gregory of Nazianzus, Ambrose and John Chrysostom all designate the misuse of reason as a major cause of heresy.[58]

At the same time, there are other voices whose estimation of reason is predominantly positive. One thinks here especially of Clement of Alexandria and his successor as head of that city's famous catechetical school, Origen.[59] These writers emphasize the fruitful maturation into Christian knowledge (*gnosis*) which is possible when the believer contemplates the deeper meanings hidden in Scripture.[60] For Origen, the intercourse between reason and the revealed word is comparable to marriage. It gives birth to the mature Christian, the one who knows, the gnostic. Nor is a positive assessment of reason entirely absent from the thought of those who point out its dangers. For example, the very texts in which Gregory of Nazianzus and John Chrysostom caution about the dangers of reason are themselves cast in literary forms (discourses and sermons) which of their nature address the minds of the listener. They attempt to convince the hearer of the truth of what they are saying by reasoned argument.

Why should reason come in for any negative comment at all by the patristic authors? Such an evaluation derives not only from the experience of the many confusions and errors which derived from rational explanations of Christianity offered by the various different heresies, but even more from the patristic conviction about the divine origin of Christian doctrine. This doctrine is based upon divine revelation, which comes from God. It is handed on to us by our forebears in the faith. The doctrine about God or about Christ which faith believes is no philosophical deduction. It is accepted ultimately on the basis of authority. This helps to explain the fact that, at the very beginning of the patristic period, Clement of Rome associated faith with humility and docility.[61] Gregory of Nyssa explained that the origin of Christian faith goes back through the apostles to Christ himself and, ultimately, to the Father.[62] For Basil, what faith believes comes from God, and therefore he insists that nothing be either added or subtracted from that which has been received.[63] Gregory of Nazianzus, so forceful in speaking on behalf of the doctrine of Nicea, himself counseled that Christians be slow to speak and instead eager to listen and to obey.[64] This sense of almost wanting to believe and of desiring to accept the word of authoritative witnesses, perhaps foreign or even distasteful to people today, is prominent also in Hilary and Ambrose.[65] This theme reaches its most eloquent and developed expression in Augustine's writings about the relation between faith and authority.[66] For Augustine, faith cannot be either understood or rationally justified outside of some reference to an authority whose teaching it is reasonable to accept.

With all of that, Augustine preserves as well the positive appreciation of the movement into greater knowledge which had been championed earlier by the Alexandrians. "Believe so that you may understand." Like so many patristic authors who commented on this text from the Septuagint version of Isaiah 7,9, Augustine envisioned faith as beginning a path which led to growth into an ever greater knowledge. *Growth* in knowledge implies a certain degree of diversity between believers who may be at different stages in their respective progress in understanding. Thus Clement of Alexandria can offer a beautiful sequence of biblical texts about children in order to explain the developing state of the believer.[67] Both Origen and John Chrysostom attribute a certain degree of diversity among believers to their diverse capacities for understanding.[68] This Chrysostom can do without ever revising his conviction that the simplest believer is far wiser and indeed knows more regarding that which is truly important to know than the most educated unbeliever.

The recognition of growth in knowledge through faith also leads Basil and Augustine to remind their readers of the eschatological limits conditioning such knowledge.[69] Basil states that, while individuals and the Church as a whole continue to advance, knowledge of God can never be perfect in this life. Augustine, in his late work *The Retractations*, accuses himself of presenting too rosy a picture in his early writings of the extent to which understanding could be achieved through following the path opened by faith. This lack of perfection is also brought into several passages which are relevant to the precise topic of unity in faith. While Origen notes that faith must be complete and that it is not sufficient to believe some doctrines and doubt others[70] and while John Chrysostom insists that his listeners accept all the dogmas of the Church and shun the company of those who would sow confusion,[71] Basil cautions that the text of the Creed not be made overly extensive or detailed[72] and Gregory of Nazianzus counsels that the most important factor for unity is to secure consensus about the doctrine concerning God—if there is agreement about the Trinity other points will naturally fall into place. [73]

All of these reflections which developed around the general theme of the evaluation of reason suggest a number of aspects which need to be taken into consideration when one reflects upon unity in faith today. Surely the Church must respect the intelligence of people today. Divided Christians must seek unity in a faith which is credible and believable because to some extent reasonable. At the same time, the patristic experience both about the positive capacity and role of reason in understanding revealed truth as well its limitations and potentially erroneous tendencies should not be forgotten. Concretely, patristic thought would seem to suggest that all Christian communities today could help the prospects of reestablishing full unity by fostering a positive appreciation of authority as this relates to faith. To be a believer at all inevitably entails, and always has entailed, accepting the Word of God ultimately not on the basis of some rational demonstration but on the authority of God. Moreover, faith trusts that God's authoritative word does "get through" to us today by means of the witnesses which God raised up to hand it on over the centuries. It is difficult if not impossible to see how unity in faith could ever come about outside of a context which genuinely values authority, ultimately the authority of God, but also any ways that God shares that authority with the Church (Mt 28,18–20).

Patristic thought about reason also highlights the possibility and fact of growth in the knowledge of the faith. It explicitly acknowledges a certain diversity or plurality without which it would be senseless to speak of growth. Unity in faith today, therefore, should take into consideration the fact that individuals will be at different stages in their growth in faith. Such diversity among individuals is understood as quite a normal consequence of the fact that the believer matures, in a way analogous to the maturation of a child into an adult. Within the precise context of the contemporary ecumenical movement, which attempts to restore unity between communities (and not simply between isolated individuals) which have experienced a divided history, oftentimes for centuries, an important question which Church leaders need to discern is whether or not and the extent to which this normal and legitimate diversity in faith among individuals may be analogously applied to the diversity in faith among divided communities.

Here the delicate problem is to discern what practical consequences may possibly be drawn from two principles which can seem to argue for opposing solutions. The fact that faith responds as full acceptance of all that God reveals on the basis of God's authority suggests that all communities must recognize and affirm all which any community has come to know as belonging to revealed truth. On the other hand, the fact that faith comes to understand revelation only gradually with the consequence that a) some ignorance of the fullness of revelation and b) some diversity among believers, whose paths in faith have not been similar enough to lead to common confession of some doctrines, are both legitimate and to be expected—all of this suggests that there may be some possibility for diversity in the extent of the doctrinal content that long-divided communities would need to explicitly profess as the condition for the reestablishment of full communion. Thus the two principles seem to argue for two opposing solutions: unanimity (which is not the same as uniformity, but rather that "being of one heart and mind" of Acts 4,32), on the one hand, and diversity (which does not mean open contradiction but rather simply lack of explicit confession of all doctrines), on the other.

There would seem to be at least two issues which need to be

considered in addressing this question, one theological and one pastoral. From a theological point of view, one needs to discern whether the principle that God's own authority underlies the truth of revelation enjoys such a hegemony over the historicity which qualifies the reception of revelation in faith that full doctrinal unanimity, at least at the level of the leaders of the various uniting communities, is a sine qua non for the reestablishment of unity. Or, on the other hand, is it possible that such a conclusion forces an opposition between authority and historicity in a way that is neither necessary nor justified by the experience of the Church throughout the ages? In this second case, one would discern that, because of the historicity which conditions the faith of the Church, a full respect for the authority of God would not preclude some doctrinal difference, not in the sense of some Christians contradicting others but in the sense of some not explicitly professing all that may be professed by others. Ultimately only those guided by the Holy Spirit with the various charisms given to official ministers for the purpose of leading and maintaining the Church in unity (Eph 4,11–13), making use of the advice of theologians and the sense of the whole community, can make this determination.

A second issue which looms very important with regard to this question is less theological than pastoral. How could Church leaders propose or sanction a degree of doctrinal diversity without thereby conveying the impression of doctrinal indifferentism or relativism? The fact that a degree of diversity in grasping truth, grounded in the historical conditions within which human knowing occurs, is not equivalent to historical relativism is an insight which is rather subtle. It requires careful and exacting thought to understand this distinction and it is possible that even many who have had the opportunity of years of study may not recognize it. Thus the way in which the Church treats the possibility of doctrinal diversity is a very delicate pastoral issue which would have to be handled with great prudence.

One should not close this section without at least a brief comment about the eschatological backdrop to faith which various patristic authors bring out in different ways. Their insistence upon the eschatological limits to human knowledge of revealed truth in the present age suggests that our contemporary understanding of unity in faith preserve a certain element of modesty. Faith accepts all of the Word of God. At the same time, paradoxically, faith never fully understands the Word of God in its totality. As Augustine would say, human knowledge in this life can never bring complete happiness because what remains yet unknown is incomparably greater than what is known.[74] This being so, unity in faith is then a goal which requires unanimity in comprehensively accepting and professing faith in the whole of revelation without, however, misconstruing such acceptance as a comprehensive profession of doctrinal content which may be impossible in this pilgrim state. One must resist a possible tendency that insistence upon the acceptance of all that God reveals imperceptibly becomes understood in such a "complete" way that it would almost amount to making the beatific vision into the condition for Church unity.

ii. Scripture. It would perhaps be easy to fashion an argument that the patristic literature witnesses to the insufficiency of Scripture alone as an ultimate basis for unity in faith. After all, it is strikingly clear from so much of this literature that scripture can be interpreted in a variety of ways and that much division within the Church is directly related to such differences in interpretation. However, to give predominant emphasis to this point in assessing what the fathers have to say about Scripture would be highly misleading.

The authority par excellence for the patristic writers which we have studied in this book is the Bible. This remains true even for the first three authors which we considered (Clement of Rome, Ignatius and Justin), who did not have what we know as the New Testament canon. The vast predominance of the writings from these early centuries are chock full of the Scriptures, to such an extent that some major authors like John Chrysostom present us with almost nothing other than reflections and meditations upon the Scriptures. Even those authors who make ample use of Greek philosophy, history and literature, such as Justin or Clement of Alexandria or Theodoret, consider the Bible as their principal authority.

Concerning the topic of faith, the use of the Bible by the patristic authors is evident in two ways. First of all, their reflections upon faith as such are quite scriptural. Characters from the Bible such as Abraham or Peter are regularly employed to explain such themes as justification by faith or the relation of faith to the Church. Moreover, one finds recourse to a number of passages which are used to highlight some specific aspect of faith, such as Is 7,9 ("Unless you believe, you shall not remain firm— understand"); Heb 11,1 ("Faith is the assurance of things hoped for, the conviction of things not seen"); Rom 10,9 ("If you confess with your lips that Jesus is Lord and believe in your heart that God raised him from the dead, you will be saved"); and Mt 5,8 ("Blessed are the pure in heart, for they shall see God"). The touch of the woman who struggles to get to

Jesus in the crowd and is healed (Mk 5,24-34 "Your faith has made you well") and the desire of Mary Magdalene to touch Jesus in the garden on Easter morning (Jn 20,16-18) as well as many other images serve as points of departure for striking and often quite beautiful reflections about faith.

Secondly, and perhaps more directly relevant to the issue of unity in faith, the patristic authors propose the doctrine which should be held by the whole Church as doctrine based upon Scripture. The anti-Arian treatises about the incarnation by Athanasius, the exposition of the doctrine about the Holy Spirit by Basil, the five great dogmatic discourses of Gregory of Nazianzus and the developed tracts on the Trinity by Hilary and Augustine are all, without exception, consciously and profoundly rooted in the Scriptures. The fact that the doctrinal errors against which they argue are also proposed on the basis of Scripture should not be allowed to obscure the fact that Scripture remains the primary source for the fathers. The issue which comes naturally to the fore because of the appearance of doctrinal error claiming biblical support is that of the correct interpretation of Scripture.

Here a number of points are worth noting. First of all, the "correct" interpretation of Scripture is not understood within the patristic literature as one particular or sole method of interpretation. At times specific rules for interpretation are given, as when Irenaeus proposes the principle of interpreting the less clear passages in light of those which are clearer or when Augustine closes the third book of his *Christian Instruction* (III, 30,42-37,56) with seven rules for interpretation which he borrows from the Donatist(!) Tyconius.[75] But generally speaking the patristic literature in no way attempts to limit interpretation to one particular school or one set of hermeneutical rules. In fact, one may describe the vast array of patristic interpretations of Scripture as one of its most convincing and persistent witnesses to legitimate diversity. If one wanted to demonstrate how variety of thought is compatible with unity of faith, one could simply place side by side a selection of patristic commentaries on some specific biblical text.

Along with this overall trait of pluriformity, one may speak of several major schools or emphases in the patristic interpretation of Scripture. One often refers, for example, to the more allegorical or the more literal approaches characteristic respectively of the schools of Alexandria and Antioch.[76] More helpful to the purpose of the present study, especially with regard to understanding unity in faith, are three distinct approaches to the interpretation of Scripture which successively emerge in the period of patristic writing which we have considered.

A first approach is especially at home among the earliest authors who wrote before the canon of the New Testament was firmly established as well as among apologists in dialogue with Judaism.[77] This is the tendency to focus on the events in the life of Christ as the fulfillment of the Old Testament and thus as an argument in favor of Christian faith in Jesus as the Christ and Son of God. This approach also seeks to render comprehensible such difficult themes as the "disgraceful" suffering and death of Jesus and the share which Christians should expect to have in Jesus' fate. This is obviously quite close to the type of biblical interpretation which one finds already within the New Testament. This apologetic approach to interpretation tends to build unity in faith by explaining the Scriptures so as to show the credibility and reasonability of the doctrine which the interpreter is proposing. Grasping this credibility, others will be drawn to accept and share his point of view.

A second thrust discernible in patristic interpretation is to attempt to counter the rather fantastic interpretations proposed by the various groups of gnostics. Here the most ready examples which come to mind are Irenaeus and Tertullian.[78] The distinctive trait of these two authors is to reject gnostic interpretations principally on the grounds that they do not conform to that interpretation commonly held by the apostolic churches—meaning those founded by the apostles or those sharing the same faith as taught by the apostles. One might call this an "ecclesial" method of interpretation. Tertullian goes so far as to affirm that argument between individuals about the precise meaning of specific texts cannot, of itself, lead to the resolution of doctrinal issues. Thus, for him, interpretations which are not compatible with the apostolic tradition simply have no right to a hearing. Unity in faith is here fostered by an interpretation of the scripture which harmonizes with that which is held by the "apostolic churches."

A third approach emerges when the fundamental argument of referring to the apostolic churches breaks down, a situation which occurs if the particular author against whom one is arguing happens to be the bishop of an ancient and undeniably apostolic church. This is precisely the situation which came to be during the course of the great Trinitarian and Christological debates of the fourth and fifth centuries. Here Tertullian's principle of simply denying one's opponent the right to speak on the basis of lack of apostolicity does not quite fit. In these great controversies, the orthodox writers needed once again to argue for the divinity of the Son and of the Holy Spirit or for the unity of person and duality of natures of the incarnate Word on the basis of a correct interpretation of the biblical texts. Thus here one finds the attempt to show how texts which, for example, could seem to imply a subordination of the Son to the Father can be interpreted in such a way that is compatible with their consubstantiality.[79] In this process of biblical interpretation several points became clear. First, while the inspired Word of God maintained its primacy in the realm of authoritativeness, nevertheless, some non-biblical words such as "consubstantial" were seen as legitimate and even necessary to express more adequately the faith of the Church. Secondly, the conviction that the proper doctrine, based upon a correct interpretation of Scripture, could be discerned by bishops gathered together in council was quite explicitly an operative principle in the minds of these fathers. Finally, support for what was judged to be the correct interpretation was sought more and more from the consensus present in earlier patristic literature. This approach seeks to foster and maintain unity in faith both by reasonable arguments concerning the correct meaning of specific texts as well as by employing various ecclesial factors and structures such as consensus with earlier patristic literature or the decision of bishops gathered in council.

Perhaps one can see in these three approaches a form of progression. The first approach emphasizes the power of the Word to convince. The second approach, noting the seeming futility of endless controversies about the relative legitimacy of conflicting interpretations, takes refuge in the sense of the Church as the decisive criterion. The third approach, returning to a thinking-through of particular texts relevant to doctrine about God or Christ, does so in light of the tradition, thereby preserving the values of both earlier approaches.

In conclusion, one may say that the patristic approach to the interpretation of Scripture as that is relevant to understanding faith and its unity suggests that today as well the Church should recognize the Bible as the principal source of its reflection about faith and of its exposition of doctrine. Regardless of the possibility of divergent interpretation, one cannot simply retrench into an exaggerated position which would make Church authority an isolated criterion, almost above the Word of God, as was overstated by Tertullian in his *Prescription against the Heretics*.[80] Scripture as the inspired and normative written expression of the Word of God will remain the principal source of doctrinal unity among Christians. But the patristic experience shows that Scripture's correct meaning needs to be discerned within the life of the community under the guidance of its leaders.

 iii. Ministerial Leadership. This topic is much broader and its adequate treatment would have to consider much more than the sources which we have examined in the foregoing chapters. There our attention was directed to texts from patristic literature which directly concern faith and its unity and not other relevant topics such as the role of ordained ministers and bishops in the Church, their relation to the Church's apostolicity, the overall activity of teaching within the Church, the particular teaching function of those exercising ministries of leadership and so forth. One could very fruitfully study the patristic writings under any of these headings and glean much which would be relevant to the theme of ministerial leadership as that relates to unity in faith.[81] Nevertheless, our more limited investigation into what this literature can say precisely about faith and its unity has not been without at least a few significant indications relevant to the role of ministerial leadership.

 A first observation worth noting is the fact that, while in continuity with the later strands of the New Testament,[82] the earliest patristic writers went quite a bit further in their emphasis upon the existence of an episcopal ministry of leadership and its importance for maintaining Church unity in general and unity in faith in particular. While the New Testament may leave room for uncertainty about the precise meaning of bishops, presbyters and deacons as well as about the extent of the presence and exercise of these ministries throughout the Church,[83] the view given already by Clement of Rome and Ignatius of Antioch seems much less ambiguous. Chapters 42–44 of Clement's *Letter to the Corinthians* speak of a certain continuity from God to Christ to the apostles and, finally, to the bishops and deacons whom the apostles chose (so paragraph 44) to lead the local churches. We saw that it is within the context of encouraging the acceptance of these ministers as leaders of the community that Clement goes on to speak of faith as involving elements of humility and docility. For Clement there seems to be a strong connection between the apostolicity of the Church and the fact that it is guided by bishops chosen originally by the apostles. Ignatius follows a similar if not even more emphatic line about ministerial leadership. One should follow the bishop as Christ followed the Father; no specifically ecclesial activities, such as the eucharist or baptism, should be performed apart from the bishop (*Smyrneans* 8; see also *Magnesians* 7 and *Ephesians* 5–6).[84] We saw that doctrinal divisions were one of the contexts within which the letters of Ignatius discuss faith and that, for him, obedience to the bishop is the principal means for promoting unity in faith and, consequently, also the unity of the Church. Writing several generations later, Irenaeus and Tertullian make specific reference to the sequence of bishops presiding over "apostolic churches" in succession to the apostles as the principal defense against heresies and thus also the principal factor promoting unity in faith.[85] Eno has argued that, in the period spanning roughly from 100 to 250, the main task facing the Christian community was that of stabilizing and preserving its identity and that three factors contributed in a special way to accomplishing this: the development of the Creed, the discernment of the canon of Scripture and the activity of ministerial leadership.[86] Of these three, all of which were important, it was the third which ultimately proved decisive.[87] What we saw of the viewpoints of Irenaeus and Tertullian with regard to the role of bishops argues in favor of Eno's conclusion.

The positive assessment of the role of ministerial leadership with regard to unity in faith continues among later patristic authors, particularly those after Nicea who, like Irenaeus and Tertullian earlier, were more occupied with questions of orthodoxy and heresy than were third century authors such as Clement of Alexandria and Origen. Even these latter two treasure the antiquity of the apostolic doctrine as that has been handed down by Church leaders from the time of the apostles.[88] But the writings of Basil, Gregory of Nyssa, Hilary, Ambrose, John Chrysostom and Augustine all provide specific passages which emphasize the apostolicity of the doctrine which is handed on in the Church and the relation between this process of tradition and the role of bishops.[89] None would see the episcopacy as merely incidental or indifferent to this process.

Nevertheless, at the time in which these later authors lived, an important and potentially alarming new development occurs: the fundamental argument of Irenaeus and Tertullian that unity in faith can be found in the doctrinal harmony which exists among the churches led by bishops in succession to the apostles proves to be no longer adequate. This is so for the simple fact that such bishops were at times the originators or proponents of what were eventually judged to be heresies. John Henry Newman opens the fifth of the notes appendixed to his *The Arians of the Fourth Century* with the words:

The episcopate, whose action was so prompt and concordant at Nicaea on the rise of Arianism, did not, as a class or order of men, play a good part in the troubles consequent upon the Council; and the laity did. The Catholic people, in the length

and breadth of Christendom, were the obstinate champions
of Catholic truth, and the bishops were not. Of course there
were great and illustrious exceptions...but on the whole,
taking a wide view of the history, we are obliged to say that the
governing body of the Church came short, and the governed
were pre-eminent in faith, zeal, courage, and constancy.[90]

While Newman's phrases "the governing body" and "the governed" may
be less than felicitous, given an understanding of ministry in terms of
service, the important point for the present discussion about the role of
ministerial leaders in fostering unity in faith is that sheer legitimacy of
authority within a line of apostolic succession would not appear to be
sufficient for "guaranteeing" correctness of doctrine. Indeed, from
roughly 250 on, one sees the emergence of local and regional councils as
means by which the consensus of a number of bishops gathered together
for the purpose of deciding potentially divisive questions serves as a
means for maintaining unity, especially in faith.

But even here, the local or regional exercise of what might be
called the collegial principle for fostering unity falls short. At times local
councils are themselves "heretical." The appendix by Newman to which
we have just referred is but one of many sources for information about
the doctrinal developments of the patristic period which list regional
councils which were Arian (for example, the Council of Antioch in 341
or that of Ariminum [Rimini] in 359, about which Jerome wrote that the
whole world woke up one day to find itself Arian[91]) or monophysite (for
example, the "robber council" of Ephesus, as Leo the Great called it, in
449). Moreover, such councils usually condemned other councils and
deposed individual bishops who actually championed what would
become recognized as orthodox doctrine. Thus the local or regional
council as such proved insufficient to the task of maintaining unity in
faith. That required recourse to a yet higher court of appeal.

Such a higher court of appeal was found in two forms: either a
universal or ecumenical council in which the leaders of the whole
Church concurred in a decision about the controversial doctrine in
question or, secondly, an appeal for a decision by the bishop of Rome.
Naturally much greater detail could be provided by studies which would
focus not simply upon what the patristic writers say about faith, as we
have attempted to do here, but rather upon the role of the ecumenical
councils and of the papacy as means for resolving doctrinal issues during
the patristic period.[92] Nevertheless, the authors studied in Chapters Six
and Seven do provide some evidence of both of these means. The way in

which the Cappadocians and Hilary championed the formula of Nicea stands as a witness to their conviction about the decisive role which ecumenical councils can play regarding unity in faith. The appeals to the bishop of Rome made by Athanasius, Basil and Cyril of Alexandria, and the various passages about Peter in authors such as Ambrose, John Chrysostom and Augustine, all serve as evidence that these fathers would not only see the appropriateness of making such an appeal but also would ground this practice in their interpretation of biblical material relevant to Peter. Moreover, it does not appear that these two means for overcoming division between individual bishops or local councils of bishops were seen as antagonistic to each other during the period which we have studied. The protagonists of three of the first four ecumenical councils (Athanasius after Nicea, Cyril of Alexandria before Ephesus and Flavian before Chalcedon) all appealed to the pope to support their position.[93] While there may at times have been different understandings of the respective roles or authority of ecumenical councils or of papal interventions, one does not find the kind of opposition between the two which would emerge in the West in the wake of the Great Western Schism and the subsequent rise of conciliarism in the early fifteenth century.[94]

Nor, looking back with the advantage of hindsight, can one say that these ultimate instances for preserving unity in faith—be they ecumenical councils or papal interventions—always functioned perfectly. The rather confusing sequence of events at the Council of Ephesus (431) which required in the end a subsequent formula of union to heal the divisions of those who had leveled excommunications at one another during the council is but one illustration of the very human character of this means of safeguarding unity in faith. Moreover, the surface clarity or sharpness of a conciliar decision may be misleading. The peculiar conciliar fate of Theodoret of Cyrus—who resisted the condemnation of Nestorius at Ephesus, participated with full rights, after overcoming opposition by some bishops, at Chalcedon and yet several of whose works were later condemned by the Second Council of Constantinople one hundred years after his death—cautions against oversimplifying the issues and the results of the councils. Ecumenical councils retain the complexity, subtlety and difficulty which qualifies any attempt by a large number of human beings to arrive at consensus on a particular issue. Moreover, human imperfection also characterized the papacy as an instance for maintaining unity, as is illustrated in the case of Pope Liberius who was pressured into condemning Athanasius in 357, for which at times in history he had been labeled a heretic.[95]

But in the end, ministerial leadership was by and large effective for maintaining the faith unity of the Church. One can and should assert this, even though it is necessary to admit that not all divisions were healed by means of such leadership and that some even remain to the present day. Nevertheless, such failures and imperfections should not be construed as an argument against this means for fostering unity in faith, nor should they obscure the fact that the patristic writers were convinced of the decisiveness of ministerial leadership for this purpose, especially in the ultimate instances of ecumenical councils and of recourse to a decision by the bishop of Rome. These two instances might be referred to respectively as the collegial and primatial expressions of ministerial leadership at the level of the universal unity of the Church. Thinking about unity in faith today, the patristic material suggests that we will need to acknowledge a distinctive role exercised by ministerial leadership in fostering such unity. Moreover, to the extent that unity in faith is a characteristic of the universal Church, this role needs to include also instances which serve the community as a whole, whether collegially, as in the case of an ecumenical council, or primatially, as in the case of an ongoing, daily ministry which bears a unique responsibility for promoting the unity of the whole community.

CONCLUSION

While, as a general rule, the precise theme of unity in faith is not the explicit object of reflection in biblical and patristic writings, a careful reexamination of these sources has led to the uncovering of a number of insights which, taken together, constitute what might be called "biblical and patristic foundations for understanding unity in faith." These foundations include the following affirmations about unity in faith.

A. Such unity should be conceived as incorporating important aspects which derive from the nature of faith itself:

    i. it should reflect faith's richness and polyvalence as an act which involves the whole being of believers, including their minds, hearts and wills, and which therefore includes both cognitive and existential dimensions;

    ii. it should incorporate the modesty and capacity for growth which derives from the fact that believers belong to a pilgrim people who undertake their journey of faith in history;

    iii. it should preserve the confessional conviction by which faith affirms, even to the point of heroic martyrdom, the revealed, salvific truth which God makes known through Christ in the Holy Spirit.

B. Such unity in faith should also be understood in light of what the biblical and patristic literature suggests about the process through which it is fostered, a process which utilizes creeds, dialogue, the exercise of a variety of charisms and ministries, recourse to sacred Scripture and guidance by those charged with leadership in the Church.

C. Finally, such unity in faith should be conceived in a way that incorporates several specific advances which appear during the patristic period:

    i. it should reflect both a balanced estimation of the strengths and weaknesses of reason in expressing revelation as well as a healthy appreciation for authority, not only that of God but also that which God shares with the Church;

    ii. it should be attentive to the ecclesial nature of the interpretation of Scripture;

    iii. it should acknowledge a significant role for the pastorally motivated doctrinal contributions of ministerial leadership.

These biblical and patristic foundations can serve the Church today in approaching the topic of unity in faith in a more informed and effective way. Collectively, they suggest that unity of faith needs to be viewed most of all as the result of an ecclesial process. If this is so, then the common acceptance of and participation in the principal elements at work in this process constitute the most urgent and necessary tasks before us so that Christians may at last reach the goal of unity in faith.

This book has been limited to sources which enjoy an almost universal authority among Christians—the Bible and the patristic literature. As such, it will hopefully appeal to and invite further investigation and reflection on the part of a wide range of people who are interested in Christian unity. But it should be added that the biblical and patristic literature does not exhaust the relevant material which can be fruitfully examined in order to understand and promote unity in faith. To the study of these privileged texts should be added an investigation of other sources which might be qualified as aspects of the daily life of the Church throughout the ages. These sources seem to me to consist principally of the following: liturgy, catechesis, the witness of holy lives, theology and the official teaching of pastors. Each of these has a long history of exercising, in a variety of ways, a profound effect upon the Church's unity in faith. To consider each of them from this perspective would provide valuable insight not only toward a better understanding of unity in faith, but also toward undertaking concrete steps to foster such unity more effectively and to advance toward the complete healing of the divisions which currently separate Christian communities from one another. Such a study must be left for another book (or books). For the moment, it is hoped that these points from our commonly prized biblical and patristic heritage may serve to shed greater light upon the unity we seek—a communion in faith, life and witness, which not only is the joyful possession which Jesus gives to his body and spouse, the Church, but which also is the condition for the full effectiveness of the Church's mission to invite all women and men to new life in Christ. "May they all be one, even as you, Father, are in me and I in you; may they be one in us, so that the world may believe that you have sent me" (Jn 17,21).

NOTES

Introduction

1. In William H. Prescott, *History of the Reign of Philip the Second, King of Spain*, Vol. I (Philadelphia: J.B.Lippincott Company, 1890) 267.

Part One: Introduction

1. A useful bibliographical listing of 334 studies about faith in the Scriptures can be found under the heading "Foi" in Paul-Émile Langevin, *Bibliographie Biblique 1930–1970* (Québec: Les presses de l'Université Laval, 1972) 653–659; Id., *Bibliographie Biblique 1930–1975*, II (Québec: Les presses de l'Université Laval, 1978) 1146–1153; and Id., *Bibliographie Biblique 1930–1983*, III (Québec: Les presses de l'Université Laval, 1985) 1296–1300. Additional listings, especially with the more recent works which have appeared since 1983, can be found in standard reference tools such as the bibliography published in the scholarly journal *Biblica* and in the notes and indices of various studies devoted to the topic of faith according to the Scriptures.

2. See, for example, S. Virgulin, *La "Fede" nella profezia di Isaia* (Milan: "Bibbia e Oriente," 1961) and Christopher D. Marshall, *Faith as a Theme in Mark's Narrative* (New York: Cambridge University Press, 1989).

1. The Old Testament on Faith and Its Unity

1. Jürgen Hermisson and Edward Lohse, *Faith* (Nashville: Abingdon, 1981) 7.

2. See E. Perry, "The Meaning of '*emuna* in the Old Testament," *JBR* 21 (1953) 252–256; J.B. Bauer, "Der Glaube im Alten Testament," *BiLit* 23 (1955–1956) 226–230; A. Weiser, "pisteuo.... B. The Old Testament Concept," in *Theological Dictionary of the New Testament*, ed. G. Kittel and G. Friedrich, Vol. VI (Grand Rapids: Eerdmans, 1959) 182–196; Egon Pfeiffer, "Glaube im Alten Testament: eine grammatikalisch-lexikalische Nachprüfung gegenwärtiger Theorien," *ZAW* 71 (1959) 151–164; Juan Alfaro, "Fides in terminologia biblica," *Gregorianum* 42 (1961) 463–505 at 463–475; H. Wildberger, "'Glauben', Erwägungen zu h'myn," *Supp VT* 16

229

(1967) 372–386; R. Smend, "Zur Geschichte von h'myn," Ibid., 284–290; Alfred Jepsen, "âman...," in G.J. Botterweck and H. Ringgren, ed. *Theological Dictionary of the Old Testament*, Vol. I (Grand Rapids: Eerdmans, 1974) 292–323.

3. See Weiser, "pisteuo.... B. The Old Testament Concept," 183. Weiser discusses six Hebrew stems which are used to express the OT relation of human beings to God, noting that: "None of the stems mentioned is specifically religious in origin. In each the religious use seems to have secular roots" (183). He focuses on the stems *'âman* and *batah* and concludes that "The LXX and NT were right when they related their term for faith (*pisteúein*) to the OT stem *'âman*, for in this word is expressed the most distinctive and profound thing which the OT has to say about faith" (196).

4. Weiser, "pisteuo.... B. The Old Testament Concept," 186. E.C. Blackman, "Faith," *The Interpreter's Dictionary of the Bible*, Vol. 2 (Nashville: Abingdon, 1962) 222–234, at 222 agrees: "A relationship is implied, and ultimately a personal one, for behind the object which is the basis of trust there is a person."

5. Weiser, "pisteuo.... B. The Old Testament Concept," 187.

6. Weiser, "pisteuo.... B. The Old Testament Concept," 187–188.

7. Weiser, "pisteuo.... B. The Old Testament Concept," 188.

8. Weiser, "pisteuo.... B. The Old Testament Concept," 188. On the covenantal context for Old Testament faith, J. Bauer writes: "In the Old Testament faith is grounded upon a historical religion—that of the covenant. Faith is, therefore, in the first place, the response of the people to the covenant." In "Faith in the Old Testament," in J. Bauer, ed., *Sacramentum verbi* (New York: Herder, 1970) 243–247 at 243.

9. Weiser, "pisteuo.... B. The Old Testament Concept," 189.

10. Thus Johannes Bauer, "Faith," 244; Jean Duplacy, "Faith," in Xavier Léon-Dufour, ed., *Dictionary of Biblical Theology* (New York: The Seabury Press, 1973²) 158; Weiser, "pisteuo.... B. The Old Testament Concept," 191–192.

11. Weiser, "pisteuo.... B. The Old Testament Concept," 191.

12. In addition to Weiser, "pisteuo.... B. The Old Testament Concept,"

191, a useful collection of OT texts which employ *batah* can be found in J. van der Ploeg, "L'Esperance dans l'Ancien Testament," *RB* 61 (1954) 481–507, at 488–490.

13. J. Bauer, "Faith," 244.

14. Weiser, "pisteuo.... B. The Old Testament Concept," 192.

15. The similarity between faith and hope or trust in the Old Testament is brought out in a striking way by J. van der Ploeg's description of the latter in "L'Espérance dans l'Ancien Testament," 481–507, especially on pages 492–493 where he provides texts in which *'âman* has the sense of "placing one's trust in," as well as in the résumé on pages 506–507, where the author remarks: "Dans tout ceci foi, attente et espérance se mêlaient toujours, sans que la dernière fût jamais absente." Hermisson and Lohse, p. 99, add: "Faith always includes trust, and there is no faith in the Old Testament without trust." A similar proximity of faith and hope or trust can be seen in W. Grossouw, "L'Espérance dans le Nouveau Testament," *RB* 61 (1954) 508–532, explicitly at 528.

16. See R. Schnackenburg, "Glaube," *Lexikon für Theologie und Kirche*, Vol. IV (Breiburg: Herder, 1960) 913–917 at 914 for a brief summary of these terms, with examples, which leads to the conclusion: "Faith is thus steadfastness and fidelity to God as response to God's own fidelity."

17. J. Alfaro, "Fides in terminologia biblica," 474–475. Alfaro adds in note 20 that this summary of OT faith is supported by many scholars; he lists references to E. Jacob, A. Weiser, T. Vriezen, W. Eichrodt, R. Bultmann, H. Menoud, P. van Imschoot, J. Bauer and O. Procksch.

18. André de Bovis, "Foi," *Dictionnaire de Spiritualité* V (Paris: Beauchesne, 1964) col. 530.

19. This theme constitutes the overarching thesis of Werner H. Schmidt's *The Faith of the Old Testament. A History* (Philadelphia: Westminster, 1983), a translation of the fourth edition of *Alttestamentlicher Glaube in seiner Geschichte* (Neukirchen-Vluyn: Neukirchener Verlag, 1982). Schmidt notes that the insights provided by exegesis into the individuality of the various periods and books of the Old Testament, the difference between the pre-exilic and post-exilic periods, the distinctive character of prophecy and similar gains regarding the historical conditions behind the various texts all lead to the recognition that "the

religion of Israel really had a history and was not complete from the beginning as if fallen from heaven..." (3).

20. Hermisson and Lohse, 10.

21. Joseph Schreiner, "The Development of the Israelite 'Credo'," *Concilium* 20 (1967) 29, writes: "If the people of the old covenant is asked about the content of its faith, the answer comes in the form of narratives and reports. Not, of course, that theoretical statements about the nature of God, the order of the world, human existence and the conduct of life are lacking....nevertheless, Israel's thinking from its very origin was otherwise oriented....Israel was filled with the experiences that had befallen it from God. This experience had to be expressed; this insight had to be grasped in mental forms." Hermisson and Lohse, 10, also note that the principal expression of Israel's faith, since it is based upon her experience of God in history, takes the form of narrative.

22. Walter Eichrodt, *Theology of the Old Testament*, Vol. II (Philadelphia: Westminster, 1967) 277–278, notes that the Elohist historian made "the word of faith the outstanding theme of his patriarchal history," adding: "in *Abraham* therefore he presented his contemporaries with *the type of the faithful*, the man who takes his stand on the promises of God, and who lives by his assurance of God's will, whatever appearances may suggest to the contrary. In the writer's powerful symbolism the silent starry heaven points to the illimitable power of the hidden God who manifests himself only in his word, and who in this way elicits the venture of personal trust in which Man gives himself wholly into God's hand."

23. An interpretation of this passage within the context of the priestly material of cultic declarations of righteousness can be found in Gerhard von Rad, "Faith Reckoned as Righteousness," in *The Problem of the Hexateuch and Other Essays* (New York: McGraw-Hill, 1966) 125–130.

24. Blackman, "Faith," 226.

25. Duplacy, "Faith," 158.

26. Blackman, "Faith," 225–226.

27. Bauer, "Faith," 243.

28. De Bovis, "Foi," 531–532, who points out that the idea of finding solidity in God corresponds nicely with the original notion conveyed by

the stem *'âman*; God's governance of history is emphasized by Bauer, "Faith," 243.

29. De Bovis, "Foi," 534. Eichrodt, *Theology of the Old Testament*, Vol. II, 279, also speaks of faith as an individual act, but in the context of contrasting such a faith with a more global view of faith as "Man's permanent attitude toward God."

30. De Bovis, "Foi," 535–537, provides a rich listing of texts, grouped under the headings: Attaching oneself to the promises of God (Future); Remembrance of the past (Past); and Attention to the present. The following paragraph of the text borrows from this rich collection.

31. Several authors, when writing about the meaning of faith in the Old Testament, explicitly relate it to the keeping of God's law. See Weiser, "pisteuo.... B. The Old Testament Concept," 185, 187; Blackman, "Faith," 227. Eichrodt, *Theology of the Old Testament*, Vol. II, 277–290, under the heading "Faith in God" devotes several pages to the discussion of the relation between faith and the law (288–290), concluding "...it is no longer fear but the faith-relationship which has become normative for the personal relation of Man to God in obedient subjection to the Law" (290).

32. Hermisson and Lohse, 99, call the book of the psalms "a textbook of the language of faith." Duplacy, "Faith," 160, writes: "The whole Psalter proclaims the faith of Israel in Yahweh, sole God (Ps 18,32; 115), Creator (8; 104), all-powerful (29), faithful Lord (89), and merciful (136) for His people (105), universal king of the future (47; 96–99)." Blackman, "Faith," 226: "As used in the organized worship of Israel, particularly the greater temple festivals, the Psalms are unique expressions of Israel's faith."

33. Schnackenburg, "Glaube," 914. See also, Rudolph Schnackenburg, "Biblical Perspectives of Faith," in *Toward a Theology of Christian Faith. Readings in Theology* (New York: P.J. Kenedy & Sons, 1968) 36–54 at 41: "Because Isaias expounds a faith in the *hidden* God of salvation, a faith that endures through periods of distress and darkness, he is called the 'prophet of faith'." Duplacy, "Faith," 159: "Isaiah was the most striking of the heralds of the faith." Bauer, "Faith," 246: "It is *the prophet Isaiah* who teaches and himself fully embodies heroic faith." Franco Festorazzi, "'WE ARE SAFE' (Jer. 7,10) The Faith of Both Testaments as Salvific Experience," *Concilium* 30 (1967) 45–59 at 49, writes: "The theme of faith acquires a consecration and a special depth especially in prophetic

literature and in the lives of the 'poor of Yahweh.' Isaiah represents the most illustrative example because he combines the various recorded aspects in a rich synthesis, thus bringing the line begun by Abraham to its Old Testament apex." The topic of faith according to Isaiah has generated the following studies: J. Böhmer, "Der Glaube und Jesaja," *ZAW* 41 (1923) 84-93; S. Virgulin, "La 'fede' nel profeta Isaia," *Biblica* 31 (1950) 346-364 and 483-503; C.A. Keller, "Das quietistische Element in der Botschaft des Jesaja," *ThZ* 11 (1955) 81-97; D. Loretz, "Der Glaube des Propheten Isaias an das Gottersreich," *ZKT* 82 (1960) 40-73 and 159-181; S. Virgulin, *La 'fede' nella profezia d'Isaia* (Milan: "Bibbia Oriente," 1961); M. Prager, "Jesajah, der Prophet des Glaubens," *BiLit* 37 (1963-1964) 143-150; M.-L. Henry, *Glaubenskrise und Glaubensbewährung in den Dichtungen der Jesaja-apokalkypse* BWANT, 5/6 (Stuttgart: Kohlhammer, 1967); G. Segalla, "La fede come opzione fondamentale in Isaia e Giovanni," *Studia Patavina* 15 (1968) 355-381; D.A. Cress, "Isaiah 7:9 and Propositional Accounts of the Nature of Religious Faith," in Elizabeth A. Livingstone, ed., *Studia biblica 1978 I. Papers on Old Testament* (Sheffield: Journal for the Study of Old Testament, supplement series 11, 1979) 111-117.

34. So Bauer, "Faith," 246.

35. So Schnackenburg, "Glaube," 914.

36. Eichrodt, *Theology of the Old Testament*, Vol. II, 281.

37. A good summary of this discussion can be found in J.I. Durham, "Credo, Ancient Israelite," *The Interpreter's Dictionary of the Bible, Supplementary Volume* (Nashville: Abingdon, 1976) 197-199.

38. See Gerhard von Rad, *The Problem of the Hexateuch and Other Essays* (New York: McGraw-Hill, 1966) 1-78.

39. Durham, 197, concludes his treatment of von Rad's position with the words: "Thus was the Hexateuch, for all its complex combination of originally separate traditions, shaped primarily by preoccupation with the theme of land settlement, itself given ancient summary in the short historical credo." Joseph Schreiner, "The Development of the Israelite 'Credo'," 37, echoes this summation: "In celebrating this gift of salvation in the minor credo, Israel followed its historical course: from the time when the fathers were strangers in Canaan, by way of the Egyptian bondage, Yahweh's liberation of the people and his leading of them through the desert, up to the grant of the promised land. Almost the

whole Pentateuch—of course, in the utmost brevity—is contained in this confession."

40. Noth's view, in *Überlieferungsgeschichte des Pentateuch* (Stuttgart: Kohlhammer, 1948) [English: *A History of Pentateuchal Traditions* (Englewood Cliffs: Prentice-Hall, 1972)] altered von Rad's on a number of details, such as positing an integration of these various traditions at a stage earlier than that of the Yahwist. An interesting account of the views of von Rad and Noth which also highlights the dissemination of their views in various college and seminary textbooks is Philip J. Hyatt, "Were There an Ancient Historical Credo in Israel and an Independent Sinai Tradition?" in H.T. Frank and W.L. Reed, ed. *Translating & Understanding the Old Testament* (Nashville: Abingdon, 1970) 152-170. The thrust of Hyatt's article is to proceed to the presentation of several studies which call the basic thesis of von Rad and Noth into question.

41. The crucial study here is L. Rost, *Das kleine Credo und andere Studien zum Alten Testament* (Heidelberg, 1965). See also T.C. Vriezen, "The Credo in the OT," in AA.VV., *Studies on the Psalms* (Leiden: Brill, 1963) 1-11; and N. Lohfink, "Zum 'kleinen geschichtlichen Credo' Dtn 26,5-9," *ThPh* 46 (1970) 1-31.

42. See C. Brekelmans, "Het 'historische Credo' van Israël," *TvT* 3 (1963) 1-11. Brekelmans relies in part on the work of J.A. Soggin for his criticism of von Rad; see Hyatt, p. 164, who summarizes his presentation of Brekelmans' criticism with the words: "These criticisms of von Rad on form-critical grounds seem to me to be valid. We must agree with Brekelmans that von Rad has not successfully isolated a *Gattung* that can be correctly called 'historical Credo.' What he calls by this name are in fact historical summaries, short or long, embedded within the *Gattungen* that should be designated as catechesis, covenant formulary (or more fully: the form for the ceremony of covenant making or renewal), or prayer to be made with the offering of firstfruits."

43. See A. Weiser, *The Old Testament: Its Formation and Development* (New York, 1961) 81-99; Hyatt, 165-167; E. Nicholson, *Exodus and Sinai in History and Tradition* (Oxford: Blackwell, 1973); W. Beyerlin, *Origins and History of the Oldest Sinaitic Traditions* (Oxford: Blackwell, 1965) esp. 145-170; J. Schmidt, "Erwägungen zum Verhältnis von Auszugs- und Sinaitradition," *ZAW* 82 (1970) 1-31; and H. Huffmon, "The Exodus, Sinai and the Credo," *CBQ* 27 (1965) 101-113.

44. C. Larcher, "La profession de la foi dans l'Ancien Testament,"

Lumière et vie 2 (1952) 15–38 at 18–19 speaks about the freedom with which later summaries utilize the traditional material. See also Hyatt, 153–154.

45. See Schreiner, 38.

46. See Schreiner, 39.

47. Schreiner, 39.

48. Schreiner, 39–40.

49. See Larcher, "La profession de la foi dans l'Ancien Testament," 22.

50. Schreiner, 31, who also makes reference to M. Noth, *Uberliefe-rungsgeschichte des Pentateuch* (Darmstadt, 1960²) 52.

51. These examples and the ones to follow in the next sentences are offered by Bernhard Lang, "Professions of Faith in the Old and New Testaments," *Concilium* 118 (1979) 3–12 at 5.

52. Lang, "Professions of Faith in the Old and New Testaments," 6.

53. Larcher, "La profession de la foi dans l'Ancien Testament," 20, calls the *Shema* "le credo par excellence de l'Ancien Testament." The text itself reads: "Hear, O Israel! The Lord is God, the Lord alone! Therefore, you shall love the Lord, your God, with all your heart, and with all your soul, and with all your strength. Take to heart these words which I enjoin on you today. Drill them into your children. Speak of them at home and abroad, whether you are busy or at rest. Bind them at your wrist as a sign and let them be as a pendant on your forehead. Write them on the doorposts of your houses and on your gates" (Dt 6,4–9).

54. Hyatt, 168.

55. Durham, 197.

56. Thus Larcher, "La profession de la foi dans l'Ancien Testament," 17, registers caution about the word "credo" and adds, on 25: "It does not seem that the people of the Old Covenant delimited in a rigorous, official way the content of their faith, nor that they elaborated an authorized creed summarizing the essential truths and dogmatic facts, nor that they felt obliged to profess such a creed because of their personal faith." Larcher goes on to develop four reasons to explain why the Israelite

religion did *not* elaborate what might properly be called a "creed" (31–38): 1) Old Testament religion is primarily one of works, focused upon rectitude by means of obeying the Law. The accent was not on beliefs. 2) It was a religion held together by the notion of nation-hood; the unity of the people was not based upon any list of doctrines. 3) Old Testament religion was framed and lived within the context of semitic psychology, which regards the whole and does not seek to distill out and hierarchize what amount to the central truths of its faith. 4) Israelite religion does not convey the sense of being based upon definitive revelation. Rather, it is directed toward the future; it includes the dimension of being unfinished, which imparts a dynamic instability to its doctrines and mitigates against the establishment of a listing of essential beliefs. Hyatt, 168, also wonders whether "indeed we may refer to Israelite religion as a creedalistic religion."

57. Durham, 198.

58. Schmidt, 72, to which he adds the following quotation from Wellhausen: "Monotheism was unknown to ancient Israel....Yahweh only came into consideration for them as the founder of Israel. Certainly they believed that the power of Yahweh extended far beyond Israel; this was why he was God, to help his own people if their own strengths were not sufficient. But this faith was not theoretically generalized."

59. Bernhard Lang, "No God but Yahweh! The Origin and Character of Biblical Monotheism," *Concilium* 177 (1985) 41–49 at 45. Lang proposes that Israel's monotheism is less concerned about doctrine than about hope. He writes: "But even when the doctrinal aspect of monotheism is stressed, Yahweh-alone supporters and early Jewish monotheists were not interested in dogma....The theology of the Yahweh-alone movement is a theology of hope; one which wagers everything on *one* person, on Yahweh. Everything is hoped of him. Hosea and Deutero-Isaiah emphasise it: there is no god other than Yahweh who will act as a saviour (Hos. 13,14; Isa. 45,21). In theological jargon we might put it thus: soteriological monotheism is older than dogmatic monotheism. Or: hope is older and more original than belief."

60. So Jacques Guillet, "God," in X. Léon-Dufour, ed. *Dictionary of Biblical Theology* (New York: Seabury, 1973²) 205–212 at 208. Guillet writes: "Israelite monotheism is not the fruit either of a metaphysical reflection or of a political integration or of a religious evolution. In Israel it is an affirmation of faith as ancient as its belief, that is, the certitude of its

election, the certainty of having been from among all the nations chosen by a God to whom all nations belong" (207–208). This contrasts rather sharply with the comment by Lang, 48: "The history of the rise of monotheism is part of a broader history: that of the destruction of a small State."

61. Lang, "No God but Yahweh! The Origin and Character of Biblical Monotheism," 45.

62. Weiser, "pisteuo.... B. The Old Testament Concept," 182–183.

63. Martin Buber, *Two Types of Faith*, trans. N.P. Goldhawk (London: Routledge and Kegan Paul, 1951).

64. Buber, 7.

65. Buber, 9.

66. See, especially, Eduard Lohse, "Emuna and Pistis" *TD* 27 (1979) 148–150 = "Emuna und Pistis—Jüdisches und urchristliches Verständnis des Glauben," *ZNW* 68 (1978) 147–163. Lohse attempts to show the continuity between what "faith" means in the Old and New Testaments respectively. The fundamental roots of Christian faith are not to be found within Hellenism, as Buber goes on to suggest, but within the faith of Israel. Paul, in particular, takes pains to relate the faith of Christians to that of Abraham. Lohse concludes: "So instead of speaking of two different kinds of faith (as Buber), we should perhaps speak of two different times: faith before and faith after Christ. While one still awaits the Messiah, the other confesses the crucified and risen Christ as Lord who will come at the end of time" (150).

67. See, for example, M. Löhr, *Sozialismus und Individualismus im Alten Testament* (B.Z.A.W., No. 10), 1906; H. Causse, *Du Groupe ethnique à la communauté religieuse* (Paris: F. Alcan, 1937); J. de Fraine, "Individu et société dans la religion de l'Ancien Testament," *Biblica* 33 (1952) 324–355 and 445–475; F. Spadafora, *Collettivismo e individualismo nel Vecchio Testamento* (Rovigo: Istituto Padano di Arti Grafiche, 1953); G.E. Wright and others, *The Biblical Doctrine of Man in Society* (London: SCM, 1954); H.H. Rowley, "Individual and Community," in *The Faith of Israel. Aspects of Old Testament Thought* (London: SCM, 1956) 99–123.

68. Eichrodt, "The Individual and the Community in the Old Testament God-Man Relationship," in *Theology of the Old Testament*, Vol. II, 231–267.

69. Eichrodt, *Theology of the Old Testament*, Vol. II, 239.

70. Eichrodt, *Theology of the Old Testament*, Vol. II, 247–251. H.H. Rowley, "Individual and Community," 99–123, argues against making too much of a development in the Old Testament in the direction of individualism. While not mentioning Eichrodt, he criticizes a number of authors who speak of Jeremiah as the "father of individualism in religion," attempting to show that there was some attention to the individual right from the beginning of Israel's history. Rowley's focus is not so much upon faith as upon such matters as personal responsibility, sin, innocent suffering, the effect of the individual's sin upon the community and the possibility of vicarious suffering by an individual on behalf of the community. Rowley sums up his findings on the relation of the individual to the community in the following way: "If the well-being of the individual lies in his harmony with the will of God, and if that well-being is bound up with the well-being of the society of which he forms a part, it is of importance to him that the whole society should be in harmony with the divine will. By the same token, it is of importance to society that all its individuals should be in harmony with God's will, since an individual could involve the community in dishonour or suffering. No man could be indifferent whether his neighbour walked in God's way or not, and there could be no delusion that a man's religion was merely his own affair....It is important that we should not think of all this as something wholly new that came into the religion of Israel at a particular date, but should recognize that it developed from a seed which was already there, and that it grew from the fundamental thought of the Old Testament on the nature of man as created in God's image, for his fellowship and service, but as a member of a corporate society and not merely as an individual, bearing his own measure of responsibility both for himself and for that society, and involved in the corporate life of society and in the life of the individuals that comprised it, and ultimately concerned with the life of nations other than his own. In the biblical conception of man there is a grandeur and a wholeness that excites ever new wonder. It is the murderer, Cain, who asks, 'Am I my brother's keeper?' (Gen 4,9). In the true faith of Israel every man was his brother's keeper, and his brother was every man" (122–123).

71. Eichrodt, *Theology of the Old Testament*, Vol. II, 255.

72. Eichrodt, *Theology of the Old Testament*, Vol. II, 265.

73. Eichrodt, *Theology of the Old Testament*, Vol. II, 266. Eichrodt adds: "Furthermore, the writers of the Psalms are so conscious of standing

within the community of the pious that it is from her that they derive their highest powers" (267).

74. De Bovis, "Foi," 553.

75. Schmidt, *The Faith of the Old Testament. A History*, 93; the quotation is from A. Alt, *Essays on Old Testament History and Religion* (Oxford: Blackwell, 1966) 3.

76. Schmidt, *The Faith of the Old Testament. A History*, 4.

77. Schmidt, *The Faith of the Old Testament. A History*, 2. In support, Schmidt offers the following quotation from Martin Noth, *The History of Israel* (London: Adam & Charles, 1965²), 2–3: "Yet in spite of all these historical connections and possibilities for comparison, 'Israel' still appears a stranger in the world of its own time...; not merely in the sense that every historical reality has its own individual character, and therefore an element of uniqueness, but rather that at the very centre of the history of 'Israel' we encounter phenomena for which there is no parallel at all elsewhere, not because the material for comparison has not yet come to light but because, so far as we know, such things have simply never happened elsewhere."

78. See, for example, Schmidt, *The Faith of the Old Testament. A History*, 53–92: "The Characteristic Features of Yahwistic Faith," or Ibid., 144–181: "The New Beliefs about God" (in the period of monarchy).

79. Schmidt, *The Faith of the Old Testament. A History*, 76–77.

80. Schmidt, *The Faith of the Old Testament. A History*, 278.

81. Georg Fohrer, "Die Vielfalt der Daseinshaltungen," in his *Theologische Grundstrukturen des Alten Testaments* (Berlin: Walter de Gruyter, 1972) 51–94.

82. Some useful summaries which treat Old Testament theology are: C.T. Craigk, "Biblical Theology and the Rise of Historicism," *JBL* 62 (1943) 281–294; N.W. Porteous, "OT Theology," in H.H. Rowley, ed. *The Old Testament and Modern Study* (Oxford: Clarendon, 1951) 311–345; C. Spicq, "L'avènement de la théologie biblique," *RSPT* 35 (1951) 561–574; C. Spicq, "Nouvelles réflexions sur la théologie biblique," *RSPT* 43 (1958) 209–219; F.M. Braun, "La théologie biblique," *RT* 61 (1953) 221–253; G. Ebeling, "The Meaning of 'Biblical Theology'," *JTL* 6 (1955) 79–97; H. Gross, "Was ist alttestamentliche Theologie?" *TTZ* 67 (1958) 355–363; R.

Martin-Achard, "Les voies de la théologie de l'Ancien Testament," *RThPh* 3 (1959) 217-226; H. Wildberger, "Auf dem Wege zu einer biblischen Theologie," *EvTh* 19 (1959) 70-90; F. Festorazzi, "Rassegna di teologia dell'Antico Testamento," *RivB* 10 (1962) 297-316 and 12 (1964) 27-48; R.C. Dentan, *Preface to Old Testament Theology* (New York: Seabury, 1963²); C. Barth, "Grundprobleme einer Theologie des Alten Testaments," *EvTh* 23 (1963) 342-372; D. Wallace, "Biblical Theology: Past and Future," *TZ* 19 (1963) 88-105; J. Barr, *Old and New in Interpretation* (London: SCM, 1966) 65-102; R.B. Laurin, *Contemporary Old Testament Theologians* (Valley Forge: Judson Press, 1970); H.-J. Kraus, *Die Biblische Theologie. Ihre Geschichte und Problematik* (Neukirchen-Vluyn: Neukirchener Verlag, 1970); J. Harvey, "The New Diachronic Biblical Theology of the Old Testament," *BTB* 1 (1971) 5-29; F.C. Prussner, "The Covenant of David and the Problem of Unity in Old Testament Theology," in J.C. Rylaarsdam, ed. *Transition in Biblical Scholarship* (Chicago: University of Chicago Press, 1968) 17-44; R. Davidson, "The Theology of the Old Testament," in R. Davidson and A.R.C. Leany, ed. *Biblical Criticism* (London, 1970) 138-165; H. Gese, "Erwägungen zur Einheit der biblischen Theologie," *ZTK* 67 (1970) 417-436; H.W. Wolff, ed. *Probleme biblischer Theologie. Gerhard von Rad zum 70. Geburtstag* (München: Kaiser, 1971); Gerhard F. Hasel, "The Center of the OT and OT Theology," in *Old Testament Theology: Basic Issues in the Current Debate* (Grand Rapids: Eerdmans, 1984) 117-143; Robert Martin-Achard, "Old Testament Theologies and Faith Confessions," *TD* 33 (1986) 145-148 [= "Théologies de l'Ancien Testament et confessions de foi," *RThPh* 117 (1985) 81-91]; and B.C. Ollenburger et al. (ed.), *The Flowering of Old Testament Theology: A Reader in Twentieth-Century Old Testament Theology, 1930-1990* (Winona Lake: Eisenbrauns, 1992).

83. Roland de Vaux, "Is it Possible to Write a 'Theology of the Old Testament?'" in his *The Bible and the Ancient Near East* (Garden City: Doubleday, 1971) 49-62 at 50.

84. Martin-Achard, "Old Testament Theologies and Faith Confessions," 145.

85. Hasel, 117-118, citing Eichrodt, *Theology of the Old Testament*, Vol. 1 (London: SCM, 1961) 14. See also Martin-Achard, "Old Testament Theologies and Faith Confessions," 145-146.

86. Hasel, 119, referring to Ernst Sellin, *Theologie des Alten Testaments* (Leipzig: Quelle & Meyer, 1936²) 19.

87. Hasel, 119, citing L. Köhler, *Old Testament Theology* (Philadelphia: Westminster, 1957) 30 and Hans Wildberger, "Auf dem Wege zu einer biblischen Theologie," *EvTh* 19 (1959) 77–78.

88. Hasel, 121, citing T. Vriezen, *An Outline of Old Testament Theology* (Newton, Mass.: Charles Branford, 1970²) 8, 160, 164 and 170.

89. Martin-Achard, "Old Testament Theologies and Faith Confessions," 146–147, referring to Georg Fohrer, *Theologische Grundstrukturen des Alten Testaments* (see note 83 above) and Hasel, 120, citing Fohrer's "Der Mittlepunkt einer Theologie des Alten Testaments," *ThZ* 24 (1968) 163 and "Das Alte Testament und das Thema 'Christologie'," *EvTh* 30 (1970) 295.

90. Hasel, 122, citing Rudolf Smend, *Die Mitte des alten Testaments* (Zürich: EVZ Verlag, 1970) 49 and 55.

91. Hasel, 120, in reference to G. Klein, "'Reich Gottes' als biblischer Zentralbegriff," *EvTh* 30 (1970) 642–670.

92. Martin-Achard, "Old Testament Theologies and Faith Confessions," 147, referring to Walther Zimmerli, *Grundriss der alttestamentlichen Theologie* (Stuttgart: Kohlhammer, 1972), later translated into English as *Old Testament Theology in Outline* (Edinburgh: T. & T. Clark, 1977).

93. Martin-Achard, "Old Testament Theologies and Faith Confessions," 147–148, in reference to C. Westermann, *Theologie des Alten Testaments in Grundzugen* (Göttingen: Vandenhoeck & Ruprecht, 1978); later translated into English as *Elements of Old Testament Theology* (Atlanta: John Knox, 1982).

94. Gerhard von Rad, *Old Testament Theology*, 2 Vols. (Edinburgh: Oliver & Boyd, 1962–1965), Vol. 2, 362; cf. Hasel, 55–62.

95. *Old Testament Theology*, Vol. II, 411.

96. Martin-Achard, "Old Testament Theologies and Faith Confessions," 148.

97. De Vaux, 58–59.

98. De Vaux, 61.

2. New Testament Terminology for and Nuances Concerning Faith

1. Institut für neutestamentliche Textforschung und vom Rechenzentrum der Universität Münster [esp. H. Bochmann and W.A. Scaby], ed. *Computer-Konkordanz zum Novum Testamentum Graece* (Berlin & New York: Walter De Gruyter, 1980) cols. 1532–1545. Other indications of statistical data are found in J. Alfaro, "Fides in Terminologia Biblica," *Greg* 42 (1961) 475 (the synoptics), 479 (Acts), 483–485 (Paul), 490–491 (Hebrews), 495–497 (Peter and James), and 497–500 (John); and Joseph Bonsirven, *Theology of the New Testament* (Westminster: The Newman Press, 1963) 128, note 1 and 288, note 3. A table comparing the synoptics with other New Testament writings as to the frequency of the use of the words "to believe" and "faith" can be found in Joachim Jeremias, *New Testament Theology. The Proclamation of Jesus* (New York: Charles Scribner's Sons, 1971) 160.

2. J. Alfaro, "Fides in Terminologia Biblica," *Greg* 42 (1961) 483, note 54, remarks that only the words God (548 times), Christ (379 times), Lord (275 times), Jesus (213 times) and Spirit (146 times) occur more frequently than faith (142 times) in the Pauline literature.

3. Jean Duplacy, "D'où vient l'importance centrale de la foi dans le nouveau testament?" in J. Coppens, A. Descamps & É. Massaux, ed., *Sacra Pagina. Miscellanea Biblica congressus internationalis catholici de re biblica* II (Paris: Gabalda et Cie; Gembloux: Duculot, 1959) 430–439 at 432.

4. Interestingly enough, Johannine literature uses almost exclusively the verb "to believe" (*pisteuô*): 107 of the 243 NT occurrences are in the gospel and letters of John; the noun appears only once: 1 Jn 5,4. While Pauline literature accounts for a significant number of the uses of the verb "to believe" (54, 21 of which are in Romans), it is by far the most predominant user of the noun "faith" (*pistis*—142 of the entire NT total of 243, with 40 occurrences in Romans and 22 in Galatians).

5. Rudolf Bultmann, "*pisteuô* ..." in G. Kittel, ed., *Theological Dictionary of the New Testament*, Vol. VI (Grand Rapids: Eerdmans, 1959) 203–204.

6. Joseph A. Burgess, "Faith: New Testament Perspectives," *American Baptist Quarterly* 1 (1982) 143–148 at 143–144. Burgess appears to be referring to the Bultmann article in the *Theological Dictionary of the New Testament* (cited in our previous note) and to the now famous work by A. Schlatter, *Der Glaube im Neuen Testament* (Darmstadt: Wissenschaftliche Buchgesellschaft, 1963).

7. Burgess, 144. Jean Duplacy, "D'où vient l'importance centrale de la foi dans le nouveau testament?" 435, says that to speak of New Testament faith without differentiating that which distinguishes the various New Testament books is to deal with an abstraction.

8. An older listing of bibliographical titles can be found in R. Schnackenburg, *La Théologie du Nouveau Testament* (Paris: Desclée, 1961) concerning Paul (70–73) and John (86–87). More recently, see F. Hahn and H. Klein, ed., *Glaube im Neuen Testament* (Neukirchen-Vluyn: Neukirchener Verlag, 1982); E. Lohse, "The Meaning of Faith in the Theology of Saint Paul," *The Journal of the Moscow Patriarchate* 8 (1982) 64–70; P. Tragan, ed., *Fede e sacramenti negli scritti giovanei* (Roma: Edizioni Abbazia S. Paolo, 1985).

9. Jeremias, *New Testament Theology*, 160. For studies of faith in the synoptic gospels, see: Mary Ann Beavis, "Mark's Teaching on Faith," *BTB* 16 (1986) 139–142; P. Benoit, "La foi dans les évangiles synoptiques," *LumVie* 22 (1955) 45–64; S. Brown, "The Lucan Use of *pistis-pisteuô*," in Id., *Apostasy and Perseverance in the Theology of Luke* (Rome: Pontifical Biblical Institute, 1969) 36–48; J. Duplacy, "La foi qui déplace les montagnes (Mt., XVII,20; XXI,21)," in AA.VV., *A la rencontre de Dieu. Mémoire Albert Gelin* (Le Puy: Mappus, 1961) 273–287; P. Lamarche, "L'appel à la conversion et à la foi. La vocation de Lévi (Mc., 2,13–17)," *Lumen vitae* 25 (1970) 125–136; Christopher D. Marshall, *Faith as a Theme in Mark's Narrative* (Cambridge: University Press, 1989); Johannes M. Nuetzel, "Vom Hören zum Glauben: Der Weg zum Osterglauben in der Sicht des Lukas," L. Lies ed. *Praesentia Christi* (Düsseldorf: Patmos, 1984) 37–49; E.D. O'Connor, *Faith in the Synoptic Gospels. A Problem in the Correlation of Scripture and Theology* (Notre-Dame: Univ. of ND Press, 1961); J. Riedl, "Wirklich der Herr ist auferweckt worden und dem Simon erschienen (Lk 24,34). Entstehung und Inhalt des neutestamentlichen Osterglaubens," *BiLit* 40 (1967) 81–110; F. Van Segbroeck, "Le scandale de l'incroyance. La signification de Mt. XIII,35," *ETL* 41 (1965) 344-372.

10. Christopher D. Marshall, *Faith as a Theme in Mark's Narrative*, 227–228. On the synoptic "encounter" setting for faith, see Marshall, 238; Jürgen Hermisson and Eduard Lohse, *Faith* (Nashville: Abingdon, 1981) 16–21; and Pierre Benoit, "Faith in the Synoptic Gospels," in his *Jesus and the Gospel*, Vol. I (London: Darton, Todd & Longman, 1973) 72–74.

11. See Hermisson and Lohse, 125-131; Heinrich Zimmermann, "Faith in the New Testament," in J. Bauer, ed., *Sacramentum Verbi* (New York: Herder, 1970) 247-257 at 248. Jeremias, *New Testament Theology*, 162-163, writes: "If we turn to the word-group *pistis/pisteuein/oligopistis/apistos* in the synoptic gospels, it is striking how more than half the examples fall either in miracle stories or in *logia* dealing with miracles. This is remarkable, because faith does not play a role either in Jewish or in Hellenistic miracle stories."

12. See Jeremias, *New Testament Theology*, 165-166, entitled "Jesus' evaluation of faith."

13. Hermisson & Lohse, 121-124; see also Jean Duplacy, "La foi qui déplace les montagnes (Mt., XVII,20; XXI,21)" 273-287; and F. Hahn, "Jesu Wort vom bergeverstetzenden Glauben," *Zeitschrift für die neutestamentliche Wissenschaft und die Kunde der Älteren Kirche* 76 (1985) 149-169.

14. Marshall, 233-234.

15. See Jeremias, *New Testament Theology*, 162-163. André De Bovis, "Foi," *DSSupp*, col. 542, talks of the Christocentric dimension of faith in the synoptics.

16. J. Duplacy, "D'où vient l'importance centrale de la foi dans le nouveau testament?" 438, nicely locates the origin of the centrality of faith for Christians in the relationship between Jesus and his disciples. See also P. Lamarche, "L'appel à la conversion et à la foi. La vocation de Lévi (Mc., 2,13-17)," 125-136, as an example of this connection between discipleship and faith.

17. Some texts which offer help in entering the Pauline understanding of faith are: M. Barth, C.K. Barrett, C. Butler, J. Dupont, J. Gnilka, J. Jeremias, S. Lyonnet, P.H. Menoud and B. Rigaux, *Foi et salut selon S. Paul* [Colloque oecuménique à l'Abbaye de S. Paul hors les Murs, 16-21 avril 1968] (Roma: Biblical Institute Press, 1970); H. Binder, *Der Glaube bei Paulus* (Berlin: Evangelische Verlagsanstalt, 1968); M.E. Boismard, "La foi selon saint Paul," *Lumière et Vie* 22 (1955) 65-90; G. Bornkamm, "Faith and Reason in Paul's Epistles," *NTS* 4 (1957-1958) 93-100; Glenn N. Davies, *Faith and Obedience in Romans. A Study in Romans 1-4* (Sheffield: Sheffield Academic Press, 1990), with bibliography 205-218; Axel von Dobbeler, *Glaube als Teilhabe: historische und semantische Grundlagen der paulinischen Theologie und Ekklesiologie des Glaubens* (Tübingen: JCB Mohr, 1987); T. Fahy, "Faith and the Law: Epistle to the

Romans, ch. 4," *ITQ* 28 (1961) 207–214; Ernst Fuchs, "Glaube sans phrase: zur Auslegung von 2 Kor 5,1–5," in E. Bizer and L. Abramowski, ed., *Studien zur Geschichte und Theologie der Reformation* (Neukirchen-Vluyn: Neukirchener Verlag, 1969) 21–31; Ernst Fuchs, "Die Logik des Paulinischen Glaubens," in H. Rückert and H. Leibing ed., *Geist und Geschichte der Reformation* (Berlin: de Gruyter, 1966) 1–14; W.H.P. Hatch, *The Pauline Idea of Faith in Its Relation to Jewish and Hellenistic Religion* (London: Harvard Univ., 1917); O. Kuss, "Der Glaube nach den paulinischen Hauptbriefen," *TG* 46 (1956) 1–26 [also in *Auslegung und Verkündigung* (Regensburg: Pustet, 1963) I, 187–212]; H. Ljungman, *Pistis. A Study of Its Presuppositions and Its Meaning in Pauline Use* (Lund: Gleerup 1964); E. Lohse, "The Meaning of Faith in the Theology of Saint Paul," *The Journal of the Moscow Patriarchate* 8 (1982) 64–70; S. Lyonnet, S., "Foi et charité chez saint Paul," *Christus* 61 (1969) 107–120; A.L. Mulka, "Fides quae per caritatem operatur (Gal 5,6)," *CBQ* 28 (1966) 174–188; Franz Mussner, "Der Glaube Mariens im Lichte des Römerbriefes," *Catholica/Mr* 18 (1964) 258–68; H. Schlier, "Der Glaube," in Id., *Grundzüge einer paulinischen Theologie* (Freiburg-Basel-Wien: Herder, 1978) 216–223; Anton Terstiege, *Hoffen und Glauben: eine biblisch-theologische Studie über die Wechselbeziehungen zwischen Hoffen und Glauben in den Hauptbriefen des heiligen Paulus* (Münster: Aschendorffsche Buchdrucherei, 1964); G. Wagner, "Paul and the Apostolic Faith," *Africa Theological Journal* 13 (1984) 115–135.

18. Rudolf Bultmann, *Theology of the New Testament*, Vol. I (New York: Charles Scribner's Sons, 1951) 315, speaks of this acceptance as "obedience": "For Paul the acceptance of the message in faith takes the form of an act of obedience because of the fact that the message which demands acknowledgment of the crucified Jesus as Lord demands of man the surrender of his previous understanding of himself, the reversal of the direction his will has previously had."

19. Zimmermann, 250, states: "It would not be too wide of the mark to assume that Rom. 10:4–17 is the passage in which the apostle sets out in general terms his view of faith."

20. Some studies which touch upon the relationship between faith and works/justification/salvation in Paul are: F. Amiot, *Les idées maîtresses de saint Paul* (Paris: Cerf, 1959) ["Abraham et la justification par la foi," 62–67; "L'accès à la justification: la foi et le baptême," 111–123]; J. Bonsirven, *L'évangile de Paul* (Paris: Aubier, 1948) ["La foi," 177–185; "Justice de la foi: sa nature," 198–212]; J. Cambier, *L'Évangile de Dieu*

selon l'épître aux Romains I (Bruges: Desclée de Brouwer, 1967) ["La manifestation de la justice de Dieu par le Christ en régime de foi. Rom. 3,12-4,25," 61-175; "Le régime de foi," 146-175; "Foi et justice," 339-429]; T. Fahy, "Faith and the Law: Epistle to the Romans, ch. 4," *ITQ* 28 (1961) 207-214; F. Prat, *La théologie de saint Paul*, Vol. I (Paris: Beauchesne, 1949) ["Justification par la foi sans les oeuvres de la Loi," 197-214; "La foi principe de justification: la foi justifiante," 279-291; "La justification par la foi," 291-301; and "La foi dans saint Paul," 536-545]; see also Zimmermann, 251-252. More recent works include John Reumann, *Righteousness in the New Testament: Justification in the Lutheran-Catholic Dialogue* (Philadelphia: Fortress, 1982), and Mark A. Seifrid, *Justification by Faith. The Origin and Development of a Central Pauline Theme* (Leiden: Brill, 1992).

21. E.C. Blackman, "Faith," *The Interpreter's Dictionary of the Bible*, Vol. 2 (Nashville: Abingdon, 1962) 231.

22. Rudolf Bultmann, *Theology of the New Testament*, Vol. I, 324.

23. Bultmann, "*pisteuô* ...," 218, writes: "Faith, then, is not exhausted by acceptance of the kerygma as though this were a mere declaration on joining a new religion. It has to establish itself continually against assaults as an attitude which controls all life."

24. See Bultmann, *Theology of the New Testament*, Vol. I, 326-327.

25. Bultmann, *Theology of the New Testament*, Vol. I, 318.

26. This point is mentioned by Hermisson & Lohse, 160; R. Bultmann, *Theology of the New Testament*, Vol. II (New York: Charles Scribner's Sons, 1955) 70; and Zimmermann, 254. Some studies which are devoted to faith according to John are: AA.VV., Pius-Ramon Tragan, ed., *Fede e Sacramenti negli Scritti Giovannei* (Rome: Abbazia S Paulo, 1985) [= Studia Anselmiana 90; Series: Sacramentum 8]; M. Baron, "La progressions des confessions de foi dans les dialogues de saint Jean," *BVC* 82 (1968) 32-44; T. Barrosse, "The Relationship of Love to Faith in St. John," *TS* 18 (1957) 538-559; Brendan J. Byrne, "The Faith of the Beloved Disciple and the Community in John 20," *JSNT* 23 (1985) 83-97; A. Decourtray, "La conception johannique de la foi," *NRT* 81 (1959) 561-576; C.H. Dodd, "Faith," in Id., *The Interpretation of the Fourth Gospel* (Cambridge: University Press, 1953) 179-186; J. Gaffney, "Believing and Knowing in the Fourth Gospel," *TS* 26 (1965) 215-241; Prosper Grech, "L'itinerario della fede in Giovanni," in N. Loss, L. Pacomio, E. Cortese, ed., *Quaerere*

Deum (Brescia: Paideia, 1980) 437–446; P. Grelot, "Le problème de la foi dans le quatrième Évangile," *BVC* 52 (1963) 60–71; F. Hahn, "Das Glaubensverständnis im Johannesevangelium," in E. Grässer and O. Merk, ed., *Glaube und Eschatologie* (Tübingen: Mohr, 1985) 51–69; F. Hahn, "Sehen und Glauben im Johannesevangelium," in H. Baltensweiler, ed., *Neues Testament und Geschichte* (Zürich: Theologische Verlag, 1972) 125–141; J. Huby, "De la connaissance de foi dans saint Jean," *RSR* 21 (1931) 385–421; J. Leal, "El clima de la fe en la Redaktionsgeschichte del IV Evangelio," *EstB* 22 (1963) 141–177; C. Lo Giudice, "La fede degli Apostoli nel IV Vangelo," *Biblica* 28 (1947) 59–82; Horacio E. Lona, "Glaube und Sprache des Glaubens im Johannesevangelium," *BZ* 28 (1984) 168–184; D. Mollat, "La foi dans le quatrième Évangile," *LV* 22 (1955) 91–107; F.J. Moloney, "From Cana to Cana (John 2:1–4:45) and the Fourth Evangelist's Concept of Correct (and Incorrect) Faith," in E.A. Livingstone, ed., *Studia Biblica 1978*, Vol. II: *Papers on the Gospels* (Sheffield: JSOT Press, 1989) 185–213 [= *Salesianum* 40 (1978) 817–843]; John Painter, "Eschatological Faith in the Gospel of John," in Robert Banks, ed., *Reconciliation and Hope* (Grand Rapids: Eerdmans, 1974) 36–52; Heinrich Schlier, "Glauben, Erkennen, Lieben nach dem Johannesevangelium," in J. Ratzinger, ed., *Einsicht und Glaube: Festgabe G. Söhngen* (Freiburg: Herder, 1962) 98–111; R. Schnackenburg, *Der Glaube im vierten Evangelium* (Breslau, 1937 [dissertation]); R. Schnackenburg, "Offenbarung und Glaube im Johannesevangelium," *Bibel und Leben* 7 (1966) 165–180; A. Vanhoye, "Notre foi, oeuvre divine, d'après le quatrième évangile," *NRT* 86 (1964) 337–354; A. Wurzinger, "Glauben nach Johannes," *BiLit* 39 (1966) 203–208.

27. On the aspect of self-communication, see Blackman, 232–233. J. Alfaro, "Fides in terminologia Biblica," 497, writes: "The center of Johannine theology is Jesus Christ, the Word made flesh and Son of God sent by the Father so that he might give human beings eternal life. Faith is very much in harmony to this doctrinal nucleus: by believing, a person accepts the man Jesus as Christ, the Son of God, and has eternal life."

28. A number of authors focus on the importance of testimony for understanding faith in John. See, for example, Blackman, 233.

29. So Blackman, 256.

30. Blackman, 256.

31. So Zimmermann, p. 255; Blackman, 233; see also: M. Baron, "La progressions des confessions de foi dans les dialogues de saint Jean," 32-44; F.-M. Braun, "L'accueil de la foi selon saint Jean," *VS* 92 (1955) 344-363; Prosper Grech, "L'itinerario della fede in Giovanni," 437-446; C. Lo Giudice, "La fede degli Apostoli nel IV Vangelo," 59-82; F.J. Moloney, "From Cana to Cana (John 2:1-4:45) and the Fourth Evangelist's Concept of Correct (and Incorrect) Faith," 185-213; F. Roustang, "Les moments de l'acte de foi et ses conditions de possibilité. Essai d'interprétation du dialogue avec la Samaritaine," *RSR* 46 (1958) 344-378.

32. Zimmermann, 256.

33. Bultmann, "pisteuô...," 227.

34. See Bultmann, "pisteuô...," 227-228; and Zimmermann, 257.

35. According to J. Alfaro, "Fides in Terminologia Biblica," 490-491, this definition of faith must be understood in the context of the whole of chapter 11. As such it shows a continuity between faith in the Old Testament and faith in the New. Blackman, 234, notes that "there is nothing distinctively Christian" in the view of faith presented in the letter to the Hebrews. Studies of faith in Hebrews include: Otto Betz, "Firmness in Faith: Hebrews 11:1 and Isaiah 28:16," in B. Thompson ed., *Scripture: Meaning and Method* (Hull: Hull University Press, 1987) 92-113; Raymond Brown, "Pilgrimage in Faith: the Christian Life in Hebrews," *Southwestern Journal of Theology* 28 (1985) 28-35; E. Grässer, *Der Glaube im Hebräerbrief* (Marburg: N.G. Elwert Verlag, 1965); C. Spicq, *L'Epître aux Hébreux*, Vol. II (Paris: J. Gabalda, 1953) 371-381 [on 534, Spicq states that chapter 11 of Hebrews, on faith, is one of the most beautiful pieces of literature in history]; Donald Medford Stine, *The finality of the Christian faith. A study of the unfolding argument of the epistle to the Hebrews, Chapters 1-7* (Dissertation, Princeton/NJ: Princeton Theological Seminary, 1964).

36. So Burgess, 143-144, and Duplacy, "D'où vient l'importance centrale de la foi dans le nouveau testament?," 436-438.

37. So Burgess, 146. On the meaning of faith in Hebrews see also Zimmermann, 253-254.

38. See Computer-Konkordanz, cols. 1535-36 and 1538; also J. Alfaro, "Fides in Terminologia Biblica," 479-482.

39. For example, Hermisson & Lohse, 155–156, and Burgess, 147.

40. So reports Blackman, 234; also Burgess, 147.

41. So Zimmermann, 254. The U.S. Lutheran-Roman Catholic Dialogue document of 1983, entitled "Justification by Faith," addresses this question in paragraph 142, concluding: "Thus it can now be agreed that James did not directly attack Paul's concept of faith or of justification by faith, although it may be difficult to reconcile James' overall understanding of law, works and sin with Paul's teaching on the same themes." Reprinted in *Origins* 13 (1983) 277–304 at 295–296.

42. So Blackman, 234. See also Jürgen Roloff, *Der erste Brief an Timotheus* (Zürich: Benzinger, 1988).

43. Juan Alfaro, "Fides in Terminologia Biblica," 504–505. Much of the material in the following paragraph is a loose translation of Alfaro's conclusion.

44. On the fundamental continuity between the Old and New Testaments with regard to faith, many more specific elements could be pointed out. Thus Bultmann, "pisteuô...," 205–208, provides quotations to show the continuation of Old Testament and Jewish usage along five lines:

> A) faith as *believing God's words* (the scripture: Jn 2,22; the Law and prophets: Lk 24,25; Acts 24,14; 26,27; Moses or his writings: Jn 5,46f; God's message through an angel: Lk 1,20.45; Acts 27,25);
>
> B) faith *as to obey* (Heb 11; Rom 1,8; 15,18; 16,19; 1 Th 1,8; 2 Cor 10,5f.);
>
> C) faith *as to trust* (Heb 11,11.17–19.29f.; trust in the wonder working power of Jesus' name: Acts 3,16; 14,9; as trusting prayer: Mk 11,22.24);
>
> D) faith *as to hope* (Heb 11; Rom 4,18-19; 1 Th 1,3; 1 Cor 13,13; 1 Pt 1,21); and
>
> E) faith *as faithfulness* (Heb 6,12; 11; 12,1; 13,7; 2 Tim 4,7).

Blackman, 229, offers additional references under the same five categories. De Bovis structures the entire biblical section of his article "Foi" in the *Dictionnaire de Spiritualité* on the presupposition of a basic continuity between the two Testaments. He joins examples from the New Testament (col. 540–546) to the various aspects which he had already elaborated in his description of faith in the Old Testament, so as to show the distinctive elements which appear in the New.

45. Bultmann, "*pisteuô...*," 209; for material contrasting Old and New Testament usage about faith, see 208–217.

46. Bultmann, "*pisteuô...*," 211.

47. Bultmann, "*pisteuô...*," 212–213.

48. Bultmann, "*pisteuô...*," 214–215. What Blackman, 230, says of the new aspects of faith in the New Testament is quite similar to the view of Bultmann.

49. Zimmermann, 247.

50. De Bovis, col. 540–546. These two elements appear substantially the same as those of Zimmermann.

51. Bernhard Lang, "Professions of Faith in the Old and New Testaments," *Concilium* 118 (1979) 3–12 at 7.

3. The New Testament Profession of Faith

1. Thus several biblical studies begin with remarks about late nineteenth–early twentieth century research into the Creed, such as P. Benoit, "The Origins of the Apostles' Creed in the New Testament," in his *Jesus and the Gospel*, Vol. 2 (New York: Seabury, 1974) 104–105; or O. Cullmann, "Les premières confessions de foi chrétiennes," in his *Foi et le culte de l'Église primitive* (Neuchatel: Delachaux & Niestlé, 1963) 49–50. Cullmann lists several of the now classic publications which emerged from this interest: A. Hahn, *Bibliothek der Symbole und Glaubensregeln der alten Kirche* (1897³); F. Kattenbusch, *Das apostolische Symbol*, 2 Vols. (1894 and 1900); A.E. Burn, *An Introduction to the Creeds and the Te Deum* (1899); F. Loofs, *Symbolik oder christliche Konfessionskunde* (1902); J. Haussleiter, *Trinitarischer Glaube und Christusbekenntnis in der alten Kirche* (1920); and, finally, the various essays by H. Lietzmann under the title "Symbolstudien," which appeared in the *Zeitschrift für die neutestamentliche Wissenschaft* in 1922, 1923, 1925 and 1927. J.N.D. Kelly, *Early*

Christian Creeds (New York: David McKay Company, Inc. 1960²) 6, speaks of "the great efflorescence of credal studies" at that time and the various notes of his book contain much of the extensive bibliography which emerged concerning the creeds. A recent essay which reflects upon the gradual reception and binding character of creeds in the ancient Church, in light of both the studies from the turn of the century as well as some insights from Thomas Aquinas, is Christoph Schönborn, "L'unità della confessione di fede nel mutamento della storia," which is Chapter II of his *Unità nella fede* (Casale Monferrato: Piemme, 1990) 37–58.

2. *Apostolic Constitutions* VI,14, in F.X. Funk, ed., *Didaskalia et Constitutiones Apostolorum*, Vol. I (Paderborn: Schoeningh, 1905) 335–337, mentions an original decision on the part of the apostles to set down briefly a common expression of faith. The most charming account is that in a sermon attributed to Augustine in PL 39:2189, in which, on Pentecost morning, each apostle is actually presented as voicing one of the articles of the Apostles' Creed. Benoit, "The Origins of the Apostles' Creed in the New Testament," 104, and Cullmann, "Les premières confessions de foi chrétiennes," 54, mention this story; Kelly, *Early Christian Creeds*, 1–4, quotes the text from PL 39.

3. Kelly, *Early Christian Creeds*, 4–5.

4. One cannot fix very precisely the date of the origin of the Apostles' Creed. Kelly has summarized in a convincing way the earlier investigations into this question, concluding that the formula which we use today derives from the eighth century and was gradually received, with minor alterations, over the period of several centuries. This is the burden of the argument in the last two chapters of *Early Christian Creeds* ("The Apostles' Creed" and "The Origins of the Apostles' Creed") 368–434. It should be added, however, that the basic wording and structure of this creed is already established much earlier, in the ancient Roman creed, which came into fixed form in the latter part of the second century (see Ibid., 100–130).

5. Kelly, *Early Christian Creeds*, 6, describing the approach of researchers at the beginning of the twentieth century, notes: "The prevailing temper, it must be remembered, under the influence of men like Harnack, was dominated by a peculiar theory of Christian origins. A sharp antithesis was often drawn between the Spirit-guided, spontaneous New Testament phase and the second-century epoch of incipient formalism

and institutionalism. So long as this was the accepted historical framework, there was no room for anything like a full-dress creed at the nursery-stage of Christianity."

6. Kelly, *Early Christian Creeds*, 7–8. Kelly's expression "separated themselves from Judaism" perhaps requires more nuance. A number of scholars today would say that, for some time, the first Christian community continued to understand itself as Jewish; so Hans Conzelmann, *The History of Primitive Christianity* (Nashville: Abingdon, 1973), 43. E. Schweizer, *Church Order in the New Testament* (London: SCM, 1961), 34–50, shares this view, but notes that Christology was eventually bound to divide the primitive Church from Judaism. F. Mussner, "'Bekenntnisstand' und Heilige Schrift," *Catholica* 21 (1967) 127–137, writes that the very confessional nature of Christianity led inexorably and rather quickly to the development of public and normative credal statements which in turn necessarily differentiated Christianity from Judaism. For his part, Conzelmann, *History*, 46–47, affirms that the way Christians interpreted Jesus' death led inevitably to a split with Judaism.

7. In addition to the works by Benoit, Cullmann, Kelly and Mussner already cited, some of the more important interventions concerning the credal material in the New Testament include: O.S., Barr, *From the Apostles' Faith to the Apostles' Creed* (London: Oxford, 1964); Hans-Werner Bartsch, "Inhalt u. Funktion des urchristlicher Osterglaubens," in E. Livingstone ed. *Studia Biblica 1978*, Vol. III (Sheffield: JSOT Press, 1980) 9–31; Hans-Werner Bartsch, "Zur vorpaulinischen Bekenntnisformel im Eingang des Römerbriefes," *ThZ* 23 (1967) 329–339; G. Bornkamm, "Glaube und Vernunft bei Paulus," 119–138 and "Das Bekenntnis im Hebräerbrief," 188–203 in *Studien zu Antike und Urchristentum* (München: Kaiser, 1954); R. Bultmann, "Bekenntnis- und Liedfragmente im ersten Petrusbrief," in *Exegetica. Aufsätze zur Erforschung des Neuen Testaments* (Tübingen: Mohr, 1967) 285–297; H. Conzelmann, "Was glaubte die frühe Christenheit?" *Schweizerische Theol. Umschau* 25 (1955) 61–74 [= *Theologie als Schriftauslegung* (München: Kaiser, 1974), 106–119]; H. Diem, "Schrift und Bekenntnis," *EvT* 2 (1935) 441–467; Arnold Ehrhardt, "Christianity Before the Apostles' Creed," *HTR* 55 (1962) 73–119; E. Fuchs, "Die Spannung im neutestamentlichen Christusglauben," *ZTK* 59 (1962) 32–45 [= *Glaube und Erfahrung* (Tübingen: Mohr, 1965), 280–297]; E. Fuchs, "Der Ursprung des christlichen Glaubens," in *Zum hermeneutischen Problem in der Theologie* (Tübingen: Mohr, 1959) 45–64; J. Gnilka, *Jesus Christus nach frühen Zeugnissen des Glaubens* (München: Kösel, 1970); F. Hahn,

"Bekenntnisformeln im Neuen Testament," in AA.VV., *Studien zur Bekenntnisbildung* (Wiesbaden: Franz Steines Verlag GMBH, 1980) 1–15; Alfons Kemmer, *The Creed in the Gospels* (New York: Paulist, 1986); K. Kleisch, *Das heilsgeschichtliche Credo in den Reden der Apostelgeschichte* (Köln, 1975); H. Koester, "The Structure and Criteria of Early Christian Beliefs," in J.M. Robinson and H. Koester, *Trajectories through Early Christianity* (Philadelphia: Fortress, 1971) 205–231; F. Mussner, "Christologische Homologese und evangelische Vita Jesu," in AA.VV., *Zur Frühgeschichte der Christologie* [Quaestiones Disputatae 51] (Freiburg: Herder, 1970) 59–73; V.H. Neufeld, *The Earliest Christian Confessions* (Leiden: Brill, 1963); H. Schlier, "Die Anfänge des christologischen Credo," in *Zur Frühgeschichte der Christologie*, 13–58; H. Von Campenhausen, "Das Bekenntnis im Urchristentum," *ZNW* 63 (1972) 210–253; H. Von Campenhausen, "Der Herrentitel und das urchristliche Bekenntnis," *ZNW* 66 (1975) 127–129; H.F. Weiss, "Bekenntnis und Uberlieferung im Neuen Testament," *Theologische Literaturzeitung* 99 (1974) 321–330; K. Wengst, *Christologische Formeln und Lieder des Urchristentums* (Gütersloh, 1972).

8. Schlier, "Die Anfänge des christologischen Credo," 13–14.

9. Conzelmann, *History of Primitive Christianity*, 43, notes that formulations of faith "are found scattered throughout primitive Christian literature. Since their content is concentrated on the person of Jesus (as the Messiah, Son of God, and so forth) and the work of salvation (death and resurrection), it is a simple matter to survey the primitive Christian doctrine of faith." See also 44–45 of the same work as well as Conzelmann's "Was glaubte die frühe Christenheit?" 109–114.

10. Benoit, "The Origins of the Apostles' Creed in the New Testament": "The Apostolic 'Kerygma,'" 105–113, and "The Confessions of Faith," 113–119.

11. Mussner, "Christologische Homologese und evangelische Vita Jesu," 69.

12. So Schlier, "Die Anfänge des christologischen Credo," 36–44; Conzelman, "Was glaubte die frühe Christenheit?" 109–112; Kelly, *Early Christian Creeds*, 13–23; however, von Campenhausen, "Der Herrentitel Jesu und das urchristliche Bekenntnis," 127–129, rejects the title "Lord" as christologically important since it did not necessarily imply a distinctive identification of Jesus. In another work, von Campenhausen, "Das Bekenntnis im Urchristentum," 218, provides an interesting list of the

titles "Christ" and "Son of God" when these are used as predicates of the verbs "I am–you are–he is"–verbs which indicate a confessional stance with regard to the identity of Jesus.

13. D.J. Harrington, "The Gospel according to Mark," in R. Brown, J. Fitzmyer and R. Murphy, ed., *The New Jerome Biblical Commentary* (London: Geoffrey Chapman, 1989) 596–629 at 597, briefly describes this "secret" in terms of W. Wrede's attempt (in *The Messianic Secret* [Cambridge, 1971]) to explain Jesus' commands that people be silent about his action or his identity (Mk 1,34.44; 3,12; 5,43; 7,36; 8,26.30; 9,9). According to Harrington's summary of Wrede, such commands should be understood as "Mark's way of accounting for the fact that Jesus in his public ministry neither claimed to be the Messiah nor was recognized as such" and, indeed, that "the real meaning of Jesus' messiahship became clear only with his death and resurrection." John P. Meier, "Jesus," in *The New Jerome Biblical Commentary*, 1316–1328 at 1323–1324, comments upon the ambiguities regarding the meaning of the title "Christ-Messiah" in the Palestinian ambient of Jesus' day as well as the likelihood that, at least in some sense, not only Jesus' disciples but also his adversaries considered him within the interpretative framework of this title.

14. So J. Fitzmyer, "Pauline Theology," in *The New Jerome Biblical Commentary*, 1394.

15. See Fitzmyer, "Pauline Theology," 1395–1396; F. Hahn, *The Titles of Jesus in Christology* (London: Lutterworth Press, 1969); W. Kramer, *Christus, Kyrios, Gottessohn* (Zürich: Zwingli, 1963); G.P. Wetter, *Der Sohn Gottes* (FRLANT 26; Göttingen, 1916).

16. So John Meier, "Jesus," 1324.

17. Nevertheless, this title has a special significance because of the religious meaning that was associated with it. John L. McKenzie, *Dictionary of the Bible* (Milwaukee: Bruce, 1965) 516–518 at 516, recalls the often mentioned fact that "The Gk *kurios*, 'lord,' is used in the LXX [the Septuagint, the most common Greek version of the Hebrew Bible at Jesus' time] as a translation of the divine name Yahweh." O. Cullmann's "Jesus the Lord (*kúrios*)," in his *The Christology of the New Testament* (London: SCM, 1963²) 195-237 at 195 and 213–215 refers to the view of W. Bousset, *Kyrios Christos* (1921²), later adopted by R. Bultmann, *Theology of the New Testament*, Vol. I, that the title "Lord" could only have been predicated of Jesus in its secular meaning by the earliest Christians

and that its application to him as a specific religious title was an effect of the influence of Hellenism upon Christianity. Cullmann argues that the Aramaic liturgical expression *Maranatha* ("Come, Lord") in reference to Jesus is the Achilles heel which shows the insufficiency of the view of Bousset and Bultmann, and that the title Lord, therefore, was already a liturgical title rich in religious meaning among the earliest Aramaic speaking Christian communities. Cullmann's entire chapter is quite informative about the presence and meaning of this title both in the New Testament itself and in the Hellenic and Judaic contexts of the first century.

18. Meier, "Jesus," 1325, says that Jesus could have been called "Lord" during his lifetime because of the wide spectrum of meanings associated with the term, "extending from a polite 'sir' to a title for God." McKenzie, *Dictionary*, 517, adds: "The use of *kyrios* in the Synoptic Gospels offers no new development. It is common as a form of address of Jesus; this reflects Aramaic usage and is no more than 'Sir.'"

19. Von Campenhausen, "Der Herrentitel Jesu und das urchristliche Bekenntnis," 127–129.

20. Cullmann, "Jesus the Lord," 232, sees Thomas' confession in Jn 20,28 as the culmination of the whole gospel of John.

21. Cullmann, "Jesus the Lord (*kúrios*)," 236–237, writes: "The designation of Jesus as *Kyrios* has the further consequence that actually all the titles of honour for God himself (with the exception of 'Father') may be transferred to Jesus. Once he was given the 'name which is above every name', God's own name ('Lord', *Adonai*, *Kyrios*), then no limitations at all could be set for the transfer of divine attributes to him." See also Fitzmyer, "Pauline Theology," 1395.

22. Kelly, *Early Christian Creeds*, 23; Schlier, "Die Anfänge des christlichen Credo," 16, who calls the expression "kurios Iesous" the "Grundform" of Christian confession; see also F. Mussner, "'Bekenntnisstand' und die Heilige Schrift," 127–128; and J. Gnilka, "Älteste Bekenntnissätze," in *Jesus Christus nach frühen Zeugnissen des Glaubens*, 27–43; Cullmann, "Les premières confessions de foi chrétiennes," 61–64; Benoit, "The Origins of the Apostles' Creed in the New Testament," 114.

23. The second part of Schlier's "Die Anfänge des christologischen Credo," 33–48, provides a list of some fourteen names or titles which

were applied to Jesus in the New Testament, insisting that only a few of them were used to convey the very core of who Jesus is, especially the titles Christ, Lord and Son of God.

24. See also, above, the many Pauline passages which refer to Jesus Christ our Lord, the use of both Son and Christ by the various gospels and such texts as Acts 2,36: "God has made him both Lord and Christ." This having been said, it is nevertheless important to acknowledge that different contexts can be more or less congenial to the specific titles. R.H. Fuller, *The Foundations of New Testament Christology* (New York: Scribner, 1965) and J.D.G. Dunn, *Unity and Diversity in the New Testament* (Philadelphia: Westminster, 1991²), offer a number of confirmations of this (for example, that the "son of Man" title would have considerable meaning within a context familiar with apocalyptic literature and not outside of such a context). Koester, "The Structure and Criteria of Early Christian Beliefs," 211-229, suggests that the four designations of Jesus as Lord, divine man, wisdom and the one who has been raised were competing and thus, to some degree, contrasting titles or ways of inter- preting Jesus. Koester emphasizes their diversity, arguing, after the fash- ion of Walter Bauer, that only one point of view eventually won out and that the others had to conform to it. Mussner, "Christologische Homologese und evangelische Vita Jesu," 70, offers an assessment which appears to be quite in contrast with that of Koester. While Mussner acknowledges that the respective missions to Jews and to Gentiles led to confessional titles for Jesus which would have been dif- ferent because of their respective meaningfulness within the different religious-historical environments of Jews or Gentiles, he maintains, how- ever, the ultimate criterion for the appropriateness of specific titles was the reality, the "Sache," of Jesus himself. Thus it was not ultimately a question of one point of view simply winning out over other contrasting but equally convincing or legitimate views.

25. Conzelmann, "Zur Analyse der Bekenntnisformel 1 Kor. 15,3-5," in *Theologie als Schriftauslegung*, 131-141 at 134-136, discusses and rejects Jeremias' suggestion about the possibility of an Aramaic original of 1 Cor 15,3-5. On 138-139 of the same work, Conzelmann insists that, though Greek in origin, this text nevertheless binds the proclamation of the death and resurrection of Jesus to Peter and the Twelve.

26. For further discussion of this passage, see Gnilka, "Das christologis- che Glaubensbekenntnis. 1 Kor 15,3-5," in his *Jesus Christus nach frühen Zeugnissen des Glaubens*, 44-60, who discusses it as a "Christological con-

fession." Campenhausen, "Das Bekenntnis im Urchristentum," 210–211, criticizes Gnilka on this point, warning that it is anachronistic to identify these verses as anything like a creed; rather they are simply one of the various pieces of tradition which form the pre-history of the New Testament. Campenhausen's objection seems to concern the identification of this text as an example of the particular literary form "confession." He is not disputing that it reflects the faith of the early community. Kelly, *Early Christian Creeds*, 13–23, discusses 1 Cor 15,3–8 under the heading "Fragments of Creeds," calling it a summary used for catechetical purposes or for preaching, with the list of witnesses serving as an apologetic element. Vernon Neufeld, *The Earliest Christian Confessions*, 47–48, treats this passage as a Pauline homologia or confession.

27. One of the most often cited studies about this material is C.H. Dodd, *The Apostolic Preaching and its Development* (New York: Harper and Row, 1964).

28. Norman Perrin, "The Literary *Gattung* 'Gospel'—Some Observations," *The Expository Times* 82 (1970/71) 4–7 at 6 speaks of Kähler's designation of the gospels as "passion narratives with long introductions," but fails to include any reference to Kähler himself. One might also include here the conviction of Koester, "The Structure and Criteria of Early Christian Beliefs," 223–229, that the "creed" concerning the resurrection of Jesus from the dead became the central criterion of faith for the "canonical" writers whose works eventually were received as the New Testament. Thus Koester's theory too may be said to support the centrality of the death and resurrection in New Testament faith.

29. Schlier, "Die Anfänge des christologischen Credo," 46: "Wir sehen, die Glaubensformeln, so sehr sie aus verschiedenen Zeiten und Gegenden stammen, bringen in einer unterschiedlichen Begrifflichkeit bestimmte Geschehnisse der Geschichte Jesu Christi in erstaunlicher Übereinstimmung zur Sprache." On the deep agreement about the fundamental Christian beliefs and the events to which they refer, see Benoit, "The Origins of the Apostles' Creed in the New Testament," 104–105; Cullmann, "Les premières confessions de foi chrétiennes," 83; and Kelly, *Early Christian Creeds*, 23–24.

30. The assertion that the first Christian community at a rather *early* point arrived at a relatively clear and homogeneous confession of its fundamental faith is emphasized by Mussner, "'Bekenntnisstand' und

Heilige Schrift," 129-130; Bornkamm, "Das Bekenntnis im Hebräerbrief," 191; Cullmann, "Les premières confessions de foi chrétiennes," 51; and Kelly, *Early Christian Creeds*, 25-28, who on 10-11 writes: "In this sense at any rate it is legitimate to speak of the creed of the primitive Church. Nor was it something vague and nebulous, without precision of contour: its main features were clearly enough defined. The Epistles and Gospels are, of course, rarely if ever concerned to set out the faith in its fulness: they rather presuppose and hint at it. Even so, it is possible to reconstruct, with a fair degree of confidence, what must have been its chief constituents."

31. Benoit, "The Origins of the Apostles' Creed in the New Testament," 105-113, states that the kerygma focuses on the central proclamation of the death and resurrection of Jesus as presented in the sermons of Acts. This kerygma soon is enveloped concentrically, first, by statements about the work of the Holy Spirit in the preparation for Christ (the prophets) and in the witness of the post-Easter community and, secondly, by the more universal, cosmic perspectives of the creation and the eschaton. Benoit sees prefigured in these three concentric layers of the kerygma already a hint of the later tripartite form of the Creed! He goes on to speak about a second category of New Testament statements which underlie the eventual development of the creed, a category which he entitles "confessions of faith" (113-119). In contrast with the various statements of the kerygma, these focus more upon the acknowledgment of Jesus' identity as Lord, Christ and Son of God and include both binitarian (i.e. 1 Cor 8,6) and Trinitarian (i.e. 2 Cor 13,13) formulae.

32. So Benoit, "The Origins of the Apostles' Creed in the New Testament," 105, 113, 119-120; Cullmann, "Les premières confessions de foi chrétiennes," 55; and Kelly, *Early Christian Creeds*, 29.

33. Schlier closes his "Die Anfänge des christologischen Credo," 58, with the words: "Im Grunde ist das Credo Evangelium, genauer: Evangelium in der Form normativer Tradition der Kirche." [Ultimately the creed is the gospel, better: gospel in the form of the normative tradition of the Church]. See also Benoit, "The Origins of the Apostles' Creed in the New Testament," 105, 119-120, to the effect that the Creed reflects the message which the apostles gave to the Church. Koester, "The Structure and Criteria of Early Christian Beliefs," 229-230, concludes his own particular theory concerning the origins of that faith which is expressed in the New Testament by stating that the "cross-resurrection creed," championed by Paul, became the dominant framework for understanding

Jesus into which other reflection about Jesus was then integrated in the
course of the process leading to the composition of the various books of
the New Testament. Thus, again, although in a quite contrasting way
from that of Schlier and Benoit who posit a fundamental credal harmony at the origins of the New Testament, Koester too serves as a witness
that, in some way, creed precedes and exerts an influence upon the formation of the gospels. Finally, Mussner, "Christologische Homologese
und evangelische Vita Jesu," 59–73, adds an additional and quite distinct
consideration to the question of the relation between creed and gospel.
Responding to the question: "what is the need for the gospel narrative if
one already has the essential aspects of Christian faith summarized in
credal formulas?" Mussner responds that the gospel in a way verifies the
Creed in history, safeguarding it from being an abstract collection of
essentialist truths: "In der Urkirche sind deshalb Evangelien, evangelische Jesusviten geschrieben worden, weil mit ihrer Hilfe die Sätze der
christologischen Homologese am besten verifiziert werden konnten.
Die Evangelien zeigen, daß die homologischen Sätze über Jesus von
Nazareth zu Recht bestehen" (60). At the same time, the confessions
(Homologese) concerning Jesus need not only to be verified but also to
be interpreted. The words and deeds of Jesus reported in the gospels
provide a context for the never-ending task of interpreting the confession about Jesus: "Die indirekte Christologie der evangelischen Vita Jesu
läßt die direkte der christologischen Homologese nie zur Ruhe kom-
men. Die Vita Jesu bleibt der notwendige Kontext der Homologese. Die
Christologie kann von der Homologese allein her nicht aufgebaut werden; denn das Jesusphänomen kann nicht ausgeschöpft werden. Das
zeigt im übrigen auch die Tatsache, daß in der Urkirche nicht nur eine
Vita Jesu geschrieben worden ist, sondern vier" (72).

34. This is the point of both Conzelmann, "Was glaubte die frühe
Christenheit?" 112–114 and Schlier, "Die Anfänge des christologischen
Credo," 46–48. Similarly for Cullmann, "Les premières confessions de
foi chrétiennes," 80, Jesus' Lordship and divine filiation are both related
to his death and resurrection. This may suggest that our treatment of
this material has been lopsided, giving over twice as much space to the
Christological titles as to the salvation deed of the death and resurrection. However, in point of fact, the incidence of the three titles Christ
(531 times), Son (379 times) and Lord (719 times) is much higher than
that of the words resurrection (42 times) or *egeiro* (144 times) or *anaste-
nai* (108 times). Thus, a more extensive presentation of the titles is somewhat inevitable and appropriate.

35. "Das ganz Sein Jesu ist Funktion des 'Für uns,' aber auch die Funktion ist—eben darum—ganz Sein." Quoted in Schlier, "Die Anfänge des christologischen Credo," 48, in reference to J. Ratzinger, *Einführung in das Christentum* (München: Kösel Verlag, 1968), 163. From a rather different perspective but along the same line, see Mussner's idea that the *vita Jesu*, as portrayed in the gospels, which one could perhaps categorize as expressive of Jesus' activity (function) on behalf of human salvation, stands always as the context within which the various homologies (ontology) must be continually interpreted; see Mussner, "Christologische Homologese und evangelische Vita Jesu," 63 and 72 (the text from the latter page is quoted above in note 33).

36. Cullmann, "Les premières confessions de foi chrétiennes," 56–65; Benoit, "The Origins of the Apostles' Creed in the New Testament," 113–116. See also Campenhausen, "Das Bekenntnis im Urchristentum," 231; Kelly, *Early Christian Creeds*, 13–15; and Bornkamm, "Das Bekenntnis im Hebräerbrief," 188–200.

37. See also the textually problematic verse which includes a profession of faith by the Ethiopian prior to his baptism by Philip: "And Philip said, 'If you believe with all your heart, you may [be baptized].' And he replied, 'I believe that Jesus Christ is the Son of God'" (Acts 8,37).

38. Kelly, *Early Christian Creeds*, 18, says of 1 Pt 3,18–22 that it "reads like a part-paraphrase and part-quotation of an instruction preparatory to baptism."

39. Bornkamm, "Das Bekenntnis im Hebräerbrief," 189–191 and 200.

40. Benoit, "The Origins of the Apostles' Creed in the New Testament," 113.

41. Benoit, "The Origins of the Apostles' Creed in the New Testament," 116.

42. On the various hymns in the New Testament which reflect a confession of faith about Christ, see J.T. Sanders, *The New Testament Christological Hymns* (Cambridge: University Press, 1971). R.P. Martin, *Carmen Christi: Philippians 2:5–11* (Cambridge: University Press, 1967), begins with a general overview and classification of New Testament hymns and proceeds to demonstrate that the Philippians hymn is an ancient Christian cultic hymn, probably of Palestinian derivation, which already was arranged in rhythmic strophes by the time it fell into Paul's

hands. On the significance of worship as a guide to understanding faith in the New Testament, see A.N. Wainwright, *The Trinity in the New Testament* (London: SPCK, 1962) 93–104. See also R. Deichgräber, *Gotteshymnus und Christushymnus in der frühen Christenheit* (Göttingen: Vandenhoeck & Ruprecht, 1967); G. Schille, *Frühchristliche Hymnen* (Berlin: Evangelische Verlagsanstalt, 1965).

43. Several passages are of particular interest and relevance insofar as they employ the verb *omologein*: "So every one who acknowledges me before men, I also will acknowledge before my Father who is in heaven; but whoever denies me before men, I also will deny before my Father who is in heaven" Mt 10,32–33; par Lk 12,8–9. Some texts present a similar idea but only in a negative form, without mentioning the positive confession. See Mk 8,38: "For whoever is ashamed of me and of my words in this adulterous and sinful generation, of him will the Son of man also be ashamed, when he comes in the glory of his Father with the holy angels" (par Lk 9,26) and 2 Tim 2,11–13: "If we have died with him we shall also live with him; if we hold out to the end we shall also reign with him. But if we deny him he will deny us. If we are unfaithful he will still remain faithful, for he cannot deny himself."

44. Benoit, "The Origins of the Apostles' Creed in the New Testament," 114. Also Cullmann, "Les premières confessions de foi chrétiennes," 63.

45. See the final section of Cullmann, "Les premières confessions de foi chrétiennes," 76–85, which attempts to distill the "essence of Christian faith" according to the earliest confessions.

46. Cullmann, "Les premières confessions de foi chrétiennes," 77.

47. As an example, Cullmann, "Les premières confessions de foi chrétiennes," 80, notes that in the Apostles' and later creeds the forgiveness of sins falls under the third article, which speaks of the Spirit and of the Church, a placement which obscures the New Testament teaching associating the forgiveness of sins with Jesus' death (1 Cor 15,3; 1 Pet 3,18; 1 Tim 2,6), prior to any consideration of the Church or of baptism. Thus, according to Cullmann, the forgiveness of sins was transferred in the later creeds from the second article to the third.

48. Campenhausen, "Das Bekenntnis im Urchristentum," 215; Conzelmann, "Was glaubte die frühe Christenheit?" 114, Mussner, "Christologische Homologese und evangelische Vita Jesu," 70.

49. Kelly, *Early Christian Creeds*, 28. On the earliness of the credal faith see Mussner, "'Bekenntnisstand' und Heilige Schrift," 129–130. Benoit, "The Origins of the Apostles' Creed in the New Testament," 25–27, joins Kelly in arguing explicitly against Cullmann's suggestion that the binitarian and Trinitarian formulae were relatively late.

50. That Christian faith always maintained this element of being faith in God, the transcendent Other, see Bornkamm, "Das Bekenntnis im Hebräerbrief," 193, and Campenhausen, "Das Bekenntnis im Urchristentum," 211.

51. On this point see Conzelmann, "Was glaubte die frühe Christenheit?" 117–119, who explores two strains within the Christian community which called for such resistance: docetism and apocalypticism. Also Ehrhardt, 92; Schlier, "Die Anfänge des christologischen Credo," 19; Cullmann, "Les premières confessions de foi chrétiennes," 65; and Campenhausen, "Das Bekenntnis im Urchristentum," 235–252.

52. For more on this topic, see the role of dialogue in sorting out sound from false doctrine which appears several times in the following chapter, especially in connection with the articles by Giblet (note 34) and Grech (notes 39–40).

53. Cullmann, "Les premières confessions de foi chrétiennes," 80 and 83 mentions the common kernel or nucleus; also Benoit, "The Origins of the Apostles' Creed in the New Testament," 104–105, and Kelly, *Early Christian Creeds*, 29. Even Koester, "The Structure and Criteria of Early Christian Beliefs," whose theory posits a diversity of four distinct early approaches to belief about Jesus (211–229), nevertheless concludes that one such approach, centering upon the death and resurrection and espoused by St. Paul, won the day and became the framework into which material from the other approaches had to fit in order to be integrated into the writings eventually accepted as part of the New Testament canon (229–231).

4. Diversity and Unity in Faith According to the New Testament

1. The following provide a fairly representative sample of the many entries which relate to unity and diversity in the New Testament, particularly with regard to the precise topic of faith: P.J. Achtemeier, *The Quest for Unity in the New Testament Church* (Philadelphia: Fortress, 1987); Hans

Urs von Balthasar, "Unity and Diversity in New Testament Theology," *Communio* 10 (1983) 106–116; J. Bogart, *Orthodox and Heretical Perfectionism in the Johannine Community as Evident in the First Epistle of John* (Missoula: Scholars Press, 1977); D. Carson, "Unity and Diversity in the New Testament: The Possibility of Synthesis," in J. D. Woodbridge, ed., *Scriptures and Truth* (Grand Rapids: Academie, 1983) 63–95; J. Charlot, *New Testament Disunity: Its Significance for Christianity Today* (New York: Dutton, 1970); O. Cullmann, *Unity through Diversity* (Philadelphia: Fortress, 1988); Axel von Dobbeler, *Glaube als Teilhabe: historische und semantische Grundlagen der paulinischen Theologie und Ekklesiologie des Glaubens* (Tübingen: JCB Mohr, 1987); James D.G. Dunn, *Unity and Diversity in the New Testament* (Philadelphia: The Westminster Press, 1977, 1991[2]); S. De Ausejo, "La 'unidad de fe' en Eph. 4,5–13," in AA.VV. *El movimiento ecumenista* (Madrid: Consejo, 1953) 155–194; Dieter Georgi, *Die Gegner des Paulus im 2. Korintherbrief: Studien zur religiösen Propaganda in der Spätantike*, WMANT 11 (Neukirchen: Neukirchener Verlag, 1964); Leonard Goppelt, "The Plurality of New Testament Theologies and the Unity of the Gospel as an Ecumenical Problem," in Vilmer Vajta, ed., *The Gospel and Unity* (Minneapolis: Augsburg, 1971) 106–130; Robert A. Guelich, *Unity and Diversity in New Testament Theology: Essays in Honor of George E. Ladd* (Grand Rapids: Eerdmanns, 1978); Ferdinand Hahn, "Die Bedeutung des Apostelkonvents [Act AP 15] für die Einheit der Christenheit," in *Exegetische Beiträge zum ökumenischen Gespräch*, Gesammelte Aufsätze I (Göttingen: Vandenhoeck, 1986) 95–116; Ferdinand Hahn, "Die Einheit der Kirche und Kirchengemeinschaft in neutestamentlicher Sicht," in *Ibid.*, 116–158; A. Houtepen, "Koinonia and Consensus: Towards Communion in One Faith," in AA.VV., *Sharing in One Hope*, Faith and Order paper 92 (Geneva: WCC, 1978) 205–208; Ernst Käsemann, "The Canon of the New Testament and the Unity of the Church," in *Essays on New Testament Themes* (London: SCM, 1964) 95–107; Ernst Käsemann, "Ketzer und Zeuge: zum johanneischen Verfasserproblem," *ZTK* 48 (1951) 292–311, reprinted in *Exegetische Versuche und Besinnungen* (Göttingen: Vandenhoeck & Ruprecht, 1960) 168–187; W. Kern, "Die Mitte des christlichen Glaubens," *StdZ* 195 (1977) 105–118; Helmut Koester, "The Purpose of the Polemic of a Pauline Fragment (Phil. 3)," *NTS* 8 (1961/62) 317–332; Helmut Koester, "The Structure and Criteria of Early Christian Beliefs," in J.M. Robinson and H. Koester, *Trajectories through Early Christianity* (Philadelphia: Fortress, 1971) 205–231; Helmut Koester, "The Theological Aspects of Primitive Christian Heresy," in J.M. Robinson, ed., *The Future of Our Religious Past: Essays in Honour of*

Rudolf Bultmann (London: SCM, 1971) 65–83; E. Lohse, *Die Einheit des Neuen Testaments* (Göttingen: Vandenhouck & Ruprecht, 1973); H. Lubsczyk, "Die Einheit der Schrift. Zur hermeneutischen Relevanz der Urbekenntnis im Alten und Neuen Testament," in F. Hoffmann, L. Scheffczyk and K. Feiereis, ed., *Sapienter ordinare* (Leipzig: St. Benno Verlag, 1969), 73–104; H. Lubsczyk, *Die Einheit der Schrift. Viele Theologien–ein Bekenntnis* (Stuttgart, 1970); V. Luz and H. Weder, ed., *Die Mitte des Neuen Testaments. Einheit und Vielfalt neutestamentlicher Theologie* (Göttingen: Vandenhoeck & Ruprecht, 1983); I. Howard Marshall, "Orthodoxy and Heresy in Earlier Christianity," *Themelios* 2 (1976) 5–14; Brice L. Martin, "Some Reflections on the Unity of the New Testament," *Studies in Religion/Sciences religieuses* 8 (1979) 143–152; F. Martin, "Pauline Trinitarian Formulas and Christian Unity," *CBQ* 30 (1968) 199–219; N.J. McEleney, "Orthodoxy and Heresy in the New Testament," *Proceedings of the CTSA* 25 (1970) 54–77; M. Meinertz, "Schisma und Hairesis im Neuen Testament," *BZ* 1 (1957) 114–118; N.M. Pritchard, "Profession of Faith and Admission to Communion in the Light of I Cor II and Other Passages," *Scottish Journal of Theology* 33 (1980) 55–70; H. Schlier, "Die Einheit der Kirche in Denken des Apostels Paulus," in *Die Zeit der Kirche* (Freiburg: Herder, 1956) 287–299; Walter Schmithals, *Die Gnosis in Korinth*, FRLANT 66 (Göttingen: Vandenhoeck & Ruprecht, 1956, 1965²); Walter Schmithals, "Die Häretiker in Galatien," *ZNW* 47 (1956) 25-67; Walter Schmithals, "Die Irrlehrer des Philipperbriefes," *ZTK* 54 (1957) 297–341; Walter Schmithals, "Die Irrlehrer von Rm. 16,17–20," *Studia Theologica* 13 (1959) 51–69 [the preceding three articles are reprinted in his collection of essays: *Paulus und die Gnostiker,* Theologische Forschung 35 (Hamburg: Evangelischer Verlag, 1965)]; Walter Schmithals, "Zur Abfassung und ältesten Sammlung der paulinischen Hauptbriefe," *ZNW* 51 (1960) 225–245; R. Schnackenburg, "Pluralität und Einheit im Glauben," in *Glaubensimpulse aus dem Neuen Testament* (Düsseldorf: Patmos, 1973) 16–46; W. Trilling, *Vielfalt und Einheit im Neuen Testament* (Einsiedeln: Benziger, 1968); Paul Wells, "Le pluralisme, l'écriture et l'unité de l'église," *Revue Réformée* 25 (1974/'75) 99, 119–141.

2. A helpful table of the differences in the resurrection narratives can be found in R. Brown, "Aspects of New Testament Thought: The Resurrection of Jesus," in R.E. Brown, J.A. Fitzmyer and R.E. Murphy, ed., *The New Jerome Biblical Commentary* (London: Chapman, 1990) 1373–1377 at 1376.

3. On the discrepancies in the infancy narratives see R. Brown, *The Birth of the Messiah* (Garden City: Doubleday, 1977) 33–37.

4. "Größer kann die Differenz kaum sein!" writes W. Trilling of these two interpretations; in "Vielfalt und Einheit im Neuen Testament," in *Vielfalt und Einheit im Neuen Testament* 32–60 at 41. Jean Giblet, "Einheit des Glaubens und Verschiedenartigkeit des Ausprucks in den Schriften des Neuen Testaments," in AA.VV., *Auf dem Weg zur Einheit des Glaubens* (Innsbruck-Basel-Wien: Tyrolia Verlag, 1976) 25–36 at 25 also refers to this scene as an example of the striking diversity to be found in the New Testament.

5. To the extent that historical-critical method seeks to uncover the literal sense of the text, that is, the intention of the author, it will tend to focus upon what is distinctive about each author and, thus, upon differences. Goppelt, "The Plurality of New Testament Theologies," 108–109, notes that the problem of diversity emerges naturally with the application of the historical critical method to the New Testament. See also A. Stock, *Einheit des Neuen Testaments* (Zürich: Benzinger, 1969) 160, and Giblet, "Einheit des Glaubens und Verschiedenartigkeit des Ausprucks in den Schriften des Neuen Testaments," 25. However, both Goppelt and Giblet add that the problem of explaining diversity within the New Testament is an ancient one, not deriving solely from contemporary exegesis, and that there is a history of proposed solutions.

6. This is the aim, for example, of the development of redaction criticism with respect to the four gospels. See N. Perrin, *What Is Redaction Criticism?* (Philadelphia: Fortress, 1969).

7. Attempts to reconstruct the communities to which the various New Testament texts were addressed include R.E. Brown, *The Community of the Beloved Disciple* (New York: Paulist, 1979); R.E. Brown and J.P. Meier, *Antioch and Rome* (New York: Paulist, 1982); and R.E. Brown, *The Churches the Apostles Left Behind* (New York: Paulist, 1984).

8. See E.F. Scott, *The Varieties of New Testament Religion* (New York: Scribner's, 1944) and Hans Conzelmann, *History of Primitive Christianity* (Nashville: Abingdon, 1973). A more recent text very similar in outline to that of Conzelmann is Frederick J. Cwiekowski, *The Beginnings of the Church* (New York: Paulist, 1988).

9. F. Porsch, *Viele Stimmen–ein Glaube. Anfänge, Entfaltung und Grundzüge neutestamentlicher Theologie* (Stuttgart: Katholisches Bibelwerk, 1982).

Such is also the overall plan of some of the more influential New Testament theologies: R. Bultmann, *Theology of the New Testament*, 2 Vols. (London: SCM, 1965); Hans Conzelmann, *An Outline of the Theology of the New Testament* (New York: Harper and Row, 1969); Joachim Jeremias, *New Testament Theology* (London: SCM, 1971).

10. See, for example, the various "christologies" outlined by Reginald Fuller, *The Foundations of New Testament Christology* (New York: Scribner, 1965); see also J.A. Fitzmyer, *Scripture and Christology. A Statement of the Biblical Commission with a Commentary* (New York: Paulist, 1986). R.E. Brown, "Aspects of New Testament Thought," in R.E. Brown, J.A. Fitzmyer and R.E. Murphy, ed., *The New Jerome Biblical Commentary* (London: Geoffrey Chapman, 1989), 1357–1359, summarizes the following six "christologies": Second-coming, Resurrection, Ministry, Boyhood, Conception and Preexistence.

11. A walk through the various views of the Church in the New Testament can be found in Eduard Schweizer, *Church Order in the New Testament* (London: SCM, 1961); Rudolf Schnackenberg, *The Church in the New Testament* (New York: Herder, 1965); and R.E. Brown, *The Churches the Apostles Left Behind* (New York: Paulist, 1984).

12. John Charlot, *New Testament Disunity. Its Significance for Christianity Today*, 17–97.

13. Helmut Koester, "The Structure and Criteria of Early Christian Beliefs," 205–231 at 205. See also his "Gnomai Diaphoroi. The Origin and Nature of Diversification in the History of Early Christianity," in James M. Robinson and Helmut Koester, ed., *Trajectories through Early Christianity*, 114–157.

14. In drawing support from Koester here and thereby also obviously acknowledging as valid some of the points in his discussion of the diversity in the New Testament, I do not mean to give the impression that I am in fundamental agreement with him. Koester argues in favor of carrying the "Bauer thesis" back into the New Testament (he claims that Bauer was "essentially right" in "Gnomai Diaphoroi. The Origins of Diversification in the History of Early Christianity," 114). The "Bauer thesis" refers to the position of Walter Bauer, *Orthodoxy and Heresy in Earliest Christianity* (Philadelphia: Fortress, 1971; original 1934), in which the famous New Testament philologist proposed that what came to be known throughout Christianity as "orthodoxy" was really only that particular doctrinal position which eventually gained hegemony over

the others. Bauer wanted to refute the position of Eusebius of Caesarea, shared by other patristic writers, that originally Christianity began with a relatively "pure" doctrine and that the various "heresies" were later deformations of this original orthodoxy. That Eusebius' view is historically insufficient can be granted. But Bauer argues that, in fact, from what we know of the doctrine which was dominant in the more prominent Christian centers of the second century, heretical views were stronger than what eventually came to be known as orthodoxy. The victors, whose theology and doctrine was that associated with the Church of Rome, were able to rewrite history after the fact and to destroy most of the writings of the "heretics." A recent study by Thomas A. Robinson, *The Bauer Thesis Examined: The Geography of Heresy in the Early Christian Church* (Lewiston: Edwin Mellen, 1988), has examined the various particulars of Bauer's argument and has concluded that the thesis can hardly be said to be convincing. (Nevertheless, the Bauer thesis has generated an impressive bibliography of responses.) Explaining his reasons for examining the Bauer thesis, Robinson notes that it had gained recent support from Koester (Robinson, page ix). The "Bauer thesis" seems to me to offer an historical argument in favor of a fundamentally relativistic view of Christian doctrine. "Orthodoxy" is simply that particular view which happens to have won and whose protagonists rewrote history in the aftermath. Ultimately such a view amounts to a relativism which is epistemologically self-defeating. A view is true not because it "wins" over other views but because it reflects reality, which is ultimately the reason why a particular viewpoint can "win." Koester's "The Structure and Criteria of Early Christian Beliefs" seems in fact to embrace Bauer's relativism, in that he presents the view that Jesus rose from the dead as that one of four different views (Jesus as the Lord of the Future; Jesus as the Divine Man; Jesus as Wisdom's Envoy and as Wisdom; Jesus Raised from the Dead) which happened to win out in the end and so control the writing of the New Testament and the process of identifying the canon. The crucial point, of course, is the reason why one or another particular viewpoint gains acceptance (along with the question of whether or not various differentiated viewpoints are in fact mutually exclusive). Koester seems to identify such a reason in the forcefulness of St. Paul, the prominent proponent of the resurrection interpretation, which became the controlling position in the end. It seems to me epistemologically untenable to relegate the truth about Christ, or indeed about anything, to a struggle which is ultimately settled by the victory of one side over the other. Reality is ultimately the criterion of truth.

15. Koester, "The Structure and Criteria of Early Christian Beliefs," 205. Again, it is worth noting that, in the brief list of essential data relative to Jesus (life, works, words and death), Koester does not add the resurrection. For him, the resurrection is already part of the faith interpretation of the Jesus event; one of four, as we have indicated in the previous note (see Ibid., 211–239). The material from the other three interpretations is subsumed into the four canonical gospels. It can be found in purer, more original form in the apocryphal gospels. Koester's whole approach to the origins of Christianity is influenced and enriched by his careful study of the New Testament apocryphal literature, a study which was encouraged "for thirty years" by his one-time professor Rudolf Bultmann. See H. Koester, *Introduction to the New Testament*, Vol. 2 (Philadelphia: Fortress, 1982), the Introduction, xxi, which contains this anecdote about Bultmann as well as the following comment about the sixty apocryphal books which he uses in that work: "These non-canonical works are witnesses to early Christian history no less valuable than the New Testament."

16. A fine summary of Schlier's account of New Testament unity and diversity drawing upon a variety of Schlier's publications can be found in Stock, *Einheit des Neuen Testaments*, 42–47. In the first section of his book, 13–59, Stock provides summaries of the positions of Käsemann, Ebeling, Braun, Marxsen, Diem, Pannenberg, Schlier and Balthasar.

17. Giblet, "Einheit des Glaubens und Verschiedenartigkeit des Ausprucks in den Schriften des Neuen Testaments," 35: "Somit stellt die Verschiedenartigkeit der ursprünglichen Theologien einen notwendigen und erhellenden Umstand dar—keine dieser Theologien könnte jedoch von sich behaupten, alles zu sagen—jede weiß, wie sehr sie, im Schoße der einen Kirche, die anderen braucht."

18. Perhaps L. Goppelt might be considered a good example of this approach, in his "The Plurality of New Testament Theologies and the Unity of the Gospel as an Ecumenical Problem," 106–130. He emphasizes that the multiplicity of theologies does not place the unity of the Church in doubt (121). The various teachings of the New Testament are formulated and passed on by responsible witnesses and teachers. They are dynamic forces which have an outward, Church building dynamism: "Consequently, the New Testament's theological plurality does not lead us to seek a minimum standard theology, but rather the center of the proclamation and of faith, which gathers the Church together and unifies it" (123). Goppelt cites Käsemann's famous dictum that, from an his-

torical point of view, the New Testament grounds not Church unity but rather the multiplicity of confessions. The thrust of his article suggests that, while he maintains that a wide diversity among Christians is possible within the one koinonia of the Church according to the New Testament, nevertheless he would not share Käsemann's view. Indeed, he writes that, while none of the New Testament authors gives a theological norm which all must recognize, "Yet all hold it as an established fact that the Church in the whole world is a unity" (121).

19. Wolfgang Trilling, "Die Verschiedenartigkeit der Evangelien in ihrer theologischen Bedeutung," in *Veilfalt und Einheit im Neuen Testament* (Einsiedeln: Benziger, 1968) 9–31 at 26–27. Another rather optimistic viewpoint is that of Schlier, as presented in Stock, *Einheit des Neuen Testaments*, 42–51.

20. Conzelmann, "Was glaubte die frühe Christenheit?" 106. It should be remembered that Conzelmann's study does not end in despair of a positive answer to this question; rather he shows that there is a fundamental unity in the confessions of faith.

21. Achtemeier, *The Quest for Unity in the New Testament*, chooses the issue of the disunity between Jewish and Gentile Christians (2) to illustrate his overall thesis that the view which posits an original doctrinal unity among Christians is overly romanticized and contrary to the facts. Achtemeier also opens his book with a footnote referring to the thesis of Walter Bauer. Other scholars also note a discrepancy between the accounts of Galatians and Acts. J.P. Meier, in *Antioch and Rome*, 36, notes that "almost all exegetes would agree that Paul's presentation in Galatians 2...must be our primary source" and continues, on pages 36–44, to give a careful account of the main agreements and disagreements between Acts and Galatians, with copious reference to the various opinions of exegetes regarding the details.

22. With the exception of the council at Jerusalem being held by James alone, Meier's account of this sequence of events, cited in the previous note, is substantially the same as that of Achtemeier. Naturally, such accounts raise the question of the accuracy and importance of historical reconstructions of the events which lay behind the text of the New Testament. How sure can we be of the precise sequence of events? Reconstructions attempt to explain as accurately as possible all the relevant data. At the same time, they have a certain "hypothetical" quality, in the sense that, like any scholarly hypothesis, they stand upon the validity

of the arguments presented and, consequently, await the recognition of the relevant community of scholars. This kind of admission is explicitly acknowledged in the preface to R.E. Brown and J.P. Meier, *Antioch and Rome*, ix: "*Second*, there is an element of speculation in this work, and so constructive disagreement is expected and hoped for. We invite scholars to add to and modify our historical pictures of the two churches. We are aware that, in a way, we are breaking new ground; and our goal is to attract interest so that the investigation will be carried on by many others." Along this line, H. Koester, *Introduction to the New Testament*, Vol. 2, p. xxii, notes: "In view of the present situation of New Testament scholarship, it would be misleading to suggest to the students of early Christian history that they can expect largely secure results.... Nevertheless, it is much better to advance scholarship, and thus our understanding, through hypothetical reconstruction than to ignore new and apparently problematic materials." This raises an important question for theology. Theology cannot contradict historically established facts. Thus one must ask to what extent is a particular reconstruction yet "hypothetical" and to what extent is it established. A further question concerns the relation between strictly historical method and theological method. In other words, even when one knows with relative surety what the facts were underlying a particular biblical text, must not the specific theological task be an interpretation of those facts in the light of faith? To this task we must eventually turn in drawing this chapter to a close.

23. Achtemeier, 66. Brown and Meier offer a similar, but seemingly more nuanced, judgment. They write that the assumption that Paul's thought "won out" in the discussions in the early community "will be severely tested by the independent work of the two authors of this volume" (viii), adding: "Such an analysis does not detract from the enormous power and challenge of Paul's letters and thought; but it warns that a purely Pauline Christianity was not dominant in NT times or afterwards. To some, the failure of Paul to dominate represents the loss of Christian vitality. Others of us believe that the only Christianity that can do justice to a NT containing diversity is one that resists sectarian purism in favor of constructively holding together tensions. Blending Paul into a wider mix, therefore, is what made the Pauline Epistles biblical, i.e., part of a Bible meant to guide, serve, and challenge the church catholic." Meier's survey of the data, *Antioch and Rome*, 36–44, concludes that, after the incident, Paul made himself independent of Antioch, but not of Jerusalem (40).

24. Achtemeier, 79. Meier, 39: "We are not directly informed as to the

upshot of this, but certain subsequent events in Paul's career give us clues. Paul soon undertakes a lengthy mission into Asia Minor and Europe without Barnabas. He returns to Antioch only once for a brief visit (Acts 18:22). He never mentions Syrian Antioch again in his letters. Whatever relations he does have are with Jerusalem rather than with Antioch. Most glaringly, in Galatians 2 [Paul] is silent about who won the debate. We can reasonably infer from these facts that Paul lost the argument, found himself isolated at Antioch, separated himself from Barnabas, and undertook a wide-ranging mission with new coworkers."

25. Achtemeier, 62.

26. Achtemeier, 2, gives this preliminary statement of what his book intends to demonstrate.

27. Achtemeier, 66. Achtemeier attempts to respond to the question which may be raised against his view of the Acts account: Is the author of Acts then convicted of deliberately falsifying history? See Chapter 9, "Reflections on some untraditional conclusions," 75–82. His response is twofold. First, Acts should not be judged on the basis of the accuracy of its historical details; rather it presents a theological reflection on the early church as a "community called into being by God's Son" and "continually guided by God's Spirit" (76). Second, the author of Acts should not be accused of deliberately distorting the facts to support his theological reflection. Rather, he was working with fragmentary materials (he probably didn't have or even know of Paul's letters [76]) and had to make certain assumptions which "he then used to organize those traditions into a coherent narrative" (77). "If it were possible to find additional evidence that Luke did not have, so that he had instead to rely on his assumptions, the possibility would arise that one could show, on the basis of that new evidence, that Luke's assumptions had, at that particular point, led him astray" (77–78). This is precisely what happened, according to Achtemeier. Paul's letters provide us with additional evidence which was lacking to Luke and which allow us to reconstruct a more adequate account. This does not detract from the theological value of Luke's view. He expresses the enormous desire within the Christian community for the unity of the Church as well as the attempts to compromise between dissident factions which did occur. However, "Luke assumed the desire for a unified church had been accomplished within the first decades of the existence of the church. That assumption proved not to be the case, as Luke would also have known had he possessed, for example, the Letters of John or the Gospel of Matthew, with

their evidence of the fractured nature of the earliest Christian com-
munty" (78-79).

28. On the way in which various exegetes describe diversity and the con-
clusions which they draw on the basis of its presence in the New
Testament, see the useful summaries by Stock, *Einheit des Neuen
Testaments*, 13-59. A. Ehrhardt, "Christianity Before the Apostles'
Creed," 73-119 at 78, states that already within the first two decades of
Christianity, "the unanimity about the content of its message to the
world was lost, if it had ever existed." W. Marxsen, "Das Neue Testament
und die Einheit der Kirche," in AA.VV., *Einheit der Kirche?* (Witten:
Luther-Verlag, 1964), 9-30 at 30, states that the diversity in the New
Testament and, indeed, throughout history is such that Christian unity
can never hope to be built upon uniformity. Such uniformity, he adds,
has never even once been present throughout the entire history of the
Church.

29. Koester, "Gnomai Diaphoroi. The Origin and Nature of Diversification in the History of Early Christianity," 114. Bultmann cites
Bauer approvingly in *Theology of the New Testament*, Vol. II, 137, which
suggests that he too considers Bauer's view of orthodoxy as valid also for
the New Testament. Dunn opens his *Unity and Diversity in the New
Testament* with reference to Bauer, implying that his own study will test
the validity of that thesis in the New Testament writings. Thomas A.
Robinson, *The Bauer Thesis Examined: The Geography of Heresy in the Early
Church*, 24-27, characterizes the works cited here by Koester and Dunn
as efforts to carry the Bauer thesis back into the New Testament. Bauer's
own study is entitled *Rechtgläubigkeit und Ketzerei im ältesten Christentum*,
Georg Strecker, ed. (Tübingen: Mohr, 1964²), English translation by
Robert A. Kraft and Gerhard Krodel, *Orthodoxy and Heresy in Earliest
Christianity* (Philadelphia: Fortress, 1971).

30. Ernst Käsemann, "The Canon of the New Testament and the Unity
of the Church," 103. This comment is quoted as an established judgment by Bultmann, *Theology of the New Testament*, Vol. II, 142, and
approvingly by James Dunn, *Unity and Diversity in the New Testament*,
376, although, by arguing for a certain degree of unity in the New
Testament, Dunn's position seems not as absolute as that of Käsemann.
Goppelt, "The Plurality of New Testament Theologies and the Unity of
the Gospel as an Ecumenical Problem," 106, also quotes this text from
Käsemann, but the thrust of Goppelt's article is to argue against it. So
also do Giblet, "Einheit des Glaubens und Verschiedenartigkeit des

Ausprucks in den Schriften des Neuen Testaments," 26, and Trilling, *Vielfalt und Einheit im Neuen Testament*, 57, who refers also to the response to Käsemann by Walter Kasper, *Dogma unter dem Wort Gottes* (Mainz: Grünewald, 1965), 18–20.

31. Dunn, *Unity and Diversity in the New Testament*, 376 (emphasis his).

32. Dunn, *Unity and Diversity in the New Testament*, 377 (emphasis his).

33. Käsemann, "Unity and Diversity in New Testament Ecclesiology," 295. This is also the position of Schlier; see the references in Stock, *Einheit des Neuen Testaments*, 50. Stock's own position, 167, states that the task of dogmatic theology is to show the unity of the New Testament, thus placing this effort to indicate unity in the hands of the theologian and not of the historian. G. Clarke Chapman, "Some Theological Reflections on Walter Bauer's *Rechtgläubigkeit und Ketzerei im ältesten Christentum*: A Review Article," *JES* 7 (1970) 564–574 at 572, speaks about the more-than-historical method needed for confronting this issue by commenting on divine providence: "'Providence' simply means that, after all is said and done in the arena of historical investigation, a theological viewpoint may be added; that all power struggles are not entirely fortuitous, and that the Christ-centered purpose of God may also be discernible here and there in the tumult of humanity." See also M. Simon and A. Benoit, "Orthodoxie et hérésie dans le christianisme des premiers siècles," *Le Judaïsme et le Christianisme antique d'Antiochie Epiphane à Constantin* (Paris: Presses Univ. de France, 1968), 289–307 at 301.

34. Giblet, "Einheit des Glaubens und Verschiedenartigkeit des Ausprucks in den Schriften des Neuen Testaments," 28–31. The rest of the present paragraph and part of the following paragraph in the text is a rough paraphrase of Giblet, 30, with some additions of my own.

35. See the previous chapter.

36. This is the gist of Koester's, "The Structure and Criteria of Early Christian Beliefs," 207–211. But Koester himself admitted that his four types of expressions of faith (Jesus as Lord of the Future, as Divine Man, as Wisdom's Envoy and as Raised from the Dead) were harmonized, at least to some extent, by the writers of the canonical gospels, under the aegis of the fourth type. Indeed, it was the death-resurrection type that "created the literary genre 'gospel'" (228). Again: "...the emerging gospel literature of the orthodox church did not restrict itself to a passion and resurrection narrative, but tried to incorporate materials which

actually had heretical tendencies, according to the standards of that creed: the divine man type of miracle stories, and the future-oriented apocalyptic predications which Mark appropriated for his gospel, collections of sayings of the wise which Luke and Matthew incorporated, and the myth of Wisdom humiliated and glorified, which is a main theme of the Fourth Gospel" (230). Still Koester insists that the variety within such viewpoints represents divergent convictions which are not easily reconcilable ("Gnomai Diaphoroi. The Origin and Nature of Diversification in the History of Early Christianity," 115-116). While one may grant that themes such as "Wisdom's Envoy" or the "Divine Man" may well be, in a purer and more isolated form, the source of the apocryphal gospels (Koester, "One Jesus and Four Primitive Gospels," in James M. Robinson and Helmut Koester, *Trajectories through Early Christianity* 158-204 at 166), the very position that they were incorporated into the canonical, "orthodox" gospels points to the conclusion that, at least for the authors of those canonical gospels, these various themes were not mutually incompatible. They saw no necessity in a forced choice between Jesus working a miracle or teaching wisdom or being Lord of the future and being raised from the dead. This suggests that Achtemeier's statement ("early unity existed...only in the optimistic historical imagination of scholars" [66]) might be turned upside down: the incompatibility of various New Testament expressions of faith may lie in the pessimistic historical imagination of scholars. If Koester's account of the writers of the canonical gospels is correct, they themselves did not grant that incompatibility which seems to serve as the basis for his assertion that the Bauer thesis was "essentially right" ("Gnomai Diaphoroi. The Origin and Nature of Diversification in the History of Early Christianity," 114).

37. On the combining of various titles in Mark, see Joachim Gnilka, *Jesus Christus nach frühen Zeugnissen des Glaubens* (München: Kösel, 1970) 20-21.

38. H. Schlier, "Die Anfänge der christologischen Credo," in AA.VV. *Zur Frühgeschichte der Christologie* (Freiburg: Herder, 1970), 46, states that the various New Testament professions of faith "bring to expression in an astonishing agreement" ("bringen...in erstaunlicher Übereinstimmung zur Sprache") the basic events concerning Jesus. P. Benoit, "The Origins of the Apostles' Creed in the New Testament," in *Jesus and the Gospel*, Vol. 2 (New York: Scribner's, 1965), 104-105, affirms a profound unity concerning essentials reigning throughout the New Testament and underlying the various theologies contained therein.

39. Prosper Grech, "Criteri di ortodossia ed eresia nel Nuovo Testamento," *Augustinianum* 25 (1985) 583-596.

40. Grech, "Criteri di ortodossia ed eresia nel Nuovo Testamento," 595.

41. For a fine presentation of the theme of unity in the letter to the Ephesians, see P. Benoit, "L'unité de l'Église selon l'Épître aux Éphésiens," in *Studiorum Paulinorum* (Roma: PIB, 1963), Vol. I, pp. 57-77.

42. Goppelt, "The Plurality of New Testament Theologies and the Unity of the Gospel as an Ecumenical Problem," 121, states that all New Testament writers hold it as an established fact that the Church in the whole world forms a unity. Eduard Lohse, *Die Einheit des Neuen Testaments* (Göttingen: Vandenhoeck & Ruprecht, 1973) 336-337, states that the Church's self understanding, in all of the New Testament writings without exception, is that it is and can only be one.

43. See Trilling, *Vielfalt und Einheit im Neuen Testament*, 11.

44. Gnilka, *Jesus Christus nach frühen Zeugnissen des Glaubens*, 22, speaks of "der vereinheitlichende Sammlerwille des Evangelisten."

45. Trilling, *Vielfalt und Einheit im Neuen Testament*, 10-13.

46. Dunn, *Unity and Diversity in the New Testament*, 384.

47. Dunn, *Unity and Diversity in the New Testament*, 384.

48. Dunn, *Unity and Diversity in the New Testament*, 384-385.

49. Thus, one is a bit perplexed by Dunn's comment: "We cannot claim to accept the authority of the NT unless we are willing to accept as valid *whatever* form of Christianity can justifiably claim to be rooted in one of the strands that make up the NT" (*Unity and Diversity in the New Testament*, 377). Why should it be sufficient to be rooted in only one strand? Why, at the least, should it not be required that such valid forms of Christianity not directly contradict any of the strands? Perhaps the adverb "justifiably" might resolve part of the difficulty, but still the history of Christianity includes a host of "forms," not a few of which contain contradictory convictions on a range of specific issues. It is difficult to see how Dunn's principle of validity here would not result in considering them all as "valid." In which case, "valid" forms of Christianity could embrace a range of contradictory convictions. This would have serious

consequences for the credibility of Christianity, for the claim that Christianity offers truth to human beings.

50. On teaching in the New Testament, see Joseph Fitzmyer, "The Office of Teaching in the Christian Church According to the New Testament," in P.C. Empie, T. Austin Murphy and J.A. Burgess, ed., *Teaching Authority and Infallibility in the Church*, "Lutherans and Catholics in Dialogue VI" (Minneapolis: Augsburg, 1978), 186–212, with its accompanying essay by John Reumann, "Teaching Office in the New Testament? A Response to Professor Fitzmyer's Essay," *Ibid.*, pp. 213–231.

51. A useful summary of Paul's life is Joseph Fitzmyer, "Paul," in *NJBC*, 1329–1337, especially the chart comparing details from Paul's letters with those contained in Acts (1331).

52. This understanding of the events surrounding the Jerusalem meeting on the part of the author of Acts must be given its proper weight, regardless of the outcome of research into the historical accuracy of his presentation of the events, an investigation we have mentioned earlier in this chapter in connection with the publications of Achtemeier and Meier.

53. Bultmann, *Theology of the New Testament*, Vol. II, 128.

54. Bultmann, *Theology of the New Testament*, Vol. II, 128.

55. Bultmann, *Theology of the New Testament*, Vol. II, 129.

56. Bultmann, *Theology of the New Testament*, Vol. II, 131.

57. Bultmann, *Theology of the New Testament*, Vol. II, 138.

58. Bultmann, *Theology of the New Testament*, Vol. II, 139.

59. Bultmann, *Theology of the New Testament*, Vol. II, 139.

60. Bultmann, *Theology of the New Testament*, Vol. II, 135.

61. Hans Conzelmann, *An Outline of the Theology of the New Testament* (New York: Harper & Row, 1969), 297.

62. Conzelmann, *An Outline of the Theology of the New Testament*, 298–300.

63. Conzelmann, *An Outline of the Theology of the New Testament*, 290: "In

crude terms: we do not have early Catholicism simply where there is the notion of tradition. This notion is part of theology itself. The decisive turning point occurs where the tradition is assured institutionally, by being bound to a ministry and a succession in this ministry. Early Catholicism...first appears where the ministry has the quality of communicating salvation, where the working of the Spirit and the sacrament are bound up with the ministry. As Bultmann puts it: the decisive process is the transformation of the regulative significance of church law into a constitutive one."

64. Dunn, *Unity and Diversity in the New Testament*, 341.

65. Dunn, *Unity and Diversity in the New Testament*, 365–366.

66. Perhaps there already is sufficient warning against an exaggerated "early catholicism" in the irrepressible presence of such themes as apocalyptic eschatology in any number of the New Testament writings, the action of the Holy Spirit in Luke-Acts, and the growth and hence provisionality of Christian knowledge of the faith in Paul, not to mention the emphasis upon the individual believer in John.

67. This would appear to be the basic thrust of E. Schweizer's, *Church Order in the New Testament* (see above, note 11), whose final remarks, 229-230, include the following statements: "A wrong development may, as we have seen, lead to a gnostic group just as well as to an institutional Church. It makes no final difference whether the official or the ecstatic— or as a variant, the ascetic—is made absolute, whether the view of the Pastoral Letters or the Johannine writings—or, as a variant, that of the Matthean fulfilment of the law—is developed one-sidedly. Whether the presence of God's Spirit is guaranteed by the group of regularly ordered persons or by a company of complete pneumatics or ascetics, any such idea is merely a form of a wrong concept of the Church. The Church will therefore have to seek a way through between Rome and Sohm; and it will be able to do so successfully only where it lives, with the utmost determination, on *God's* freedom and faithfulness, and not on its own order or on its own religious vitality." Schweizer cautions against seeking "guarantees" of the presence of God's Spirit in either a gnostic group or an institutional Church. This element of guarantee seems also to be the negative element which Conzelmann would reject and which constitutes for him the core of early Catholicism, as we have seen above. Perhaps Dunn's language about "crystallization" falls along this line as well. It seems that one needs to explore the ways in which enduring structures

or doctrinal decisions (faith and order) may be compatible with *"God's freedom and faithfulness,"* as Schweizer puts it.

68. Dunn, *Unity and Diversity in the New Testament*, 341.

69. Dunn, *Unity and Diversity in the New Testament*, 381.

70. Käsemann's thought on this point is summarized by Stock, *Einheit des Neuen Testaments*, 23–24.

71. Dunn, *Unity and Diversity in the New Testament*, 378, 380–381.

Part Two: Introduction

1. Ignacio Escribano-Alberca, *Glaube und Gotteserkenntnis in der Schrift und Patristik* (Freiburg-Basel-Wien: Herder, 1974), Handbuch der Dogmengeschichte, Band I, Fasz. 2a, 138 pages, and Dieter Lührmann, "Glaube," *Reallexikon für Antike und Christentum* Band XI (Stuttgart: Anton Hiersemann, 1981), 48–122, have served as my principal guides in mapping out the route which I shall follow through the patristic literature. Both of these studies contain rich additional bibliography about the topic of faith in patristic literature. A shorter and much sketchier summary, but which nevertheless adds some insights not found in either Escribano-Alberca or Lührmann, is R.J. De Simone, "Fede," in Angelo di Berardino, ed., *Dizionario patristico e di antichità christiane*, Vol. 1 (Casale Monferrato: Marietti, 1983), 1338–1347.

2. Johannes Quasten, *Patrology*, Vol. I: *The Beginnings of Patristic Literature* (Utrecht: Spectrum, 1950), 349 pages; Vol. II: *The Ante-Nicene Literature after Irenaeus* (Utrecht–Antwerp: Spectrum, 1953), 450 pages; Vol. III: *The Golden Age of Greek Patristic Literature from the Council of Nicea to the Council of Chalcedon* (Utrecht-Antwerp: Spectrum, 1960), 605 pages, and M.J. Rouët de Journel, *Enchiridion Patristicum* (Barcelona: Editorial Herder, 1946[14]) 802 pages. The Quasten trilogy was translated into *two* volumes in Italian by the Patristic Institute of the Augustianum in Rome, the faculty of which then also produced a third volume (in Italian) which covers Latin patrology in the period after Nicea and which follows the same format which Quasten used in his three volumes. Quasten wrote the presentation to this text, acknowledging it as a kind of completion to the three volumes which he wrote. See A. Di Berardino, ed., *Patrologia. Vol. III, Dal Concilio di Nicea (325) al Concilio di Calcedonia (451). I Padri latini* (Torino: Marietti, 1978), page v.

3. This list is compiled on the basis of the surveys by Escribano-Alberca and Lührmann, but it is also confirmed by De Simone and by the indices of the *Enchiridion Patristicum* and of W.A. Jurgens, *The Faith of the Early Fathers*, Vol. I: *A Sourcebook of Theological and Historical Passages from the Christian Writings of the Pre-Nicene and Nicene Eras* (Collegeville: The Liturgical Press, 1970); Vol. II: *A Sourcebook of Theological and Historical Passages from the Christian Writings of the Post-Nicene and Constantinopolitan Eras through St. Jerome* (Collegeville: The Liturgical Press, 1979); Vol. III: *A Sourcebook of Theological and Historical Passages from the Writings of St. Augustine to the End of the Patristic Age* (Collegeville: The Liturgical Press, 1979). Jurgens' three volumes are in large part a translation of the *Enchiridion Patristicum*, although it does provide a fair number of additional passages.

5. Faith and Its Unity According to Pre–Nicean Writers

1. A critical Greek text for Clement's letter to the Corinthians can be found in F. X. Funk, ed., *Patres Apostolici*, Vol. I (Tübingen: Laupp, 1901) 98–185. A Greek text with Latin translation is also available in PG 1, 199–328. The numbers within parentheses in the text refer to the numbered chapters of Clement's letter.

2. English translation is by Maxwell Staniforth, in his *Early Christian Writings. The Apostolic Fathers* (Harmondsworth: Penguin Books, 1968) 23.

3. See Quasten, *Patrology*, Vol. I, 47, and Escribano-Alberca, 15–16, on the influence of stoic and other Greek cosmology upon 1 Clement; Escribano-Alberca, 18–25, adds data about stoic influence upon the Christian apologists.

4. Lührmann, col. 80, states that, for Clement, the object of faith is always God (so paragraphs 3, 12, 10, 34) and never Christ (the expression faith "in Christ" of paragraph 22, referring merely to the realm within which faith works, as in Eph 1,15 or Col 1,4).

5. The seven letters were written respectively to the Ephesians, the Magnesians, the Trallians, the Romans, the Philadelphians, the Smyrneans and to the bishop Polycarp. These letters will be referred to henceforth by using the abbreviations Eph, Mag, Trall, Rom, Phil, Smy and Poly, followed by the paragraph number where the text in question

can be found. Any English quotations will be from the translation of Maxwell Staniforth (see above, note 2). The Greek text can be found in Funk, 212–295, and also in PG 5, 643–728.

6. This point is made by Lührmann, col. 80, and De Simone, 1341.

7. This theme is dear to Escribano-Alberca (see his page 16, note 21), as it fits with the whole thrust of his study—that faith leads to intimate knowledge of God.

8. The Greek text with a Latin translation for these works can be found in PG 6, 327–440 (*Apologia prima pro christianis* = *First Apology*) and PG 6, 471–800 (*Dialogus cum Tryphone Judaeo* = *Dialogue with Trypho, a Jew*). Numbers within parentheses in the text refer to the numbered chapters of these two works. English translations will be taken from *The Ante-Nicene Fathers*, Volume I: *The Apostolic Fathers - Justin Martyr - Irenaeus*, American reprint of the Edinburgh Edition, Revised and chronologically arranged, with brief prefaces and occasional notes by A. Cleveland Coxe (Grand Rapids: Eerdmans, 1975). This volume will be referred to hereafter as ANF I, followed by the page number.

9. This famous passage notes that all those who lived according to reason—Justin includes Socrates among other examples—were in some way Christian, even should they have lived before the time of Christ or may have been explicit atheists. Christ is the Logos, the Word, who enlightens every reasonable person. For more on this theme, with reference to Justin's doctrine of the *logos spermatikos*, that is, that Christ the Logos sows seeds of moral and religious illumination throughout creation, see the useful summary by L.W. Barnard, "The Logos Theology of Justin Martyr," *Downside Review* 89 (1971) 132–141. See also R. Holte, "Logos Spermatikos. Christianity and Ancient Philosophy according to St. Justin's Apologies," *Studia Theologica* 12 (1958) 109-168; E. Osborn, "Justin Martyr and the Logos Spermatikos," in *Studia Missionalia*, Vol. 42 (Roma: Editrice Pontificia Università Gregoriana, 1993), pp. 143-159; and R.M. Price, "'Hellenization' and Logos Doctrine in Justin Martyr," *Vigiliae Christianae* 42 (1988) 18–23.

10. Lührmann, col. 84.

11. The critical text can be found in *Sources chrétiennes* as follows: for Book I, volumes 263–264; Book II, volumes 293–294; Book III, volumes 210–211; Book IV, volumes 100,1-100,2; Book V, volumes 152–153. A Greek and Latin version of this work can also be found in PG 7,

433–1224. References to *Adversus haereses* within the text will follow the standard procedure of using the acronym AH, followed by a roman numeral indicating the book, an arabic number for the chapter and usually a third arabic number for the paragraph in question. When no third arabic number is used, the reference is to the entire chapter or chapters. English translations are from ANF I.

12. So Joseph Smith, in the "Introduction" to his translation of the *Proof of the Apostolic Preaching* (Westminster: Newman, 1952), 44. A similarity between the writings of Justin and of Irenaeus (died c. 202–203) is the many references to the Old Testament prophecies understood as referring to and as fulfilled in Jesus Christ. This similarity is noted by Smith, 37–38. Comparing Irenaeus' two works, the *Proof* cuts a rather striking contrast with *Adversus haereses* in its use of Scripture, insofar as the latter makes heavy use of the New Testament, the first Christian writing which clearly does so (see Lührmann, col. 86). *Proof* makes very little use of the New Testament (Smith, 32–34). The *Proof*, known of by references from other patristic writings, was thought to have perished, when an Armenian version was discovered in 1904 by Karapet Ter Mekerttschian. This was published, along with a German translation and notes, as *Des heiligen Irenaeus Schrift zum Erweise der apostolischen Verkündigung* in *Texte und Untersuchungen* 31.1 (Leipzig, 1907). A translation from the Armenian into French can be found in *Sources chrétiennes*, volume 62. Information about the publication history of this work in various languages can be found in Smith, 3–12. In our text, this work will be referred to as *Proof*, followed by the chapter number. The English translation will be taken from Smith.

13. This is emphasized by Escribano-Alberca, 34–36, who attributes to O. Cullmann an important role in bringing to awareness this particular Irenaean emphasis upon salvation history and recapitulation.

14. On these three closely related factors (the New Testament, the apostolic Tradition and the *regula fidei*), see Lührmann, col. 86. Concerning the scriptures, Edgar J. Goodspeed, *A History of Early Christian Literature*, revised and enlarged by Robert M. Grant (Chicago: University of Chicago Press, 1966 [orig. 1942]), 120, states that Irenaeus was the first Christian writer who can be shown to have known and cited most of the books which we accept as the New Testament: four gospels, Acts, thirteen letters of Paul (Ephesians, Colossians, Hebrews and the pastorals being included in this number), 1 John, 1 Peter, Revelation and the Shepherd of Hermas. With Irenaeus it is clear that Christians have now

begun to call these books Scriptures, on a par with the writings of the Old Testament.

15. De Simone, col. 1342, emphasizes this continuity with the faith of Abraham. Examples of references by Clement and Justin to Abraham within the context of discussing faith are Clement of Rome, *Letter to the Corinthians*, 10 and 31, and Justin Martyr, *Dialogue with Trypho, a Jew*, 11 and 119.

16. On the fact that he was the first, see De Simone, col. 1342. On the importance of patristic use of this verse in understanding faith, see the brief sketch provided by P. Parente, "La teologia patristica della fede e il testo d'Isaia 7,9," *Doctor Communis* 1 (1948) 185–190.

17. The future tense is used here in light of J.N.D. Kelly, *Early Christian Creeds* (New York: David McKay Company, Inc., 1960[2] [orig. 1950]), 30–49, which argues that the profession of faith used in baptism originally took an interrogatory form and that one can only speak of a declaratory creed from the time of the liturgical practice of the *traditio* and *redditio* of the creed, which Kelly dates in the mid 200's. Kelly, 49, adds: "Scholars have often assumed that the ceremonies of the tradition and reddition of the Creed were established from the earliest times. But the catechumenate itself, in its evolved and fully articulated form, was a relatively late development. The gulf between the catechetical arrangements presupposed by St. Justin, for example, and those envisaged in the rubrics of St. Hippolytus' *Apostolic Tradition* is enormous: even so the process was not complete. The tradition and reddition of the Creed, as the absence of these ceremonies from the *Apostolic Tradition* shows, belong to the heyday of the fully mature catechumenate, that is, to the second generation of the third century at the earliest."

18. Lührmann, col. 87, points out that, in Irenaeus, a certain fluidity or freedom of expression is yet characteristic of the regula fidei. The adoption of the creeds of Nicea and 1 Constantinople for the purpose of distinguishing orthodox faith from heresies relative to the persons of the Trinity introduced a motive, not present in the earlier history of the Creed, for considering the Creed as a relatively fixed formula.

19. Irenaeus writes: "For how should it be if the apostles themselves had not left us writings? Would it not be necessary, [in that case,] to follow the course of the tradition which they handed down to those to whom they did commit the Churches?" In AH III,4,1 [SC 211, 46–47]; ANF I, 417.

20. Some have pointed out that Irenaeus here speaks of the apostles appointing bishops as their successors in the Churches but does not use the word "bishop" for the apostles themselves. For them, this fact would suggest a fundamental difference between the apostles and the bishops. While it is surely true that any theory of apostolic succession can and should point out some differences between the apostles and bishops as their successors, nevertheless, it is clear that the whole thrust of Irenaeus' argument here is to underline a certain type of succession, which serves to maintain the Churches in the apostolicity of their faith. Y. Congar, "Apostolicità di ministero e apostolicità di dottrina," in *Ministeri e comunione ecclesiale* (Bologna: EDB, 1973) 60, notes that, while Irenaeus did not originate the idea of apostolic succession, he may be called its great teacher. The use of AH III,3,1-3 in support of the view that the bishop of Rome is the successor to Peter is a bit more complicated, since both Peter and Paul are mentioned as the two apostles who founded the Church at Rome, a point made by James F. McCue, "The Roman Primacy in the Patristic Era," in Paul C. Empie and T. Austin Murphy, ed., *Papal Primacy and the Universal Church* (Minneapolis: Augsburg, 1974) 44-72 at 60.

21. The further question of how these texts by Irenaeus might have an impact on the question of a certain primacy of the Church of Rome with regard to the maintainance of unity in faith is somewhat complicated by the fact that Irenaeus prefaces his presentation of the "pedigree" of the Roman Church with the comment that it would be tedious to "reckon up the successions of all the Churches," as well as by the fact that various arguments have been proposed as to Irenaeus' intention for saying that "every Church should agree with this Church" (i.e. the Church of Rome). Nevertheless, it would be difficult to deny that Irenaeus is here pointing to some specific churches which, because of their succession, serve as a measure of correct faith. Thus one can see evidence here of a certain "primatial" principle in Irenaeus' understanding of the apostolic ecclesiality of the faith and its unity. This dimension of "primacy" will become clearer in the later conciliar recognition of the pentarchy and even of a certain papal primacy, which has been understood in various ways over the course of history and which was particularly developed in the West during the second millennium and in counter-position to conciliarism. On the role of the Church of Rome in the period in which Irenaeus was writing, see Roland Minnerath, "La position de l'Église de Rome aux trois premiers siècles," in Michele Maccarrone, ed., *Il primato del vescovo di Roma nel primo millennio* (Vatican City: Libreria Editrice Vaticana, 1991) 139-171.

22. Johannes Quasten, *Patrology*, Vol. II: *The Ante-Nicene Literature after Irenaeus* (Utrecht-Antwerp: Spectrum Publishers, 1953) 247.

23. Quasten, *Patrology*, Vol. II, 247, gives the year 207 for this change; Patrick Hamell, *Handbook of Patrology* (Staten Island: Alba House, 1968) 70, gives "about 202 or 205" as the year.

24. Concerning the consequences on his terminology for faith which stemmed from the fact that Tertullian was the first to use Latin as a theological language, see Lührmann, col. 96.

25. Quasten, *Patrology*, Vol. II, 247-248. On 247 he writes: "Of fiery temperament and burning energy he develops a fanatical passion for truth. In one of his works the word *veritas* occurs one hundred and sixty-two times. The whole problem of Christianity or paganism is to him identical with *vera vel falsa divinitas*. When Christ founded the new religion He did it in order to lead mankind *in agnitionem veritatis* (*Apol.* 21,30). The Christian God is the *Deus verus*; those who find Him find the fullness of truth. *Veritas* is what the demons hate, what the pagans reject, and what the Christian suffers and dies for. *Veritas* separates the Christian from the pagan."

26. Quasten lists 31 in the synopsis which he presents in *Patrology*, Vol. II, 255–317. The "Introductory Note" to *The Ante-Nicene Fathers*, Vol III: *Latin Christianity: Its Founder, Tertullian*, A. Roberts and J. Donaldson, ed., American reprint of the Edinburgh edition revised by A. Cleveland Coxe (Grand Rapids: Eerdmans, 1976) 11, lists 38 works, but this is simply because the various books of the works *Ad uxorem*, *Ad nationes*, *De cultu Feminarum* and *Adversus Marcionem* are listed individually. The Latin text for all of the works of Tertullian can be found in volumes 1 and 2 of PL. Critical editions for the works cited in the following exposition can be located as follows: *Apology* in CSEL (= *Corpus Scriptorum ecclesticorum latinorum*) 69, 1–121; *Prescription of the Heretics* CCL (= *Corpus Christianorum. Series latina*) 1, 187–224; *On the flesh of Christ* in CCL 1, 871-917; *On Baptism* in CSEL 20, 201–218; *On flight in persecution* in CSEL 76, 17–43; *The chaplet* in CCL 1, 1039–1065; *On patience* in CSEL 47, 1–24; *Against Marcion* in CSEL 47, 290–650; *Against Praxaeus* in CSEL 47, 227–289; *On the veiling of virgins* in CSEL 76, 79–103; and *On modesty* in CSEL 20, 219–273. English translations will be taken from the Roberts and Donaldson edition cited in the present note which will be referred to as ANF III.

27. "Qui audierit, inveniet Deum; qui etiam studuerit intellegere, coge-tur et credere" (*Apology* 18,9 [CSEL 69, 48]; ANF III, 33).

28. Escribano-Alberca, 43, lists five other texts from Tertullian which associate faith with hearing: *Adv Jud* 3,7; 3,11; *3 Adv Marc* 6,5; *4 Ad Marc* 8,10; 19,1-3.

29. Escribano-Alberca, 39-43.

30. Quasten, *Patrology*, Vol. II, 324.

31. On the legal procedure here in use, see R.F. Refoulé's "Introduction" to the "Sources chrétiennes" edition *Traité de la prescription contre les héré-tiques* (Paris: Cerf, 1957) 20-45.

32. See *On Modesty* (= *De pudicitia*) 21,17 (CCL 2, 1368) and the com-ments surrounding this view of the Church in Quasten, *Patrology*, Vol. II, 331.

33. The Greek text of *Exhortation* (= *Protreptikos pros Hellenas*) can be found in GCS (= Die griechischen christlischen Schriftssteller) 12, 1-86, in SC 2 and in PG 8, 49-246; of *Instructor* (= *Paidagogos*) in GCS 12, 87-292, in SC 70, 108 and 158 and in PG 8, 247-684; and of the *Stromata* in GCS 15 (for Books I-VI) and 17² (for Books VII-VIII) as well as in PG 8, 685-1382 and PG 9, 9-602. Book I of the *Stromata* can also be found in SC 30; Book II in SC 38; and Book V in SC 278-279. English transla-tions for these works will be taken from *The Ante-Nicene Fathers*, Vol. II: *Fathers of the Second Century: Hermes, Tatian, Athenagoras, Theophilus, and Clement of Alexandria (Entire)*, A. Roberts and J. Donaldson, ed., American Reprint of the Edinburgh Edition, Revised and Chronologi-cally Arranged, with Brief Prefaces and Occasional Notes, by A. Cleveland Coxe (Grand Rapids: Wm. B. Eerdmans Publishing Company, 1975) 171-567. Hereafter this volume will be referred to as ANF II, followed by the page number.

34. So the Introduction to Clement of Alexandria, in ANF II, 168. See Quasten, *Patrology*, Vol. II, 7-14, on the interrelation of the three books. Quasten translates stromata as "carpets."

35. So Thomas Camelot, OP, in his "Introduction" to the edition of Book II of the *Stromata* in Sources chrétiennes, 38 (Paris: Cerf, 1954) 12-19, entitled "Une théologie de la foi" (especially page 15) and 20-26, "Les vertus du gnostique."

36. Quasten, *Patrology*, Vol. II, 43, writes: "The Origenistic Controversies caused most of the literary output of the great Alexandrian to disappear. The remains are mostly preserved, not in the original Greek, but in Latin translations. The complete list of his writings that Eusebius added to the biography of his friend and teacher Pamphilus was also lost. According to Jerome (*Adv. Ruf.* 2,22), who used it, the treatises numbered two thousand. Epiphanius (*Haer.* 64,63) estimates his literary productions at six thousand. We know only the titles of eight hundred, itemized in St. Jerome's Letter to Paula (*Epist.* 33)."

37. See Eusebius, *Hist. eccl.* 6,23,1-2; cited in Quasten, *Patrology*, Vol. II, 43.

38. So Damien Van den Eynde, *Les normes de l'Enseignement Chrétien* (Gembloux: Duculot, 1933) 155.

39. See Quasten, *Patrology*, Vol. II, 41-42. Also Van den Eynde, 150.

40. This is suggested by Gustave Bardy, "La règle de foi d'Origène," *RSR* 9 (1919) 162-196 at 164-168.

41. Escribano-Alberca, 63-84 at 63-69. That this section is the longest in Escribano-Alberca's contribution to the *Handbuch der Dogmengeschichte* betrays his particular interest, that is, to focus upon faith as personal or even mystical knowledge of God (hence, the title *Glaube und Gotteserkenntnis in der Schrift und Patristik*). He is not so much interested in faith conceived in terms of doctrine. Because Origen's view of faith culminates in something of a mystical vision of God, in ecstasy, something which comes out especially in his biblical commentaries relevant to passages which speak of the experience of the apostles with Jesus on Mount Tabor, Origen is particularly important for the specific topic in which Escribano-Alberca is interested (see 75-79, with Origen's comments about Tabor).

42. *In Exodum*, Homilia III,1 (SC 321, 90-91).

43. See Escribano-Alberca, 66, for various texts, such as *Com. in Jo.* XX,42,398 (SC 290, 348-349); *Com. in Jo.* X,28,174-175 (SC 157, 488-491); *Hom. in Jer.* IX,1 (SC 232, 376-379); and *Hom. in Gen.* XIV,1 (SC 7bis, 336-337). On this point, see also Van Den Eynde, 116, who provides several further texts from Origen's commentaries on the gospel of John and on the Canticle of Canticles which argue that there is such a profound harmony between the two Testaments that Moses and the

prophets can be said to have the same faith as that of the apostles or of Christians today.

44. *In Exodum*, Homilia VII,5 (SC 321, 222–223).

45. This is the way in which Escribano-Alberca, 69, interprets Origen's *Com. in Jo.* I,38,277–279 (SC 120, 198–201).

46. *In Genesim*, Homilia X,5 (SC 7bis, 270–273); see the comment by De Simone, col. 1343.

47. English translation from *The Ante-Nicene Fathers*, Vol. IV: *Tertullian, Part Fourth; Minucius Felix; Commodian; Origen, Parts First and Second*, ed. Alexander Roberts and James Donaldson; American Reprint of the Edinburgh Edition, Revised and Chronologically Arranged with Brief Prefaces and Accompanying Notes by A. Cleveland Coxe (Grand Rapids: Eerdmans, 1989) 628–629. Hereafter, this work will be cited as ANF IV.

48. Van den Eynde, 151.

49. Van den Eynde, 152.

50. Van den Eynde, 153; citing W. Völker, *Das Vollkommenheitsideal des Origenes* (Tübingen, 1931) 76–144. Lührmann, col. 93, points out that the precise relationship between faith (pistis) and knowledge (either as episteme or as gnosis) is never thematically worked out in Origen.

51. J. Lebreton, "Les degrés de la connaissance religieuse d'après Origène," *RSR* 12 (1922) 265–296; Van den Eynde, 230–232.

52. Van den Eynde, 153; also Lührmann, col. 94.

53. See Van den Eynde, 304–311, on Origen's possible knowledge and use of baptismal creeds. See also the article by G. Bardy cited above in note 40.

54. So Robert Girod, in his Introduction to *Commentaire sur l'évangile selon Matthieu*, Sources chrétiennes, 162 (Paris: Cerf, 1970), 88–89. The entire subsection of Girod's introduction, entitled "L'Église, maîtresse de vérité," 88–93, is extremely rich in quotations from Origen on the relationship of the Church to Scripture, on Origen's intense desire to be "ecclesiastic" and "orthodox," on his revulsion at heresy, on his appreci-

ation of the Church as "mother" despite the presence of sinners within the Church and on the necessity of the Church for salvation.

55. Girod, 93.

6. Faith and Its Unity in Eastern Patristic Writers After Nicea

1. The chart of ancient ecclesiastical writers first prepared by P. Doncoeur and later reedited by G. Dumeige under the title *Synopsis Scriptorum Ecclesiae Antiquae ab A.D. 60 ad A.D. 460* (Uccle: Éditions Willy Rousseau, 1953) graphically depicts the ebb and flow of the appearance and production of various patristic writers, confirming this judgment about the late third century.

2. J. Quasten, *Patrology*, Vol. III: *The Golden Age of Greek Patristic Literature* (Westminster: The Newman Press, 1960) 1.

3. My access to this book is through the Italian translation, *Atanasio il Grande e la chiesa del suo tempo*, 2 vols. (Milano, 1843–1844), which was based upon the second edition of Möhler's *Athanasius der Große*. Möhler gives a summary of Athanasius' doctrine on pages 139–205 of Volume I of this Italian edition.

4. Some of Newman's translations and explanatory comments can be found in Philip Schaff and Henry Wace, ed., *A Select Library of Nicene and Post-Nicene Fathers of the Christian Church*, Vol. IV., *St. Athanasius. Select Works and Letters* (Grand Rapids: Eerdmans, 1978). Hereafter this series of translations will be referred to with the acronym LNPF, followed by the volume number and page number. See also Newman's *Select Treatises of St. Athanasius in Controversy with the Arians*, Vol. I (London, 1887[4]). Quasten, *Patrology*, Vol. III, 20, states: "The Greek Church called him later 'the Father of Orthodoxy,' whereas the Roman Church counts him among the four great Fathers of the East."

5. Athanasius is not treated at all by Escribano-Alberca and De Simone; Lührmann, col. 102–103, devotes a mere thirty–three lines of text to him.

6. The one major exception to this would appear to be Athanasius' *Life of Anthony*, where "faith" appears not so much as doctrine but as St. Anthony's principal virtue. See Lührmann, col. 103.

7. English translation taken from Quasten, *Patrology*, Vol. III, 66.

8. This date is according to Quasten, *Patrology*, Vol. III, 25. The *Discourse against the Greeks* can be found in PG 25, 3–96 and SC 18, 107–317; the *Discourse on the Incarnation* in PG 25, 96–197 and SC 199, 257–469.

9. See J. Ruwet, "Le canon alexandrin des Écritures. S. Athanase," *Biblica* 33 (1952) 1–29. Also Quasten, *Patrology*, Vol. III, 54.

10. Several sections of this letter (PG 25, 459–468; LNPF IV, 166–169) list a number of earlier authorities whose teachings support the decision of Nicea.

11. See the material which appears in Quasten, *Patrology*, Vol. III, 55–64, for more details on this aspect of Athanasius' promotion of unity in faith by means of letters to other bishops.

12. A Greek and Latin text for the catecheses can be found in PG 33, 331–1128. A critical edition of the final five lectures is presented in SC 126, 82–175. The English translation here used for Cyril's works is that of Leo McCauley and Anthony Stephenson in *The Fathers of the Church* series, Vols. 61 and 64, *The Works of Saint Cyril of Jerusalem*, 2 vols. (Washington: CUA Press, 1969, 1970). Quasten, *Patrology*, Vol. III, 363, states that the lectures were delivered in the Church of the Holy Sepulchre in Jerusalem.

13. There is some discussion about whether Cyril is the author of the last five lectures or whether, instead, they are to be attributed to his successor, John. For a brief history of this discussion based upon textual as well as theological considerations, as well as some of the relevant bibliography surrounding this debate, see the "Introduction" to "The Mystagogical Lectures" by Anthony Stephenson in *The Writings of Saint Cyril of Jerusalem*, Vol. 2, 143–151, as well as Auguste Piédagnel's introduction, chapter II, "Le problème de l'auteur des Catéchèses Mystagogiques," in the "Sources chrétiennes" edition of this work, Vol. 126 (Paris: Cerf, 1966) 18–40.

14. This leads Anthony Stephenson to write: "Cyril's teaching was severely biblical." In "General Introduction," to *The Works of Saint Cyril of Jerusalem*, Vol. 1, p. 4. Stephenson bolsters his argument with a reference to Catechesis IV, 17, which reads: "For in regard to the divine and holy mysteries of the Faith, not even a casual statement should be delivered without the Scriptures, and we must not be drawn aside merely by

probabilities and artificial arguments. Do not believe even me merely because I tell you these things, unless you receive from the inspired Scriptures the proof of the assertions. For this saving faith of ours depends not on ingenious reasoning but on proof from the inspired Scriptures" (PG 33, 475–478; McCauley, 127–128).

15. See Rufinus, *A Commentary on the Apostles' Creed,* translated and annotated by J.N.D. Kelly, "Ancient Christian Writers, No. 20" (London: Longmans, Green and Co., 1955) 9–10.

16. There are 366 letters of St. Basil printed in PG 32, 219–1112. The English translation is taken from *Letters. Volume I (1–185),* translated by Agnes Clare Way with notes by Roy J. Deferrari, "The Fathers of the Church, 13" (New York: Fathers of the Church, Inc., 1951) 169. English text for the letters will be taken from this volume as well as from Saint Basil, *Letters. Volume II (186-368),* translation and notes by the same, "Fathers of the Church, 28" (New York: Fathers of the Church, Inc., 1955). These two translations will be referred to as Way I and Way II respectively.

17. On the identity of the addressee, see Quasten, *Patrology,* Vol. III, 206, as well as note 1 on page 168 of Way I.

18. See *De fide* 5 (PG 31, 689–690), translated into English under the title "Concerning Faith" in Saint Basil, *Ascetical Works,* by M. Monica Wagner, C.S.C., "The Fathers of the Church, 9" (New York: Fathers of the Church, Inc., 1950) 57–69 at 67. The complete text of *De fide* can be found in PG 31, 675–692. See also *Moralia,* Rule 40 (PG 31, 759–760) and Rule 70, chapter 5 (PG 31, 821–822), translated under the title "Herewith Begins the Morals," in Ibid., 71–205, Rule Forty on p. 118 and Rule Seventy, Cap. 5 on p. 166. The whole of the *Moralia* can be found in PG 31, 699–870.

19. See also Rule Twelve: "but every word of the Lord ought to be received with complete assent" (PG 31, 721–722; Wagner, 89).

20. See also Letter 92, 3, to the bishops of Italy and Gaul, which speaks of "those professing the faith of the Apostles" (PG 32, 48; Way I, 207) and Letter 105, which refers to the "apostolic pronounciation of the faith" (PG 32, 513–514; Way I, 230).

21. There are forty-five discourses in all, contained in Volumes 35 and

36 of Migne's *Patrologia greca*. Discourses 1–5 and 20–43 have also appeared in eight different volumes of *Sources chrétiennes*.

22. Quasten, *Patrology*, Vol. III, 236.

23. On the date of this discourse relative to the presence of Theodosius and his decree against Arianism, see the comment of Claudio Moreschini, "Introduction," to SC 318, pp. 48 and 61.

24. See Quasten, *Patrology*, Vol. III, 254.

25. Quasten, *Patrology*, Vol. III, 283. A Greek and Latin text for this work can be found in PG 45, 9–106.

26. Escribano-Alberca, 91–105, 111–115.

27. Escribano-Alberca, 94, citing W. Völker, *Gregor von Nyssa als Mystiker* (Wiesbaden: Steiner Verlag, 1955) 140.

28. PG 44, 1267–1268 B-C. English translation is that of Hilda C. Graef, St. Gregory of Nyssa, *The Lord's Prayer. The Beatitudes*, "Ancient Christian Writers, 18" (London: Longmans, Green and Co., 1954) 146. A Greek and Latin version of the *De beatitudinibus* can be found in PG 44, 1193–1302.

29. J. Daniélou, *Platonisme et théologie mystique. Doctrine spirituelle de saint Grégoire de Nysse* (Aubier: Éditions Montaigne, 1944), 143.

30. Daniélou, 143: "Dans le VI° *Homélie sur les Béatitudes*, Grégoire distingue deux modes de connaissance de Dieu: il ya a d'abord la connaissance symbolique dont nous venons de parler et qui s'élève à la connaissance des attributs de Dieu par l'intermédiaire de ses manifestations dans le monde visible; il y a ensuite la connaissance que nous appelons mystique et qui est l'expérience de la présence de Dieu dans l'âme par la grâce....une double voie, celle du monde visible...et celle de l'amour, accessible à tout chrétien, qui unit, dans la ténèbre de la foi, au Dieu présent dans l'âme."

31. PG 44, 427–428 B-C. English text from Gregory of Nyssa, *The Life of Moses*, translation, introduction and notes by A.J. Malherbe and E. Ferguson, "Classics of Western Spirituality" (New York: Paulist, 1978) 135. A Greek and Latin text for the complete *De vita Moysis* can be found in PG 44, 297–430.

32. PG 44, 893–894 B-C. A Greek and Latin text of the fifteen homilies of *In Canticum Canticorum* can be found in PG 44, 755–1120.

33. Escribano-Alberca, 96, makes this point, giving as examples three texts from *The Life of Moses*: II, 34 (PG 44, 335-336 C; Malherbe and Ferguson, 62); II, 193 (PG 44, 389–390 B; Malherbe and Ferguson, 104); II, 266–267 (PG 44, 411–412 D; Malherbe and Ferguson, 122–123).

34. PG 45, 465–468 A-C. See also, *In psalmos* I, VIII (PG 44, 475–476 C-D), which states that faith is confirmed in hearers, who listen to the proclamation of the marvelous deeds of God by and within the Church.

35. *In Epistolam I ad Corinthios*, Homilia IV,2 (PG 61, 32). English translation from Philip Schaff, ed., *A Select Library of the Nicene and Post-Nicene Fathers*, Vol. XII, *Saint Chrysostom: Homilies on the Epistles of Paul to the Corinthians* (Grand Rapids: Eerdmans, 1979) 17.

36. See Quasten, *Patrology*, Vol. III, 457–458, for the context surrounding these sermons as well as for the judgment: "Delivered at the beginning of his presbyterate these courageous homilies *On the Statues* made his name as an orator."

37. See also *In illud, Paulus vocatus, et de mutat. nominum* IV,5 (PG 51, 152–153), where Chrysostom points to a widow who is begging at the door of the church and says: "Ask her about the immortality of the soul, the resurrection of the body, the providence of God, the retribution according to merits....She will respond with exactitude and great assurance; but the philosopher, all proud with his long hair and staff, after many long discourses...will not be able even to open his mouth...."

38. *In epistolam ad Romanos*, Homilia VIII, ver. 21 (PG 60, 462). English from *Saint Chrysostom: Homilies on the Acts of the Apostles and the Epistle to the Romans*, "A Select Library of the Nicene and Post-Nicene Fathers of the Christian Church," First Series, Vol. XI, Philip Schaff, ed. (Grand Rapids: Eerdmans, 1979) 391.

39. The conflicts which caused John Chrysostom such a difficult time in Constantinople were not fundamentally of a doctrinal nature, but rather seem to have stemmed from personal enmity, perhaps aroused by his zeal to promote moral reform and his effectiveness and forcefulness as a preacher. Thus John's writings are not the products of strenuous struggles with "heretics," a fact which distinguishes him from many of the patristic writers which we have been reviewing in this chapter. Quasten,

Vol. III, 474, writes: "He was not involved in any of the great dogmatic controversies of the fourth century. If he refutes heresies, he does it in order to provide the necessary information and instruction for his listeners."

40. Quasten, *Patrology*, Vol. III, 474, writes: "Among the great number of Chrysostom's writings there is none that could be properly called an investigation or study of a theological problem as such....He was by nature and by predeliction a pastor of souls and a born reformer of human society. Though no one has ever interpreted Holy Scripture as successfully as he, he had no speculative bent nor any interest in the abstract. However, this lack of inclination for systematic presentation does not exclude a deep understanding of difficult theological questions. Since this greatest pulpit orator of the Ancient Church bases his entire preaching on Scripture, the study of his literary bequest is of great importance for positive theology."

41. Lührmann, col. 107, writes that in no place does Chrysostom systematically develop precisely what faith means for him and that his interest lies less in the doctrinal formulation of faith than in its ethical impact. Ephrem Boularand writes: "Saint Jean Chrysostome n'a pas étudié le problème de la foi pour lui-même et dans son ensemble, à la manière d'un théologien moderne. Il ne l'aborde guère qu'en passant, au hasard du passage de l'Ecriture qu'il explique aux fidèles. A ce point qu'on ne trove dans les treize tomes de ses oeuvres, ni un traité complet, ni même une homélie entière qui s'y rapporte. Mais s'il n'a jamais songé à élaborer une théorie générale de la foi, il s'est pourtant demandé, à tout propos, comment l'on y parvient." In E. Boularand, *La venue de l'homme à la foi d'après saint Jean Chrysostome* (Rome: PUG, 1939) 1. This study by Boularand is quite impressive in that it reflects a wide knowledge of and sympathy for the works of Chrysostom. Nevertheless, the author admits that, in attempting to bring into a systematic whole some of the important insights of Chrysostom about faith, he may be imposing a structure which, simply as a structure, is somewhat foreign to Chrysostom himself. Another helpful publication is T. Spácil, "Fides catholica S. Joannis Chrysostomi et recens quoddam opus auctoris orthodoxi," *Gregorianum* 17 (1936) 176–194; 355–376; and 18 (1937) 70–87, which focuses on the doctrinal content of the writings of John Chrysostom, especially with a view to showing their consonance with Roman Catholic teaching. These works are useful tools for entering into Chrysostom's understanding of faith, and my own presentation owes much to them, especially to that of Boularand.

42. *In Joannem*, Homilia V,4 (PG 59,58). English text is taken from Saint John Chrysostom, *Commentary on Saint John the Apostle and Evangelist. Homilies 1-47*, translated by Sister Thomas Aquinas Goggin (New York: Fathers of the Church, Inc., 1957) 67. Hereafter, this translation will be referred to as Goggin I.

43. St. John Chrysostom, *Baptismal Instructions*, translated and annotated by Paul W. Harkins (London: Longmans, Green and Co., 1963), "Ancient Christian Writers, no. 31," 164. This particular instruction is listed as "The Eleventh Instruction" in the Harkins translation and it is the third in the Papadopoulos-Kerameus series, the original Greek of which was published in a collection entitled *Varia graeca sacra* (St. Petersburg, 1909). For details about the discovery, authenticity and publication of this instruction as well as the arrangement and numbering of the 12 instructions in the "Ancient Christian Writers" edition, see Harkins' "Introduction" to that volume, 3-19. A more extensive introduction to John Chrysostom's baptismal catechesis, as well as the Greek text for the first eight lectures found in the Harkins translation, is provided in Jean Chrysostome, *Huit catéchèses baptismales inédites*, Introduction, texte critique, traduction et notes de Antoine Wenger (Paris: Cerf, 1957), "Sources chrétiennes 50," 7-107.

44. Boularand, 12-21.

45. Boularand, 12-16, with many references to Chrysostom.

46. This sentence is a loose translation of the summary provided by Boularand, 19. A number of references to this mysterious nature of redemption, taken particularly from Chrysostom's comments on 1 Corinthians, Ephesians and Colossians, can be found on pages 20-21 of Boularand.

47. See also *In epistulam ad Romanos*, Homilia VI on Rom 2,17ff (PG 60, 438-439).

48. Other passages which speak of the transformative grace and knowledge which come from being a Christian and which raise one to a higher level of knowing and living, thus implying a certain superiority of faith to reason, are *In epistolam ad Romanos*, Homilia XIII on Rom 8,5ff (PG 60, 515-518) and *In epistolam ad Philippenses*, Homilia XII, 2 (PG 62, 271-273).

49. Chrysostom's precise view about Peter and the "primacy" of Peter

and of his successors has been the topic of some dispute, particularly between Orthodox and Catholic authors. The second part of T. Spácil, "Fides catholica S. Ioannis Chrysostomi et recens quoddam opus auctoris orthodoxi," entitled "II. De Primatu S. Petri eiusque successorum" and appearing in *Gregorianum* 17 (1936) 355–376, argues for an explicit recognition of Peter's primacy but only an implicit recognition of that of his successors, against the opposite view of D.N. Jaksic, *Zivot i ucenie sv. Joanna Zlatousta* (Karlovci, 1934), 311 pages. This theme was earlier taken up by Niccolò Marini in his *Il primato di S. Pietro e de' suoi successori in San Giovanni Crisostomo* (Roma: Tipografia Poliglotta Vaticana, 1922²), 373 pages. For Marini, the decisive indication of Chrysostom's view on this question can be found in the final homily (88) on the gospel of John, where Jesus three times asks Peter whether he loves him and three times entrusts to him the care of his sheep: "Now why in the world did He pass over the other Apostles, and speak to this one about these matters? He was the chosen one of the Apostles, the mouthpiece of the disciples, and the head of the band. That is why Paul also came, on that later occasion, to make inquiries of him rather than of the others. At the same time, also, Christ entrusted to Peter the primacy over his brethren to show him that in the future he must have no fear, because his denial had been completely forgiven....And, if someone should say: 'How is it, then, that it was James who received the bishop's chair in Jerusalem?' I would make this reply: that Christ appointed this man, not merely to a chair, but as teacher of the world." English taken from Saint John Chrysostom, *Commentary on Saint John the Apostle and Evangelist. Homilies 48–88*, translated by Sister Thomas Aquinas Goggin (New York: Fathers of the Church, Inc., 1950) 470 and 473. (Hereafter this translation will be referred to as Goggin II.) The question about Peter is important for the topic of the relationship between faith and the Church, insofar as Chrysostom sees the faith of Peter's confession as the rock on which the Church is built. The question of the primacy would seem to be less related to the topic of faith in the mind of Chrysostom. The similarity, according to Spácil and Marini, between Chrysostom's thought and later Roman Catholic doctrine, is so striking that one cannot help but be at least a bit suspicious as to the accuracy of their interpretations.

50. *In martyres* 1 (PG 50, 646). I have taken this English from note 34 of the Harkins translation of the *Baptismal Instructions*, 203.

51. Cyril is absent from the studies by Escribano-Alberca and De Simone and receives even less mention (merely 13 lines on col. 107) by Lührmann than did Athanasius (see above, page 289, note 5).

52. William J. Malley, *Hellenism and Christianity. The Conflict Between Hellenic and Christian Wisdom in the "Contra Galilaeos" of Julian the Apostate and the "Contra Julianum" of St. Cyril of Alexandria* (Rome: Università Gregoriana Editrice, 1978), 466 pages, at 422. Malley's book is quite refreshing in that it examines a dimension of Cyril which is somewhat obscured by the more predominant interest in his Christological thought, that is, his contribution as an apologist in response to the Hellenism of his day.

53. For a brief but authoritative account of Cyril's appeal to the pope and his role in the Council of Ephesus, see Hubert Jedin, *Ecumenical Councils of the Catholic Church. An Historical Outline* (New York: Herder and Herder, 1960) 30–36. Much later in the West and in no small part as a result of the Western Schism of 1378–1415, the idea of an opposition between pope and ecumenical council made its appearance. See Jedin, "The Council above the Pope?" in Ibid. 105–141. The ecclesiological outlook or movement which grew from this supposed tension and which came to be known as conciliarism bore significant influence upon the way in which the doctrine of papal primacy and infallibility would eventually be expressed at Vatican I (1869–1870). The fourth part of Hubert du Manoir de Juaye's *Dogme et spiritualité chez saint Cyrille d'Alexandrie* (Paris: J. Vrin, 1944), 594 pages, while admitting that Cyril did not elaborate any explicit and systematic treatment of the Church as he had in the areas of Christology or Trinitarian theology, nevertheless attempts, by means of gathering together comments which appear in various places, to sketch out Cyril's ecclesiology. Germane to the present study, Du Manoir emphasizes Cyril's insistence upon the doctrinal authority of bishops as successors to the apostles (pp. 336–343) as well as the primacy of the bishop of Rome (pp. 347–366), noting in the latter case that Cyril comments some thirty times on the passage of Matt 16,13–20, in which Peter professes faith in Jesus as the Christ, the Son of the living God, and Jesus gives Simon the name Peter, the rock upon which he will build his Church (pp. 354–356).

54. Quasten, *Patrology*, Vol. III, 135.

55. Quasten, *Patrology*, Vol. III, 538 and 536 respectively.

56. John Henry Cardinal Newman, "Trials of Theodoret," in Id., *Historical Sketches*, Vol. II (London: Longmans, Green and Co., 1917) 303–362 at 307–308. This short biography by Newman is characterized

by that charm of style and comprehensive familiarity with the fathers which typifies his works as a whole.

57. For a wealth of background information to this work, see Pierre Canivet SI, "Introduction" to Théodoret de Cyr, *Thérapeutique des maladies helléniques* (Paris: Cerf, 1958), "Sources chrétiennes 57,1," 7–99. On 28–31 of this introduction Canivet argues from external and internal evidence in favor of a date prior to Ephesus. However, earlier commentators had suggested arguments in favor of a number of other dates; see Quasten, *Patrology*, Vol. III, 544 (with some pertinent bibliography) and Nicola Festa, "Introduzione" to Teodoreto, *Terapia dei morbi pagani*, Vol. I (Libri I.-VI.), a cura di Nicola Festa (Firenze: Edizioni "Testi Cristiani," 1931) 5–45 at 36–39.

58. For the title and date of Julian's work, see Quasten, *Patrology*, Vol. III, 129. For Julian's characterization of Christianity as an illness, see Canivet, 43–45. J.R. Asmus argues that the *Curatio* is in response to Julian, in "Theodorets Therapeutik und ihr Verhältnis zu Julian," *ByzZ* 3 (1894) 116–145; against whom argues J. Schulte, "Das Verhältnis von Theodorets Therapeutik zu den Schriften Kaiser Julians," *ThQ* 88 (1906) 349–356. These studies are listed in the bibliography provided by Quasten, *Patrology*, Vol. III, 544.

59. According to Canivet, 42, there is little likelihood that Theodoret had read Julian's *Against the Galilaeans*. Such a detailed refutation was provided by Theodoret's "enemy" Cyril of Alexandria during the 430's; see Quasten, *Patrology*, Vol. III, 129–130. Others who similarly responded to Julian were Gregory of Nazianzus, Apollinaris of Laodicea and Philip Sidetes (see Ibid. 242, 378 and 530 respectively).

60. These figures are given by Quasten, *Patrology*, Vol. III, 544, though Quasten says "more than one hundred" authors. This is slightly exaggerated, which one sees by consulting Canivet's excellent "Index des citations d'auteurs anciens," at the end of Volume II of his translation of the *Thérapeutique des malades helléniques* (Paris: Cerf, 1958), "Sources chrétiennes 57.2," 451–466. Canivet lists over seventy authors, but some of them are quoted from more than one of their books. Plato is especially an example of this; more than twenty of his works are cited. Regarding these quotations, Canivet's index shows that, with the exception of a very few authors (most notably Homer), almost all of the quotations found in Theodoret were cited earlier in Clement of Alexandria's *Stromata* and Eusebius of Caesarea's *Preparatio evangelica*, obviously two of his princi-

pal sources in writing the *Curatio*. Indeed, Festa, p. 30, even notes that such similarities have at times raised the charge that Theodoret was guilty of plagiarism, a charge which Festa himself sees as unfounded.

61. For both Lührmann, cols. 107–109, and Escribano-Alberca, 128, the cognitive is the dimension of faith which is prominent in Theodoret. Neither of them mentions the texts of a more existential tonality, which we will add in this paragraph.

62. His comment on Eph 4,13 ("...until we attain to the unity of the faith and of the knowledge of the Son of God, to mature manhood, to the measure of the stature of the fullness of Christ") is illuminating: "we will reach perfection only in the future life. In the present, therefore, we have need of the help of apostles, prophets and teachers" (*Interpretatio epistolae ad Ephesios* 4,13 [PG 82, 535–536]). This suggests that, in Theodoret's view, during the imperfect state of the Church on earth, ministry is the necessary, if provisional, help for unity and maturity in faith.

63. For the profession of faith required of Theodoret at Chalcedon, see J. Mansi et alii, *Sacrorum Conciliorum Nova et Amplissima Collectio*, VII (Florence, 1762) 189-190. For brief accounts of the difficulties of Theodoret regarding the condemnation of Nestorius as well as his eventual acquiescence in that condemnation, see Newman, "Trials of Theodoret," 333–362; Quasten, *Patrology*, Vol. III, 537–538; Festa, 9–13; Canivet, 20–23.

64. For the texts of these condemnations see *Conciliorum Oecumenicorum Decreta*, a cura di Giuseppe Alberigo et alii (Bologna: EDB, c. 1991), 111, 113 and 121. Constantinople II does not identify these writings by name. In Quasten's account of Theodoret, *Patrology*, Vol. III, 536–554 at 546, he identifies these as the *Refutation of the Twelve Anathemas of Cyril of Alexandria against Nestorius* and the *Pentalogium*, both of which were subsequently lost because of this condemnation, although much if not all of the former is preserved in Cyril's detailed rejoinder to it.

65. Texts in *Conciliorum Oecumenicorum Decreta*, 69–74. On Theodoret's authorship of the formula, see Quasten, *Patrology*, Vol. III, 118 and 537.

7. Faith and Its Unity in Post-Nicean Latin Writers

1. This title is given to him, with various qualifiers, by F. Cayré, in *Patrologie et histoire de la théologie*, Tome premier, Livres I et II (Paris:

Desclée, 1938[3]) 346. M. Simonetti writes that all of the historical data which we have about Hilary is connected with the Arian controversy and that his writings are also reflective of this engagement. See "Ilario de Poitiers e la crisi ariana in occidente," in A. Di Berardino, ed. *Patrologia. Vol. III, Dal Concilio di Nicea (325) al Concilio di Calcedonia (451). I Padri latini* (Torino: Marietti, 1978) 36.

2. Simonetti, 43, writes that Hilary's *De synodis* reveals for the first time a full awareness on the part of a Western thinker of the complex religious reality in the East, an example, he adds, which was to remain unique.

3. On the date of the writing of this work as well as its breaking new ground in the West, see Simonetti, 38–41. Interestingly enough, Hilary in *De synodis*, 91, claims that, long after he was a Christian (he converted to Christianity around the year 345; so Cayré, 344) and even for a while after he became bishop of Poitier in 355, he had not even heard of Nicea. Thus, at least thirty years after its occurrence a Western bishop was unaware of the first ecumenical council!

4. A. Gardeil, "Credibilité," in *Dictionnaire de théologie catholique*, Vol. III.2 (Paris: Letouzey et Ané, 1938) 2201–2310 at 2251. This index was simply reprinted from the Benedictine edition, *Sancti Hilarii Pictavorum Episcopi Opera* (Paris, 1693).

5. A. Peñamaría, "*Fides* en Hilario de Poitiers," *Miscelánea Comillas* 55 (1971) 5–102; and Idem, "Exegesis alegorica y significados de *fides* en San Hilario de Poitiers," *Miscelánea Comillas* 56 (1972) 65–91.

6. "*Fides* en Hilario de Poitiers," 5. Peñamaría claims that there seems to be a theology of faith in Hilary's writings, but one must make the effort to extract it ("libarla") from his so abundant use of the vocabulary of faith. He adds: "If there is an exegesis concerning faith in Hilary, it is hidden in the typology of the Tract on the Mysteries or in the symbolism of persons and events in the gospels as that appears in the Commentary on Matthew or in the refined anthropological analysis of the spirituality of the Christian so widespread in the Tract on the Psalms" (Ibid., 7). Peñamaría's second article is devoted to this biblically-oriented task.

7. English text for *De Trinitate* will be taken from the translation of S. McKenna, *Saint Hilary of Poitiers. The Trinity*, "The Fathers of the Church, Volume 25" (New York: Fathers of the Church, Inc., 1954), here at 12–13. The critical text is Sancti Hilarii Pictaviensis Episcopi, *De*

Trinitate, P. Smulders, ed. (Turnholt: Brepols, 1979), Corpus Christianorum. Series Latina, 62 and 62A (1980).

8. This according to the conclusion of Peñamaría, "Exégesis alegórica y significados de *Fides* en San Hilario de Poitiers," 91.

9. Here there may be a point of departure for seeing the relation between bishops and the apostles in the writings of Hilary. In *In Matthaeum* 27,1-2 (PL 9,1058-1059), commenting on the good servant which the master places over his household (Mt 24,45-51), Hilary speaks of the role of the bishop in the church as comparable to that of the laborers in the harvest. An enlightening elaboration of Hilary's view of bishops can be found in L. Padovese, "Ministero episcopale e 'memoria' nel pensiero d'Ilario di Poitiers," *Compostellanum* 35 (1990) 461-477.

10. The scope of this work has been presented in a very concise and helpful way by Simonetti, 42-43; see also 33-35 on the general context of the different situations of the Eastern and Western Churches respectively vis-à-vis Arianism.

11. See *Vita Sancti Ambrosii a Paulino eius notario*, a revised text, and commentary, with an Introduction and Translation by Sister Mary Simplicia Kaniecka (Washington: CUA Press, 1928) nos. 6-11 (on pages 45-51 of Kaniecka's translation). This work can also be found in PL 14, 27-46.

12. For this material, see Giuseppe Toscani, *Teologia della chiesa in sant'Ambrogio* (Milano: Vita e Pensiero, 1974) 17-18, who summarizes the results of several other scholars concerning these two stages in the literary production of Ambrose.

13. This was only natural insofar as he himself had been a public official, even governor of Liguria and Emilia at the time when he was elected bishop, and thus would have had many ties with those involved in government. See F. Cayré, *Patrologie et Histoire de la théologie*, 508-509 and 522.

14. These two works, written during the years 378-382, have sometimes been considered as one under the title of *The Trinity*, according to Roy J. Deferrari's "Introduction" to *The Holy Spirit* in Saint Ambrose, *Theological and Dogmatic Works*, translated by Roy J. Deferrari (Washington: CUA Press, 1963) 31.

15. An excellent brief summary of this activity is Manlio Simonetti, "La

politica antiariana di Ambrogio," in *Ambrosius Episcopus. Atti del Congresso internazionale di studi ambrosiani nel XVI centenario della elevazione di sant'Ambrogio alla cattedra episcopale*, a cura di Giuseppe Lazzati (Milano: Vita e Pensiero, 1976) 266–285. Hereafter, this book, which contains other studies to which we will refer, will be cited as *Ambrosius Episcopus*.

16. A brief account of some of this material can be found in Toscani, 4–8. An influential book concerning Ambrose's role in the events of his time was H. von Campenhausen's *Ambrosius von Mailand als Kirchenpolitiker* (Berlin: Walter de Gruyter, 1929), which, as the title suggests, attempted to draw out the ecclesiastical politics reflected in Ambrose's actions.

17. The connection to Philo is outlined by Ernst Dassmann, *Die Frömmigkeit des Kirchenvaters Ambrosius von Mailand* (Münster: Aschendorff, 1965) 61–62. Dassmann's book is a very helpful tool for exploring Ambrose's understanding of faith, as is Chapter Eight, "La 'plantatio ecclesiae' mediante la fede," of Toscani's *Teologia della chiesa in sant'Ambrogio*, 355–399 (see note 12 above).

18. Ambrose interprets the post-resurrection encounter between Jesus and Mary Magdalene again using this metaphor. Jesus says to Mary "Do not touch me" because her faith in the resurrection was yet wavering. "Illa igitur tangit Christum quae fide tangit" (= She therefore touches Christ who touches him with faith; *De virginitate* 15 [PL 16, 284]).

19. Translation is by Michael P. McHugh for the "Fathers of the Church, Vol. 65": Saint Ambrose, *Seven Exegetical Works* (Washington: CUA Press, 1971) 38.

20. In *De Abraham* I,3 and 10 (CSEL 32,1, 503 and 509–510), Abraham's fundamental relation to God is spoken of as devotion rather than as faith; in *De Abraham* I,32 (CSEL 32,1, 526) the two words are listed side by side. This relation between fides and devotio is explained by Dassmann, 58–64, 84, 110 and 294.

21. This work is listed as Letter 75a in CSEL 82.3; it is listed as Letter 21a in the Maurist collection.

22. In *De Spiritu sancto* II,26–28 (CSEL 79, 96–97) Ambrose freely applies Jn 17,3 to the Holy Spirit as well. Not only is eternal life in know-

ing the Father and the Son, but also in knowing, i.e. acknowledging the divinity of, the Holy Spirit.

23. He was an ardent defender of Nicea, claiming that precisely 318 bishops were present there and that this number was prefigured in the number of soldiers with which Abraham, that symbol par excellence of the faith, defeated innumerable enemies (Gn 14,14; cf. *De fide* I,3–5 [CSEL 78, 5–6]; see also *De Abraham* I,15 [CSEL 32,1, 512-513] on the symbolism of the number 318 and its relation to the victory of faith). There are varying accounts of how many participated in the Council of Nicea, which came to be recognized as the first ecumenical council. For a brief overview, see Lorenzo Perrone, "Da Nicea (325) a Calcedonia (451). I primi quattro concili ecumenici: istituzioni, dottrine, processi di ricezione," in Giuseppe Alberigo (ed.), *Storia dei concili ecumenici* (Brescia: Queriniana, 1990) 11–118 at 24–26.

24. For example, Jn 15,1 ("I am the true vine and my Father is the vine-grower") was used by Arians to show a level of subordination of the Son to the Father to which Ambrose replies by explaining the text in a way which does not require such a subordination; cf. *De fide* IV,157-168 (CSEL 78, 212–216). Much of the argumentation of Ambrose's dogmatic writings is devoted to an interpretation of Scripture which is in harmony with the doctrine of Nicea and a response to those who interpret it in a different way.

25. In this regard, one is amazed by the strongly apophatic tone of the final sections of *De fide*, a work of five books in which Ambrose has tried to argue at considerable length about true and false doctrine, hence about what we know and must confess about God. Yet, in the end, his argument against Arius is that the latter claims to know too much. For example, *De fide* V,228 (CSEL 78, 303–304): "Almighty Father, in tears I now direct my words to you. I would say without hesitation that you are 'inaccessible,' 'incomprehensible,' 'inestimable,' but I would not dare to say that your Son is less. For since I read that he is the 'reflection of your glory and the image of your substance' I fear lest by saying that the image of your substance is inferior I may appear to say the same of your substance, of which your Son is the image, for in the Son is every fullness of your divinity. I have often read and willingly believe that you and your Son and the Holy Spirit are immense, immeasurable, beyond thought or description. Then I cannot make a judgment about you so as to fully understand you." In presuming to know the mysteries of generation within the divinity, Arius' "sacrilege" is yet greater than that of the devil:

"The devil, in fact, confessed him to be truly 'Son of God'; Arius denies it!" (*De fide* V, 230 [CSEL 78, 305]). Again: "Paul, speaking about matters of less importance, says: 'Our knowledge is imperfect and our prophesying is imperfect.' Arius says: 'I have known God completely, not in part.' Is Paul then inferior to Arius—the vessel of election knows in part while the vessel of perdition knows the whole?" (*De fide* V,237 [CSEL 78, 307]). Finally, commenting on Paul's statement in 2 Cor 12,3 ("I know a man in Christ who, fourteen years ago, was caught up into the third heaven— whether in the body or out of the body I do not know, God knows"), Ambrose adds the gloss: "Paul says about himself: 'God knows him.' Arius says about God: 'I know him'" (*De fide* V,237 [CSEL 78, 307]). These texts from the closing section of Ambrose's vigorous defense of Nicean orthodoxy show that, for him, the affirmation that one can know something of God and that correct doctrine can and indeed must be distinguished from false doctrine in no way eliminates the limited and imperfect nature of human knowledge of God. For Ambrose, it is precisely the vanity of not recognizing this which lies at the root of the false doctrines which he condemns as, therefore, "impious" (cf. *De fide* I,74; IV,78; V,27 [CSEL 78: 32, 183 and 226]; and *De Spiritu sancto* I,164; II,81; III,73; III,122 [CSEL 79: 84–85, 118, 180 and 202]).

26. Dassmann, 81, where he says that *cognoscere* is not so much *comprehendere* as *accipere, tenere, confiteri*; it is not a question of *discutere causas* but of *servare sacramenta*.

27. English translation is that of Michael P. McHugh, in *Seven Exegetical Works*, 348.

28. English translation of *De incarnatione dominicae sacramento*, 89, is that of Roy J. Deferrari, Saint Ambrose, *Theological and Dogmatic Works*, 252.

29. Perhaps within the context of his arguing against the Arians it is appropriate to raise the question of Ambrose's place in the overall panorama of the theology of his time. It is known that St. Jerome "took a rather dim view of St. Ambrose." For this comment and further details, see Roy J. Deferrari, "Introduction" to *De Spiritu sancto* in *Theological and Dogmatic Works*, 32. Cayré, 531, says that Ambrose was not, properly speaking, a theologian in the sense of one whose thought was truly original in that it applied high philosophical investigation to some specific aspect or aspects of the mysteries of the faith. An impressively careful study of this question which concludes to a very positive evaluation of

Ambrose is Raniero Cantalamessa, "Sant'Ambrogio di fronte ai grandi dibattiti teologici del suo secolo," in *Ambrosius Episcopus*, 483–539.

30. What a powerful text is *Expositio evangelii secundum Lucam* X,92 (CSEL 32,1, 490): "From where shall I ask you to come, Peter, to teach me what you were thinking amid your tears? Yes, I say, from where shall I call you? From heaven, where you are already inserted among the choirs of angels? Or are you still in the tomb? For you did not think it an injury to stay in that place from where your Lord rose. Teach us what good your tears were to you. Ah, but you have already taught that to us very quickly. For you who had fallen before you wept and who earlier had been unable to keep yourself on a straight course were chosen, after you wept, to be the guide to others."

31. A well balanced analysis of Ambrose's texts, without however going into a discussion of the various interpretations of others, is the subsection of Chapter Eight of Toscani's book, entitled "La fede di Pietro modello e sostegno per tutta la chiesa di Cristo." In Toscani, pp 391–399. Toscani also presents some texts which give a certain preeminence to the Church of Rome, such as *Explanatio symboli* 7 (CSEL 73, 10); *De sacramentis* III,5-6 (CSEL 73, 40–41); *De paenitentia* I,33 (CSEL 73, 135); *Epistola* XI,2-5 (CSEL 82,3, 182–185); *De excessu fratris* I,47 (CSEL 73, 235). Toscani's general conclusion is that, with regard to the question of Peter's relation to the Twelve, Ambrose simply repeats the New Testament data, placing a special emphasis upon Peter's faith. With regard to the question of the role of the bishops of Rome or of the Church of Rome, Ambrose seems to be more interested in the faith which has been handed on and preserved in Rome than upon Church structure as such. See Toscani, 397.

32. English text is taken from the translation by Sister Mary Melchior Beyenka: Saint Ambrose, *Letters* (New York: Fathers of the Church, Inc., 1954) 52–53. Because of editorial decisions concerning the arrangement of letters in this particular collection, *Epistula* XXI is listed as letter 9.

33. One may smile (without however shaking the feeling of intimidation which it can inspire) at the way in which Agostino Trapè opens his study of Augustine in the volume produced by the Institutum Patristicum Augustinianum in Rome and intended as the concluding volume of Quasten's great *Patrology*: "Augustine is undoubtedly the greatest of the Fathers and one of the brightest geniuses of all time. His influence on posterity has been profound and unending. The studies about him have

multiplied, and continue to do so, at such a rate that it becomes impossible to give a complete account of them." A. Trapè, "S. Agostino," in *Patrologia. Vol. III. Dal Concilio di Nicea (325) al Concilio di Calcedonia (451). I Padri latini*, 325.

34. On this commitment to seek wisdom from the age of nineteen, see Augustine's *Confessions* VI,11 [CSEL 33, 132].

35. *Confessions* VIII,12 (CSEL 33, 195). English translation of this work is by Rex Warner, *The Confessions of St. Augustine* (New York: Mentor-Omega, 1963) 183.

36. In *The Advantage of Believing* I,2, Augustine writes: "For, what else forced me for almost nine years, during which time I rejected the religion which my parents had implanted in me as a child, to follow these men and diligently to listen to them, save that they said we were terrified by superstition, and that faith was demanded of us before reason, while they, on the other hand, were forcing faith on no one without first hunting for and disentangling the truth. Who would not be enticed by these promises?" The English translation used here is that of Luanne Meagher in *Writings of Saint Augustine. Volume 2* (New York: Cima, 1947), 392. Another of many texts about this promise of knowledge by the Manichaeans can be found in *Confessions* VI,5.

37. These English titles are those given in the translations contained in several volumes of "The Fathers of the Church" series. *The Advantage of Believing = De utilitate credendi* (CSEL 25, 3–48), translated by Luanne Meagher in *Writings of Saint Augustine. Volume 2* (New York: Cima, 1947), 381–442; *On Faith in Things Unseen = De fide rerum invisibilium* (CCL 46, 1–19), translated by Roy J. Deferrari and Mary Francis McDonald, in *Ibid.*, 443–469; *Faith and the Creed = De fide et symbolo* (CSEL 41, 1–32), translated by Robert P. Russell in *Saint Augustine. Treatises on Marriage and Other Subjects* (New York: Fathers of the Church, 1955), 309–345 (hereafter, Russell I); *Faith and Works = De fide et operibus* (CSEL 41, 33–97), translated by Sr. Marie Liguori, in *Ibid.*, 213–282; *The Christian Combat = De agone christiano* (CSEL 41, 99–138), translated by Robert P. Russell, in *Writings of Saint Augustine. Volume 4* (New York: Cima, 1947), 307–353 (hereafter, Russell II); *Faith, Hope and Charity = Enchiridion de fide, spe et caritate* (CCL 46, 49–114), translated by Bernard M. Peebles, in *Ibid.*, 355–472.

38. Abundant references to Augustine's conviction that the Church is one and extends throughout the world and to Augustine's use of the

adjective *catholica* are provided by Maurice Pontet in "Extension visible de l'Église," which is chapter 8 of his *L'exégèse de S. Augustin prédicateur* (Paris: Aubier, 1945) 419–446. An often cited study which begins with the premise that, because of his many contributions about the nature of the Church, Augustine could as justly be called "doctor of ecclesiology" as he is by the common and widely accepted designation "doctor of grace" is Pierre Batiffol, *Le catholicisme de saint Augustin* (Paris: Lecoffre, 1920²) vi. Augustine's first anti-Donatist work, at least according to order of appearance in his *Retractationes*, is the *Psalmus contra partem Donati, liber unus* [CSEL 51, 1–15], the title of which indicates his view that the Donatists represented only a "part" and therefore cannot be considered truly the Church, which of its nature includes the whole. Of the 93 works discussed in the *Retractationes* [CSEL 36, 1–204], 19 are directed against the Donatists! See the comments by Sr. Mary Inez Bogan, in her translation and notes entitled *Saint Augustine. The Retractations* (Washington: Catholic University of America Press, 1968) 87.

39. *The Advantage of Believing* (391) may be seen as a first draft of sections of the later *Confessions* (397–401); see P. Batiffol, "Autour du 'De utilitate credendi' de St. Augustin," *Revue Biblique* 14 (1917) 9–53 at 11.

40. Lührmann, col. 113, emphasizes the connection between faith and history in Augustine: "Erkenntnis von Geschichte aber, und um eine solche handelt es sich beim Christentum, ist nur als credere, nicht als intelligere möglich, da solches Erkennen immer auf Zeugen angewiesen ist, nicht auf eigener Anschauung beruhen kann (fid. invis. 1/4; ep. 120,9)." Thus for Lührmann, both the epistemological context which led to Augustine's becoming a Manichaean and the historical nature of Christianity lead to the conclusion that, for Augustine, Christianity *is* faith: "Auch für Augustinus ist das Christentum, dem er sich nach seiner Darstellung in den Confessiones zuwendet, fides. Er ist dabei genötigt, den fides-Charakter des Christentums gegenüber dem Anspruch der Manichäer, ratio zu bieten, zu verteidigen (util. cred. 21f)." A text which supports the analysis that, for Augustine, history can only be known through belief is *De diversis quaestionibus LXXXIII,* XLVIII [CCL 44A, 75]: "Three classes of things are objects of belief. First, there are those things which always are believed and never understood, e.g., history, which deals with events both temporal and human. Second, there are those things which are understood as soon as they are believed, e.g., all human reasonings either in mathematics or in any of the sciences. Third, there are those things which are first believed and afterwards understood. Of such a character is that which cannot be understood of

divine things except by those who are pure in heart. This understanding is achieved through observing those commandments which concern virtuous living." English from David L. Mosher, trans., *St. Augustine. Eighty-Three Different Questions* (Washington: CUA Press, 1977) 83.

41. Cf. *Advantage* XI,25 (CSEL 25, 32; Meagher, 425), which adds that opinion "is very base for two reasons: both in that he who has convinced himself that he already knows cannot learn (even if it were possible for the thing to be learned), and the very rashness is of itself a sign of a mind ill disposed."

42. On the distinction between credulity and belief, see *Advantage* IX,22 [CSEL 25, 26–28]. The reasonability of believing is a conviction which Augustine maintains throughout his life, which can be seen from the famous line from one of his last works, *De praedestinatione sanctorum* 5 [PL 44, 962–963]: "No one indeed believes anything, unless he thought that it is to be believed." English translation is taken from Erich Przywara, *An Augustine Synthesis* (New York: Harper and Brothers, 1958) 61.

43. One of the most carefully researched studies in this area, Magnus Löhrer's *Der Glaubensbegriff des hl. Augustinus in seinen ersten Schriften bis zu den Confessiones* (Einsiedeln-Zürich-Köln: Benziger, 1955), a doctoral dissertation defended at the Benedictine faculty Anselmianum in 1954, places considerable emphasis on the relation between auctoritas and ratio in Augustine's view of faith. See especially Chapter Two, part I: "Der Autoritätsbegriff," 79–117.

44. The English translation is that of Donald Gallagher and Idella Gallagher, *Saint Augustine. The Catholic and Manichaean Ways of Life (= De moribus ecclesiae catholicae et de moribus manichaeorum* [CSEL 40,3–156]) (Washington: Catholic University of America, 1966) 5.

45. An English translation of this text is that of Joseph Christopher, *St. Augustine. The First Catechetical Instruction* (Westminster: Newman Press, 1952) 26–27.

46. An English translation of this text from Letter 137 can be found in Przywara, 44–46.

47. *De quantitate animae* (CSEL 89, 129-231) was written in Rome sometime during 387 or 388. An English translation, entitled *The Magnitude of*

the Soul, by John McMahon, is available in *Writings of St. Augustine. Volume 2* (New York: Cima, 1947) 49–149.

48. As one might expect given the gnoseological-mystical thrust of his monograph, this aspect of mind's coming to know God receives prominent treatment in the discussion of Augustine's thought on faith by Escribano-Alberca, 116–125. Augustine may be said to harmonize the Western caution about reason's ability to know God (see above, Tertullian, for example) with certain strains from the East which convey a certain optimism about the possibility of genuine Christian *gnosis* (see above, Clement of Alexandria and Origen, for example). Augustine's requirement of faith reflects the Western caution; his insistence that faith leads to understanding reflects the Eastern optimism.

49. English translation is by Robert P. Russell in Saint Augustine, *The Teacher. The Free Choice of the Will. Grace and Free* Will (Washington: The Catholic University of America Press, 1968), "The Fathers of the Church 59," 72–241 at 113.

50. Some fine examples can be found in *Christian Instruction* I, 37,41–38,42 [CSEL 80, 31–32]: "'For we walk by faith, not by sight.' Faith will totter if the authority of Sacred Scriptures wavers. Indeed, even charity itself grows weak, if faith totters. If anyone falls from faith, it is inevitable that he also falls from charity. For, he cannot love what he does not believe exists. But if he believes and loves, he has reason to hope....But the vision which we shall see takes the place of faith and that blessedness to which we shall attain takes the place of hope, but charity will be all the more increased as those former die away." English translation by John J. Gavigan, in *Christian Instruction* (= De doctrina Christiana) in *Writings of Saint Augustine. Volume 4*, 58 (bibliographical data in note 37 above).

51. This work closes with the following words, also relevant to the present point of the value of the Creed as an indication of the doctrinal quality of Christian faith. "This is the faith imparted to Christian neophytes. They are to make profession of it in the few words contained in the Creed; to believers, these few words are well known. By believing them they are made subject to God, by being subject to God they live a good life, by a good life they obtain purity of heart, and with a pure heart they understand the things they believe" (X,25 [CSEL 41, 32] Russell I, 345).

52. See the fifth and final chapter of Löhrer's *Der Glaubensbegriff...*,

224–270, entitled simply "Glaube und Gnade." In his conclusion, Löhrer notes: "Von entscheidender Bedeutung ist der Fortschritt, den Augustinus von den Propositiones zur Schrift Ad Simplicianum gemacht hat, indem nun auch die Glaubensbewegung als ein Werk der göttlichen Gnade erscheint, einer Gnade freilich, die den Willen nicht vergewaltigt, sondern aus der Knechtschaft der Sünde unter dem Gesetz befreit" (269). Also Lührmann, col. 115.

53. English translation from "On the Spirit and the Letter," *A Select Library of the Nicene and Post-Nicene Fathers*, Vol. V: *St. Augustine: Anti-Pelagian Writings* (Grand Rapids: Eerdmans, 1977) 110 (page 107 for XXXI, 54).

54. English translation by Sr. Wilfrid Parsons, *St. Augustine. Letters. Volume IV (165–203)* (New York: Fathers of the Church, 1955) 307.

55. This three-part structure is suggested by Sister Marie Liguori in the introduction to her translation of *Faith and Works* in *Saint Augustine. Treatises on Marriage and Other Subjects*, 216 (see above, note 37).

56. The text cited is from *Epistula CXX* II,8 (CSEL 34, 704–722 at 711), addressed to Consentius and packed with insights into Augustine's thought on the respective roles of and harmonious collaboration between faith and reason. The English translation used here is that of Sister Wilfrid Parsons, *Saint Augustine. Letters. Volume II (83–130)* (New York: Fathers of the Church, Inc., 1953) 300–317 at 306 (hereafter, Parsons II). Pierre Rousselot began what was to become his famous article "Les yeux de la foi," *Recherches de science religieuse* 1 (1910) 241–259 and 444–475, with the words "Habet namque fides oculos suos," attributing them to St. Augustine, without however indicating *Epistula CXX*, from which they obviously come. On the connection between faith and sight in Augustine, see also *In Ps. XLIV* 11, 25: "For it is to this end we hearken to that which we are to believe, before we see it, that by believing we may purify the heart, whereby we may be able to see" (CCL 38, 512; Przywara, 41). Or again, *In Ps. XXXVI*, Serm. II, 2, states: "Have the eyes of a believing mind. That which God sees, be thou ready to believe" (CCL 38, 348; Przywara, 42).

57. Some of Augustine's texts which utilize this passage are *Christian Instruction* II,12,17 (CSEL 80, 44); *Faith and the Creed* I,1 (CSEL 41, 4); *De magistro* 46 (CSEL 77A, 54). The text from *Christian Instruction* underscores the ultimate priority of reason over faith. Augustine is well aware that the more exact translation of the Hebrew is: "you will not contin-

ue/stand firm," instead of "you will not understand." Yet he finds "something valuable" in harmonizing the two translations: "Now, the essence of knowledge is the eternal Vision, while faith nourishes us as babes, upon milk, in the cradles of earthly things (for now 'we walk by faith and not by sight' [2 Cor 5,7]). If, however, we do walk by faith, we shall not be able to arrive at sight, which does not vanish, but continues through our intellect once cleansed by our union with the Truth. Therefore, it is that one translator says: 'If ye will not believe, ye shall not understand,' and the other declares: 'If you will not believe, you shall not continue'" (*De doctrina Christiana* II,12,17). This work is translated under the title *Christian Instruction* by John J. Gavigan in *Writings of Saint Augustine. Volume 4* (see above, note 37) 1–235, and is quite fascinating in that its first three books offer Augustine's view on interpreting the Scripture, a kind of patristic manual of hermeneutics, while the fourth and final book is a handbook for preaching.

58. James Lehrberger, "Intelligo ut credam: St. Augustine's *Confessions,*" *Thomist* 52 (1988) 23–39 at 23 notes that the expression "credo ut intelligam" was Anselm's formulation of Augustine's overall approach to the question of the relation between faith and reason. As the title of his article indicates, Lehrberger's concern is to indicate the role of reason in assisting one to come to faith. Reason functions as a "norma negativa," which leads Lehrberger to comment: "While faith alone may be able to give wisdom, reason of itself can discover folly" (25).

59. That Augustine himself understood the vast majority of his writings as being "against" the positions of other Christians is easily verifiable by glancing through the *Retractations*. Here, in reviewing his various works toward the end of his life, he gives the context within which each was written. Very often that context is to respond to or to refute the views of pagans, Jews, Manichaeans, Donatists, Pelagians or Arians.

60. One finds a variety of attitudes in Augustine regarding those whom he labels as heretics. Here in *The Christian Combat* as in many of his writings the tone seems quite harsh and condemnatory. But this must be nuanced by other much more conciliatory texts, as, for example, in *Against the Epistle of Manichaeus Called Fundamental* (CSEL 25, 193–248), the first chapter of which proposes that it is better to heal than to destroy and that his own aim in writing against the Manichaeans is to bring about their recovery. Here he also notes that one may be a heretic more from thoughtlessness than from malice. The point is that

Augustine's view toward those whom he considers as erring in faith cannot be limited to his more sharply negative comments.

61. Trapè, 401–403.

62. While not denying this assertion about Augustine's study of the
Scriptures at the time of his conversion, H. Chadwick remarks that
Augustine's earliest works tend to be more philosophical in content and
that only after he became a bishop did he seriously begin to grapple with
the exegesis of the Bible. In Henry Chadwick, *The Early Church*
(Middlesex: Penguin, 1967) 219. Chadwick's valid observation need not
obscure the fact that Augustine himself testifies that the discovery of a
more reasonably satisfying way of interpreting the Scriptures was instru-
mental for his entrance into the Church.

63. For a brief sketch of Augustine's view of non-scriptural traditions
and universality as the criterion of their authenticity, see, Y. Congar,
Tradition and Traditions (London: Burns & Oates, 1966) 53–55. More
developed is P. Batiffol, *Le catholicisme de Saint Augustin*, 29–42. Letter
LIV contains a short passage which reflects Augustine's mind on this
question of tradition and its authority: "But, regarding those other
observances which we keep and all the world keeps, and which do not
derive from Scripture but from tradition, we are given to understand
that they have been ordained or recommended to be kept by the apostles themselves, or by plenary councils, whose authority is well founded
in the Church. Such are the annual commemorations of the Lord's
Passion, Resurrection and Ascension into heaven, the descent of the
Holy Spirit from heaven, and other such observances as are kept by the
universal Church wherever it is found" (CSEL 34, 159–160); English
translation by Sr. Wilfrid Parsons, in *Saint Augustine. Letters. Volume I
(1–82)* (New York: Fathers of the Church, 1951) 252–253; hereafter
Parsons I. Obviously, in this passage, Augustine is thinking of tradition
as something distinct from Scripture and not as the all-encompassing
process of handing on what has happened and been revealed in Christ
which would include Scripture, and which is the more generally
employed concept of tradition within ecumenical circles since the
famous statement by the Fourth World Conference on Faith and Order
at Montreal in 1963. The description of revelation in Vatican II's *Dei verbum*, focusing as it does on God's self-manifestation, tends to play down
any view of tradition which would sharply isolate it from Scripture.

64. "Against the Epistle of the Manichaeans called Fundamental," trans-

lated by R. Stothert in P. Schaff, ed., *A Select Library of the Nicene and Post-Nicene Fathers. Vol. IV. St. Augustine: The Writings Against the Manichaeans and Against the Donatists* (Grand Rapids: Eerdmans, 1979) 129-150 at 131.

65. On the divine origin, inerrancy, depth and richness of Scripture for Augustine, see Trapè, 401. *Christian Instruction* II,8,12-13 (CSEL 80, 39-41) provides Augustine's list of the canonical books of the Bible, a list which for him is able to be known upon the basis of the authority of the churches.

66. Batiffol, *Le catholicisme*, 31-33, develops this notion of the relation of Church authority to tradition. See also Trapè, 402, in reference to *De Genesi ad litteram liber imperfectus*, 1,1 (CSEL 28.1, 459-461), though the text from Augustine in this case seems to me a less clear example of the point that Trapè wishes to make.

67. The first chapter of Batiffol's *Le catholicisme*, entitled "L'Église, Règle de foi," 1-75, develops this last point at considerable length.

68. English translation by Sister Mary Patricia Garvey, *Saint Augustine. Against the Academicians* (Milwaukee: Marquette University Press, 1957) 82. *The Magnitude of the Soul* closes with comments focusing more upon God the creator, rather than upon Christ, as the one who is supreme and true (XXXVI,80 [CSEL 89, 229]). In these same pages, one also finds various references to the role of the Church in the soul's ascent toward truth. For example: "Even though all these visible things, considered in themselves, are marvelous and beautiful, having been created by God their Maker, still, in comparison with the unseen realities, they are as nothing. From this we shall realize how full of truth are the things we are commanded to believe, how excellently and healthfully we were nourished by Mother Church; else, what is the worth of that 'milk' which St. Paul declared he gave as drink to little ones" (*Magnitude* XXXIII, 76 [CSEL 89, 224]; English by McMahon, 143).

69. Quapropter securus iudicat orbis terrarum bonos non esse, qui se dividunt ab orbe terrarum in quacumque parte terrarum. The French translation in *Oeuvres de saint Augustin*, Vol. 28 *Traités Anti-Donatistes. Volume 1* (Paris: Desclée, 1963) 457 reads: "En toute sûreté l'univers juge donc qu'ils ne sont pas bons, ceux qui se séparent de l'univers en quelque contrée de l'univers que ce soit." Newman compared the effect of this phrase upon his own life to that exercised on Augustine at the moment of his conversion by the words "Tolle, lege." See John Henry

Cardinal Newman, *Apologia pro vita sua* (Oxford: Clarendon, 1967), "Chapter Three: History of my Religious Opinions from 1839–1841," 109–111.

70. On Augustinian texts which address the "chair of Peter," see P. Batiffol, "La *cathedra Petri* dans la controverse antidonatiste d'Augustin," in *Le catholicisme de S. Augustin*, 192–209; and A. Trapè, "La 'Sedes Petri' in S. Agostino," in *Miscellanea Antonio Piolanti* (Roma: Facultas Theologica Pontificiae Universitatis Lateranensis, 1964) Vol. II, 57–76.

71. See Batiffol's Chapter Six, "Augustin, Pèlage et le siège apostolique (411–417)," in *Le Catholicisme de S. Augustin*, 349–410, especially 402–410. Augustine's text: Jam enim de hac causa duo concilia missa sunt ad Sedem Apostolicam: inde etiam rescripta venerunt. Causa finita est: utinam aliquando finiatur error! (PL 38,734).

8. Toward a Biblical and Patristic Understanding of Unity in Faith

1. In this sentence I am admitting one of the limits of the entire study: that I have focused upon texts and secondary literature which can be identified by their use of words such as "faith" and "to believe." Obviously there can be literature which is relevant to the theme of the present book which would only be identifiable under different terminology, for example, texts and relevant secondary sources which can be located under terminology such as regula fidei, heresy, orthodoxy and so forth. It is true that some of this material has been considered, although much more could be done in exploring such themes. Unfortunately one must eventually make a choice to limit a topic or face a research project which is, for all practical purposes, impossible.

2. See above, 14–18.

3. See above, 21–27.

4. Once again, this point about the scarcity of the occurrence of the precise expression "unity in faith" should not obscure the fact that the same idea can be conveyed in other terminology, such as Acts 4,32: "Now the company of those who believed were of one heart and soul...." Nevertheless, the general point seems to hold true: what makes for "unity in faith" is less an object of explicit reflection in the Scriptures and more a matter of general presupposition.

5. Another approach, in addition to that of considering the unity and diversity of New Testament "theologies," might be that of examining the topic of unity and diversity in the Church according to the New Testament. The Pontifical Biblical Commission has done an exemplary job of this in its *Unité et Diversité dans l'Église* (Città del Vaticano: Libreria Editrice Vaticana, 1989), 348 pages, which includes a summary statement of the commission's conclusions and twenty essays by individual exegetes concerning various aspects of the Church's unity. What is quite surprising is that the summary statement, while directed to an affirmation of the substantial unity of the Church according to the New Testament, says very little about unity in faith. This can be explained, no doubt, by the fact that the commission attempted to reflect the thought of the Scriptures themselves as accurately as possible. And the Bible itself offers much more explicit material about the unity of the Church as such than it offers about the fact that this unity includes, as one of its essential elements, unity in faith. It is only by noting the prominence of faith in the New Testament that one can conclude that Church unity also requires a fundamental unity in faith, as we have done in the first of our conclusions to the New Testament material at the end of Chapter Four.

6. One cannot but recall here the forceful statements by Leonard Goppelt, "The Plurality of New Testament Theologies and the Unity of the Gospel as an Ecumenical Problem," in Vilmer Vajta, ed., *The Gospel and Unity* (Minneapolis: Augsburg Press, 1971) 121, and Eduard Lohse, *Die Einheit des Neuen Testaments* (Göttingen: Vandenhoeck & Ruprecht, 1973) 336–337, that every New Testament writer and writing, without exception, understand the Church of Christ as a whole which is united throughout the world.

7. See above, Chapter One, 7–10, on the variety in Old Testament terminology for faith; the quotation from Van der Leeuw is at 10.

8. See above, 31.

9. See above, 31–39.

10. Concerning the presence of this polyvalence of the meaning of faith, see our earlier comments about Clement of Rome, 90–91, Ignatius of Antioch, 92–93, Irenaeus, 98, Tertullian, 103–104, Cyril of Jerusalem, 128, Gregory of Nyssa, 137-140, Cyril of Alexandria, 150–151, Theodoret, 155–156, Hilary, 161 and 164, Ambrose, 168–170, and Augustine, 181–184.

11. So, for example, texts from the Johannine letters on Jesus coming in the flesh (1 Jn 4,2–3; 2 Jn 7–11; see also 1 Jn 2,22), or the attitude of Basil (especially!), 131, Ambrose, 170, Gregory of Nazianzus, 133–134, in the earlier chapters of this book with regard to the formula of faith of the 318 fathers of Nicea.

12. I am attempting here to paraphrase closely the description of faith contained in Vatican II's Dogmatic Constitution on Revelation, *Dei verbum*, paragraph 5: "By faith man freely commits his entire self to God, making 'the full submission of his intellect and will to God who reveals,' and willingly assenting to the Revelation given by him." (Latin: "qua homo se totum libere Deo committit 'plenum revelanti Deo intellectus et voluntatis obsequium' praestando et voluntarie revelationi ab Eo datae assentiendo.") English translation from A. Flannery, ed., *Vatican Council II: The Conciliar and Post Conciliar Documents* (Northport: Costello, 1975), p. 752.

13. On the Old Testament roots of this theme, see above, 10–14.

14. Thomas Aquinas' "tract" on faith, which appears as the first seven articles of his *Summa Theologica*, II-II (although one may add those articles up to and including number sixteen, since they speak of other virtues or vices insofar as they relate to faith), provides a marvelous discussion of the object toward which faith is directed, the internal and external acts of faith, faith as a virtue, those who believe, and the causes and effects of faith. It could offer a valuable contribution to contemporary ecumenical reflection upon faith and its unity. II-II, 2, 1 addresses the question "Whether to believe is to think with assent?" Here Aquinas argues that this is an appropriate description of faith since, like acquired knowledge, one firmly assents to the truths of faith and yet, at least in the present life, "its knowledge does not attain the perfection of clear vision" and so is characterized by ongoing thinking, investigating or pondering. If "thought" may be described as "the movement of the soul while yet deliberating, and not yet perfected by the clear vision of the truth," and if assent means to hold a truth firmly and without doubt, then faith may be described as "thinking with assent." English translation has been taken from Anton Pegis, ed., *Basic Writings of St. Thomas Aquinas*, Vol. II (New York: Random, 1945), 1075. The theme of growth in love is nicely developed by Bonaventure, *The Soul's Journey into God. The Tree of Life. The Life of St. Francis*, Translation and Introduction by Ewert Cousins (New York: Paulist, 1978), 51–116.

15. See above, 18-19.

16. See above, 110-113, on Clement of Alexandria; 116-118, on Origen; and 138-139 on Gregory of Nyssa, although Gregory can be said to part ways with Clement and Origen to the extent that he is more apophatic in his view of drawing near to God; see Daniélou's comment, above, 139.

17. See, above, this emphasis in the writings of Irenaeus, 101-102, Tertullian, 105-109, Clement of Alexandria, 113-114, Origen, 118-119 and 121, Basil, 133, Gregory of Nazianzus, 135-136, John Chrysostom, 147-148, Cyril of Alexandria, 149 and 151-152 and (on fidelity to the apostolic foundations) Ambrose, 171-172.

18. All of Chapter Three above, 43-59, is devoted to developing this theme.

19. J.N.D. Kelly's *Early Christian Creeds* (New York: David McKay, 1960²), of which extensive use was made above in Part I, Chapter Three, is a highly regarded and frequently cited account of the emergence of various creeds in the first Christian centuries. Important collections and sources for many subsequent studies are A. Hahn, *Bibliothek der Symbole und Glaubensregeln der alten Kirche* (Breslau: Morgenstern, 1897³); H. Lietzmann, *Symbole der alten Kirche* (Berlin: Gruyter, 1968⁶); and F. Kattenbusch, *Das Apostolische Symbol*, 2 Vol. (Leipzig: J.C. Hinriches'sche Buchhandlung, 1894 and 1900). A more recent work which opens with a bibliographical note listing many of the more important publications concerned with creeds in general and the Apostles' Creed in particular is P. Smulders, "Some Riddles in the Apostles' Creed," *Bijdragen* 31 (1970) 234-260, and Idem, "Some Riddles in the Apostles' Creed. II. Creeds and Rules of Faith," *Bijdragen* 32 (1971) 350-366. For an attempt to explicate the Creed as a means toward arriving at greater unity of faith within the specifically ecumenical context, see the Faith and Order Commission, *Confessing the One Faith. An Ecumenical Explication of the Apostolic Faith as it is Confessed in the Nicene-Constantinopolitan Creed (381)* (Geneva: WCC Publications, 1991), 139 pages. This document may be considered as the result of many years of multi-lateral dialogue and publication concerning the Creed, which are nicely summarized in two of the appendices of Gennadios Limouris which appear at the end of the *Confessing the One Faith* document: "Appendix I: Historical Background of the Apostolic Faith Today," 105-111, and "Appendix III: Bibliography," 121-124. Furthermore, greater use of this study was highly encouraged at the Fifth World Conference of Faith and Order, held in Santiago

de Compostela, August 2–13, 1993 (See the "Report of Section II," paragraphs 2, 5.2 and 5.3). This suggests that a common explication of and profession of the Creed may continue to serve as an important factor for the ecumenical movement in the years ahead.

20. See above, 52, especially note 33, on the views of Schlier and others. See also the extended quote from Kelly, above, 56–57. Kelly, *Early Christian Creeds*, 29, concludes his chapter on the credal material in the New Testament by stating that the legend that the Apostles' Creed stemmed from the apostles turns out, after a fashion, to have been fundamentally correct. Cullmann, Benoit, Mussner and Koester, to name a few, seem to hold that a type of "creed" exerted a formative influence upon the writing of the New Testament, even though they may evaluate this in quite different ways.

21. See, above, the comments about the Creed by Cyril of Jerusalem, 127, and Augustine, 181–182.

22. As Denzinger's title suggests, being a collection of "symbols" in the plural, there are some differences between the various creeds which emerged in various places and at various times in the early Church. At the same time, one can note much similarity and compatibility among them. Since our study focused upon writings by a selected number of authors on the topic of faith, it would not have been quite appropriate to introduce reflections about the plurality of distinct creeds in the early centuries of the Church and the possible implications of this fact for what creeds can suggest to us about unity in faith. Perhaps it can suffice merely to point out that the fact that a number of creeds emerged during the early period of Christianity would seem to continue a pattern which was already established in both the Old and New Testaments. An extensive collection of ancient creeds and rules of faith can be found in Hahn, *Bibliothek der Symbole und Glaubensregeln der alten Kirche* (see above, note 19).

23. See above, 130–131.

24. See above, 166–167.

25. See above, 53–55.

26. On the Old Testament way of contextualizing the profession of the faith within the life of the community, see above, 16–17.

27. For several patristic commentaries on the Creed, see above, 129–130.

28. See above, 21–27.

29. This was a point very clearly made by Augustine: among his original difficulties with accepting the Scriptures was the presence of apparent contradictions in them. Only by seeing that a more discerning way of interpretation could remove apparent contradictions was it possible for him to accept the Scriptures as the Word of God. See above, 186.

30. A number of the criteria which go into this process of discernment, such as apostolic origin, liturgical use, orthodoxy and so forth, are listed by Robert Eno, "Preservazione ed interpretazione: la chiesa dei padri," *Concilium* (1976) 38–50 (1074–1086). [The Italian edition of *Concilium* indicates pagination in this double form, the first numbers referring to the pagination in the individual fascicle, the numbers in parentheses referring to the pagination for the year as a whole (in this case 1976). I have not been able to find this particular fascicle in English.]

31. On this topic, see Hans Dieter Betz, "Orthodoxy and Heresy in Primitive Christianity," *Interpretation* 19 (1965) 299–311; Prosper Grech, "Criteri di ortodossia ed eresia nel Nuovo Testamento," *Augustinianum* 25 (1985) 583–596; I. Howard Marshall, "Orthodoxy and Heresy in Earlier Christianity," *Themelios* 2 (1976) 5–14; N.J. McEleney, "Orthodoxy and Heresy in the New Testament," *Proceedings of the Catholic Theological Society of America* 25 (1970) 54–77; M. Meinertz, "Schisma und Haeresis im Neuen Testament," *BZ* 1 (1957) 114–118; Walter Schmithals, *Paulus und die Gnostiker* (Hamburg: Evangelischer Verlag, 1965); H.E.W. Turner, *The Pattern of Christian Truth: A Study in the Relationship between Orthodoxy and Heresy in the Early Church* (London: Mowbray, 1954).

32. See above, 67–79, on factors favoring unity.

33. See above, 99–100, and 101–102.

34. See above, 105–108.

35. See above, 113, for Clement of Alexandria's reference to the canon of the Church and 119 for Origen's list of the more important points of doctrine. The latter also speaks of the canon of the Church; see above, 121.

36. See above, 127–128, as well as 128–129 for Cyril of Jerusalem's over-all appreciation and use of scripture.

37. See above, 135–136.

38. See above, 140–141.

39. See above, 164–165, about Hilary and 171, about Ambrose.

40. See above, 147–148.

41. See above, 188. Eugene TeSelle, "Some Reflections on Augustine's Use of Scripture," in *Augustinian Studies (Annual Publication of the Augustinian Institute. Villanova University)* 7 (1976) 165–178 at 173, writes: "Augustine confidently assumes that the Bible is the Church's book....The two Testaments are the breasts of mother Church, from which one may suck the milk of all the mysteries enacted temporally for eternal salvation (tr. 3,1)." The abbreviation "tr. 3,1" is to the first sec-tion of Homily 3 on the First Epistle of St. John. An English translation of this text can be found in *A Select Library of Nicene and Post-Nicene Fathers*, Vol. VII: *St. Augustine: Homilies on the Gospel of John. Homilies on the First Epistle of John. Soliloquies* (Grand Rapids: Eerdmans, 1986) 476. See also, Robert Eno, "Scripture and the Church," in Chapter Seven, "Augustine of Hippo (354–430)," of his *Teaching Authority in the Early Church* (Wilmington: Glazier, 1984) 132–136.

42. See above, 130–131.

43. See above, 126–127, for Cyril of Jerusalem, and 181–182 for Augustine.

44. For a conciliatory, reconciling note in several of the patristic writers, see above, 130–131 on Basil, 134–136 on Gregory of Nazianzus, 166–167 on Hilary and 311–312, note 60, on Augustine.

45. See above, 107.

46. On the regula fidei, see above, 98, for Irenaeus and 104–105, for Tertullian. Still one of the most referred to studies in this area is one of those rare doctoral theses which became a standard reference work in its particular field: Damien Van den Eynde, *Les normes de l'enseignement Chrétien* (Gembloux: Duculot, 1933).

47. Chapter Two of J.N.D. Kelly's *Early Christian Creeds*, 30–61, entitled "Creeds and Baptism," is a good, concise introduction to the baptismal-

liturgical context for the emergence of creeds. For essays around the general topic of the way that liturgy relates to the expression and formation of faith, see A.M. Triacca and A. Pistoia, ed., *La liturgie. Expression de la foi* (Rome: Edizioni Liturgiche, 1979).

48. See above, 107 for Tertullian, 114 for Clement of Alexandria, 133 for Basil and 182, 186–187 for Augustine. For a fine listing of many references to the way in which the patristic writers understood tradition and called upon it as an authority, see Yves Congar, *Tradition and Traditions* (London: Burns & Oates, 1966), Chapter Two: "The Fathers and the Early Church," 23–85.

49. See above, 151–152, on Cyril of Alexandria. Athanasius already began to move in this direction; see above, 125 and 290, note 10.

50. While the literature on the emergence and history of councils is quite vast and scientifically advanced (one thinks immediately of the two series of books published by the Schöningh publishing house of Paderborn under the editorship of Walter Brandmüller: *Konziliengeschichte, Reihe A: Darstellungen* and *Reihe B: Untersuchungen*, as well as of the many scholarly essays published by the *Annuarium Historiae Conciliorum*), a useful introduction including essays by some of the most recognized authorities concerning the councils and treating also the continuity of the ecumenical councils with the New Testament and the regional councils before Nicea is AA.VV. *Le concile et les conciles* (Paris: Cerf, 1960). More recently, see G. Alberigo, ed., *Storia dei concili ecumenici* (Brescia: Queriniana, 1990), with extensive bibliography. These books treat ecumenical councils from a Roman Catholic perspective and thus include all of those which Catholics consider to be ecumenical (twenty-one), up to and including Vatican II (for the book edited by Alberigo).

51. On the question of primacy, see the various comments with regard to a primatial role in connection with certain Churches or with Peter or with the Church of Rome by Irenaeus, 102; Athanasius, 125–126; Hilary, 165–166; Basil, 130; Ambrose, 172–173; John Chrysostom, 147–148; Augustine, 189–190; and Cyril of Alexandria, 151. The essays of the symposium held in Rome from October 9–12, 1989 and devoted to the consideration of the primacy of the bishop of Rome during the first millennium have been published as Michele Maccarrone, ed., *Il Primato*

del vescovo di Roma nel primo millennio. Richerche e testimonianze (Città del Vaticano: Libreria Editrice Vaticana, 1991), 782 pages.

52. See again the interesting work by Prosper Grech, "Criteri di ortodossia ed eresia nel Nuovo Testamento," 583–596, which shows that sometimes very important issues can be at stake without arriving at the point of breaking off communion.

53. See above, 311–312, note 60.

54. See above, 103.

55. See above, 162.

56. See above, 146.

57. See above, 135.

58. On the misuse of reason as a cause of false doctrine, see above, 101 for Irenaeus, 162–163 for Hilary, 135–136 for Gregory of Nazianzus, 170–171 for Ambrose, 145–146 for John Chrysostom.

59. See above, 110 and 112–113, for Clement of Alexandria and 116–118 for Origen, although Origen is less enthusiastic than Clement: see 115 and 287, note 39.

60. This more positive assessment relating faith to knowledge seems to be best traced through the wide scope of patristic literature as a whole by Ignacio Escribano-Alberca, *Glaube und Gotteserkenntnis in der Schrift und Patristik* (Freiburg-Basel-Wien: Herder, 1974), Handbuch der Dogmengeschichte, Band I, Fasz. 2a, 138 pages. This work contains much additional bibliography.

61. See above, 90.

62. See above, 140–141. Irenaeus speaks of the antiquity of the origins of Christian teaching (above, 101–102) and Tertullian traces it back to Christ (above, 105).

63. See above, 131–132.

64. See above, 135.

65. See above, 162, where faith is humble submission for Hilary and

168–169 where Ambrose speaks of faith as the desire of the woman with the hemorrhage to touch Jesus or as the longing of the bride for the groom.

66. See above, 177–179.

67. See above, 110–112.

68. See above, 116–118, for Origen and 148, for John Chrysostom.

69. See above, 132–133, for Basil and 180–181, for Augustine.

70. See above, 120

71. See above, 147.

72. See above, 131, as well as the extended quote on 130–131 saying that not much more than the profession of the Creed should be asked of those with whom Basil was seeking to reestablish unity.

73. See above, 136–137.

74. See above, 181.

75. For Irenaeus, see above, 101.

76. A concise, authoritative overview of patristic methods of interpreting the Bible can be found in Manlio Simonetti, "Esegesi patristica," in *Dizionario patristico di antichità cristiane*, a cura di Angelo di Bernardino, Vol. I: A-F (Casale Monferrato: Marietti, 1983) 1211–1223. For a bibliography which includes 2,000 entries of publications concerning patristic exegesis, see Herman Josef Sieben, *Exegesis Patrum. Saggio bibliografico sull'esegesi biblica dei Padri della Chiesa* (Roma: Istituto Patristico Augustinianum, 1983).

77. See above, 94–96, for examples of Justin's use of scripture.

78. See above, 101, for Irenaeus' view of the faulty interpretation of his opponents and 101–102 for his proposal of adhering to the teachings of the ancient churches; see above, 105–108, for Tertullian's suggestion to reject a priori the biblical interpretations of the heretics.

79. See above, 125, on Athanasius; 162–163 on Hilary and 170, especially note 24, on Ambrose. There is a huge amount of patristic material which could illustrate this point but, since the precise scope of the present study is not to focus upon the way these writers interpreted scripture

but rather upon the way in which they understood faith and its unity, this extensive material was not explored at great depth.

80. See above, 105–106 and 108.

81. A good example of a study which collects and briefly comments upon patristic texts which are relevant to the present issue and which does not approach this literature simply from the angle of faith and its unity but from the somewhat different angle of teaching authority is Robert B. Eno, *Teaching Authority in the Early Church* (see above, 320, note 41).

82. See the presentation of the interventions by Bultmann, Conzelmann and Dunn and our attempt to respond to what seems to be a derogatory view of "early Catholicism," at the close of Chapter Four above, 75–79.

83. For some useful summaries of the complexity of the New Testament data concerning these ministries, see R. Brown, *Priest and Bishop* (New York: Paulist, 1970); R. Brown, "An Example: Rethinking the Episcopate of the NT Churches," in *The Critical Meaning of the Bible* (New York: Paulist, 1981) 124–126; and Nathan Mitchell, *Mission and Ministry* (Wilmington: Glazier, 1982), Chapter Two, "The Earliest Patterns of Christian Ministry," and Chapter Three, "Ministry in the Later New Testament Period," 72–200.

84. In this context, Y. Congar, "The Historical Development of Authority in the Church. Points for Christian Reflection," in John M. Todd, ed., *Problems of Authority* (London: Darton, Long & Todd, 1962) 119–155 at 124, observes that the affirmation of the authority of bishops has never been more strongly made than by Ignatius of Antioch, writing in the early second century.

85. See above, 101–102, for Irenaeus, and 107–108 for Tertullian.

86. See Robert Eno, "Preservazione ed interpretazione: la chiesa dei padri," 38–50 (1074–1086).

87. So Eno, "Preservazione ed interpretazione," 39. A fine essay relevant to the emergence of the role of bishops as authoritative teachers in the second century and attentive to potential objections to "apostolic succession" from the historical point of view is Francis A. Sullivan, "Biblical and Historical Basis for the Teaching Authority of Bishops," in his

Magisterium. Teaching Authority in the Catholic Church (Mahwah: Paulist, 1983), 35-51.

88. See above, 114 for Clement; 119 and 121 for Origen.

89. See above, 133 for Basil, 140–141 for Gregory of Nyssa, 164–165 (especially note 9) for Hilary, 171–172 for Ambrose, 147–148 for John Chrysostom and 187–190 for Augustine. Since my concern here has been to concentrate upon faith and its unity and not upon episcopacy, apostolicity or tradition, the references on these pages merely hint at the wealth of patristic material which can be found on the relation between the handing on of the apostolic faith and the role of bishops. The works of Eno (cf. notes 30 and 47 of this chapter) contribute some helpful documentation here. Similarly fine points of departure for further development of these themes can be found in J. Colson, *Les fonctions ecclésiales aux deux premier siècles* (Bruges: Desclée de Brouwer, 1956); Agnes Cunningham, *The Bishop in the Church: Patristic Texts on the Role of the Episkopos* (Wilmington: Glazier, 1985); P. Delhaye and L. Elders, ed., *Episcopale Munus* (Assen: Van Gorcum, 1982); and Willy Rordorf and André Schneider, *L'évolution du concept de tradition dans l'Eglise ancienne* (Berne and Frankfurt am Main: Peter Lang, 1982).

90. The entire note is entitled "The Orthodoxy of the Body of the Faithful during the Supremacy of Arianism," in John Henry Newman, *The Arians of the Fourth Century* (London: Longmans, Green and Co., 1919), 445–468, quotation at 445.

91. See Newman, 450, with reference to Jerome's *In Lucif.* 19.

92. Highly regarded works on the ecumenical councils are W. De Vries, *Orient et Occident. Les structures ecclésiales vue dans l'histoire des sept premiers conciles oecuméniques* (Paris: Cerf, 1974) and H.J. Sieben, *Die Konzilsidee der Alten Kirche* (Paderborn: Schöningh, 1979). Regarding the role of the papacy, much relevant material can be found in *Il primato del vescovo di Roma nel primo Millennio*, cited above on page 321, note 51, as well as in Paul C. Empie and T. Austin Murphy, ed., *Papal Primacy and the Universal Church*, "Lutherans and Catholics in Dialogue V" (Minneapolis: Augsburg, 1974).

93. Thus, of the first four ecumenical councils, only the second (Constantinople I in 381) does not fall into this pattern of collaboration between the leader of the orthodox party at the council and the bishop of Rome. However, this exception is explained by the fact that the plan

leading up to Constantinople I called for the holding of parallel councils in the East and the West, the bishop of Rome naturally being involved in that in the West (held at Aquileia several months after the Eastern bishops met at Constantinople). See Lorenzo Perrone, "Da Nicea (325) a Calcedonia (451)," in Giuseppe Alberigo, ed., *Storia dei concili ecumenici* (Brescia: Queriniana, 1990) 11–118 at 58–59.

94. As a case in point, see our earlier discussion of Cyril of Alexandria's positive attitude toward both kinds of intervention above in Chapter Six, 151.

95. For Liberius' resistance to condemning Athanasius, see Perrone, 51. That he subscribed to the condemnation after two years of banishment, see Newman, 448–449, who presents texts from Baronius, Athanasius and Jerome to this effect. Robert B. Eno, "Some Elements in the Pre-History of Papal Infallibility," in Paul C. Empie, T. Austin Murphy and Joseph A. Burgess, ed., *Teaching Authority & Infallibility in the Church*, "Lutherans and Catholics in Dialogue VI" (Minneapolis: Augsburg, c. 1978), 238–258, at 248–249, also speaks of this episode and Arthur Carl Piepkorn, "The Roman Primacy in the Patristic Era. II. From Nicaea to Leo the Great," in *Papal Primacy and the Universal Church*, 73–97, at 80, states that "the Middle Ages regarded [Liberius] as a heretic," without providing, however, further documentation.

INDEX

Benoit, A. 274
Benoit, Pierre 44, 52-54, 67, 206,
244, 251-254, 256, 258-263,
275-276, 318
Betz, Otto 249
Betz, Hans Dieter 319
Beyenka, Sr. Mary Melchior 305
Beyerlin, W. 235
Binder, H. 245
Blackman, E.C. 11-12, 34, 40,
230, 232-233, 247-251
Bogan, Sr. Mary Inez 181, 307
Bogart, J. 264
Böhmer, J. 234
Boismard, M.E. 245
Bonaventure of Bagnoregio 316
Bonsirven, Joseph 243, 246
Bornkamm, Günther 54, 245,
253, 259, 261, 263
Boularand, Ephrem 144, 294-295
Bousset, W. 255-256
Brandmüller, Walter 321
Braun, F.M. 240, 249, 269
Brekelmans, C. 15, 235
Brown, Raymond 249, 265-267,
271, 324
Brown, S. 244
Buber, Martin 19, 238
Bultmann, Rudolf 31, 34, 37, 40,
75-76, 231, 243, 246-247, 249-
251, 253, 255-256, 267, 269,
273, 277-278, 324
Burgess, Joseph 31, 243-244, 249-
250
Burn, A.E. 251
Butler, C. 245
Byrne, Brendan 247

Caecilan, Bishop 190
Cambier, J. 246
Camelot, Thomas 286

Canivet, Pierre 298-299
Cantalamessa, Raniero 305
Carson, D. 264
Causse, H. 238
Cayré, F. 299-301, 304
Celestine I, Pope 151
Celsus 116
Chadwick, H. 312
Chapman, G. Clarke 274
Charles the Fifth, Emperor 1
Charlot, John 61, 264, 267
Christopher, Joseph 308
Clement of Alexandria 2-3, 88-89,
109-115, 122, 124, 138-139,
197, 202, 210-212, 213, 215,
218, 223, 286, 298, 309, 317,
319, 321-322, 325
Clement of Rome 3, 75, 89-91,
93, 98, 121, 197, 210, 214, 218,
222, 280, 283, 315
Congar, Y. 284, 312, 321, 324
Colson, J. 325
Consentius 310
Conzelmann, Hans 44, 61-62, 64,
76, 82, 253-254, 257, 260, 262-
263, 266-267, 270, 277-278,
324
Craigk, C.T. 240
Cress, D.A. 234
Cullmann, Oscar 53, 55-56, 83,
205, 251-253, 255-256, 258-
264, 282, 318
Cunningham, Agnes 325
Cwiekowski, Frederick J. 266
Cyril of Alexandria 3, 123, 149-
152, 156-158, 191, 211, 225,
296-297, 299, 315, 317, 321,
326
Cyril of Jerusalem 3, 88, 123, 126-
130, 158, 197, 206, 210, 290,
315, 318, 320

DATE DUE